BYRON
A Self-Portrait

ILLUSTRATION TO BYRON'S POEMS BY RICHARD WESTALL

BYRON
A Self-Portrait

LETTERS AND DIARIES
1798 TO 1824

WITH HITHERTO UNPUBLISHED LETTERS
IN TWO VOLUMES EDITED BY
PETER QUENNELL

★ ★

VOLUME II

★ ★

NEW YORK
CHARLES SCRIBNER'S SONS

MADE AND PRINTED IN GREAT BRITAIN
BY MESSRS. R. & R. CLARK, LTD., EDINBURGH

CONTENTS

VOLUME II

★ ★

FRONTISPIECE : ILLUSTRATION TO BYRON'S POEMS, BY
RICHARD WESTALL

NOTE : *Unpublished letters are marked by a star ; letters to which passages
have been restored, by a dagger.*

4

Venice

October 1816 to December 1819

After a romantic tour in the Bernese Alps, Byron left Switzerland in October 1816, passed through Milan (where he encountered Henri Beyle and discarded Dr. Polidori) and came to rest in Venice on the 11th of November. The city delighted him; and, as a relief from remorse and introspection, he at once plunged into a series of highly stimulating love-affairs. Two of his earlier Venetian mistresses—Marianna Segati, with her " large, black, oriental eyes ", the wife of a draper in the Frezzeria, and Margarita Cogni, the baker's runaway wife, a magnificent amazon, who installed herself in his palace on the Grand Canal, where she ruled her good-humoured lover and terrorized his household—are graphically portrayed in a celebrated letter to John Murray. Their successors and rivals were unconscionably numerous; and Byron's debaucheries presently began to surprise and alarm even his Venetian intimates. His health suffered; his temper did not improve; and Shelley, who visited him in 1818, found him lamentably the worse for wear. " He says he disapproves ", wrote Shelley, " but he endures. He is heartily and deeply discontented with himself. . . ." Yet, although, following Shelley's example, it is customary to deplore Byron's existence at the Palazzo Mocenigo, we must not forget that throughout this period he was busily and profitably occupied, and had triumphantly launched Don Juan, beyond a doubt his finest long poem. Work and dissipation, nevertheless, had overtaxed his energies; and he had already resolved on reform when, at the beginning of April 1819, he was caught up in a quasi-domestic liaison with the Countess Guiccioli, an ardent and impulsive young woman, recently married to a rich and elderly Romagnol landowner. His new mistress was a determined sentimentalist; Byron, an easy-going and self-indulgent cynic. He soon accepted the rôle to which Teresa Guiccioli assigned him—that of an accredited *lover in the recognized Italian style. Returning home to Ravenna, she fell seriously ill; and Byron, though not without some grumbling, obeyed her urgent summons.*

TO THE HON. AUGUSTA LEIGH *   *Milan, Oct. 13th, 1816*

·MY DEAREST AUGUSTA,—You see I have got to Milan. We came by the Simplon, escaping all perils of precipices and robbers, of which last there was some talk and apprehension, a chain of English carriages having been stopped near Cesto a few weeks ago and handsomely pilfered of various chattels. We were not molested.

The Simplon, as you know, is the most superb of all possible routes ;—so I shall not describe it. I also navigated the Lago Maggiore, and went over the Borromean Islands ; the latter are fine but too artificial ; the lake itself is beautiful, as indeed is the whole country from Geneva hither, and the Alpine part most magnificent.

Close to Milan is the beginning of an unfinished triumphal arch for Napoleon, so beautiful as to make one regret its non-completion. As we only reached Milan last night, I can say little about it, but will write again in a few days. The Jerseys are here ; Made de Stael is gone to Paris (or going) from Coppet. I was more there than elsewhere during my stay at Diodati, and she has been particularly kind, and friendly towards me the whole time. When you write, address to *Geneva* still, Post *restante,* and my banker (Monsr Hentsch) will forward your letters. I have written to you so often lately that you will not regret the brevity of this. I hope that you received safely my presents for the children (by Scrope) and that you also have (by the post) a little journal of a journey in and on the Alps which I sent you early this month, having kept it on purpose for *you*—Ever my own dearest

Yrs. most B

TO THE HON. AUGUSTA LEIGH *Milan Octr 15, 1816*

MY DEAREST AUGUSTA,—I have been at Churches, Theatres, libraries, and picture galleries. The Cathedral is noble, the theatre grand, the library excellent, and the galleries I know nothing about—except as far as liking one picture out of a thousand. What has delighted me most is a manuscript collection (preserved in the Ambrosian library), of original love-letters and verses of Lucretia de Borgia and Cardinal Bembo ; and a lock of her hair—so long—and fair and beautiful —and the letters so pretty and so loving that it makes one wretched not to have been born sooner to have at least seen her. And pray what do you think is one of her *signatures?*—why this + a Cross—which she says " is to stand for her name etc." Is not this amusing? I suppose you know that she was a famous beauty, and famous for the use she made of it ; and that she was the love of this same Cardinal Bembo (besides a story about her papa Pope Alexander and her brother Cæsar Borgia—which some people don't believe—and others do), and that after all she ended with being Duchess of Ferrara, and an excellent mother and wife also ; so good as to be quite an example. All this may or may not be, but the hair and the letters are so beautiful that I have done nothing but pore over them, and have made the librarian promise me a copy of some of them ; and I mean to get some of the hair if I can. The verses are Spanish—the letters Italian—some signed—others with a cross—but all in her own hand-writing.

I am so hurried, and so sleepy, but so anxious to send you even a few lines my dearest Augusta, that you will forgive me troubling you so often ; and I shall write again soon ; but I have sent you so much lately, that you will have too many perhaps. *A thousand loves* to *you* from *me*—which is very generous for I only ask *one* in return

Ever dearest thine B.

TO THE HON. AUGUSTA LEIGH *Octr 28th, 1816*

MY DEAREST AUGUSTA,—Two days ago I wrote you the enclosed but the arrival of your letter of the 12th has revived me a little, so pray forgive the apparent " *humeur* " of the other, which I do not tear up—from lazyness—and the hurry of the post as I have hardly time to write another at present.

I really do not and cannot understand all the mysteries and alarms in your letters and more particularly in the last. All I know is—that no human power short of destruction— shall prevent me from seeing you when—where—and how— I may please—according to time and circumstance; that you are the only comfort (except the remote possibility of my daughter's being so) left me in prospect in existence, and that I can bear the rest—so that you remain; but anything which is to divide us would drive me quite out of my senses; Miss Milbanke appears in all respects to have been formed for my destruction; I have thus far—as you know—regarded her without feelings of personal bitterness towards her, but if directly or indirectly—but why do I say this?—You know she is the cause of all—whether intentionally or not is little to the purpose——You surely do not mean to say that if I come to England in Spring, that you and I shall not meet? If so I will never return to it—though I must for many reasons—business etc etc—But I quit this topic for the present.

My health is good, but I have now and then fits of giddi- ness, and deafness, which make me think like Swift—that I shall be like him and the *withered* tree he saw—which occasioned the reflection and " die at top " first. My hair is growing grey, and *not* thicker; and my teeth are sometimes *looseish* though still white and sound. Would not one think I was sixty instead of not quite nine and twenty? To talk thus— Never mind—either this must end—or I must end—but I repeat it again and again—*that woman* has destroyed me.

Milan has been made agreeable by much attention and kindness from many of the natives; but the whole tone of Italian society is so different from yours in England; that I have not time to describe it, tho' I am not sure that I do not prefer it. Direct as usual to Geneva—hope the best—and love me the most—as I ever must love you.

B.

TO THE HON. AUGUSTA LEIGH * *Milan, Nov. 2nd, 1816*

MY DEAREST AUGUSTA,—I wrote to you the other day, and I now do so to send a few lines, and request you to take particular care that Lady B. receives a letter sent in another enclosure. I feel so miserable that I must write to her—however useless.

In a day or two we set off for Venice. I have seen a good deal of Milanese society but nothing to make me forget others —or forgive myself.

Dr. Polidori (whom I dismissed some time before I left Geneva, as I had no use for him and his temper and habits were not good) had been in Milan some time before but, getting into a scrape and quarrel with some Austrians, has been sent by the Government out of the territory.

I had nothing to do with his squabble, and was not even present, though, when he sent for me, I tried of course to get him out of it, as well as Mr. Hobhouse, who tried also for him, but to no purpose. I tell you all this because in England, by some kind mistake, his squabbles may be set down to *me*, and now (if this should be the case) you have it in your power to contradict it. It happened about a week ago.

I shall probably write to you on my road to Venice—from Verona or elsewhere.

Ever, my dearest, thine, B.

TO THOMAS MOORE *Verona, November 6, 1816*

MY DEAR MOORE,—Your letter, written before my departure from England, and addressed to me in London, only reached me recently. Since that period, I have been over a portion of that part of Europe which I had not already seen. About a month since, I crossed the Alps from Switzerland to Milan, which I left a few days ago, and am thus far on my way to Venice, where I shall probably winter. Yesterday I was on the shores of the Benacus, with his *fluctibus et fremitu*. Catullus's Sirmium has still its name and site, and is remembered for his sake : but the very heavy autumnal rains and mists prevented our quitting our route, (that is, Hobhouse and myself, who are at present voyaging together,) as it was better not to see it at all than to a great disadvantage.

I found on the Benacus the same tradition of a city, still visible in calm weather below the waters, which you have preserved of Lough Neagh, " When the clear, cold eve's declining ". I do not know that it is authorised by records ; but they tell you such a story, and say that the city was swallowed up by an earthquake. We moved to-day over the frontier to Verona, by a road suspected of thieves,—" the wise *convey* it call ",—but without molestation. I shall remain here a day or two to gape at the usual marvels,—amphitheatre, paintings, and all that time-tax of travel,—though Catullus, Claudian, and Shakspeare have done more for Verona than it ever did for itself. They still pretend to show, I believe, the " tomb of all the Capulets "—we shall see.

Among many things at Milan, one pleased me particularly, viz. the correspondence (in the prettiest love-letters in the world) of Lucretia Borgia with Cardinal Bembo, (who, *you say*, made a very good cardinal,) and a lock of her hair, and some Spanish verses of hers,—the lock very fair and beautiful. I took one single hair of it as a relic, and wished sorely to get a copy of one or two of the letters ; but it is prohibited : *that* I don't mind ; but it was impracticable ; and so I only got some of them by heart. They are kept in the Ambrosian Library, which I often visited to look them over—to the scandal of the librarian, who wanted to enlighten me with sundry valuable MSS., classical, philosophical, and pious. But I stick to the Pope's daughter, and wish myself a cardinal.

I have seen the finest parts of Switzerland, the Rhine, the Rhone, and the Swiss and Italian lakes ; for the beauties of which, I refer you to the Guide-book. The north of Italy is tolerably free from the English ; but the south swarms with them, I am told. Madame de Stael I saw frequently at Copet, which she renders remarkably pleasant. She has been particularly kind to me. I was for some months her neighbour, in a country-house called Diodati, which I had on the Lake of Geneva. My plans are very uncertain ; but it is probable that you will see me in England in the spring. I have some business there. If you write to me, will you address to the care of Mons.

Hentsch, *Banquier*, Geneva, who receives and forwards my letters. Remember me to Rogers, who wrote to me lately, with a short account of your poem, which, I trust, is near the light. He speaks of it most highly.

My health is very endurable, except that I am subject to casual giddiness and faintness, which is so like a fine lady, that I am rather ashamed of the disorder. When I sailed, I had a physician with me, whom, after some months of patience, I found it expedient to part with, before I left Geneva some time. On arriving at Milan, I found this gentleman in very good society, where he prospered for some weeks; but, at length, at the theatre, he quarrelled with an Austrian officer, and was sent out by the government in twenty-four hours. I was not present at his squabble; but, on hearing that he was put under arrest, I went and got him out of his confinement, but could not prevent his being sent off, which, indeed, he partly deserved, being quite in the wrong, and having begun a row for row's sake. I had preceded the Austrian government some weeks myself, in giving him his congé from Geneva. He is not a bad fellow, but very young and hot-headed, and more likely to incur diseases than to cure them. Hobhouse and myself found it useless to intercede for him. This happened some time before we left Milan. He is gone to Florence.

At Milan I saw, and was visited by, Monti, the most celebrated of the living Italian poets. He seems near sixty; in face he is like the late Cooke the actor. His frequent changes in politics have made him very unpopular as a man. I saw many more of their literati; but none whose names are well known in England, except Acerbi. I lived much with the Italians, particularly with the Marquis of Breme's family, who are very able and intelligent men, especially the Abbate. There was a famous improvisatore who held forth while I was there. His fluency astonished me; but, although I understand Italian, and speak it (with more readiness than accuracy), I could only carry off a few very common-place mythological images, and one line about Artemisia, and another about Algiers, with sixty words of an entire tragedy about Eteocles and Polynices. Some of the Italians liked him—others called his performance " *seccatura* " (a devilish good word, by the way) and all Milan was in controversy about him.

The state of morals in these parts is in some sort lax. A mother and son were pointed out at the theatre, as being pronounced by the Milanese world to be of the Theban dynasty —but this was all. The narrator (one of the first men in Milan) seemed to be most sufficiently scandalised by the taste or the tie. All society in Milan is carried on at the opera : they have private boxes, where they play at cards, or talk, or any thing else ; but (except at the Cassino) there are no open houses, or balls, etc., etc.   * * * * *

The peasant girls have all very fine dark eyes, and many of them are beautiful. There are also two dead bodies in fine preservation—one Saint Carlo Boromeo, at Milan ; the other not a saint, but a chief, named Visconti, at Monza—both of which appeared very agreeable. In one of the Boromean isles (the Isola bella), there is a large laurel—the largest known—on which Buonaparte, staying there just before the battle of Marengo, carved with his knife the word " Battaglia ". I saw the letters, now half worn out and partly erased.

Excuse this tedious letter. To be tiresome is the privilege of old age and absence ; I avail myself of the latter, and the former I have anticipated. If I do not speak to you of my own affairs, it is not from want of confidence, but to spare you and myself. My day is over—what then?—I have had it. To be sure, I have shortened it ; and if I had done as much by this letter, it would have been as well. But you will forgive that, if not the other faults of

> Yours ever and most affectionately, B.

P.S.—*November 7, 1816*

I have been over Verona. The amphitheatre is wonderful —beats even Greece. Of the truth of Juliet's story they seem tenacious to a degree, insisting on the fact—giving a date (1303), and showing a tomb. It is a plain, open, and partly decayed sarcophagus, with withered leaves in it, in a wild and desolate conventual garden, once a cemetery, now ruined to the very graves. The situation struck me as very appropriate to the legend, being blighted as their love. I have brought away a few pieces of the granite, to give to my daughter and my nieces. Of the other marvels of this city, paintings, antiquities, etc., excepting the tombs of the Scaliger princes, I have no pretensions to judge. The Gothic monuments of the Scaligers pleased me, but " a poor virtuoso am I ", and ever yours.

TO THE HON. AUGUSTA LEIGH †　　　*Verona, Novr 6th 1816*

MY DEAREST AUGUSTA,—I am thus far on my way to Venice, and shall stay here a day to see the place, the paintings, the " tomb of all the Capulets " which they show (at least a tomb they call so after the story, from which Shakespeare drew the plot of his play), and all the sights and so forths at which it is usual to gape in passing.

I left Milan on Sunday, and have travelled but slowly over some celebrated ground; but Lombardy is not a beautiful country—at least in autumn, excepting however the Lago di Garda and its outlines which are mountainous on one side: and it is a very fine stormy lake throughout—never quiet; and I had the pleasure of seeing it in all its vexation, foaming like a little Sea, as Virgil has described it. But (thank God) you are not a blue-stocking, and I won't inflict the appropriate bit of Latin upon you.

I wrote to you a few scraps of *letterets* (I may call them they were so short) from Milan.

Dr. Polidori, whom I parted with before I left Geneva (not for any great harm, but because he was always in squabbles, and had no kind of conduct), contrived at Milan, which he reached before me, to get into a quarrel with an Austrian, and to be ordered out of the city by the government. *I did not even see his adventure,* nor had any thing to do with it, except getting him out of arrest, and trying to get him altogether out of the scrape. This I mention, because I know in England some one or other will probably transfer his adventures to me.　After what has been said already, I have a right to suspect every thing and every body; so I state all this for your satisfaction, and that you may be able to contradict any such report. Mr. Hobhouse and Trevannion, and indeed every body—Italian and English—then at Milan, can corroborate this if necessary. It occurred several days before Mr. H. and myself left it. So much for this.

When we reach Venice I shall write to thee again. I had

received your acknowledgement of the journal etc. and the trinkets by Scrope, of which I delight to hear the reception.

In health I am pretty well, except that the confounded Lombardy rains of this season (the autumn) have given me a flying rheumatism, which is troublesome at times, and makes me feel ancient. I am also growing *grey* and *giddy*, and cannot help thinking my head will decay ; I wish my memory would, at least my remembrance—except a parenthesis for *ou*—my dearest Augusta.

Ada—by the way *Ada's* name (which I found in our pedigree under King John's reign) is the same with that of the Sister of Charlemagne, as I read the other day in a book treating of the Rhine.

Ever my own—thy own B.

P.S.—I forgot to tell you that my dog (Mutz by name and Swiss by nation) shuts a door when he is told : there—that's more than Tip can do.

Remember me to the childer, and to Georgiana, who I suppose has grown a prodigious penwoman. I hope she likes her seals and all her share of Mont Blanc.

I have had so much of mountains that I am not yet reconciled to the plains—but they improve. Verona seems a fine city.

P.S.—Novr 7th I have been over Verona. The Amphitheatre is superb, and in high preservation. Of the *truth* of the story of Juliet they seem very tenacious, giving the date (1303), and shewing a tomb. It is an open granite sarcophagus in a most desolate convent garden, which looks quite wild and withered, and once was a Cimetery [*sic*] since ruined. I brought away four small pieces of it for you and the babes (at least the female part of them), and for Ada, and her mother, if she will accept it from you. I thought the situation more appropriate to the history than if it had been less blighted. This struck me more than all the antiquities, more even than the Amphitheatre.

TO THOMAS MOORE   *Venice, November 17, 1816*

I wrote to you from Verona the other day in my progress hither, which letter I hope you will receive. Some three years ago, or it may be more, I recollect your telling me that you had received a letter from our friend Sam, dated " On board his gondola ". *My* gondola is, at this present, waiting for me on the canal ; but I prefer writing to you in the house, it being autumn—and rather an English autumn than otherwise. It is my intention to remain at Venice during the winter, probably, as it has always been (next to the East) the greenest island of my imagination. It has not disappointed me ; though its evident decay would, perhaps, have that effect upon others. But I have been familiar with ruins too long to dislike desolation. Besides, I have fallen in love, which, next to falling into the canal, (which would be of no use, as I can swim,) is the best or the worst thing I could do. I have got some extremely good apartments in the house of a " Merchant of Venice ", who is a good deal occupied with business, and has a wife in her twenty-second year. Marianna [Segati] (that is her name) is in her appearance altogether like an antelope. She has the large, black, oriental eyes, with that peculiar expression in them which is seen rarely among *Europeans*—even the Italians— and which many of the Turkish women give themselves by tinging the eyelid,—an art not known out of that country, I believe. This expression she has *naturally*,—and something more than this. In short, I cannot describe the effect of this kind of eye,—at least upon me. Her features are regular, and rather aquiline—mouth small—skin clear and soft, with a kind of hectic colour—forehead remarkably good : her hair is of the dark gloss, curl, and colour of Lady J[ersey]'s : her figure is light and pretty, and she is a famous songstress—scientifically so ; her natural voice (in conversation, I mean) is very sweet ; and the naïveté of the Venetian dialect is always pleasing in the mouth of a woman.

November 23

You will perceive that my description, which was proceeding with the minuteness of a passport, has been interrupted for several days. In the mean time * * * *

December 5

Since my former dates, I do not know that I have much to add on the subject, and, luckily, nothing to take away ; for I am more pleased than ever with my Venetian, and begin to feel very serious on that point—so much so, that I shall be silent. * * * * *

By way of divertisement, I am studying daily, at an Armenian monastery, the Armenian language. I found that my mind wanted something craggy to break upon ; and this—as the most difficult thing I could discover here for an amusement—I have chosen, to torture me into attention. It is a rich language, however, and would amply repay any one the trouble of learning it. I try, and shall go on ;—but I answer for nothing, least of all for my intentions or my success. There are some very curious MSS. in the monastery, as well as books ; translations also from Greek originals, now lost, and from Persian and Syriac, etc. ; besides works of their own people. Four years ago the French instituted an Armenian professorship. Twenty pupils presented themselves on Monday morning, full of noble ardour, ingenuous youth, and impregnable industry. They persevered, with a courage worthy of the nation and of universal conquest, till Thursday ; when *fifteen* of the *twenty* succumbed to the six-and-twentieth letter of the alphabet. It is, to be sure, a Waterloo of an Alphabet—that must be said for them. But it is so like these fellows, to do by it as they did by their sovereigns—abandon both ; to parody the old rhymes, " Take a thing and give a thing "— " Take a king and give a king ". They are the worst of animals, except their conquerors.

I hear that Hodgson is your neighbour, having a living in Derbyshire. You will find him an excellent-hearted fellow, as well as one of the cleverest ; a little, perhaps, too much japanned by preferment in the church and the tuition of youth, as well as inoculated with the disease of domestic felicity, besides being over-run with fine feelings about woman and *constancy* (that small change of Love, which people exact so rigidly, receive in such counterfeit coin, and repay in baser metal) ; but, otherwise, a very worthy man, who has lately got a pretty wife, and (I suppose) a child by this time. Pray remember me to him, and say that I know not which to envy most his neighbourhood—him, or you.

Of Venice I shall say little. You must have seen many descriptions ; and they are most of them like. It is a poetical place ; and classical, to us, from Shakespeare and Otway. I have not yet sinned against it in verse, nor do I know that I shall do so, having been tuneless since I crossed the Alps, and feeling, as yet, no renewal of the *estro*. By the way, I suppose you have seen *Glenarvon*. Madame de Stael lent it me to read from Copet last autumn. It seems to me, that if the authoress had written the *truth*, and nothing but the truth—the whole truth—the romance would not only have been more *romantic*, but more entertaining. As for the likeness, the picture can't be good—I did not sit long enough. When you have leisure, let me hear from and of you, believing me,

Ever and truly yours most affectionately, B.

P.S.—Oh ! *your poem*—is it out? I hope Longman has paid his thousands ; but don't you do as H—— T——'s father did, who, having made money by a quarto tour, became a vinegar merchant ; when, lo ! his vinegar turned sweet (and be damned to it) and ruined him. My last letter to you (from Verona) was enclosed to Murray—have you got it? Direct to me *here*, *poste restante*. There are no English here at present. There were several in Switzerland—some women ; but, except Lady Dalrymple Hamilton, most of them as ugly as virtue—at least, those I saw.

TO THE HON. DOUGLAS KINNAIRD   *Venice,*
November 27th, 1816

MY DEAR KINNAIRD,—Before I left Switzerland, I answered your last letter, and feel a little anxious to know that you have received it, as it was partly on business—that is to say, on the disposition of Murray's proposed payment.

I fear there is little chance of an immediate sale of Newstead, which is to be wished for many reasons.

H[obhouse] and I have been some time in the north of Italy, and reached Venice about a fortnight ago, where I shall remain probably during the winter. It is a place which I like, and which I long anticipated that I should like—besides, I have fallen in love, and with a very pretty woman—so much so as to obtain the approbation of the not easily approving H., who is, in general, rather tardy in his applause of the fairer part of the creation.

She is married—so our arrangement was formed according to the incontinent continental system, which need not be described to you, an experienced voyager—and gifted withal with a modest self-confidence, which my bashful nature is not endowed with—but nevertheless I have got the woman—I do not very well know how, but we do exceedingly well together. She is not two-and-twenty, with great black eastern eyes, and a variety of subsidiary charms, etc., etc., and amongst her other accomplishments is a mighty and admirable singer—as most of the Italians are—(though not a public one); luckily I can speak the language fluently; and luckily (if I did not), we could employ ourselves a little without talking.

I meant to have given up gallivanting altogether on leaving your country, where I had been tolerably sickened of that and everything else; but, I know not how it is, my health growing better, and my spirits not worse, the " besoin d'aimer " came back upon my heart again, and, after all, there is nothing like it. So much for that matter.

I hear you are in a row with Dibdin and Fanny Kelly, and the devil knows whom—Humph!

I hear also that at the meeting or in the committee, you said that I was coming back in spring—it is probable—and if you have said so I *will* come, for sundry reasons—to see my daughter—my sister—and my friends—(and not least nor last —*yourself*,) to renew my proxy (if Parliament be dissolved) for the Whigs—to see Mr. Waite, and Mr. Blake—and the newest play—and the S[ub]-committee—and to sell Newstead (if I can), but not to reside in England again. It neither suits me, nor I it; my greatest error was remaining there,—that is to say, my greatest error but one. My ambition, if ever I had much—is over—or at least limited. If I could but remain as I now am, I should not merely be happy, but *contented*, which in my mind is the strangest, and most difficult attainment of the two—for any one who will hazard enough may have moments of happiness. I have books—a decent establishment—a fine country—a language which I prefer—most of the amusements and conveniences of life—as much of society as I choose to take—and a handsome woman, who is not a bore—and does not annoy me with looking like a fool, setting up for a sage. Life has little left for my curiosity; there are few things in it of which I have not had a sight, and a share—it would be silly to quarrel with my luck because it did not last—and even that was partly my own fault. If the present does—I should fall out with the past; and if I could but manage to arrange my pecuniary concerns in England, so as to pay my debts, and leave me what would be here a very fair income (though nothing remarkable at home), you might consider me as *posthumous*, for I would never willingly dwell in the " tight little Island ".

Pray write to me a line or two, addressed to Venice, *Poste Restante*. I hope to remain here the winter—remember me to Maria, and believe me,

Yours ever truly and affectionately, B.

P.S.—Colonel Finch, an English acquaintance of H[obhouse]'s and mine, has, I believe, written to you to complain of his banker (who is also mine), and has with our permission mentioned our names to you, as knowing him. I must, however, say that *I* have no complaint whatever against (Mr. Siri), the banker—who has, on the contrary, been remarkably civil and attentive to both H. and myself.

Of Col. Finch's row with him, I understand nothing but that he had one.

Pray let me hear from you, and tell me what Murray has done, and if you have received my letter from Geneva in answer to your former one.

P.S.—If you write pray do not refer to any *persons* or *events* except our own· *theatrical* — *political* — personal — *attorneycal* — *poetical*—or *diabolical* concerns.

You see I give a pretty wide range still—but what I wish to put under Quarantine are (*my*) *family events*, and all allusion thereto past—present—or to come. It is what I have laid an embargo on, with all my other friends.

It will be better that the *Author* of these lines (if spoken), be *not avowed*—pray make it a secret and keep it so.

TO JOHN MURRAY   *Venice, December 4, 1816*

DEAR SIR,—I have written to you so frequently of late, that you will think me a bore; as I think you a very impolite person for not answering my letters from Switzerland, Milan, Verona, and Venice. There are some things I wanted, and want, to know; viz. whether Mr. Davies, of inaccurate memory, had or had not delivered the MS. as delivered to him; because, if he has not, you will find that he will bountifully bestow extracts and transcriptions on all the curious of his acquaintance, in which case you may probably find your publication anticipated by the " Cambridge " or other Chronicles. In the next place,—I forget what was next; but in the 3^d place, I want to hear whether you have yet published, or when you mean to do so, or why you have not done so, because in your last (Sept. 20th,—you may be ashamed of the date) you talked of this being done immediately.

From England I hear nothing, and know nothing of any thing or any body. I have but one correspondent (except Mr. Kinnaird on business now and then), and that one is a female; [1] and her letters are so full of mysteries and miseries,—such a quantity of the trivial and conjectural, and such a dearth of any useful or even amusing information, that I know no more of your island, or city, than the Italian version of the French papers chooses to tell me, or the advertisements of Mr. Colburn tagged to the end of your *Quarterly Review* for the year *ago*. I wrote to you at some length last week; so that I have little to add, except that I have begun, and am proceeding in, a study of the Armenian language, which I acquire, as well as I can, at the Armenian convent, where I go every day to take lessons of a learned Friar, and have gained some singular and not useless information with regard to the literature and customs of that oriental people. They have an establishment here—a church and convent of ninety monks, very learned and accomplished men, some of them. They have also a press, and make great efforts for the enlightening of their nation. I find the language (which is *twin*, the *literal* and the *vulgar*) difficult, but not invincible (at least I hope not). I shall go on. I found it necessary to twist my mind round some severer study; and this, as being the hardest I could devise here, will be a file for the serpent.

I mean to remain here till the Spring, so address to me *directly* to *Venice, poste restante.*—Mr. Hobhouse, for the present,

_____
[1] Augusta Leigh.

is gone to Rome, with his brother, brother's wife, and Sister, who overtook him here: he returns in two months. I should have gone too, but I fell in love, and must stay that over. I should think that and the Armenian alphabet will last the winter. The lady has, luckily for me, been less obdurate than the language, or, between the two, I should have lost my remains of sanity. By the way, *she* is not Armenian, but a Venetian, as I believe I told you in my last. As for Italian, I am fluent enough, even in its Venetian modification, which is something like the Somersetshire version of English; and as for the more classical dialects, I had not forgot my former practice during my voyaging.

Yours, ever and truly, B.

P.S.—Remember me to Mr. Gifford. And do not forget me to—— but I don't think I have any other friends of your acquaintance.

TO THE HON. AUGUSTA LEIGH   *Venice, Dec^r, 18th 1816*

MY DEAREST AUGUSTA,—I have received one letter dated 19th Novr I think (or rather earlier by a week or two perhaps), since my arrival in Venice, where it is my intention to remain probably till the Spring. The place pleases me. I have found some pleasing society—and the *romance* of the situation—and it's extraordinary appearance—together with all the associations we are accustomed to connect with Venice, have always had a charm for me, even before I arrived here; and I have not been disappointed in what I have seen.

I go every morning to the Armenian Convent (of *friars not Nuns*—my child) to study the language, I mean the *Armenian* language, (for as you perhaps know—I am versed in the Italian which I speak with fluency rather than accuracy), and if you ask me my reason for studying this out of the way language—I can only answer that it is Oriental and difficult, and employs me—which are—as you know my Eastern and difficult way of thinking—reasons sufficient. Then I have fallen in love with a very pretty Venetian of two and twenty, with great black eyes. She is married—and so am I—which is very much to the purpose. We have formed and sworn an eternal attachment, which has already lasted a lunar month, and I am more in love than ever, and so is the lady—at least she says so. She does not plague me (which is a wonder) and I verily believe we are one of the happiest—unlawful couples on this side of the Alps.   She is very handsome, very Italian or rather Venetian, with something more of the Oriental cast of countenance ; accomplished and musical after the manner of her nation. Her spouse is a very good kind of man who occupies himself elsewhere, and thus the world goes on here as elsewhere.   This adventure came very opportunely to console me, for I was beginning to be " like Sam Jennings very *unappy* " but at present—at least for a month past—I have been very tranquil, very loving, and have not so much embarassed myself with the tortures of the last two years and that virtuous monster Miss Milbanke, who had nearly driven me out of my senses.—

Hobhouse is gone to Rome with his brother and sister— but returns here in February : you will easily suppose that I was not disposed to stir from my present position.

I have not heard recently from England and wonder if Murray has published the po's sent to him ; and I want to know if you don't think them very fine and all that—Goosey my love—don't they make you " put finger in eye " ?

You can have no idea of my thorough wretchedness from the day of my parting from you till nearly a month ago though I struggled against it with some strength.   At present I am better—thank Heaven above—and woman beneath—and I will be a very good boy.   Pray remember me to the babes, and tell me of little *Da*—who by the way—is a year old and a few days over.

My love to you all and to Aunt *Sophy* : pray tell *her* in particular that I have consoled myself ; and tell Hodgson that his prophecy is accomplished.   He said—you remember—I should be in love with an Italian—so I am.—

ever dearest yrs.   B.

P.S.—I forgot to tell you—that the *Demoiselle*—who returned to England from Geneva—went there to produce a new baby B., who is now about to make his appearance.   You wanted to hear some adventures—there are enough I think for one epistle.——Pray address direct to Venice—Poste Restante.

TO THE HON. AUGUSTA LEIGH†   *Venice, Decr 19th 1816*

MY DEAREST AUGUSTA,—I wrote to you a few days ago.
Your letter of the 1st is arrived, and you have " a *hope* " for
me, it seems : what " *hope* ", child? my dearest Sis. I remember
a methodist preacher who, on perceiving a profane grin on the
faces of part of his congregation, exclaimed " no *hopes* for *them*
as *laughs* ". And thus it is with us : we laugh too much for
hopes, and so even let them go. I am sick of sorrow, and must
even content myself as well as I can : so here goes—I won't be
woeful again if I can help it. My letter to my moral Clytemnestra required no answer, and I would rather have none. I
was wretched enough when I wrote it, and had been so for
many a long day and month : at present I am less so, for reasons
explained in my late letter (a few days ago) ; and as I never
pretend to be what I am not, you may tell her if you please that
I am recovering, and the reason also if you like it. I do not
agree with you about Ada : there was *equivocation* in the answer,
and it shall be settled one way or the other. I wrote to Hanson
to take proper steps to prevent such a removal of my daughter,
and even the probability of it. You do not know the woman
so well as I do, or you would perceive in her *very negative
answer* that she *does intend* to take Ada with her, if she should
go abroad. I have heard of Murray's squabble with one of
his brethren, who is an impudent impostor, and should be
trounced.

You do not say whether the *true po's* are out : I hope you
like them.

You are right in saying that I like Venice : it is very much
what you would imagine it, but I have no time just now for
description. The Carnival is to begin in a week, and with it
the mummery of masking.

I have not been out a great deal, but quite as much as I
like. I am going out this evening in my *cloak* and *Gondola*—
there are two nice Mrs. Radcliffe words for you. And then
there is the place of St. Mark, and conversaziones, and various
fooleries, besides many *nau* : indeed, every body is *nau*, so
much so, that a lady with only *one lover* is not reckoned to have
overstepped the modesty of marriage—that being a regular
thing. Some have two, three, and so on to twenty, beyond

which they don't account; but they generally begin by one. The husbands of course belong to any body's wives—but their own. . . . . .

My present beloved is aged two and twenty—with remarkably fine black eyes, and very regular and pretty features, figure light and pretty, hair dark, a mighty good singer, as they all are. She is married (of course) and has one child, a girl. Her temper very good (as you know it had need to be) and lively. She is a Venetian by birth, and was never further from Venice than Milan in her days. Her lord is about five years older than me, an exceeding good kind of a man. That amatory appendage called by us a lover is here denominated variously—sometimes an " Amoroso " (which is the same thing) and sometimes a Cavaliere Servente—which I need not tell you is a serving Cavalier. I told my fair one, at setting out, that as to the love and the Cavaliership I was quite of accord, but as to the *servitude* it would not suit me at all : so I begged to hear no more about it. You may easily suppose I should not at all shine in the ceremonious department—so little so that, instead of handing the Lady as in duty bound into the Gondola, I as nearly as possible conveyed her into the Canal, and this at midnight. To be sure it was as dark as possible—but if you could have seen the gravity with which I was committing her to the waves, thinking all the time of something or other not to the purpose. I always forget that the streets are canals, and was going to walk her over the water, if the servants and the Gondoliers had not awakened me.

So much for love and all that. The music here is famous, and there will be a whole tribe of singers and dancers during the Carnival, besides the usual theatres.

The Society here is something like our own, except that the women sit in a semicircle at one end of the room, and the men stand at the other.

I pass my mornings at the Armenian convent studying Armenian,—my evenings here and there. To-night I am going to the Countess Albrizzi's, one of the *noblesse*. I have also been at the Governor's, who is an Austrian, and whose wife, the Countess Goetz, appears to me in the little I have seen of her a very amiable and pleasing woman, with remarkably good manners, as many of the German women have.

There are no English here, except birds of passage, who stay a day and then go on to Florence or Rome.

I mean to remain here till Spring. When you write address *directly* here, as in your present letter.

Ever, dearest, yours, B.

TO THOMAS MOORE   *Venice, December 24, 1816*

I have taken a fit of writing to you, which portends postage —once from Verona—once from Venice, and again from Venice—*thrice* that is. For this you may thank yourself; for I heard that you complained of my silence—so, here goes for garrulity.

I trust that you received my other twain of letters. My " way of life " (or " May of life ", which is it according to the commentators?)—my " way of life " is fallen into great regularity. In the mornings I go over in my gondola to babble Armenian with the friars of the convent of St. Lazarus, and to help one of them in correcting the English of an English and Armenian grammar which he is publishing. In the evenings I do one of many nothings—either at the theatres, or some of the conversaziones, which are like our routs, or rather worse, for the women sit in a semicircle by the lady of the mansion, and the men stand about the room. To be sure, there is one improvement upon ours—instead of lemonade with their ices, they hand about stiff *rum-punch—punch*, by my palate ; and this they think *English*. I would not disabuse them of so agreeable an error,—" no, not for Venice ".

Last night I was at the Count Governor's, which, of course, comprises the best society, and is very much like other gregarious meetings in every country,—as in ours,—except that, instead of the Bishop of Winchester, you have the Patriarch of Venice, and a motley crew of Austrians, Germans, noble Venetians, foreigners, and, if you see a quiz, you may be sure he is a Consul. Oh, by the way, I forgot, when I wrote from Verona, to tell you that at Milan I met with a countryman of yours—a Colonel [Fitzgerald], a very excellent, good-natured fellow, who knows and shows all about Milan, and is, as it

were, a native there. He is particularly civil to strangers, and
this is his history,—at least, an episode of it.

Six-and-twenty years ago, Col. [Fitzgerald], then an
ensign, being in Italy, fell in love with the Marchesa [Castig-
lione], and she with him. The lady must be, at least, twenty
years his senior. The war broke out ; he returned to England,
to serve—not his country, for that's Ireland—but England,
which is a different thing ; and *she*—heaven knows what she
did. In the year 1814, the first annunciation of the Definitive
Treaty of Peace (and tyranny) was developed to the astonished
Milanese by the arrival of Col. [Fitzgerald], who, flinging
himself full length at the feet of Mad. [Castiglione], murmured
forth, in half-forgotten Irish Italian, eternal vows of indelible
constancy. The lady screamed, and exclaimed, " Who are
you? " The Colonel cried, " What ! don't you know me? I
am so and so ", etc., etc., etc. ; till, at length, the Marchesa,
mounting from reminiscence to reminiscence, through the
lovers of the intermediate twenty-five years, arrived at last at
the recollection of her *povero* sub-lieutenant. She then said,
" Was there ever such virtue? " (that was her very word) and,
being now a widow, gave him apartments in her palace, re-
instated him in all the rights of wrong, and held him up to the
admiring world as a miracle of incontinent fidelity, and the
unshaken Abdiel of absence.

Methinks this is as pretty a moral tale as any of Marmontel's.
Here is another. The same lady, several years ago, made an
escapade with a Swede, Count Fersen (the same whom the
Stockholm mob quartered and lapidated not very long since),
and they arrived at an Osteria on the road to Rome or there-
abouts. It was a summer evening, and, while they were at
supper, they were suddenly regaled by a symphony of fiddles
in an adjacent apartment, so prettily played, that, wishing to
hear them more distinctly, the Count rose, and going into the
musical society, said, " Gentlemen, I am sure that, as a company of gallant cavaliers, you will be delighted to show your
skill to a lady, who feels anxious ", etc., etc. The men of
harmony were all acquiescence—every instrument was tuned
and toned, and, striking up one of their most ambrosial airs,
the whole band followed the Count to the lady's apartment.
At their head was the first fiddler, who, bowing and fiddling at

the same moment, headed his troop and advanced up the room. Death and discord !—it was the Marquis himself, who was on a serenading party in the country, while his spouse had run away from town. The rest may be imagined—but, first of all, the lady tried to persuade him that she was there on purpose to meet him, and had chosen this method for an harmonic surprise. So much for this gossip, which amused me when I heard it, and I send it to you in the hope it may have the like effect. Now we'll return to Venice.

The day after to-morrow (to-morrow being Christmas-day) the Carnival begins. I dine with the Countess Albrizzi and a party, and go to the opera. On that day the Phenix, (not the Insurance Office, but) the theatre of that name, opens : I have got me a box there for the season, for two reasons, one of which is, that the music is remarkably good. The Contessa Albrizzi, of whom I have made mention, is the De Stael of Venice ; not young, but a very learned, unaffected, good-natured woman ; very polite to strangers, and, I believe, not at all dissolute, as most of the women are. She has written very well on the works of Canova, and also a volume of Characters, besides other printed matter. She is of Corfu, but married a dead Venetian—that is, dead since he married.

My flame (my *Donna* whom I spoke of in my former epistle, my Marianna) is still my Marianna, and I her—what she pleases. She is by far the prettiest woman I have seen here, and the most loveable I have met with any where—as well as one of the most singular. I believe I told you the rise and pro-gress of our *liaison* in my former letter. Lest that should not have reached you, I will merely repeat, that she is a Venetian, two-and-twenty years old, married to a merchant well to do in the world, and that she has great black oriental eyes, and all the qualities which her eyes promise. Whether being in love with her has steeled me or not, I do not know ; but I have not seen many other women who seem pretty. The nobility, in particular, are a sad-looking race—the gentry rather better. And now, what art *thou* doing?

> What are you doing now,
> Oh Thomas Moore?
> What are you doing now,
> Oh Thomas Moore?

Sighing or suing now,
Rhyming or wooing now,
Billing or cooing now,
        Which, Thomas Moore?

Are you not near the Luddites? By the Lord! if there's a row, but I'll be among ye! How go on the weavers—the breakers of frames—the Lutherans of politics—the reformers?

As the Liberty lads o'er the sea
Bought their freedom, and cheaply, with blood,
        So we, boys, we
    Will *die* fighting, or *live* free,
And down with all kings but King Ludd!

When the web that we weave is complete,
And the shuttle exchanged for the sword,
        We will fling the winding-sheet
    O'er the despot at our feet,
And dye it deep in the gore he has pour'd.

Though black as his heart its hue,
Since his veins are corrupted to mud,
        Yet this is the dew
    Which the tree shall renew
Of Liberty, planted by Ludd!

There's an amiable *chanson* for you—all impromptu. I have written it principally to shock your neighbour * * [Hodgson?], who is all clergy and loyalty—mirth and innocence—milk and water.

But the Carnival's coming,
    Oh Thomas Moore,
The Carnival's coming,
    Oh Thomas Moore;
Masking and mumming,
Fifing and drumming,
Guitarring and strumming,
    Oh Thomas Moore.

The other night I saw a new play,—and the author. The subject was the sacrifice of Isaac. The play succeeded, and they called for the author—according to continental custom—and he presented himself, a noble Venetian, Mali—or Malapiero, by name. Mala was his name, and *pessima* his production,—at least, I thought so ; and I ought to know, having read more or less of five hundred Drury Lane offerings, during my co-adjutorship with the sub-and-super Committee.

When does your poem of poems come out? I hear that the *Edinburgh Review* has cut up Coleridge's *Christabel*, and declared against me for praising it. I praised it, firstly, because I thought well of it ; secondly, because Coleridge was in great distress, and after doing what little I could for him in essentials, I thought that the public avowal of my good opinion might help him further, at least with the booksellers. I am very sorry that Jeffrey has attacked him, because, poor fellow, it will hurt him in mind and pocket. As for me, he's welcome—I shall never think less of Jeffrey for any thing he may say against me or mine in future.

I suppose Murray has sent you, or will send (for I do not know whether they are out or no) the poem, or poesies, of mine, of last summer. By the mass ! they are sublime—*Ganion Coheriza*—gainsay who dares ! Pray, let me hear from you, and of you, and, at least, let me know that you have received these three letters. Direct right *here, poste restante*.

Ever and ever, etc.

P.S.—I heard the other day of a pretty trick of a book-seller, who has published some damned nonsense, swearing the bastards to me, and saying he gave me five hundred guineas for them. He lies—I never wrote such stuff, never saw the poems, nor the publisher of them, in my life, nor had any communication, directly or indirectly, with the fellow. Pray say as much for me, if need be. I have written to Murray, to make him contradict the impostor.

TO JOHN MURRAY *Venice, Dec. 27, 1816*

DEAR SIR,—As the Demon of silence seems to have possessed you, I am determined to have my revenge in postage. This is my sixth or seventh letter since summer and Switzerland.

My last was an injunction to contradict and consign to confusion that Cheapside impostor, who (I heard by a letter from
your Island) had thought proper to append my name to his
spurious poesy, of which I know nothing, nor of his pretended
purchase or copyright. I hope you have, at least, received
that letter.

As the news of Venice must be very interesting to you, I
will regale you with it.

Yesterday being the feast of St. Stephen, every mouth was
put in motion. There was nothing but fiddling and playing on
the virginals, and all kinds of conceits and divertisements, on
every canal of this aquatic city. I dined with the Countess
Albrizzi and a Paduan and Venetian party, and afterwards
went to the opera, at the Fenice theatre (which opens for the
Carnival on that day),—the finest, by the way, I have ever
seen ; it beats *our* theatres hollow in beauty and scenery, and
those of Milan and Brescia bow before it. The opera and its
Syrens were much like all other operas and women, but the
subject of the said opera was something edifying ; it turned—
the plot and conduct thereof—upon a fact narrated by Livy
of a hundred and fifty married ladies having *poisoned* a hundred
and fifty husbands in the good old times. The bachelors of
Rome believed this extraordinary mortality to be merely the
common effect of matrimony or a pestilence ; but the surviving
Benedicts, being all seized with the cholic, examined into the
matter, and found that " their possets had been drugged " ;
the consequence of which was much scandal and several suits
at law. This is really and truly the subject of the Musical piece
at the Fenice ; and you can't conceive what pretty things are
sung and recitativoed about the *horrenda strage*. The conclusion
was a lady's head about to be chopped off by a Lictor, but (I
am sorry to say) he left it on, and she got up and sung a trio
with the two Consuls, the Senate in the back-ground being
chorus. The ballet was distinguished by nothing remarkable,
except that the principal she-dancer went into convulsions
because she was not applauded on her first appearance ; and
the manager came forward to ask if there was " ever a physician
in the theatre ". There was a Greek one in my box, whom I
wished very much to volunteer his services, being sure that in
this case these would have been the last convulsions which

would have troubled the *Ballerina*; but he would not. The crowd was enormous; and in coming out, having a lady under my arm, I was obliged, in making way, almost to " beat a Venetian and traduce the state ", being compelled to regale a person with an English punch in the guts, which sent him as far back as the squeeze and the passage would admit. He did not ask for another; but, with great signs of disapprobation and dismay, appealed to his compatriots, who laughed at him.

I am going on with my Armenian studies in a morning, and assisting and stimulating in the English portion of an English and Armenian grammar, now publishing at the convent of St. Lazarus.

The Superior of the Friars is a bishop, and a fine old fellow, with the beard of a meteor. My spiritual preceptor, pastor and master, Father Paschal, is also a learned and pious soul: he was two years in England.

I am still dreadfully in love with the Adriatic lady whom I spoke of in a former letter (and *not* in *this*—I add, for fear of mistakes; for the only one mentioned in the first part of this epistle is elderly and bookish, two things which I have ceased to admire), and love in this part of the world is no sinecure. This is also the season when every body make up their intrigues for the ensuing year, and cut for partners for the next deal.

And now, if you don't write, I don't know what I won't say or do, nor what I will: send me some news—good news.

Yours very truly, etc., etc., etc. B.

P.S.—Remember me to Mr. G[ifford], with all duty.

I hear that the E[*dinburgh*] R[*eview*] has cut up Coleridge's *Christabel*, and me for praising it, which omen, I think, bodes no great good to your forthcome or coming Canto and Castle (of Chillon) : my run of luck within the last year seems to have taken a turn every way; but never mind, I will bring myself through in the end—if not, I can but be where I began : in the mean time, I am not displeased to be where I am—I mean, at Venice. My Adriatic nymph is this moment here, and I must therefore repose from this letter, " rocked by the beating of her heart ".

Venice, Jan. 2, 1817

DEAR SIR,—Your letter has arrived. Pray, in publishing the 3ᵈ canto [of *Childe Harold*], have you *omitted* any passage or passages? I hope *not*; and indeed wrote to you on my way over the Alps to prevent such an accident—say in your next whether or not the *whole* of the canto (as sent to you) has been published. I wrote to you again the other day, (*twice*, I think,) and shall be glad to hear of the reception of those letters.

To-day is the 2d of January. On this day *3* years ago *The Corsair's* publication is dated, I think, in my letter to Moore. On this day *two* years I married—" Whom the Lord loveth he chasteneth—blessed be the name of the Lord ".—I sha'n't forget the day in a hurry; and wilᴵ ake care to keep the Anniversary before the Evening is over. It is odd enough that I this day received a letter from you announcing the publication of *Cd. Hd.*, etc., etc., on the day of the date of *The Corsair*; and that I also received one from my Sister, written on the 10th of Decr., my daughter's birth-day (and relative chiefly to my daughter), and arriving on the day of the date of my marriage, this present 2d of January, the month of my birth,—and various other Astrologous matters, which I have no time to enumerate.

By the way, you might as well write to Hentsch, my Genevese banker, and enquire whether the *two packets* consigned to his care were or were not delivered to Mr. St. Aubyn, or if they are still in his keeping. One contains papers, letters, and all the original MS. of your 3ᵈ canto, as first conceived; and the other, some bones from the field of Morat. Many thanks for your news, and the good spirits in which your letter is written.

Venice and I agree very well; but I do not know that I have any thing new to say, except of the last new opera, which I sent in my late letter. The Carnival is commencing, and there is a good deal of fun here and there—besides business; for all the world are making up their intrigues for the season—changing, or going on upon a renewed lease. I am very well off with Marianna, who is not at all a person to tire me; firstly, because I do not tire of a woman *personally*, but because they are generally bores in their disposition; and, secondly, because she is amiable, and has a tact which is not always the portion of the fair creation; and, thirdly, she is very pretty; and, fourthly—but there is no occasion for further specification. I have passed a great deal of my time with her since my arrival at Venice, and never a twenty-four hours without giving and receiving from one to three (and occasionally an extra or so) pretty unequivocal proofs of mutual good contentment. So far we have gone on very well; as to the future, I never anticipate—" *Carpe diem* "—the past at least is one's own, which is one reason for making sure of the present. So much for my proper liaison.

The general state of morals here is much the same as in the Doges' time; a woman is virtuous (according to the code) who limits herself to her husband and one lover; those who have two, three, or more, are a little *wild*; but it is only those who are indiscriminately diffuse, and form a low connection, such as the Princess of Wales with her courier, (who, by the way, is made a knight of Malta,) who are considered as over-stepping the modesty of marriage. In Venice, the Nobility have a trick of marrying with dancers or singers: and, truth to say, the women of their own order are by no means hand-some; but the general race—the women of the 2^d and other orders, the wives of the Advocates, merchants, and proprietors, and untitled gentry, are mostly *bel' sangue*, and it is with these that the more amatory connections are usually formed: there are also instances of stupendous constancy. I know a woman of fifty who never had but one lover, whó dying early, she be-came devout, renouncing all but her husband: she piques herself, as may be presumed, upon this miraculous fidelity, talking of it occasionally with a species of misplaced morality, which is rather amusing. There is no convincing a woman here, that she is in the smallest degree deviating from the rule of right or the fitness of things, in having an *Amoroso* : the great sin seems to lie in concealing it, or in having more than one; that is, unless such an extension of the prerogative is under-stood and approved of by the prior claimant.

In my case, I do not know that I had any predecessor, and am pretty sure that there is no participator; and am inclined to think, from the youth of the party, and from the frank un-disguised way in which every body avows everything in this part of the world, when there is anything to avow, as well as from some other circumstances, such as the marriage being recent, etc., etc., etc., that this is the *premier pas* : it does not much signify.

In another sheet, I send you some sheets of a grammar, English and Armenian, for the use of the Armenians, of which I promoted, and indeed induced, the publication : (it cost me but a thousand francs—French livres.) I still pursue my lessons in the language, without any rapid progress, but advancing a little daily. Padre Paschal, with some little help from me, as translator of his Italian into English, is also proceeding in an MS. Grammar for the *English* acquisition of Armenian, which will be printed also, when finished.

We want to know if there are any *Armenian types* or letter-press in England—at Oxford, Cambridge, or elsewhere? You know, I suppose, that, many years ago, the two Whistons published in England an original text of a history of Armenia, with their own Latin translation? Do those types still exist? and where? Pray enquire among your learned acquaintance.

When this grammar (I mean the one now printing) is done, will you have any objection to take 40 or fifty copies, which will not cost in all above five or ten guineas, and try the curiosity of the learned with a sale of them? Say yes or no, as you like. I can assure you that they have some very curious books and MS., chiefly translations from Greek originals now lost. They are, besides, a much respected and learned community, and the study of their language was taken up with great ardour by some literary Frenchmen in Buonaparte's time.

I have not done a stitch of poetry since I left Switzerland, and have not, at present, the *estro* upon me : the truth is, that you are *afraid* of having a *4th* canto *before* September, and of another copyright ; but I have at present no thoughts of resuming that poem nor of beginning any other. If I write, I think of trying prose ; but I dread introducing living people, or applications which might be made to living people : perhaps one day or other, I may attempt some work of fancy in prose, descriptive of Italian manners and of human passions ; but at present I am preoccupied. As for poesy, mine is the *dream* of my sleeping Passions ; when they are awake, I cannot speak their language, only ⅄ their Somnambulism, and just now they are not dormant.

If Mr. G[ifford] wants *Carte blanche* as to *The Siege of Corinth*, he has it, and may do as he likes with it.

I sent you a letter contradictory of the Cheapside man (who invented the story you speak of) the other day. My best respects to Mr. Gifford, and such of my friends as you may see at your house. I wish you all prosperity and new year's gratulation, and am

Yours, ever and truly, B.

TO THE HON. DOUGLAS KINNAIRD* *Venice, January 12th, 1817*

MY DEAR KINNAIRD,—Since my arrival in Venice I have written to you *twice*, to request that you would have the goodness to transmit as soon as convenient letters for the credit of such sum or sums as Murray may have paid " according to the tenor " concluded in Septr. last. Address to me here, either Poste restante, or to the care of Messrs Siri and Wilhalm, bankers of this city; it is my intention to remain here probably till Spring. Hobhouse is gone to Rome with his brother and sister but will return in March or so.

I hope that you have received at least one of my letters. In these I told you all the gossip I could think of, and should be glad to have a little in return. To my surprise Murray in a recent letter tells me that you are out of the committee,[1] an event which it requires no great sagacity to attribute to the illustrious Frances Kelly of comic memory. If you recollect (for I am a wonderful judge in all concerns but my own) I forboded long ago disasters to some of you—or us—or one or more, from the intervention of that worthy young woman, and you may also recollect, that for my own part, among the very few pieces of prudence which grace my graceless history, one was to steer very clear of any colloquy or communion with that fair favourite of elderly gentlemen. I don't mean in an im-modest way, for she is a Vestal as is well known, but in the

---

[1] *The Drury Lane Committee*, on which Byron had himself served during his last year in England.

chaster attentions which my coadjutors, including yourself, were accustomed to pay to her. I kept to distant politeness, and verily I have my reward, as you it seems have for being her friend first, and her manager afterwards.

Seriously, if this vexes you I am very sorry for it, but I know nothing of the matter, though I can't help thinking that if I had been at your elbow, and had not lost my temper at the pretty speeches you would have made me in the course of our dialogues, I could have prevented this, at least I should have tried. I say no more. Where the Devil are the other Committed? George, and Mr. Peter Moore? And my locum tenens whosoever he be? You will tell me these matters in your next.

Murray tells me the poems are out, with what success I know not except from his letter, which is written in good spirits. I wonder if he published them as *sent*; if he has made alterations or omissions, I shall not pardon him. I suspect him as a *Tory* of softening my M.S. If he has, by the Ass of Balaam! he shall endure my indignation. He tells me of a row with an Impostor, a bookseller who has been *injunctioned*, by the aid of an *oath* from Scrope Davies. I would give a trifle to see Scrope's affidavit, and to have heard half the good things he has said upon that subject. " Hath he laid perjury upon his soul? " No doubt he will say so, as he always adds his sins to the other obligations he has conferred upon me. When he left Switzerland he was determined to see a " Boa-Constrictor ", God knows why, but whatever he saw, he always wished for the addition of that amiable reptile. I hope that fortune has had the good taste to stick to him, turf or table. Doth he drink as of old?

We were sadly sober all the autumn, but I hope some day or other to revive and quench our antient thirst in the way of our youth. He promised to write; I trust that his affidavit was of a different complexion from his promise.

TO THOMAS MOORE   *Venice, January 28, 1817*

Your letter of the 8th is before me. The remedy for your plethora is simple—abstinence. I was obliged to have recourse

to the like some years ago, I mean in point of *diet*, and, with
the exception of some convivial weeks and days, (it might be
months, now and then), have kept to Pythagoras ever since.
For all this, let me hear that you are better. You must not
indulge in " filthy beer ", nor in porter, nor eat *suppers*—the
last are the devil to those who swallow dinner. * * * *

I am truly sorry to hear of your father's misfortune—cruel
at any time, but doubly cruel in advanced life. However, you
will, at least, have the satisfaction of doing your part by him,
and, depend upon it, it will not be in vain. Fortune, to be
sure, is a female, but not such a b * * as the rest (always
excepting your wife and my sister from such sweeping terms) ;
for she generally has some justice in the long run. I have no
spite against her, though between her and Nemesis I have had
some sore gauntlets to run—but then I have done my best to
deserve no better. But to *you*, she is a good deal in arrear, and
she will come round—mind if she don't : you have the vigour
of life, of independence, of talent, spirit, and character all with
you. What you can do for yourself, you have done and will
do ; and surely there are some others in the world who would
not be sorry to be of use, if you would allow them to be useful,
or at least attempt it.

I think of being in England in the spring. If there is a
row, by the sceptre of King Ludd, but I'll be there ; and if
there is none, and only a continuance of " this meek, piping
time of peace ", I will take a cottage a hundred yards to the
south of your abode, and become your neighbour ; and we will
compose such canticles, and hold such dialogues, as shall be
the terror of the *Times* (including the newspaper of that name),
and the wonder, and honour, and praise, of the *Morning
Chronicle* and posterity.

I rejoice to hear of your forthcoming in February—though
I tremble for the " magnificence ", which you attribute to the
new *Childe Harold*. I am glad you like it ; it is a fine indistinct
piece of poetical desolation, and my favourite. I was half mad
during the time of its composition, between metaphysics,
mountains, lakes, love unextinguishable, thoughts unutterable,
and the nightmare of my own delinquencies. I should, many
a good day, have blown my brains out, but for the recollection
that it would have given pleasure to my mother-in-law ; and,

even *then*, if I could have been certain to haunt her —— but I won't dwell upon these trifling family matters.

Venice is in the *estro* of her carnival, and I have been up these last two nights at the ridotto and the opera, and all that kind of thing. Now for an adventure. A few days ago a gondolier brought me a billet without a subscription, intimating a wish on the part of the writer to meet me either in gondola or at the island of San Lazaro, or at a third rendezvous, indicated in the note. " I know the country's disposition well " —in Venice " they do let Heaven see those tricks they dare not show ", etc., etc. ; so, for all response, I said that neither of the three places suited me ; but that I would either be at home at ten at night *alone*, or be at the ridotto at midnight, where the writer might meet me masked. At ten o'clock I was at home and alone (Marianna was gone with her husband to a con-versazione), when the door of my apartment opened, and in walked a well-looking and (for an Italian) *bionda* girl of about nineteen, who informed me that she was married to the brother of my *amorosa*, and wished to have some conversation with me. I made a decent reply, and we had some talk in Italian and Romaic (her mother being a Greek of Corfu), when lo ! in a very few minutes, in marches, to my very great astonishment, Marianna Segati, *in propriâ personâ*, and after making a most polite courtesy to her sister-in-law and to me, without a single word seizes her said sister-in-law by the hair, and bestows upon her some sixteen slaps, which would have made your ear ache only to hear their echo. I need not describe the screaming which ensued. The luckless visitor took flight. I seized Marianna, who, after several vain efforts to get away in pursuit of the enemy, fairly went into fits in my arms ; and, in spite of reasoning, eau de Cologne, vinegar, half a pint of water, and God knows what other waters beside, continued so till past midnight.

After damning my servants for letting people in without apprizing me, I found that Marianna in the morning had seen her sister-in-law's gondolier on the stairs, and, suspecting that his apparition boded her no good, had either returned of her own accord, or been followed by her maids or some other spy of her people to the conversazione, from whence she returned to perpetrate this piece of pugilism. I had seen fits before, and also some small scenery of the same genus in and out of our island : but this was not all. After about an hour, in comes—who? why, Signor Segati, her lord and husband, and finds me with his wife fainting upon the sofa, and all the apparatus of confusion, dishevelled hair, hats, handkerchiefs, salts, smelling-bottles—and the lady as pale as ashes, without sense or motion. His first question was, " What is all this? " The lady could not reply—so I did. I told him the explanation was the easiest thing in the world ; but in the mean time it would be as well to recover his wife—at least, her senses. This came about in due time of suspiration and respiration.

You need not be alarmed—jealousy is not the order of the day in Venice, and daggers are out of fashion ; while duels, on love matters, are unknown—at least, with the husbands. But, for all this, it was an awkward affair ; and though he must have known that I made love to Marianna, yet I believe he was not, till that evening, aware of the extent to which it had gone. It is very well known that almost all the married women have a lover ; but it is usual to keep up the forms, as in other nations. I did not, therefore, know what the devil to say. I could not out with the truth, out of regard to her, and I did not choose to lie for my sake ;—besides, the thing told itself. I thought the best way would be to let her explain it as she chose (a woman being never at a loss—the devil always sticks by them)—only determining to protect and carry her off, in case of any ferocity on the part of the Signor. I saw that he was quite calm. She went to bed, and next day—how they settled it, I know not, but settle it they did. Well—then I had to explain to Marianna about this never-to-be-sufficiently-confounded sister-in-law ; which I did by swearing innocence, eternal constancy, etc., etc. * * * But the sister-in-law, very much discomposed with being treated in such wise, has (not having her own shame before her eyes) told the affair to half Venice, and the servants (who were summoned by the fight and the fainting) to the other half. But, here, nobody minds such trifles, except to be amused by them. I don't know whether you will be so, but I have scrawled a long letter out of these follies.

Believe me ever, etc.

TO THOMAS MOORE   *Venice, February 28, 1817*

You will, perhaps, complain as much of the frequency of my letters now, as you were wont to do of their rarity. I think this is the fourth within as many moons. I feel anxious to hear from you, even more than usual, because your last indicated that you were unwell. At present, I am on the invalid regimen myself. The Carnival—that is, the latter part of it, and sitting up late o' nights, had knocked me up a little. But it is over,— and it is now Lent, with all its abstinence and sacred music.

The mumming closed with a masked ball at the Fenice, where I went, as also to most of the ridottos, etc., etc.; and, though I did not dissipate much upon the whole, yet I find " the sword wearing out the scabbard ", though I have but just turned the corner of twenty-nine.

> So we'll go no more a roving
>   So late into the night,
> Though the heart be still as loving,
>   And the moon be still as bright.
>
> For the sword outwears its sheath,
>   And the soul wears out the breast,
> And the heart must pause to breathe,
>   And Love itself have rest.
>
> Though the night was made for loving,
>   And the day returns too soon,
> Yet we'll go no more a roving
>   By the light of the moon.

I have lately had some news of litter*atoor*, as I heard the editor of the *Monthly* pronounce it once upon a time. I hear that W. W.[1] has been publishing and responding to the attacks of the *Quarterly*, in the learned Perry's *Chronicle*. I read his poesies last autumn, and, amongst them found an epitaph on his bull-dog, and another on *myself*. But I beg leave to assure him (like the astrologer Partridge) that I am not only alive now, but was alive also at the time he wrote it. * * Hobhouse has (I hear, also) expectorated a letter against the *Quarterly*,

[1] Wedderburn Webster.

addressed to me. I feel awkwardly situated between him and Gifford, both being my friends.

And this is your month of going to press—by the body of Diana! (a Venetian oath,) I feel as anxious—but not fearful for you—as if it were myself coming out in a work of humour, which would, you know, be the antipodes of all my previous publications. I don't think you have any thing to dread but your own reputation. You must keep up to that. As you never showed me a line of your work, I do not even know your measure; but you must send me a copy by Murray forthwith, and then you shall hear what I think. I dare say you are in a pucker. Of all authors, you are the only really *modest* one I ever met with,—which would sound oddly enough to those who recollect your morals when you were young—that is, when you were *extremely* young—I don't mean to stigmatise you either with years or morality.

I believe I told you that the E[*dinburgh*] R[*eview*] had attacked me, in an article on Coleridge (I have not seen it)— " *Et tu*, Jeffrey? "—" there is nothing but roguery in villanous man ". But I absolve him of all attacks, present and future; for I think he had already pushed his clemency in my behoof to the utmost, and I shall always think well of him. I only wonder he did not begin before, as my domestic destruction was a fine opening for all the world, of which all who could did well to avail themselves.

If I live ten years longer, you will see, however, that it is not over with me—I don't mean in literature, for that is no-thing; and it may seem odd enough to say, I do not think it my vocation. But you will see that I shall do something or other—the times and fortune permitting—that, " like the cosmogony, or creation of the world, will puzzle the philo-sophers of all ages ". But I doubt whether my constitution will hold out. I have, at intervals, exorcised it most devilishly.

I have not yet fixed a time of return, but I think of the spring. I shall have been away a year in April next. You never mention Rogers, nor Hodgson, your clerical neighbour, who has lately got a living near you. Has he also got a child yet?—his desideratum, when I saw him last. * * *

Pray let me hear from you, at your time and leisure, be-lieving me ever and truly and affectionately, etc.

TO THOMAS MOORE   *Venice, March 10, 1817*

I wrote again to you lately, but I hope you won't be sorry to have another epistle.   I have been unwell this last month, with a kind of slow and low fever, which fixes upon me at night, and goes off in the morning ; but, however, I am now better. In spring it is probable we may meet ; at least I intend for England, where I have business, and hope to meet you in *your* restored health and additional laurels.

Murray has sent me the *Quarterly* and the *Edinburgh*.   When I tell you that Walter Scott is the author of the article in the former, you will agree with me that such an article is still more honourable to him than to myself.   I am perfectly pleased with Jeffrey's also, which I wish you to tell him, with my remembrances—not that I suppose it is of any consequence to him, or ever could have been, whether I am pleased or not, but simply in my private relation to him, as his well-wisher, and it may be one day as his acquaintance.   I wish you would also add, what you know, that I was not, and, indeed, am not even *now*, the misanthropical and gloomy gentleman he takes me for, but a facetious companion, well to do with those with whom I am intimate, and as loquacious and laughing as if I were a much cleverer fellow.

I suppose now I shall never be able to shake off my sables in public imagination, more particularly since my moral * * [Clytemnestra?] clove down my fame.   However, nor that, nor more than that, has yet extinguished my spirit, which always rises with the rebound.

At Venice we are in Lent, and I have not lately moved out of doors, my feverishness requiring quiet, and—by way of being more quiet—here is the Signora Marianna just come in and seated at my elbow.

Have you seen * * *'s book of poesy? and, if you have seen it, are you not delighted with it?   And have you—I really cannot go on : there is a pair of great black eyes looking over my shoulder, like the angel leaning over St. Matthew's, in the old frontispieces to the Evangelists,—so that I must turn and answer them instead of you.

Ever, etc.

Venice, March 25, 1817

I have at last learned, in default of your own writing (or *not* writing—which should it be? for I am not very clear as to the application of the word *default*), from Murray two particulars of (or belonging to) you ; one, that you are removing to Hornsey, which is, I presume, to be nearer London ; and the other, that your poem is announced by the name of *Lalla Rookh*. I am glad of it,—first that we are to have it at last, and next, I like a tough title myself—witness *The Giaour* and *Childe Harold*, which choked half the Blues at starting. Besides, it is the tail of Alcibiades's dog,—not that I suppose you want either dog or tail. Talking of tail, I wish you had not called it a " *Persian Tale* ". Say a " Poem ", or " Romance ", but not " Tale ". I am very sorry that I called some of my own things " Tales ", because I think that they are something better. Besides, we have had Arabian, and Hindoo, and Turkish, and Assyrian Tales. But, after all, this is frivolous in me ; you won't, however, mind my nonsense.

Really and truly, I want you to make a great hit, if only out of self-love, because we happen to be old cronies ; and I have no doubt you will—I am sure you *can*. But you are, I'll be sworn, in a devil of a pucker ; and *I* am *not* at your elbow, and Rogers *is*. I envy him ; which is not fair, because he does not envy any body. Mind you send to me—that is, make Murray send—the moment you are forth.

I have been very ill with a slow fever, which at last took to flying, and became as quick as need be. But, at length, after a week of half-delirium, burning skin, thirst, hot headach, horrible pulsation, and no sleep, by the blessing of barley water, and refusing to see any physician, I recovered. It is an epidemic of the place, which is annual, and visits strangers. Here follow some versicles, which I made one sleepless night.

> I read the " Christabel ",
> Very well :
> I read the " Missionary " ;
> Pretty—very :
> I tried at " Ilderim " ;
> Ahem !

> I read a sheet of " Marg'ret of *Anjou* " ;
>   *Can you ?*
> I turn'd a page of Webster's " Waterloo " ;
>   Pooh ! pooh !
> I look'd at Wordsworth's milk-white " Rylstone Doe " :
>   Hillo !
> I read " Glenarvon ", too, by Caro. Lamb—
>   God damn !

*   *   *   *   *   *   *

I have not the least idea where I am going, nor what I am to do. I wished to have gone to Rome ; but at present it is pestilent with English,—a parcel of staring boobies, who go about gaping and wishing to be at once cheap and magnificent. A man is a fool who travels now in France or Italy, till this tribe of wretches is swept home again. In two or three years the first rush will be over, and the Continent will be roomy and agreeable.

I stayed at Venice chiefly because it is not one of their " dens of thieves " ; and here they but pause and pass. In Switzerland it was really noxious. Luckily, I was early, and had got the prettiest place on all the Lake before they were quickened into motion with the rest of the reptiles. But they crossed me every where. I met a family of children and old women half-way up the Wengen Alp (by the Jungfrau) upon mules, some of them too old and others too young to be the least aware of what they saw.

By the way, I think the Jungfrau, and all that region of Alps, which I traversed in September—going to the very top of the Wengen, which is not the highest (the Jungfrau itself is inaccessible) but the best point of view—much finer than Mont-Blanc and Chamouni, or the Simplon. I kept a journal of the whole for my sister Augusta, part of which she copied and let Murray see.

I wrote a sort of mad Drama,[1] for the sake of introducing the Alpine scenery in description : and this I sent lately to Murray. Almost all the *dram. pers.* are spirits, ghosts, or magicians, and the scene is in the Alps and the other world, so you may suppose what a Bedlam tragedy it must be : make him show it you. I

---

[1] *Manfred.*

399

sent him all three acts piecemeal, by the post, and suppose they have arrived.

I have now written to you at least six letters, or letter*ets*, and all I have received in return is a note about the length you used to write from Bury Street to St. James's Street, when we used to dine with Rogers, and talk laxly, and go to parties, and hear poor Sheridan now and then. Do you remember one night he was so tipsy, that I was forced to put his cocked hat on for him,—for he could not,—and I let him down at Brookes's, much as he must since have been let down into his grave. Heigh ho! I wish I was drunk—but I have nothing but this damned barley-water before me.

I am still in love,—which is a dreadful drawback in quitting a place, and I can't stay at Venice much longer. What I shall do on this point I don't know. The girl means to go with me, but I do not like this for her own sake. I have had so many conflicts in my own mind on this subject, that I am not at all sure they did not help me to the fever I mentioned above. I am certainly very much attached to her, and I have cause to be so, if you knew all. But she has a child; and though, like all the " children of the sun ", she consults nothing but passion, it is necessary I should think for both; and it is only the virtuous, like * * * *, who can afford to give up husband and child, and live happy ever after.

The Italian ethics are the most singular ever met with. The perversion, not only of action, but of reasoning, is singular in the women. It is not that they do not consider the thing itself as wrong, and very wrong, but *love* (the *sentiment* of love) is not merely an excuse for it, but makes it an *actual virtue*, provided it is disinterested, and not a *caprice*, and is confined to one object. They have awful notions of constancy; for I have seen some ancient figures of eighty pointed out as *Amorosi* of forty, fifty, and sixty years' standing. I can't say I have ever seen a husband and wife so coupled.

Ever, etc.

P.S.—Marianna, to whom I have just translated what I have written on our subject to you, says—" If you loved me thoroughly, you would not make so many fine reflections, which are only good *forbirsi i scarpi* ",—that is, " to clean shoes withal ",—a Venetian proverb of appreciation, which is applicable to reasoning of all kinds.

TO JOHN CAM HOBHOUSE †   *Venice, March 31st, 1817*

MY DEAR HOBHOUSE,—In verity, the *malaria* was a pretext, as I knew it was a summer and not a spring production, but the English crowd of the Holy Week was as sincere an excuse as need to be.

Since I wrote to you I have had a fever, like one I had from the marshes of Elis, which nearly finished me at Patras, but this was milder, and of shorter duration; it, however, left me weakly. It had been approaching by slow degrees ever since the Carnival, and at last came on rather sharply. It was not, however, the low, vulgar typhus, which is at present decimating Venice, and has half unpeopled Milan; but a sharp, gentlemanly fever that went away in a few days. I saw no physician; they sent for one without telling me, and when I heard he was below I had him sent out of the house. And so I recovered. It was not Aglietti, I believe, but you may be sure if it had [been], that prig should never have had a fee of mine.

At present I am very well, with a monstrous appetite. I think of coming on to Rome this ensuing month; in case you should be gone, will you delegate some friend to get me in without custom-house research, and will you tell me what hostel or inn I am to lay down my wallet in, and how about lodgement? Truly wroth am I to hear the rumours you wot of, particularly the first, but one is as false as the other. The origin of the latter I take to be a lie which was rife here about the *Fabre* or *Fabri* (which is it?), the singer from Milan—the girl we saw there. She sang here, at the Fenice, during the Carnival; and was in high and magnificent maintenance by a Sig^r Papadopoli, a Venetian of great wealth and concupiscence. But a man in a cloak was seen coming out of her abode one very early morning, and this man they would have to be me (I never saw her in my life but on the stage), and not content with this, it was added that I had decamped with her for Naples; and I had as much difficulty in proving my presence here, as Partridge in re-establishing his existence. The origin of these unseemly reports I take to be a translation in some Venetian gazette of the Jena review of C. L.'s *Glenarvon*, and another of the last canto of C. H^d, the one stating the scratching attempt at canicide of that " two-handed whore " at Lady Heathcote's, and the other representing me as the most decided panegyrist of Buonaparte. I have, you may be sure, noticed neither one, nor the other of these matters.

The Quarterly I have read (which is written by Walter Scott, so M[urray] says). Both it and the " Edinburgh " are as favourable as the author could wish ; and more so than could be wished by anybody else ; the Edin^h is by Jeffrey himself : I am very glad that anybody likes the Canto, but particularly glad that Baillie does, because he is a very superior if not a *supreme* man ; as for you and I, we are such old friends that " we have travelled over one another's minds long ago " ; don't you remember what a pet that sentence used to put you into ? But never mind, is it not true.

In case you should not have heard from England, I will tell you some news of litera*toor*. K[innaird] writes to me that Mrs. K., under the colours of Keppel, has become " *a* PUBLIC *character* ", at Drury Lane as well as at Covent Garden, with great success. I suppose he means, of course, as a singer, but it is as well to be distinct.

Maturin's second tragedy, he says, has not succeeded, and he gives some very good reasons why it should not, which sound remarkably well, particularly as his very last letter save this anticipated its " complete success."

For my part I say nothing ; but this I will say, Did I *ever*? No, I *never*, etc., etc., etc., etc., etc., etc., etc. Do you understand me ? No one else can.

I have heard of my daughter, who is very fine they say ; but there is a dispute about her suscitated between me and my moral Clytemnestra. Some day or other Ada will become my Orestes, and Electra too, both in one.

This dispute will probably end in a lawsuit. Having heard that they thought of voyaging, I refused to allow the child to leave the country, and demanded an explicit declaration that on no account should the attempt be made ; this was evaded, and at last a sort of half reluctant kind of paper signed, which I have refused to accept, and so we are all at, or about, law.

That old fool Noel,[1] last year, I hear for the first time, had filed a bill in Chancery against me, upon some remote question of property, purely to make my daughter a ward of the Court and circumscribe my right over her, or rather my authority. I can tell you, however, that Hanson has behaved very well, and briskly in this business, for I have copies of the correspondence.

They have begun, and, by the Lord, I must go on—pretty separation ! We are as fast as ever, only pulling the chain different ways, till one of us tumbles. My star is sure to win in the long run.

You do not say a word of your " paradoxes ", or of the Pope—only think of Dr. Polidori coming too !—well! I'm sure ! Is he any sager ? I suppose you mean that despicable lisping old ox and charlatan, Frederic North, by the successor to Ld Guilford. Of all the perambulating humbuggerers, that aged nondescript is the principal.

I send you a catalogue of some books " of poeshie of the king, my master ", as Freytag said to Voltaire :

> I read the " Christabel ".
>> Very well.
> I read the " Missionary ",
>> Somewhat visionary.
> I tried at " Ilderim ",
>> Ahem !
> I read a sheet of " Margaret of *Anjou* ",
>> Can *you* ?
> I skimmed a page of Webster's " Waterloo ",
>> Pooh ! Pooh !
> I looked at Wordsworth's milkwhite " Rylstone Doe ",
>> Hillo ! !
> I read " Glenarvon ", too, by Caro. Lamb,
>> God damn.

I have bought several books which must be left for my bankers to forward to England ; amongst others a complete Voltaire, in ninety-two volumes, whom I have been reading ; he is delightful, but dreadfully inaccurate frequently. One of

---

[1] Sir Ralph Milbanke. Lady Milbanke had assumed the name of Noel on the death of her brother, Lord Wentworth, whose heiress Annabella Byron was.

his paragraphs (in a letter) begins " *Jean Jacques* is a Jean *foutre* " which he seems to say with all his heart and soul. This is one of the things which make me laugh—being a " clever Tom Clinch " and perhaps will have the like effect on you.

Yours ever, and very truly and affectly., B.

TO JOHN MURRAY † *Venice, April 2, 1817*

DEAR SIR,—I sent you the whole of the Drama at *three several* times, act by act, in separate covers. I hope that you have, or will receive, some or the whole of it.

So Love has a conscience. By Diana! I shall make him take back the box,[1] though it were Pandora's. The discovery of its intrinsic silver occurred on sending it to have the lid adapted to admit Marianna's portrait. Of course I had the box remitted *in statu quo*, and had the picture set in another, which suits it (the picture) very well. The defaulting box is not touched, hardly,—it was not in the man's hands above an hour.

I am aware of what you say of Otway; and am a very great admirer of his,—all except of that maudlin bitch of chaste lewdness and blubbering curiosity, Belvidera, whom I utterly despise, abhor, and detest; but the story of Marino Falieri is different, and, I think, so much finer, that I wish Otway had taken it instead: the head conspiring against the body for refusal of redress for a real injury,—jealousy—treason, with the more fixed and inveterate passions (mixed with policy) of an old or elderly man—the devil himself could not have a finer subject, and he is your only tragic dramatist.

Voltaire has asked *why* no woman has ever written even a tolerable tragedy? " Ah (said the Patriarch) the composition of a tragedy requires * * *." If this be true, Lord knows what Joanna Baillie does; I suppose she borrows them.

There is still, in the Doge's Palace, the black veil painted over Falieri's picture, and the staircase whereon he was first crowned Doge, and subsequently decapitated. This was the thing that most struck my imagination in Venice—more than

---

[1] Byron had discovered that a box purchased from a London jeweller as gold was, in fact, of silver gilt.

the Rialto, which I visited for the sake of Shylock; and more, too, than Schiller's "*Armenian*", a novel which took a great hold of me when a boy. It is also called the "Ghost Seer", and I never walked down St. Mark's by moonlight without thinking of it, and "*at nine o'clock he died!*"—But I hate things *all fiction*; and therefore the *Merchant* and *Othello* have no great associations to me: but *Pierre* has. There should always be some foundation of fact for the most airy fabric, and pure invention is but the talent of a liar.

Maturin's tragedy.—By your account of him last year to me, he seemed a bit of a coxcomb, personally. Poor fellow! to be sure, he had had a long seasoning of adversity, which is not so hard to bear as t'other thing. I hope that this won't throw him back into the "slough of Despond". Let him take heart—"whom the Lord loveth he chasteneth; blessed be the name of the Lord!" This sentence, by the way, is a contrast to the other one of *Quem Deus vult perdere prius dementat*, which may be thus done into English:—

> "God maddens him whom 'tis his will to lose,
>   And gives the choice of death or phrenzy—choose."

You talk of "marriage";—ever since my own funeral, the word makes me giddy, and throws me into a cold sweat. Pray, don't repeat it.

Tell me that Walter Scott is better; I would not have him ill for the world. I suppose it was by sympathy that I had my fever at the same time. I joy in the success of your *Quarterly*; but I must still stick by the *Edinburgh*. Jeffrey has done so by me, I must say, through everything, and this is more than I deserved from him. I have more than once acknowledged to you by letter the "Article" (and articles); say that you have received the said letters, as I do not otherwise know what letters arrive. Both reviews came, but nothing more. M[aturin]'s play, and the extract not yet come.

There have been two articles in the Venice papers, one a Review of C. Lamb's *Glenarvon* (whom may it please the beneficent Giver of all Good to damn in the next world! as she has damned herself in this) with the account of her scratching attempt at *Canicide* (at Lady Heathcote's), and the other a Review of *Childe Harold*, in which it proclaims me the most

rebellious and contumacious admirer of Buonaparte now surviving in Europe. Both these articles are translations from the
Literary Gazette of German Jena. I forgot to mention them
at the time; they are some weeks old. They actually mentioned Caro: Lamb and her *mother's* name at full length. I
have conserved these papers as curiosities.

Write to say whether or no my Magician has arrived, with
all his scenes, spells, etc.

Yours ever, B.

P.S.—Will you tell Mr. Kinnaird that the two recent letters
I wrote to him were, owing to a mistake of a booby of a Partner
of Siri and Wilhalm (the Bankers here), and that one of them
called this morning to say all was right—and that there was no
occasion for a further letter; however, heaven knows whether
they are right or not. I hope I shall not have the same bother
at Rome.

You should close with Madame de Stael. This will be her
best work, and permanently historical; it is on her father,
the Revolution, and Buonaparte, etc. Bonstetten told me in
Switzerland it was *very great*. I have not seen it myself, but
the author often. She was very kind to me at Copet.

I like your delicacy—*you* who print *Margaret*—and *Ilderim*
and then demur at Corinne. The failure of poor M's play will
be a cordial to the aged heart of Saul,[1] who has been " kicking
against the pricks " of the managers so long and so vainly—
they ought to act his *Ivan*; as for Kean he is an " *infidus Scurra* ",
and his conduct on this occasion is of a piece with all one ever
heard of him. Pray look after *Mr. S*ᵗ *Aubin*. He is an Oxonian.
It is very odd and something more than negligent that he has
not consigned the letters, etc.; it was his own offer.

It is useless to send to the *Foreign Office*: nothing arrives to
me by that conveyance. I suppose some zealous clerk thinks
it a Tory duty to prevent it.

TO THE HON. AUGUSTA LEIGH *Rome, May 10ᵗʰ 1817*

My dearest Augusta,—I have taken a flight down here
(see the Map), but shall return to Venice in fifteen days from

[1] Sotheby, whose *Saul* was published in 1807.

this date, so address all answers to my usual head- (or rather heart-) quarters—that is to Venice. I am very well, quite recovered, and as is always the case after all illness—particularly fever—got large, ruddy, and robustous to a degree which would please you—and shock me. I have been on horseback several hours a day for this last ten days, besides now and then on my journey ; proof positive of high health, and curiosity, and exercise. Love me—and don't be afraid—I mean of my sicknesses. I get well, and shall always get so, and have luck enough still to beat most things ; and whether I win or not—depend upon it—I will fight to the last.

Will you tell my wife " mine excellent Wife " that she is brewing a Cataract for herself and me in these foolish equivocations about *Ada*,—a job for lawyers—and more hatred for every body, for which—(God knows), there is no occasion. She is surrounded by people who detest me—Brougham the lawyer—who never forgave me for saying that Mrs G^e Lamb was a damned fool (by the way I did not then know he was in love with her) in 1814, and for a former savage note in my foolish satire, all which is good reason for *him*—but not for *Lady B^n* ; besides her mother—etc etc etc—so that what I may say or you may say is of no great use—however—*say it.* If she supposes that I want to hate or plague her (however wroth circumstances at times may make me in words and in temporary gusts or disgusts of feeling), she is quite out—I have no such wish—and never had, and if she imagines that I now wish to become united to her again she is still more out. *I never will.* I *would* to the end of the *year* succeeding our separation— (expired nearly a month ago, *Legal reckoning*), according to a resolution I had taken thereupon—but the day and the hour is gone by—and it is irrevocable. But all this is no reason for further misery and quarrel ; Give me but a *fair share* of my daughter—the half—my natural right and authority, and I am content ; otherwise I come to England, and " law and claw before they get it ", all which will vex and out live Sir R. & L^y N. besides making Mrs Clermont bilious—and plaguing Bell herself, which I really by the great God ! wish to avoid. Now pray see her and say so—it may do good—and if not—she and I are but what we are, and God knows that is wretched enough—at least to me.

407

Of Rome I say nothing—you can read the Guide-book— which is very accurate.

I found here an old letter of yours dated November 1816 —to which the best answer I can make—is none. You are sadly timid my child, but so you all shewed yourselves when you could have been useful—particularly ———— but never mind. I shall not forget *him*, though I do not rejoice in any ill which befalls him. Is the fool's spawn a *son* or a *daughter*? you say one —and others another; so Sykes works him—*let him*—I shall live to see him and W. destroyed, and more than them—and then—but let all that pass for the present.

yrs. ever   B.

P.S.—Hobhouse is here. I travelled from V——— *quite alone* so do not fuss about women etc—I am not so rash as I have been.

TO JOHN MURRAY   *Venice, May 30, 1817*

DEAR SIR,—I returned from Rome two days ago, and have received your letter; but no sign nor tidings of the parcel sent through Sir ——— Stuart, which you mention. After an interval of months, a packet of *Tales*, etc., found me at Rome; but this is all, and may be all that ever will find me. The post seems to be the only sane conveyance; and *that only for letters*. From Florence I sent you a poem on Tasso, and from Rome the new third act of *Manfred*, and by Dr. Polidori two pictures for my sister. I left Rome, and made a rapid journey home. You will continue to direct here as usual. Mr. Hobhouse is gone to Naples: I should have run down there too for a week, but for the quantity of English whom I heard of there. I prefer hating them at a distance; unless an earthquake, or a good real eruption of Vesuvius, were insured to reconcile me to their vicinity.

I know no other situation except Hell which I should feel inclined to participate with them—as a race, always excepting several individuals. There were few of them in Rome, and I believe none whom you know, except that old Blue-*bore* Sotheby, who will give a fine account of Italy, in which he will be greatly assisted by his total ignorance of Italian, and yet this is the translator of Tasso.

The day before I left Rome I saw three robbers guillotined. The ceremony—including the *masqued* priests; the half-naked executioners; the bandaged criminals; the black Christ and his banner; the scaffold; the soldiery; the slow procession, and the quick rattle and heavy fall of the axe; the splash of the blood, and the ghastliness of the exposed heads—is altogether more impressive than the vulgar and ungentlemanly dirty " new drop ", and dog-like agony of infliction upon the sufferers of the English sentence. Two of these men behaved calmly enough, but the first of the three died with great terror and reluctance, which was very horrible. He would not lie down; then his neck was too large for the aperture, and the priest was obliged to drown his exclamations by still louder exhortations. The head was off before the eye could trace the blow; but from an attempt to draw back the head, notwithstanding it was held forward by the hair, the first head was cut off close to the ears : the other two were taken off more cleanly. It is better than the oriental way, and (I should think) than the axe of our ancestors. The pain seems little; and yet the effect to the spectator, and the preparation to the criminal, are very striking and chilling. The first turned me quite hot and thirsty, and made me shake so that I could hardly hold the opera-glass (I was close, but determined to see, as one should see every thing, once, with attention); the second and third (which shows how dreadfully soon things grow indifferent), I am ashamed to say, had no effect on me as a horror, though I would have saved them if I could.

It is some time since I heard from you—the 12*th April* I believe.

Yours ever truly, B.

TO THE HON. AUGUSTA LEIGH   *Venice, June 3ᵈ 1817*

DEAREST AUGUSTA—I returned home a few days ago from Rome but wrote to you on the road; at Florence I believe, or Bologna. The last city you know—or do not know—is celebrated for the production of Popes—Cardinals—painters—and sausages—besides a female professor of anatomy, who has left there many models of the art in waxwork, some of them not the most decent.—I have received all your letters I believe, which are full of woes, as usual, megrims and mysteries ; but my sympathies remain in suspense, for, for the life of me I can't make out whether your disorder is a broken heart or the earache—or whether it is *you* that have been ill or the children —or what your melancholy and mysterious apprehensions tend to, or refer to, whether to Caroline Lamb's novels—Mrs Clermont's evidence—Lady Byron's magnanimity—or any other piece of imposture ; I know nothing of what you are in the doldrums about at present. I should think all that could affect *you* must have been over long ago ; and as for me— leave me to take care of myself. I may be ill or well—in high or low spirits—in quick or obtuse state of feelings—like any body else, but I can battle my way through ; better than your exquisite piece of helplessness G. L.[1] or that other poor creature George Byron, who will be finely helped up in a year or two with his new state of life—I should like to know what they would do in my situation, or in any situation. I wish well to your George, who is the best of the two a devilish deal—but as for the other I shan't forget him in a hurry, and if I ever forgive or allow an opportunity to escape of evincing my sense of his conduct (and of more than his) on a certain occasion—write me down—what you will, but do not suppose me asleep. " Let them look to their bond "—sooner or later time and Nemesis will give me the ascendant—and then " let them look to their bond ". I do not of course allude only to that poor wretch, but to all—to the 3^d and 4th generation of these accursed Amalekites and the woman who has been the stumbling block of my——

June 4th 1817

I left off yesterday at the stumbling block of my Midianite marriage—but having received your letter of the 20th May I will be in good humour for the rest of this letter. I had hoped you would like the miniatures, at least one of them, which is in pretty good health ; the other is thin enough to be sure—and

[1] Colonel Leigh, Augusta's husband.

so was I—and in the ebb of a fever when I sate for it. By the
" man of fashion " I suppose you mean that poor piece of
affectation and imitation Wilmot—another disgrace to me
and mine—that fellow. I regret not having shot him, which the
persuasions of others—and circumstances which at that time
would have rendered combats presumptions against my cause
—prevented. I wish you well of your indispositions which I
hope are slight, or I should lose my senses.

Yours ever very and truly   B.

TO JOHN MURRAY   *La Mira,*[1] *near Venice, July 1, 1817*

DEAR SIR,—Since my former letter, I have been working
up my impressions into a 4th Canto of *Childe Harold*, of which I
have roughened off about rather better than thirty stanzas,
and mean to go on ; and probably to make this " Fytte " the
concluding one of the poem, so that you may propose against
the Autumn to draw out the Conscription for 1818. You must
provide monies, as this new resumption bodes you certain
disbursements ; somewhere about the end of September or
October, I propose to be under way (*i.e.* in the press) ; but I
have no idea yet of the probable length or calibre of the canto,
or what it will be good for ; but I mean to be as mercenary
as possible, an example (I do not mean of any individual in
particular, and least of all any person or persons of our mutual
acquaintance) which I should have followed in my youth, and
I might still have been a prosperous gentleman.

No tooth-powder, no packet of letters, no recent tidings of
you.

Mr. Lewis is at Venice, and I am going up to stay a week
with him there—as it is one of his enthusiasms also to like the
city.

> I stood in Venice, on the " Bridge of Sighs " ;
> A palace and a prison on each hand :
> I saw from out the wave her structures rise
> As from the stroke of $\begin{cases} an \\ the \end{cases}$ Enchanter's wand :

[1] Byron's summer residence on the Brenta.

A thousand Years their cloudy wings expand
Around me, and a dying Glory smiles
O'er the far times when many a subject land
Looked to the winged Lion's marble piles,
Where Venice sate in state, throned on her Seventy Isles.

The " Bridge of Sighs " (*i.e. Ponte dei sospiri*) is that which divides, or rather joins, the palace of the Doge to the prison of the state. It has two passages : the criminal went by the one to judgement, and returned by the other to death, being strangled in a chamber adjoining, where there was a mechanical process for the purpose.

This is the first stanza of the new canto ; and now for a line of the second :—

In Venice, Tasso's echo is no more,
And silent rows the songless gondolier,
Her palaces, etc., etc.

You know that formerly the gondoliers sang always, and Tasso's *Gerusalemme* was their ballad. Venice is built on seventy-two islands.

There ! there's a brick of your new Babel ! and now, sirrah ! what say you to the sample?

Yours most sincerely, B^N

P.S.—I shall write again by and bye.

TO THOMAS MOORE *La Mira, Venice, July 10, 1817*

Murray, the Mokanna of booksellers, has contrived to send me extracts from *Lalla Rookh* by the post. They are taken from some magazine, and contain a short outline and quotations from the two first Poems. I am very much delighted with what is before me, and very thirsty for the rest. You have caught the colours as if you had been in the rainbow, and the tone of the East is perfectly preserved. I am glad you have changed the title from " Persian Tale ". * * * *

I suspect you have written a devilish fine composition, and I rejoice in it from my heart ; because " the Douglas and the

Percy both together are confident against a world in arms ".
I hope you won't be affronted at my looking on us as " birds
of a feather " ; though, on whatever subject you had written,
I should have been very happy in your success.

There is a simile of an orange-tree's " flowers and fruits ",
which I should have liked better if I did not believe it to be a
reflection on * * *.

Do you remember Thurlow's poem to Sam—" *When
Rogers* " ; and that damned supper at Rancliffe's that ought
to have been a *dinner*?   " Ah, Master Shallow, we have heard
the chimes at midnight."   But,

> My boat is on the shore,
>   And my bark is on the sea ;
> But, before I go, Tom Moore,
>   Here's a double health to thee !
>
> Here's a sigh to those who love me,
>   And a smile to those who hate ;
> And whatever sky's above me,
>   Here's a heart for every fate.
>
> Though the ocean roar around me,
>   Yet it still shall bear me on ;
> Though a desert should surround me,
>   It hath springs that may be won.
>
> Were't the last drop in the well,
>   As I gasp'd upon the brink,
> Ere my fainting spirit fell,
>   'Tis to thee that I would drink.
>
> With that water, as this wine,
>   The libation I would pour
> Should be—peace with thine and mine,
>   And a health to thee, Tom Moore.

This should have been written fifteen moons ago—the first
stanza was.   I am just come out from an hour's swim in the
Adriatic ;   and I write to you with a black-eyed Venetian girl
before me, reading Boccaccio.   * * *

Last week I had a row on the road (I came up to Venice from my casino, a few miles on the Paduan road, this blessed day, to bathe) with a fellow in a carriage, who was impudent to my horse. I gave him a swingeing box on the ear, which sent him to the police, who dismissed his complaint. Witnesses had seen the transaction. He first shouted, in an unseemly way, to frighten my palfry. I wheeled round, rode up to the window, and asked him what he meant. He grinned, and said some foolery, which produced him an immediate slap in the face, to his utter discomfiture. Much blasphemy ensued, and some menace, which I stopped by dismounting and opening the carriage door, and intimating an intention of mending the road with his immediate remains, if he did not hold his tongue. He held it.

Monk Lewis is here—" how pleasant ! " He is a very good fellow, and very much yours. So is Sam—so is every body— and amongst the number,

Yours ever, B.

P.S.—What think you of *Manfred* ? * * * *

TO JOHN MURRAY † *La Mira, near Venice, August 21, 1817*

DEAR SIR,—I take you at your word about Mr. Hanson, and will feel obliged if you will *go* to him, and request Mr. Davies also to visit him by my desire, and repeat that I trust that neither Mr. Kinnaird's absence nor mine will prevent his taking all proper steps to accelerate and promote the sales of Newstead and Rochdale, upon which the whole of my future personal comfort depends. It is impossible for me to express how much any delays upon these points would inconvenience me ; and I do not know a greater obligation that can be conferred upon me than the pressing these things upon Hanson, and making him act according to my wishes. I wish you would *speak out*, at least to *me*, and tell me what you allude to by your odd way of mentioning him. All mysteries at such a distance are not merely tormenting but mischievous, and may be prejudicial to my interests ; so, pray expound, that I may consult with Mr. Kinnaird when he arrives ; and remember that I prefer the most disagreeable certainties to hints and inuendos. The devil take every body : I never can get any person to be explicit about any thing or any body, and my whole life is passed in conjectures of what people mean : you all talk in the style of Caroline Lamb's novels.

It is not Mr. St. John, but *Mr. St. Aubyn*, son of Sir John St. Aubyn. *Polidori* knows him, and introduced him to me. He is of Oxford, and has got my parcel. The Doctor will ferret him out, or ought. The parcel contains many letters, some of Madame de Stael's, and other people's, besides MSS., etc. By G—d, if I find the gentleman, and he don't find the parcel, I will say something he won't like to hear.

You want a " civil and delicate declension " for the medical tragedy?[1] Take it—

Dear Doctor,—I have read your play,
Which is a good one in its way,
Purges the eyes, and moves the bowels,
And drenches handkerchiefs like towels
With tears, that, in a flux of grief,
Afford hysterical relief
To shatter'd nerves and quicken'd pulses,
Which your catastrophe convulses.
I like your moral and machinery ;
Your plot, too, has such scope for Scenery !
Your dialogue is apt and smart ;
The play's concoction full of art ;
Your hero raves, your heroine cries,
All stab, and every body dies ;
In short, your tragedy would be
The very thing to hear and see ;
And for a piece of publication,
If I decline on this occasion,
It is not that I am not sensible
To merits in themselves ostensible,
But—and I grieve to speak it—plays
Are drugs—mere drugs, Sir, nowadays.

---

[1] Dr. Polidori's latest freak had been to compose a tragedy, which he submitted to Murray.

I had a heavy loss by *Manuel*,—
Too lucky if it prove not annual,—
And Sotheby, with his damned *Orestes*,
(Which, by the way, the old Bore's best is,)
Has lain so very long on hand .
That I despair of all demand;
I've advertized,—but see my books,
Or only watch my Shopman's looks;—
Still *Ivan, Ina,* and such lumber,
My back-shop glut,—my shelves encumber.
There's Byron too, who once did better,
Has sent me—folded in a letter—
A sort of—it's no more a drama
Than *Darnley, Ivan,* or *Kehama*:
So altered since last year his pen is,
I think he's lost his wits at Venice,
Or drained his brains away as stallion
To some dark-eyed and warm Italian;
In short, sir, what with one and t'other,
I dare not venture on another.
I write in haste; excuse each blunder;
The Coaches through the street so thunder!
My Room's so full; we've Gifford here
Reading MSS., with Hookham Frere,
Pronouncing on the nouns and particles
Of some of our forthcoming articles,
The *Quarterly*—Ah, sir, if you
Had but the Genius to review!—
A smart Critique upon St. Helena,
Or if you only would but tell in a
Short compass what——but, to resume;
As I was saying, Sir, the Room—
The Room's so full of wits and bards,
Crabbes, Campbells, Crokers, Freres, and Wards,
And others, neither bards nor wits:—
My humble tenement admits
All persons in the dress of Gent.,
From Mr. Hammond to Dog Dent.
A party dines with me today,
All clever men who make their way:

Crabbe, Malcolm, Hamilton, and Chantrey,
Are all partakers of my pantry.
They're at this moment in discussion
On poor De Staël's late dissolution.
Her book, they say, was in advance—
Pray Heaven! she tell the truth of France!
'Tis said she certainly was married
To Rocca, and had twice miscarried,
No—not miscarried, I opine,—
But brought to bed at forty-nine.
Some say she died a Papist; Some
Are of opinion *that's* a Hum;
I don't know that—the fellow, Schlegel,
Was very likely to inveigle
A dying person in compunction
To try the extremity of Unction.
But peace be with her! for a woman
Her talents surely were uncommon.
Her Publisher (and Public too)
The hour of her demise may rue—
For never more within his shop he—
Pray—was not she interred at Coppet?
Thus run our time and tongues away;—
But, to return, Sir, to your play;
Sorry, Sir, but I cannot deal,
Unless 'twere acted by O'Neill.
My hands are full—my head so busy,
I'm almost dead—and always dizzy;
And so, with endless truth and hurry,
Dear Doctor, I am yours,
　　　　　　　　　　JOHN MURRAY.
　　　　　　　　　　August, 1817.

P.S.—I've done the 4th and last Canto, which mounts to
133 stanzas. I desire you to name a price; if you don't, *I* will;
so I advise you in time.

　　　　　　　　　　　　　　Yours, etc.

There will be a good many notes.

September 15, 1817

DEAR SIR,—I enclose a sheet for correction, if ever you get to another edition. You will observe that the blunder in printing makes it appear as if the Château was *over* St. Gingo, instead of being on the opposite shore of the Lake, over Clarens. So, separate the paragraphs, otherwise my *to*pography will seem as inaccurate as your *ty*pography on this occasion.

The other day I wrote to convey my proposition with regard to the 4th and concluding canto. I have gone over and extended it to one hundred and fifty stanzas, which is almost as long as the two first were originally, and longer by itself than any of the smaller poems except *The Corsair*. Mr. Hobhouse has made some very valuable and accurate notes of considerable length, and you may be sure I will do for the text all that I can to finish with decency. I look upon *Childe Harold* as my best; and as I begun, I think of concluding with it. But I make no resolutions on that head, as I broke my former intention with regard to *The Corsair*. However, I fear that I shall never do better; and yet, not being thirty years of age, for some moons to come, one ought to be progressive as far as Intellect goes for many a good year. But I have had a devilish deal of wear and tear of mind and body in my time, besides having published too often and much already. God grant me some judgement! to do what may be most fitting in that and every thing else, for I doubt my own exceedingly.

I have read *Lallah Rookh*, but not with sufficient attention yet, for I ride about, and lounge, and ponder, and—two or three other things; so that my reading is very desultory, and not so attentive as it used to be. I am very glad to hear of its popularity, for Moore is a very noble fellow in all respects, and will enjoy it without any of the bad feeling which success— good or evil—sometimes engenders in the men of rhyme. Of the poem itself, I will tell you my opinion when I have mastered it: I say of the *poem*, for I don't like the *prose* at all—at all; and in the mean time, the " Fire worshippers " is the best, and the " Veiled Prophet " the worst, of the volume.

With regard to poetry in general, I am convinced, the more I think of it, that he and *all* of us—Scott, Southey, Wordsworth, Moore, Cambell, I,—are all in the wrong, one as much as another; that we are upon a wrong revolutionary poetical system, or systems, not worth a damn in itself, and from which none but Rogers and Crabbe are free; and that the present and next generations will finally be of this opinion. I am the more confirmed in this by having lately gone over some of our classics, particularly *Pope*, whom I tried in this way, —I took Moore's poems and my own and some others, and went over them side by side with Pope's, and I was really astonished (I ought not to have been so) and mortified at the ineffable distance in point of sense, harmony, effect, and even *Imagination*, passion, and *Invention*, between the little Queen Anne's man, and us of the Lower Empire. Depend upon it, it is all Horace then, and Claudian now, among us; and if I had to begin again, I would model myself accordingly. Crabbe's the man, but he has got a coarse and impracticable subject, and Rogers, the Grandfather of living Poetry, is retired upon half-pay, (I don't mean as a Banker),—

> Since pretty Miss Jaqueline,
> With her nose aquiline,

and has done enough, unless he were to do as he did formerly.

TO JOHN MURRAY †   *Venice, January 27, 1818*

DEAR SIR,—My father—that is, not God the Father, but my father in God, my Armenian father, Padre Pasquali—in the name of all the other fathers of our convent, sends you the inclosed greeting.

Inasmuch as it has pleased the translators of the long-lost and lately-found portions of the text of Eusebius to put forth the inclosed prospectus, of which I send six copies, you are hereby implored to obtain Subscribers in the two Universities, and among the learned, and the unlearned who would unlearn their ignorance.—This *they* (the Convent) request, *I* request, and *do you* request.

I sent you *Beppo* some weeks agone. You had best publish it alone; it has politics and ferocity, and won't do for your Isthmus of a Journal.

Mr. Hobhouse, if the Alps have not broken his neck, is, or ought to be, swimming with my Commentaries and his own coat of Mail in his teeth and right hand, in a cork jacket, between Calais and Dover.

It is the height of the Carnival, and I am in the *estrum* and agonies of a new intrigue with I don't exactly know whom or what, except that she is insatiate of love, and won't take money, and has light hair and blue eyes, which are not common here, and that I met her at the Masque, and that when her mask is off, I am as wise as ever. I shall make what I can of the remainder of my youth, and confess, that, like Augustus, I would rather die *standing*.

                                                                    B.

TO JOHN MURRAY   *Venice, Feb. 20, 1818*

DEAR SIR,—I have to thank Mr. Croker for the arrival, and you for the Continents, of the parcel which came last week, much quicker than any before, owing to Mr. C.'s kind attention, and the official exterior of the bags; and all safe, except much fraction amongst the magnesia, of which only two bottles came entire; but it is all very well, and I am exceedingly obliged to you.

The books I have read, or rather am reading. Pray, who may be the Sexagenarian, whose gossip is very amusing? Many of his sketches I recognise, particularly Gifford, Mackintosh, Drummond, Dutens, H. Walpole, Mrs. Inchbald, Opie, etc., with the Scotts, Loughborough, and most of the divines and lawyers, besides a few shorter hints of authors, and a few lines about a certain " *Noble Author* ", characterised as Malignant and Sceptical, according to the good old story " as it was in the beginning, is now, but *not* always shall be " : do you know such a person, Master Murray? eh?—And pray, of the Booksellers, which be *you*? the dry, the dirty, the honest, the opulent, the finical, the splendid, or the Coxcomb Bookseller? " Stap my vitals ", but the author grows scurrilous in his grand Climacteric !

I remember to have seen Porson [1] at Cambridge, in the Hall of our College, and in private parties, but not frequently : and I never can recollect him except as drunk or brutal, and generally both : I mean in an evening, for in the hall he dined at the Dean's table, and I at the Vice-master's, so that I was not near him ; and he then and there appeared sober in his demeanour, nor did I ever hear of excess or outrage on his part in public,—Commons, college, or Chapel ; but I have seen him in a private party of undergraduates, many of them freshmen and strangers—take up a poker to one of them, and heard him use language as blackguard as his action. I have seen Sheridan drunk, too, with all the world ; but his intoxication was that of Bacchus, and Porson's that of Silenus. Of all the disgusting brutes, sulky, abusive, and intolerable, Porson was the most bestial, as far as the few times that I saw him went, which were only at William Bankes's (the Nubian Discoverer's) rooms. I saw him once go away in a rage, because nobody knew the name of the " Cobbler of Messina ", insulting their ignorance with the most vulgar terms of reprobation. He was tolerated in this state amongst the young men for his talents—as the Turks think a Madman inspired, and bear with him. He used to recite, or rather vomit, pages of all languages, and could hiccup Greek like a Helot ; and certainly Sparta never shocked her children with a grosser exhibition than this man's intoxication.

[1] Professor Richard Porson, the celebrated classical scholar, 1759–1808.

I perceive, in the book you sent me, a long account of him; of Gilbert Wakefield's account of him, which is very savage, I cannot judge, as I never saw him sober, except in *Hall* or Combination-room; and then I was never near enough to hear, and hardly to see him. Of his drunken deportment I can be sure, because I saw it.

With the Reviews I have been much entertained. It requires to be as far from England as I am to relish a periodical paper properly: it is like Soda-water in an Italian Summer. But what cruel work you make with Lady Morgan!—You should recollect that she is a woman; though, to be sure, they are now and then very provoking: still, as authoresses, they can do no great harm; and I think it a pity so much good invective should have been laid out upon her, when there is such a fine field of us Jacobin gentlemen for you to work upon. It is perhaps as bitter a Critique as ever was written, and enough to make sad work for Dr. Morgan, both as a husband and an Apothecary, unless she should say as Pope did, of some attack upon him, " that it is as good for *her* as a dose of *Hartshorn* ".

I heard from Moore lately, and was very sorry to be made aware of his domestic loss. Thus it is—*medio de fonte leporum*—in the acmé of his fame and of his happiness comes a drawback as usual.

His letter, somehow or other, was more than two months on the road, so that I could only answer it the other day. What you tell me of Rogers in your last letter is like him; but he had best let *us*, that is one of us, if not both, alone. He cannot say that I have not been a sincere and a warm friend to him, till the black drop of his liver oozed through, too palpably to be overlooked. Now, if I once catch him at any of his jugglery with me or mine, let him look to it, for, if I spare him then, write me down a good-natured gentleman; and the more that I have been deceived,—the more that I once relied upon him,—I don't mean his petty friendship (what is that to me?), but his *good* will, which I really tried to obtain, thinking him at first a good fellow,—the more will I pay off the balance; and so, if he values his quiet, let him look to it; in three months I could restore him to the Catacombs.

Mr. Hoppner, whom I saw this morning, has been made the father of a very fine boy.—Mother and child doing very well

indeed.   By this time Hobhouse should be with you, and also
certain packets, letters, etc., of mine, sent since his departure.—
I am not at all well in health within this last eight days.   My
remembrances to Gifford and all friends.

Yours, B.

P.S.—In the course of a month or two, Hanson will have
probably to send off a clerk with conveyances to sign (Newstead
being sold in November last for ninety-four thousand and five
hundred pounds), in which case I supplicate supplies of articles
as usual, for which desire Mr. Kinnaird to settle from funds
in their bank, and deduct from my account with him.

P.S.—To-morrow night I am going to see *Otello*, an opera
from our *Othello*, and one of Rossini's best, it is said.   It will be
curious to see in Venice the Venetian story itself represented,
besides to discover what they will make of Shakespeare in
Music.

TO THOMAS MOORE   *Venice, March 16, 1818*

MY DEAR TOM,—Since my last, which I hope that you have
received, I have had a letter from our friend Samuel.   He talks
of Italy this summer—won't you come with him?   I don't
know whether you would like our Italian way of life or not.
* * * * *

They are an odd people.   The other day I was telling a girl,
" You must not come to-morrow, because Margueritta [Cogni]
is coming at such a time ",—(they are both about five feet ten
inches high, with great black eyes and fine figures—fit to breed
gladiators from—and I had some difficulty to prevent a battle
upon a rencontre once before)—" unless you promise to be
friends, and "—the answer was an interruption, by a declaration of war against the other, which she said would be a *Guerra
di Candia*.   Is it not odd, that the lower order of Venetians
should still allude proverbially to that famous contest, so
glorious and so fatal to the Republic?

They have singular expressions, like all Italians.   For
example, *Viscere*—as we should say, " My love ", or " My
heart ", as an expression of tenderness.   Also, " I would go for

you into the midst of a hundred *knives* ".—" *Mazza ben* ",
excessive attachment,—literally, " I wish you well even to
killing ". Then they say (instead of our way, " Do you think
I would do you such harm? ") " Do you think I would *assassinate* you in such a manner? "—" *Tempo perfido* ", bad weather ;
" *Strade perfide* ", bad roads,—with a thousand other allusions
and metaphors, taken from the state of society and habits in
the middle ages.

I am not so sure about *mazza*, whether it don't mean *massa*,
i.e. a great deal, a *mass*, instead of the interpretation I have
given it. But of the other phrases I am sure.

Three o' th' clock—I must " to bed, to bed, to bed ", as
mother Siddons, that tragical friend of the mathematical * * *,
says. * * * * *

Have you ever seen—I forget what or whom—no matter.
They tell me Lady Melbourne is very unwell. I shall be so
sorry. She was my greatest *friend*, of the feminine gender :—
when I say " friend ", I mean *not* mistress, for that's the anti-
pode. Tell me all about you and every body—how Sam is—
how you like your neighbours, the Marquis and Marchesa,
etc., etc.

Ever, etc.

TO THE HON. DOUGLAS KINNAIRD   *Venice, April 23rd, 1818*

DEAR DOUGLAS,—I will *not* go to Geneva, and I look upon
the proposition as a very gross neglect on the part of Hanson,
and an affront on that of my friends, including you, Davies,
Hobhouse, and everybody else. The messenger must come
here—is it not evident that the expense and trouble must be
less for the man and papers to come to me, than for me to go
to the man and papers? At any rate, and at any cost, I won't
stir ; and if anything occurs, it is all *your* faults for not taking
better care of my interests, besides wanting to drag me a mile
nearer to your infernal country.

" Poor Maria "—um ! I do not understand the particulars, nor wish to hear them ; all I know is that she made
your house very pleasant to your friends, and as far as I know,
made no mischief (which is saying infinitely for a woman), and
therefore whatever has, or may happen, she has my good will,

go where she will. I understand that you have provided for
her in the handsomest manner, which is in your nature, and
don't surprise me :—as far as prudence goes, you are in the
right to dissolve such a connection ; and as to provocation,
doubtless you had sufficient, but I can't help being sorry for the
woman—although she did tell you that I made love to her—
which, by the God of Scrope Davies ! was not true—for I
never dreamed of making love to anything of yours, except
sixty pints of brandy, sixty years old—all, or the greater part
of which, I consumed in your suppers. God help me, I was
very sorry when they were no more.

Now to business—" Shylock ! I must have monies ", so
have at Spooney [1] for Noel's and Newstead arrears, and have at
Murray for coming copyrights, and let me have a credit forthwith—I am in cash, but I don't like to break in upon my
circular notes—in case of a journey—or changing my residence,
but look to my finance department, and above all, *don't lecture
me*, for I won't bear it, and will run savage.

Make the *messenger proceed* to Geneva ; and send him a
letter therefor, that we may conclude the Newstead sale, and
if you can sell, or settle a sale for Rochdale—do. Newstead
has done well so far.

Do not suppose that I will be induced to return towards
England for less than the most imperious motives, but believe
me always

Yrs. B.

P.S.—Don't mind Hobhouse, he would whistle me home—
that is, to his home if he could ; but " thaut's impossible "
for the son and heir of Sir Wm Meadows. So look to it, and
don't conspire against me or my quiet.

TO JOHN MURRAY   *April 23, 1818*

DEAR SIR,—The time is past in which I could feel for the
dead,—or I should feel for the death of Lady Melbourne, the
best, and kindest, and ablest female I ever knew—old or
young. But " I have supped full of horrors ", and events of
this kind leave only a kind of numbness worse than pain,—

---

[1] Byron's nickname for Hanson.

like a violent blow on the elbow, or on the head. There is one link the less between England and myself.

Now to business. I presented you with *Beppo*, as part of the contract for Canto 4th,—considering the price you are to pay for the same, and intending it to eke you out in case of public caprice or my own poetical failure. If you choose to suppress it entirely, at Mr. Sotheby's suggestion, you may do as you please. But recollect it is not to be published in a *garbled* or *mutilated* state. I reserve to my friends and myself the right of correcting the press ;—if the publication continue, it is to continue in its present form.

If Mr. S. fancies, or feels, himself alluded to and injured by the allusion, he has his redress—by law—by reply—or by such other remedy personal or poetical as may seem good to himself, or any person or persons acting for, by, or at his suggestion.

My reasons for presuming Mr. S. to be the author of the anonymous note sent to me at Rome last Spring, with a copy of " Chillon ", etc., with marginal notes by the writer of the billet were—firstly, Similarity in the handwriting : of which I could form a recollection from correspondence between Mr. S. and myself on the subject of *Ivan* a play offered to D. L. Theatre ; 2dly, the *Style*, more especially the word " *Effulgence* ", a phrase which clinched my conjecture as decisively as any coincidence between Francis and Junius : 3dly, the paucity of English *then* at Rome, and the circumstances of Mr. S.'s return from Naples, and the delivery of this note and book occurring at the same period, he having then and there arrived with a party of Blue-Stocking Bi—women, I would say, of the same complexion whom he afterwards conveyed to the Abbate Morelli's at Venice—to view his Cameo, where they so tormented the poor old man (nearly twenty in number, all with pencil and note book in hand and questions in infamous Italian and villainous French), that it became the talk of Venice, as you may find by asking my friend Mr. Hoppner or others who were then at Venice ; 4thly, my being aware of Mr. S.'s patronage and anxiety on such occasions, which led me to the belief that, with very good intentions, he might nevertheless blunder in his mode of giving as well as taking opinions ; and 5thly, the Devil who made Mr. S. one author and me another.

As Mr. Sotheby says that he did not write this letter, etc., I am ready to believe him ; but for the firmness of my former persuasion, I refer to Mr. Hobhouse, who can inform you how sincerely I erred on this point. He has also the note—or, at least, *had* it, for I gave it to him with my verbal comments thereupon. As to *Beppo*, I will not alter or suppress a syllable for any man's pleasure but my own.

If there are resemblances between Botherby and Sotheby, or Sotheby and Botherby, the fault is not mine, but in the person who resembles,—or the persons who trace a resemblance. *Who* find out this resemblance? Mr. S.'s *friends*. *Who* go about moaning over him and laughing? Mr. S.'s *friends*. Whatever allusions Mr. S. may imagine, or whatever may or may not really exist, in the passages in question, I can assure him that there is not a literary man, or a pretender to Literature, or a reader of the day—in the World of London, who does not think and express more obnoxious opinions of his Blue-Stocking Mummeries than are to be found in print, and I for one think and say that, to the best of my knowledge and belief, from past experience and present information, Mr. Sotheby has made, and makes, himself highly ridiculous.

He may be an amiable man, a moral man, a good father, a good husband, a respectable and devout individual. I have nothing to say against all this ; but I have something to say to Mr. S.'s literary foibles, and to the wretched affectations and systematized Sophistry of many men, women, and Children, now extant and absurd in and about London and elsewhere ;— which and whom, in their false pretensions and nauseous attempts to make learning a nuisance and society a Bore, I consider as fair game—to be brought down on all fair occasions, and I doubt not, by the blessing of God on my honest purpose, and the former example of Mr. Gifford and others, my betters, before my eyes, to extirpate, extinguish and eradicate such as come within the compass of my intention. And this is my opinion, of which you will express as much or as little as you think proper.

Did you receive two additional stanzas, to be inserted towards the close of Canto 4th? Respond, that (if not) they may be sent.

Tell Mr. Hobhouse and Mr. Hanson that they may as well

expect Geneva to come to me, as that I should go to Geneva. The messenger may go on or return, as he pleases; I won't stir: and I look upon it as a piece of singular absurdity in those who know me imagining that I should;—not to say *Malice*, in attempting unnecessary torture. If, on the occasion, my interests should suffer, it is their neglect that is to blame; and they may all be damned together. You may tell them this, and add that nothing but force or necessity shall stir me one step towards the places to which they would wring me. I wonder particularly at Mr. Hobhouse's (who is in possession of my opinions) sanctioning such a conspiracy against my tranquillity.

If your literary matters prosper, let me know. If *Beppo* pleases, you shall have more in a year or two in the same mood. And so " Good morrow to you, good Master Lieutenant ".

Yours, B.

TO JOHN CAM HOBHOUSE [1]   *Venice, June, 1818*

SIR,—With great grief I inform you of the death of my late dear Master, my Lord, who died this morning at ten of the

---

[1] It is interesting to compare this letter which purports to be from Byron's valet, Fletcher, with the letter Fletcher actually wrote from Missolonghi in April, 1824:

TO JOHN MURRY ESQRE   *Missolonghi, April 21st, 1824*

SIR,—Forgive Me for this Intrusion which I now am under the Painfull Necessity of wrighting to you to Inform you of the Malloncolly News of My Lord Byron whom his no more he Departed This Miserable Life on the 19 of April after an Illness of onley 10 Days his Lordship Began by a Nervious Feavor and Terminated with an Inflammation on the Brains For want of being Bled in time which his Lordship Refused till it was Too Late I have sent The Honble. Mrs. Leighs Letter Inclosed in yours which I think would Be Better for you to open and Explain to Mrs. Leigh For I fear the Contents of the Letter will be too much For her and you will Please to Inform Lady Byron and the Honble. Miss Byron whom I am wished to see when I Return with My Lords Effects and his Dear and Noble Remains Sir you will Please Mannage in the most Mildest way Possable or I am much affraid of the Consequences Sir you will Please give my duty to Lady Byron Hoping she will allow me to see Her by My Lords Pertickeler wish and Miss Byron Likewise Please to Excuse all Deffects for I scearseley Now what I either Say or Do for after 20 Years Services To My Lord he was more to me than a father and I am too much Distressed to now give a Correct accompt of every Pertickeler which I hope to Do at my arrival in England Sir you will likewise have the Goodness to Forward the Letter To The Honble. Capt. George

Clock of a rapid decline and slow fever, caused by anxiety, sea-bathing, women, and riding in the Sun against my advice.

He is a dreadful loss to every body, mostly to me, who have lost a master and a place—also, I hope you, Sir, will give me a charakter.

I saved in his service as you know several hundred pounds. God knows how, for I don't, nor my late master neither ; and if my wage was not always paid to the day, still it was or is to be paid sometime and somehow. You, Sir, who are his executioner won't see a poor Servant wronged of his little all.

My dear Master had several phisicians and a Priest : he died a Papish, but is to be buried among the Jews in the Jewish burying ground ; for my part I don't see why—he could not abide them when living nor any other people, hating whores who asked him for money.

He suffered his illness with great patience, except that when in extremity he twice damned his friends and said they were selfish rascals—you, Sir, particularly and Mr. Kinnaird, who had never answered his letters nor complied with his repeated requests. He also said he hoped that your new tragedy would be damned—God forgive him—I hope that my master won't be damned like the tragedy.

His nine whores are already provided for, and the other servants ; but what is to become of me? I have got his Cloathes and Carriages, and Cash, and everything ; but the Consul quite against law has clapt his seal and taken an inventary and swears that *he* must account to my Lord's heirs—who they are, I don't know—but they ought to consider poor Servants and above all his Vally de Sham.

Byron whom has the Representative of the family and title I thought it my duty To send him a Line But you Sir will Please to Explain to him all Pertickelers has I have not time has the Express his now Ready to make his voyage Day and Night till he arrives in London I must Sir Praying forgiveness and Hopeing at the same time that you will so far oblige me has to Execute all my wishes which I am well Convinced you will not Refuse I Remain Sir
                    your Most Obt. and Verry Humble
                            Servant W Fletcher
                                valet to The Late
                                L.B. For 20 years

P.S.—I mention My Name and Capacity that you may Remember and forgive this when you Remember the Quantity of times I have been at your house in Albemarle Street.

My Lord never grudged me perquisites—my wage was the least I got by him; and if I did keep the Countess (she is, or ought to be, a Countess, although she is upon the town) Marietta Monetta Piretta, after passing my word to you and my Lord that I would not never no more—still he was an indulgent master, and only said I was a damned fool, and swore and forgot it again. What could I do? she said as how she should die, or kill herself if I did not go with her, and so I did— and kept her out of my Lord's washing and ironing—and nobody can deny that, although the charge was high, the linen was well got up.

Hope you are well, Sir—am, with tears in my eyes,

Yours faithfoolly to command, W^M FLETCHER

P.S.—If you know any Gentleman in want of a Wally— hope for a charakter. I saw your late Swiss Servant in the Galleys at Leghorn for robbing an Inn—he produced your recommendation at his trial.

TO THOMAS MOORE   *Palazzo Mocenigo, Grande Canal, Venice,*
June 1, 1818

Your letter is almost the only news, as yet, of Canto fourth, and it has by no means settled its fate—at least, does not tell me how the " Poeshie " has been received by the public. But, I suspect, no great things,—firstly, from Murray's " horrid stillness " ; secondly, from what you say about the stanzas running into each other, which I take *not* to be *yours*, but a notion you have been dinned with among the Blues. The fact is, that the *terza rima* of the Italians, which always *runs* on and in, may have lead me into experiments, and carelessness into conceit—or conceit into carelessness—in either of which events failure will be probable, and my fair woman, *superne*, end in a fish ; so that *Childe Harold* will be like the mermaid, my family crest, with the fourth Canto for a tail thereunto. I won't quarrel with the public, however, for the " Bulgars " are generally right ; and if I miss now, I may hit another time :— and so, the " gods give us joy ".

You like *Beppo*, that's right. I have not had the Fudges[1] yet, but live in hopes. I need not say that your successes are mine. By the way, Lydia White is here, and has just borrowed my copy of *Lalla Rookh*. * *

Hunt's letter is probably the exact piece of vulgar cox-combry you might expect from his situation. He is a good man, with some poetical elements in his chaos ; but spoilt by the Christ-Church Hospital and a Sunday newspaper,—to say nothing of the Surrey gaol, which conceited him into a martyr. But he is a good man. When I saw *Rimini* in MS., I told him that I deemed it good poetry at bottom, disfigured only by a strange style. His answer was, that his style was a system, or *upon system*, or some such cant ; and, when a man talks of system, his case is hopeless : so I said no more to him, and very little to any one else.

He believes his trash of vulgar phrases tortured into com-pound barbarisms to be *old* English ; and we may say of it as Aimwell says of Captain Gibbet's regiment, when the Captain calls it an " old corps ",—" the *oldest* in Europe, if I may judge by your uniform ". He sent out his *Foliage* by Percy Shelley * * *, and, of all the ineffable Centaurs that were ever begotten by Self-love upon a Night-mare, I think " this monstrous Sagittary " the most prodigious. *He* (Leigh H.) is an honest charlatan, who has persuaded himself into a belief of his own impostures, and talks Punch in pure simplicity of heart, taking himself (as poor Fitzgerald said of *him*self in the *Morning Post*) for *Vates* in both senses, or nonsenses, of the word. Did you look at the translations of his own which he prefers to Pope and Cowper, and says so?—Did you read his skimble-skamble about Wordsworth being at the head of his own *profession*, in the *eyes* of *those* who followed it? I thought that poetry was an *art*, or an *attribute*, and not a *profession* ;—but be it one, is that * * * * * * at the head of *your* profession in *your* eyes? I'll be curst if he is of *mine*, or ever shall be. He is the only one of us (but of us he is not) whose coronation I would oppose. Let them take Scott, Campbell, Crabbe, or you, or me, or any of the living, and throne him ;—but not this new Jacob Behmen, this * * * * * * whose pride might have kept him true, even had his principles turned as perverted as his *soi-disant* poetry.

---

[1] The reference is to Moore's *Fudge Family in Paris*, etc.

But Leigh Hunt is a good man, and a good father—see his Odes to all the Masters Hunt;—a good husband—see his Sonnet to Mrs. Hunt;—a good friend—see his Epistles to different people;—and a great coxcomb and a very vulgar person in every thing about him. But that's not his fault, but of circumstances.

* * * * * * *
* * * * * * *

I do not know any good model for a life of Sheridan but that of *Savage*. Recollect, however, that the life of such a man may be made far more amusing than if he had been a Wilberforce;—and this without offending the living, or insulting the dead. The Whigs abuse him; however, he never left them, and such blunderers deserve neither credit nor compassion.— As for his creditors,—remember, Sheridan *never had* a shilling, and was thrown, with great powers and passions, into the thick of the world, and placed upon the pinnacle of success, with no other external means to support him in his elevation. Did Fox * * * *pay his* debts?—or did Sheridan take a subscription? Was the * *'s drunkenness more excusable than his? Were his intrigues more notorious than those of all his contemporaries? and is his memory to be blasted, and theirs respected? Don't let yourself be led away by clamour, but compare him with the coalitioner Fox, and the pensioner Burke, as a man of principle, and with ten hundred thousand in personal views, and with none in talent, for he beat them all *out* and *out*. Without means, without connexion, without character, (which might be false at first, and make him mad afterwards from desperation,) he beat them all, in all he ever attempted. But alas, poor human nature! Good night or rather, morning. It is four, and the dawn gleams over the Grand Canal, and unshadows the Rialto. I must to bed; up all night—but, as George Philpot says, " it's life, though, damme it's life ! "

Ever yours, B.

Excuse errors—no time for revision. The post goes out at noon, and I shan't be up then. I will write again soon about your *plan* for a publication.

TO THE HON. DOUGLAS KINNAIRD *   *Venice, July 15th, 1818*

DEAR DOUGLAS,—I hear wonders of your popular eloquence [1]
and speeches to the mobility, from all quarters, and I see by
the papers that Captain Lemchen [2] has been well nigh slain by a
potatoe, so the Italian Gazettes have it ; it serves him right, a
fellow who has lost three ships, an Orang-outang, a Boa Con-
strictor (they both died in the passage), and an Election—he be
damned. How came Burdett not to be at the head of the poll ?

Murray's letters and the credits are come, laud we the
Gods ! If I did not know of old, Wildman [3] to be a Man of
honour, and Spooney a damned tortoise in all his proceeds, I
should suspect foul play in this delay of the man and papers ;
now that your politics are a little subsided, for God his sake,
row the man of law, spur him, kick him on the Crickle, do
something, any thing, you are my power of Attorney, and I
thereby empower you to use it and abuse Hanson, till the fellow
says or does something as a gentleman should do.

I am [staying] in Venice, instead of summering it at Este,
writing for the Clerk and the conveyances, but, " why tarry
the wheels of his Chariot ? "

I hear of Scrope and his jests, and Hobhouse and his toils ;
I wish you all the pleasure such pursuits can afford, and as
much success as usually attends them.

I have lately had a long swim (beating an Italian all to
bubbles) of more than four miles, from Lido to the other end
of the Grand Canal, that is the part which enters from Mestri.
I won by a good three quarters of a mile, and as many quarters
of an hour, knocking the Chevalier up, and coming in myself
quite fresh ; the fellow had swum the Beresina in the Bonaparte
Campaign, and thought of coping with " our Youth ", but it
would not do.

Give my love to Scrope and the rest of us ragmuffins, and
believe me yours ever and truly,

BYRON

Pray look very sharp after Spooney ; I have my suspicions, my
suspicions, Sir, my Suspicions.

[1] Kinnaird, like Hobhouse, took an active part in the Westminster election.
[2] Captain Sir Murray Maxwell, R.N., the Tory candidate.
[3] Newstead was purchased by Byron's old school-fellow, Colonel Wildman, in
November 1817 for £94,500.

TO THOMAS MOORE   *Venice, September 19, 1818*

An English newspaper here would be a prodigy, and an opposition one a monster; and except some extracts *from* extracts in the vile, garbled Paris gazettes, nothing of the kind reaches the Veneto-Lombard public, who are, perhaps, the most oppressed in Europe. My correspondences with England are mostly on business, and chiefly with my attorney, who has no very exalted notion, or extensive conception, of an author's attributes; for he once took up an *Edinburgh Review*, and, looking at it a minute, said to me, " So, I see you have got into the magazine ",—which is the only sentence I ever heard him utter upon literary matters, or the men thereof.

My first news of your Irish Apotheosis has, consequently, been from yourself. But, as it will not be forgotten in a hurry, either by your friends or your enemies, I hope to have it more in detail from some of the former, and, in the mean time, I wish you joy with all my heart. Such a moment must have been a good deal better than Westminster Abbey,—besides being an assurance of *that* one day (many years hence, I trust), into the bargain.

I am sorry to perceive, however, by the close of your letter, that even *you* have not escaped the *surgit amari*, etc., and that your damned deputy has been gathering such " dew from the still *vext* Bermoothes "—or rather *vexatious*. Pray, give me some items of the affair, as you say it is a serious one ; and, if it grows more so, you should make a trip over here for a few months, to see how things turn out. I suppose you are a violent admirer of England by your staying so long in it. For my own part, I have passed, between the age of one-and-twenty and thirty, half the intervenient years out of it without regretting any thing, except that I ever returned to it at all, and the gloomy prospect before me of business and parentage obliging me, one day, to return to it again,—at least, for the transaction of affairs, the signing of papers, and inspecting of children.

I have here my natural daughter, by name Allegra,—a pretty little girl enough, and reckoned like papa. Her mamma is English,—but it is a long story, and—there's an end. She is about twenty months old. * * *

I have finished the first canto (a long one, of about 180 octaves) of a poem in the style and manner of *Beppo*, encouraged by the good success of the same. It is called *Don Juan*, and is meant to be a little quietly facetious upon everything. But I doubt whether it is not—at least, as far as it has yet gone— too free for these very modest days. However, I shall try the experiment, anonymously; and if it don't take, it will be discontinued. It is dedicated to Southey in good, simple, savage verse, upon the Laureat's politics, and the way he got them. But the bore of copying it out is intolerable; and if I had an amanuensis he would be of no use, as my writing is so difficult to decipher.

> My poem's Epic, and is meant to be
>   Divided in twelve books, each book containing,
> With love and war, a heavy gale at sea—
>   A list of ships, and captains, and kings reigning—
> New characters, etc., etc.

The above are two stanzas, which I send you as a brick of my Babel, and by which you can judge of the texture of the structure.

In writing the *Life* of Sheridan, never mind the angry lies of the humbug Whigs. Recollect that he was an Irishman and a clever fellow, and that *we* have had some very pleasant days with him. Don't forget that he was at school at Harrow, where, in my time, we used to show his name—R. B. Sheridan, 1765,— as an honour to the walls. Remember * * * * * * *. Depend upon it that there were worse folks going, of that gang, than ever Sheridan was.

What did Parr [1] mean by "haughtiness and coldness"? I listened to him with admiring ignorance, and respectful silence. What more could a talker for fame have?—they don't like to be answered. It was at Payne Knight's I met him, where he gave me more Greek than I could carry away. But I certainly meant to (and *did*) treat him with the most respectful deference.

I wish you a good night, with a Venetian benediction, " *Benedetto te, e la terra che ti fara!* "—" May you be blessed, and the *earth* which you will *make*! "—is it not pretty? You would think it still prettier if you had heard it, as I did two hours ago,

----

[1] Dr. Samuel Parr, the celebrated pedagogue.

from the lips of a Venetian girl, with large black eyes, a face like Faustina's, and the figure of a Juno—tall and energetic as a Pythoness, with eyes flashing, and her dark hair streaming in the moonlight—one of those women who may be made any thing. I am sure if I put a poniard into the hand of this one, she would plunge it where I told her,—and into *me*, if I offended her. I like this kind of animal, and am sure that I should have preferred Medea to any woman that ever breathed. You may, perhaps, wonder that I don't in that case. * * * I could have forgiven the dagger or the bowl,—any thing, but the deliberate desolation piled upon me, when I stood alone upon my hearth, with my household gods shivered around me. * * Do you suppose I have forgotten it? It has comparatively swallowed up in me every other feeling, and I am only a spectator upon earth, till a tenfold opportunity offers. It may come yet. There are others more to be blamed than * * * *, and it is on these that my eyes are fixed unceasingly.

TO THE HON. AUGUSTA LEIGH   *Venice, Sep^{tr} 21st 1818*

DEAREST AUGUSTA,—I particularly beg that you will contrive to get the enclosed letter safely delivered to Lady Frances, and if there is an answer to let me have it. You can write to her first and state that you have such a letter—at my request—for there is no occasion for any concealment at least with *her*—and pray oblige me so far, for many reasons.

If the Queen dies you are no more a Maid of Honour—is it not so? Allegra is well, but her mother (whom the Devil confound) came prancing the other day over the Appennines— to see her *shild*; which threw my Venetian loves (who are none of the quietest) into great combustion ; and I was in a pucker till I got her to the Euganean hills, where she and the child now are, for the present. I declined seeing her for fear that the consequence might be an addition to the family ; she is to have the child a month with her and then to return herself to Lucca, or Naples, where she was with her relatives (she is English you know), and to send Allegra to Venice again. I lent her my house at Este for her maternal holidays. As troubles don't come single, here is another confusion. The chaste wife of a baker—having quarrelled with her tyrannical husband—has run away *to* me (God knows without being invited), and resists all the tears and penitence and beg-pardons of her disconsolate Lord, and the threats of the police, and the priest of the parish besides; and swears she won't give up her unlawful love (myself), for any body, or any thing. I assure you I have begged her in all possible ways too to go back to her husband, promising her all kinds of eternal fidelity into the bargain, but she only flies into a fury; and as she is a very tall and formidable Girl of three and twenty, with the large black eyes and handsome face of a pretty fiend, a correspondent figure and a carriage as haughty as a Princess—with the violent passions and capacities for mischief of an Italian when they are roused— I am a little embarrassed with my unexpected acquisition. However she keeps my household in rare order, and has already frightened the learned Fletcher out of his remnants of wits more than once; we have turned her into a housekeeper. As the morals of this place are very lax, all the women commend her and say she has done right—especially her own relations. You need not be alarmed—I know how to manage her—and can deal with anything but a cold blooded animal such as Miss Milbanke. The worst is that she won't let a woman come into the house, unless she is as old and frightful as possible; and has sent so many to the right about that my former female acquaintances are equally frightened and angry. She is extremely fond of the child, and is very cheerful and good-natured, when not jealous; but Othello himself was a fool to her in that respect. Her soubriquet in her family was *la Mora* from her colour, as she is very dark (though clear of complexion), which literally means *the Moor* so that I have " the Moor of Venice " in propria persona as part of my household. She has been here this month. I had known her (and fifty others) more than a year, but did not anticipate this escapade, which was the fault of her booby husband's treatment—who now runs about repenting and roaring like a bull calf. I told him to take her in the devil's name, but she would not stir; and made him a long speech in the Venetian dialect which was more entertaining to anybody than to him to whom it was addressed. You see Goose—that there is no quiet in this world —so be a good woman—and repent of yʳ sins.——

TO LADY BYRON   *Venice, Novr 18th 1818*

Sir Samuel Romilly has cut his throat for the loss of his wife.[1]
It is now nearly three years since he became, in the face of his
compact (by a retainer—previous, and, I believe, general),
the advocate of the measures and the Approver of the proceedings, which deprived me of mine. I would not exactly,
like Mr. Thwackum, when Philosopher Square bit his own
tongue—" saddle him with a Judgement " ; but

" This even-handed Justice
Commends the ingredients of our poisoned Chalice
To our own lips."

This Man little thought, when he was lacerating my heart
according to law, while he was poisoning my life at its sources,
aiding and abetting in the blighting, branding, and exile that
was to be the result of his counsels in their indirect effects,
that in less than thirty-six moons—in the pride of his triumph
as the highest candidate for the representation of the Sister-
City of the mightiest of Capitals—in the fullness of his professional career—in the greenness of a healthy old age—in the
radiance of fame, and the complacency of self-earned riches—
that a domestic affliction would lay him in the earth, with the
meanest of malefactors, in a cross-road with the stake in his
body, if the verdict of insanity did not redeem his ashes from
the sentence of the laws he had lived upon by interpreting or
misinterpreting, and died in violating.

This man had eight children, lately deprived of their
mother : could he not live? Perhaps, previous to his annihilation, he felt a portion of what he contributed his legal mite to
make me feel ; but I have lived—lived to see him a Sexagenary
Suicide.

It was not in vain that I invoked Nemesis in the midnight
of Rome from the awfullest of her ruins.

Fare you well.   B.

---

[1] Sir Samuel Romilly had incurred Byron's enmity because, having accepted
a retaining-fee from the poet at the beginning of the separation-proceedings, he
had subsequently acted against him.

TO JOHN CAM HOBHOUSE AND
THE HON. DOUGLAS KINNAIRD †   *Venice, January 19th, 1819*

DEAR H. AND DEAR K.,—I approve and sanction all your legal proceedings with regard to my affairs, and can only repeat my thanks and approbation. If you put off the payments of debts " till *after* Lady Noel's death ", it is well ; if till *after* her damnation, better, for that will last for ever ; yet I hope not ; for her sake as well as the creditors I am willing to believe in purgatory.

With regard to the Poeshie, I will have no " cutting and slashing ", as Perry calls it ; you may omit the stanzas on Castlereagh, indeed it is better, and the two " *Bobs* " at the end of the 3rd stanza of the dedication, which will leave " high " and " a-dry " good rhymes without any " *double* (or single) entendre ", but no more. I appeal, not " to Philip fasting ", but to Alexander drunk ; I appeal to Murray at his ledger, to the people, in short, Don Juan shall be an entire horse, or none. If the objection be to the indecency, the Age which applauds the " Bath Guide ", and Little's poems, and reads Fielding and Smollett still, may bear with that. If to the poetry, I will take my chance. I will not give way to all the cant of Christendom. I have been cloyed with applause, and sickened with abuse ; at present I care for little but the copyright ; I have imbibed a great love for money, let me have it ; if Murray loses this time, he won't the next ; he will be cautious, and I shall learn the decline of his customers by his epistolary indications. But in no case will I submit to have the poem mutilated. There is another Canto written, but not copied, in two hundred and odd Stanzas, if this succeeds ; as to the prudery of the present day, what is it? Are we more moral than when Prior wrote? Is there anything in " Don Juan " so strong as in Ariosto, or Voltaire, or Chaucer?

Tell Hobhouse his letter to Di Breme has made a great sensation, and is to be published in the Tuscan and other gazettes. Count R. came to consult with me about it last Sunday ; we think of Tuscany ; for Florence and Milan are in literary war ; but the Lombard league is headed by Marti, and would make a difficulty of insertion in the Lombard gazettes ; once published in the Pisan, it will find its way through Italy by translation or reply.

So Lauderdale has been telling a story! I suppose this is my reward for presenting him at Countess Benzoni's and showing him what attention I could. Which " piece " does he mean? Since last year I have run the gauntlet. Is it the Tarruscelli—the Da Mosto—the Spinola—the Lotti—the Mizzato—the Eleanora—the Carlotta—the Giulietta—the Aloisi—the Gambieri—the Eleanora da Bezzi (who was the King of Naples' Gioachino's mistress—at least one of them)—the Theresina of Mazzurati—the Glettenheim and her sister—the Luigia and her mother—the Fornaretta—the Santa—the Caligara—the Portiera Vedova—the Bolognese figurante—the Tintora and her sister—cum multis aliis? Some of them are countesses and some of them cobbler's wives, some noble, some middling, some low, and all whores. Which does the damned old " Ludro and porco fottato " mean? Since *he* tells a story about me, I will tell one about him. When he landed at the *Custom House* from Corfu, he called for " *Post horses, directly* ". He was told that there were no horses except mine nearer than Lido, unless he wished for the four bronze coursers of St. Mark, which *were at his service*.

I am, yours ever, B.

Let me have H.'s election immediately. I mention it *last* as being what I was least likely to forget.

P.S.—Whatever brain-money you get on my account from Murray, pray remit me. I will never consent to pay away what I *earn*. That is *mine*, and what I get by my brains I will spend * * *, as long as I have a tester or a * remaining. I shall not live long, and for that reason I must live while I can. So let him disburse, and me receive. " For the night cometh." If I had but had twenty thousand a year I should not have been living now. But all men are not born with a silver or gold spoon in their mouths. My balance also—my balance—and a copyright. I have another Canto, too, ready ; and then there will be my half year in June. Recollect I care for nothing but " monies ".

January 20ᵗʰᵉ, 1819

You say nothing of Mazeppa. Did it arrive, with one other, besides that you mention?

TO JOHN CAM HOBHOUSE †   *Venice, April 6th, 1819*

My dear Hobhouse,—I have not derived from the Scriptures of Rochefoucault that consolation which I expected " in the misfortunes of our best friends ".

I had much at heart your gaining the Election, but from " the filthy puddle " into which your patriotism had run you, I had, like Croaker, my bodings, but like old " Curry-comb " you make " so handsome a corpse ", that my wailing is changed into admiration. With the Burdettites divided, and the Whigs and Tories united, what else could be expected? If I had guessed at your opponent, I would have made one among your Cortes, and have * Caroline Lamb out of her " two hundred votes " * * * * *. I think I could have neutralised her zeal with a little management. But alas! who would have thought of that cuckoldy family's *standing* for a *member*. I suppose it is the first time that George Lamb ever *stood* for anything;—and William with his " Corni ". " Cazzo da Seno ! " (as we Venetians say. It means : * * * * * *in earnest*— a sad way of swearing). But that you who know them should have to *concur* with such dogs—well—did I ever—no I never etc. etc. etc.

I have sent my second Canto ; but I will have no gelding. Murray has my order of the day. Douglas Kinnaird with more than usual politeness writes me vivaciously that Hanson or I willed the *three per cent*, instead of the five—as if I could prefer *three* to *five* per cent !—death and fiends !—and then *he* lifts up his leg against the publication of Don Juan. " Et tu *Brute* " (*the e mute* recollect). I shall certainly hitch our dear friend into some d—d story or other, " my dear, Mr. Sneer—Mr. Sneer— my dear ". I must write again in a few days, it being now past four in the morning ; it is Passion week, and rather dull. I am dull too, for I have fallen in love with a Romagnola Countess from Ravenna,[1] who is nineteen years old, and has a Count of fifty—whom she seems disposed to qualify, the first year of marriage being just over. I knew her a little last year at her starting, but they always wait a year, at least generally. I met her first at the Albrizzi's, and this spring at the Benzona's —and I have hopes, sir,—hopes, but she wants me to come to

[1] Teresa Guiccioli.

Ravenna, and then to Bologna. Now this would be all very well for certainties; but for mere hopes; if she should plant me, and I should make a " fiasco ", never could I show my face on the Piazza. It is nothing that money can do, for the Conte is awfully rich, and would be so even in England,—but he is fifty and odd; has had two wives and children before this his third (a pretty fair-haired girl last year out of a convent; now making her second tour of the Venetian Conversazioni) and does not seem so jealous this year as he did last—when he stuck close to her side—even at the Governor's.

She is pretty, but has no tact; answers aloud, when she should whisper—talks of age to old ladies who want to pass for young; and this blessed night horrified a correct company at the Benzona's, by calling out to me " *mio Byron* " in an audible key, during a dead silence of pause in the other prattlers, who stared and whispered their respective *serventi*. One of her preliminaries is that I must never leave Italy. I have no desire to leave it, but I should not like to be frittered down into a regular Cicisbeo. What shall I do? I am in love, and tired of promiscuous concubinage, and have now an opportunity of settling for life.

Yours, B.

FRAGMENT OF A LETTER
TO JOHN CAM HOBHOUSE†   [*FPO Postmark April 20 1819*]

. . . P.S.—We have had, a fortnight ago, the devil's own row with an elephant who broke loose, ate up a fruit shop, killed his keeper; broke into a church; and was at last killed by a cannon-shot brought from the Arsenal. I saw him the day he broke open his own house; he was standing in the Riva, and his keepers trying to persuade him with *peck loaves* to go on board of a sort of ark they had got. I went close up to him that afternoon in my gondola, and he amused himself with flinging great beams that flew about over the water in all directions; he was then not *very* angry, but towards midnight he became furious, and displayed the most extraordinary strength, pulling down everything before him. All musketry proved in vain; and when he charged, the Austrians threw down their muskets and ran. At last they broke a hole and brought a field piece, the first shot missed, the second entered behind, and came out *all but* the skin at his shoulder. I saw him dead the next day, a stupendous fellow. He went mad for want of a She, it being his rutting month.

Fletcher is well. I have got two monkeys, a fox, and two new mastiffs, Mutz is still in high old age. The monkeys are charming. Last month I had a business about a Venetian girl who wanted to marry me, a circumstance prevented, like Dr. Blifil's espousals, not only by my previous marriage, but by Mr. Allworthy's being acquainted with the existence of Mrs. Dr. Blifil. I was very honest, and gave her no hopes, but there was a scene, I having been found at her window at midnight, and they sent me a priest, and a friend of the family's, to talk with me the next day, both of whom I treated with coffee.

TO THE HON. DOUGLAS KINNAIRD †   *Venice,*
                                          April 24th, 1819
DEAR DOUGLAS,—

" When that the Captain came for to know it
    He very much applauded what she had done "

and I only want the command " of the gallant Thunder Bomb " to make you my " first Lieutenant ". I meant " five thousand pounds " and never intend to have so much meaning again. In short, I refer you Gentlemen to my original letter of instructions which, by the blessing of God, seems to bear as many constructions as a Delphic Oracle; I say I refer you to that when you are at a loss how to avoid paying my money away; I hate paying and you are quite right to encourage me. As to Hanson & *Son*, I make no distinctions—it would be a sort of blasphemy—I should as soon think of untwisting the Trinity. What do they mean by separate bills? With regard to the Rochdale suit—and the " large discretion " or Indiscretion of " a thousand pounds "—what could I do? I want to gain my suit; but I will be guided by you. If you think " pounds Scottish " will do better, let me know—I am docile.

443

Pray what could make Farebrother say that Seventeen thousand pounds had been bidden for the undisputed part of Rochdale manor? It may be so, but I never heard of it before, not even from Spooney. If anybody bids, take it, and send it me by post; but don't pay away to those low people of tradesmen. They may survive Lady Noel, or me, and get it from the executors and heirs. But I don't approve of any living liquidations—a damned deal too much has been paid already—the fact is that the villains owe me money—and not I to them. Damn "*the Vampire*". What do I know of Vampires?[1] It must be some bookselling imposture; contradict it in a solemn paragraph.

I sent off on April 3rd the 2nd canto of "Don Juan" addressed to Murray, I hope it is arrived—by the Lord it is a Capo d'Opera, so "full of pastime and prodigality", but you sha'n't decimate nor mutilate, no—"rather than that, come critics into the list, and champion me to the uttermost".

Nor you, nor that rugged rhinoceros Murray, have ever told me, in answer to *fifty* times the question, if he ever received the additions to Canto *first*, entitled "Julia's letter" and also some four stanzas for the beginning.

I have fallen in love, within the last month, with a Romagnuola Countess from Ravenna, the spouse of a year of Count Guiccioli, who is sixty—the girl twenty. He has eighty thousand ducats of rent, and has had two wives before. But he is sixty. He is the first of Ravenna nobles, but he is sixty. She is as fair as sunrise, and warm as noon, we had but ten days to manage all our little matters in beginning, middle and end; and we managed them; and I have done my duty with the proper consummation. But she is young, and was not content with what she had done, unless it was to be turned to the advantage of the public, and so she made an éclat, which rather astonished even the Venetians, and electrified the Conversazioni of the Benzona, the Albrizzi, and the Michelli, and made her husband look embarrassed. They have been gone back to Ravenna some time, but they return in the winter. She is the queerest woman I ever met with, for in general they cost one something one way or other, whereas by an odd combina-

[1] Polidori's romance, *The Vampyre*, published in 1819, was popularly credited to Byron.

tion of circumstances, I have proved an expense to *her*, which is
not *my* custom, but an accident ; however it don't matter. She
is a sort of Italian Caroline Lamb, except that she is much
prettier, and not so savage. But she has the same red-hot
head, the same noble disdain of public opinion, with the
superstructure of all that Italy can add to such natural dispositions. To be sure, they may go much further here with
impunity, as her husband's rank ensured them reception at all
societies including the Court ; and it was her first outbreak
since marriage, the sympathizing world was liberal. She is
also of the Ravenna noblesse, educated in a convent, sacrifice to wealth, filial duty, and all that. I am damnably in
love, but they are gone—gone—for many months—and nothing
but Hope keeps me alive *seriously*.

Yours ever, B.

TO THE COUNTESS GUICCIOLI * [1]   *Venice, 25th April, 1819*

My Love,—I hope you have received my letter of the 22nd,
addressed to the person in Ravenna of whom you told me,
before leaving Venice. You scold me for not having written
to you in the country—but—how could I ? My sweetest
treasure, you gave me no other address but that of Ravenna.
If you knew how great is the love I feel for you, you would
not believe me capable of forgetting you for a single instant ;
you must become better acquainted with me. Perhaps one day
you will know that, although I do not deserve you, I do indeed
love you.

You want to know whom I most enjoy seeing, since you
have gone away ? who makes me tremble and feel—not what
you alone can arouse in my soul—but something like it ?
Well, I will tell you—it is the *old porter* whom Fanny [2] used to
send with your notes when you were in Venice, and who now
brings your letters—still dear, but not so dear as those which
brought the hope of seeing you that same day at the usual

---

[1] This and the letter of August 7, 1820, in the Gamba collection, have
been translated from the Italian by the Marchesa Origo, and are included in
her study of Teresa Guiccioli and Byron, *The Last Attachment* (Murray and
Cape, 1949).
[2] Fanny Silvestrini, Teresa Guiccioli's confidante.

time. My Teresa, where are you? Everything here reminds me of you, everything is the same, but you are not here and I still am. In separation the one who goes away suffers less than the one who stays behind. The distraction of the journey, the change of scene, the landscape, the movement, perhaps even the separation, distracts the mind and lightens the heart. But the One who stays behind is surrounded by the same things, tomorrow as yesterday, while only that is lacking which made me forget that a tomorrow would ever come. When I go to the Conversazione I give myself up to tedium, too happy to suffer ennui, rather than grief. I see the same faces—hear the same voices—but no longer dare to look towards the sofa where I shall not see *you* any more, but instead some old crone who might be Calumny personified. I hear, without the slightest emotion, the opening of that door which I used to watch with so much anxiety when I was there before you, hoping to see you come in. I will not speak of *much dearer* places still, for *there* I shall not go—unless you return ; I have no other pleasure than thinking of you, but I do not see how I could see again the places where we have been together—especially those most consecrated to our love—without dying of grief.

Fanny is now in Treviso, and God knows when I shall have any more letters from you ; but meanwhile I have received three ; you must by now have arrived in Ravenna—I long to hear of your arrival ; my fate depends upon your decision. Fanny will be back in a few days ; but tomorrow I shall send her a note by a friend's hand to ask her not to forget to send me your news, if she receives any letters before returning to Venice.

My Treasure, my life has become most monotonous and sad ; neither books, nor music, nor *horses* (rare things in Venice —but you know that mine are at the Lido), nor dogs, give me any pleasure ; the society of women does not attract me ; I won't speak of the society of men, for that I have always despised. For some years I have been trying systematically to avoid strong passions, having suffered too much from the tyranny of Love. *Never to feel* admiration [1]—and to enjoy myself without giving too much importance to the enjoyment in itself— to feel indifference toward human affairs—contempt for many—

---

[1] " Not to admire is all the art I know."—*Don Juan.*

but hatred for none, this was the basis of my philosophy. I did not mean to love any more, nor did I hope to receive Love. You have put to flight all my resolutions ; now I am all yours ; I will become what you wish—perhaps happy in your love, but never at peace again. You should not have re-awakened my heart, for (at least in my own country) my love has been fatal to those I love—and to myself. But these reflections come too late. You have been mine—and whatever the outcome—I am, and eternally shall be, entirely yours. I kiss you a thousand and a thousand times—but—

> Che giova a te, cor mio, l' esser amato ?
> Che giova a me l' aver si caro amante ?
> Perchè crudo destino—
> Ne disunisci tu s' Amor ne stringe ? [1]

Love me—as always your tender and faithful,

B

TO THE LORD KINNAIRD *   *Venice, May 15, 1819*

My dear Lord,[2]—Three years and some months ago, when you were reading " Bertram " at your brother's, on my exclaiming in the words of Parson Adams to his Son, " *Lege Dick, Lege* " (on occasion of some interruption that had occurred) you replied to me " my name is *not Richard*, my Lord ", thus converting my luckless quotation into an intentional liberty, and reproving me there*for*. This was a hint to me to address you in future with all Aristocratical decorum as becomes our birth, parentage, and education, and now I pay you back in your own coin, and say unto you, my dear Lord, " my name is *not Lady* " with which you commence your letter, which I am nevertheless as glad to receive, as I shall be to see the writer.

" Your Lordship will be right welcome back to Denmark."

Your good nature to the chaste [? Arpalice] has been very serviceable to her, for without it she would have never rejoined

---

[1] " What does it profit you, my heart, to be beloved ?
What good to me, to have so dear a lover ?
Why should a cruel fate
Separate those whom love has once united ? "
　　　　　　　　　　　　　　—Guarini, *Il Pastor Fido*.
[2] The brother of Douglas Kinnaird.

her principal Performer.   I had a letter from her soon after her arrival at Milan, but have heard nothing since.   She may probably write from Munich.

It was my intention to have left Venice tomorrow, on my journey to R. but the Lady has miscarried, and her recovery seems more remote than was expected, being still in bed.   I have been ordered to come at all events, but what the deuce should I do in the mean time without the possibility of seeing her, or at least of seeing her to any purpose in her present state. However, on the mere chance of seeing her only, I shall set out about the 20th and leave the rest to the protecting deities.

I hope that you will arrive in Venice before I set out, and would wait a day or two on purpose, if you will let me know by return of post, where are you going?   To *Reggio*?   I should like greatly to see you on your route, and will lay to till you come within hail, if you will make the Signal.   But pray respond by the first ordinary.

There is the devil to do here at present, an Englishman— son of a Baronet—robbed a Baronet (Sir W. Drummond) at his " Hostel or Inn " of goods and monies, and is like " to be troubled at Size " about it; the young man is a damned Rascal and is to be treated accordingly, by being permitted to get off.   At least I suppose so.

Don't forget to answer and believe me, dear Kinnaird, very truly

and affectly.,   yrs., BYRON

P.S.—If they open our letters at the post they will be edified by the correspondence—it is all hitherto about whores and rogues.

TO JOHN MURRAY   *Venice, May 15, 1819*

DEAR SIR,—I have received and return by this post, under another Cover, the first proof of *Don Juan*.   Before the Second can arrive, it is probable that I may have left Venice, and the length of my absence is so uncertain, that you had better proceed to the publication without boring me with more proofs.

448

I send by last post an addition—and a new copy of "Julia's Letter ", perceiving or supposing the former one in winter did not arrive.

Mr. Hobhouse is at it again about indelicacy. There is *no indelicacy*; if he wants *that*, let him read Swift, his great Idol; but his Imagination must be a dunghill, with a Viper's nest in the middle, to engender such a supposition about this poem. For my part, I think you are all crazed. * * * Request him not " to put me in a phrenzy ", as Sir Anthony Absolute says, " though he was not the indulgent father that I am."

I have got your extract, and the *Vampire*. I need not say it is *not mine*. There is a rule to go by : you are my publisher (till we quarrel), and what is not published by you is not written by me.

The story of Shelley's agitation is true.[1] I can't tell what seized him, for he don't want courage. He was once with me in a gale of Wind, in a small boat, right under the rocks between Meillerie and St. Gingo. We were five in the boat— a servant, two boatmen, and ourselves. The sail was mismanaged, and the boat was filling fast. He can't swim. I stripped off my coat—made him strip off his and take hold of an oar, telling him that I thought (being myself an expert swimmer) I could save him, if he would not struggle when I took hold of him—unless we got smashed against the rocks, which were high and sharp, with an awkward surf on them at that minute. We were then about a hundred yards from shore, and the boat in peril. He answered me with the greatest coolness, that " he had no notion of being saved, and that I would have enough to do to save myself, and begged not to trouble me ". Luckily, the boat righted, and, baling, we got round a point into St. Gingo, where the inhabitants came down and embraced the boatmen on their escape, the Wind having been high enough to tear up some huge trees from the Alps above us, as we saw next day.

And yet the same Shelley, who was as cool as it was possible to be in such circumstances, (of which I am no judge myself,

[1] During the summer of 1816, when they were both in Switzerland, Shelley, after an evening of ghost-stories, had been seized with sudden panic. Later, he explained that, while gazing at Mary, he had remembered a tale he had been told of a woman who " had eyes instead of nipples, which taking hold of his mind horrified him. . . ."

as the chance of swimming naturally gives self possession when near shore), certainly had the fit of phantasy which Polidori describes, though *not exactly* as he describes it.

The story of the agreement to write the Ghost-books is true ; but the ladies are *not* sisters. One is Godwin's daughter by Mary Wolstonecraft, and the other the *present* Mrs. Godwin's daughter by a former husband. So much for Scoundrel Southey's story of " *incest* " ; neither was there *any promiscuous intercourse* whatever. Both are an invention of that execrable villain Southey, whom I will term so as publicly as he deserves. Mary Godwin (now Mrs. Shelley) wrote *Frankenstein*, which you have reviewed, thinking it Shelley's. Methinks it is a wonderful work for a girl of nineteen,—*not* nineteen, indeed, at that time. I enclose you the beginning of mine, by which you will see how far it resembles Mr. Colburn's publication. If you choose to publish it in the *Edinburgh Magazine* (*Wilson's and Blackwood's*) you may, *stating why*, and with such explanatory proem as you please. I never went on with it, as you will perceive by the date. I began it in an old account-book of Miss Milbanke's, which I kept because it contains the word " Household ", written by her twice on the inside blank page of the covers, being the only two scraps I have in the world in her writing, except her name to the Deed of Separation. Her letters I sent back except those of the quarrelling correspondence, and those, being documents, are placed in possession of a third person (Mr. Hobhouse), with copies of several of my own ; so that I have no kind of memorial whatever of her, but these *two* words,—and her actions. I have torn the leaves containing the part of the Tale out of the book, and enclose them with this sheet.

Next week I set out for Romagna—at least in all probability. You had better go on with the publications without waiting to hear farther, for I have other things in my head. " Mazeppa " and " The Ode " *Separate*—what think you? *Juan anonymously*, without the dedication, for I won't be shabby and attack Southey under Cloud of night.

What do you mean? First you seem hurt by my letter, and then, in your next, you talk of its " power ", and so forth. " This is a damned blind story, Jack ; but never mind, go on." You may be sure I said nothing *on purpose* to plague you ; but

if you will put me " in a phrenzy, I will never call you Beck
[*sic*] again ". I remember nothing of the epistle at present.

What do you mean by Polidori's *Diary*? [1] Why, I defy him
to say any thing about me, but he is welcome. I have nothing
to reproach me with on his score, and I am much mistaken if
that is not his *own* opinion. But why publish the names of the
two girls? and in such a manner?—what a blundering piece of
exculpation! *He* asked Pictet, etc., to dinner, and of course was
left to entertain them. I went into Society *solely* to present
him (as I told him), that he might return into good company
if he chose; it was the best thing for his youth and circumstances: for myself, I had done with Society, and, having
presented him, withdrew to my own " way of life ". It is true
that I returned without entering Lady Dalrymple Hamilton's,
because I saw it full. It is true that Mrs. Hervey (she writes
novels) fainted at my entrance into Coppet, and then came back
again. On her fainting, the Duchesse de Broglie exclaimed,
" This is *too much*—at *sixty-five* years of age! "—I never gave
" the English " an opportunity of " avoiding " me; but I
trust that, if ever I do, they will seize it.

I am, yours very truly, B.

TO ——[2]   *Venice [Monday], May 17th 1819*

MY DEAREST LOVE,—I have been negligent in not writing,
but what can I say? Three years absence—and the total change
of scene and habit make such a difference—that we have now
nothing in common but our affections and our relationship.—

But I have never ceased nor can cease to feel for a moment
that perfect and boundless attachment which bound and binds
me to you—which renders me utterly incapable of *real* love for
any other human being—for what could they be to me after
you? My own xxxx we may have been very wrong—but I
repent of nothing except that cursed marriage—and your

[1] Dr. Polidori had originally been commissioned by Murray to produce a
journal of his journey with the poet. His *Diary* was eventually published under
the editorship of W. M. Rossetti.
[2] This letter, originally published by Lord Lovelace in *Astarte*, was addressed,
it has been assumed, to Augusta Leigh.

refusing to continue to love me as you had loved me—I can neither forget nor *quite forgive* you for that precious piece of reformation.—but I can never be other than I have been—and whenever I lóve anything it is because it reminds me in some way or other of yourself—for instance I not long ago attached myself to a Venetian for no earthly reason (although a pretty woman) but because she was called xxxx and she often remarked (without knowing the reason) how fond I was of the name.—It is heart-breaking to think of our long Separation—and I am sure more than punishment enough for all our sins—Dante is more humane in his " Hell " for he places his unfortunate lovers (Francesca of Rimini and Paolo whose case fell a good deal short of *ours*—though sufficiently naughty) in company—and though they suffer—it is at least together.—If ever I return to England—it will be to see you—and recollect that in all time—and place—and feelings—I have never ceased to be the same to you in heart—Circumstances may have ruffled my manner—and hardened my spirit—you may have seen me harsh and exasperated with all things around me ; grieved and tortured with *your new resolution,*—and the soon after persecution of that infamous fiend who drove me from my Country and conspired against my life—by endeavouring to deprive me of all that could render it precious—but remember that even then *you* were the sole object that cost me a tear? and *what tears* ! do you remember *our* parting? I have not spirits now to write to you upon other subjects—I am well in health—and have no cause of grief but the reflection that we are not together—When you write to me speak to me of yourself—and say that you love me—never mind commonplace people and topics—which can be in no degree interesting—to me who see nothing in England but the country which holds *you*—or around it but the sea which divides us.—They say absence destroys weak passions—and confirms strong ones—Alas ! *mine* for you is the union of all passions and of all affections—Has strengthened itself but will destroy me—I do not speak of *physical* destruction—for I have endured and can endure much —but of the annihilation of all thoughts feelings or hopes—which have not more or less a reference to you and to *our recollections*—

Ever dearest.   [Signature erased]

TO JOHN MURRAY   *Venice, May 18, 1819*

DEAR SIR,—Yesterday I wrote to Mr. Hobhouse and returned the proof under cover to you. Tell Mr. Hobhouse that
in the Ferrara Story I told him, the phrase was *Vi riveresco
Signor Cognato* and *not Cognato mio* as I stated yesterday by
mistake.

I wrote to you in haste and at past two in the morning
having besides had an accident. In going, about an hour and
a half ago, to a rendezvous with a Venetian girl (unmarried
and the daughter of one of their nobles), I tumbled into the
Grand Canal, and, not choosing to miss my appointment by
the delays of changing, I have been perched in a balcony with
my wet clothes on ever since, till this minute that on my return
I have slipped into my dressing-gown. My foot slipped in
getting into my Gondola to set out (owing to the cursed slippery
steps of their palaces), and in I flounced like a Carp, and went
dripping like a Triton to my Sea nymph and had to scramble
up to a grated window :—

> Fenced with iron within and without
> Lest the lover get in or the Lady get out.

She is a very dear friend of mine, and I have undergone some
trouble on her account, for last winter the truculent tyrant her
flinty-hearted father, having been informed by an infernal
German, Countess Vorsperg (their next neighbour), of our
meetings, they sent a priest to me, and a Commissary of police,
and they locked the Girl up, and gave her prayers and bread
and water, and our connection was cut off for some time ;
but the father hath lately been laid up, and the brother is at
Milan, and the mother falls asleep, and the Servants are naturally on the wrong side of the question, and there is no Moon at
Midnight just now, so that we have lately been able to re-
commence ; the fair one is eighteen ; her name, Angelina ; the
family name, of course, I don't tell you.

She proposed to me to divorce my mathematical wife, and
I told her that in England we can't divorce except for *female*
infidelity. " And pray, (said she), how do you know what she
may have been doing these last three years? " I answered that
I could not tell, but that the state of Cuckoldom was not quite

so flourishing in Great Britain as with us here. " But ", she said, " can't you get rid of her? " " Not more than is done already (I answered) : You would not have me *poison her* ? " Would you believe it? She made me *no answer*. Is not that a true and odd national trait? It spoke more than a thousand words, and yet this is a little, pretty, sweet-tempered, quiet feminine being as ever you saw, but the Passions of a Sunny Soil are paramount to all other considerations. An unmarried Girl naturally wishes to be married : if she can marry and love at the same time it is well, but at any rate she must love. I am not sure that my pretty paramour was herself fully aware of the inference to be drawn from her dead Silence, but even the unconsciousness of the latent idea was striking to an observer of the Passions ; and I never strike out a thought of another's or of my own without trying to trace it to its Source.

I wrote to Mr. H. pretty fully about our matters. In a few days I leave Venice for Romagna. Excuse this scrawl, for I write in a state of shivering from having sat in my dripping drapery, and from some other little accessories which affect this husk of our immortal Kernel.

Tell Augusta that I wrote to her by yesterday's post, addressed to your care. Let me know if you come out this Summer that I may be in the way, and come to me ; don't go to an Inn. I do not know that I can promise you any pleasure ; " our way of life " is so different in these parts, but I insure to myself a great deal in seeing you, and in endeavouring (however vainly) to prove to you that I am, very truly

Yours ever, B.

P.S.—I have read Parson Hodgson's *Friends* in which he seems to display his knowledge of the subject by a Covert attack or two on some of his own. He probably wants another Living ; at least I judge so by the prominence of his piety, although he was always pious—even when he was kept by a Washerwoman on the New Road. I have seen him cry over her picture, which he generally wore under his left Armpit. But he is a good man, and I have no doubt does his duty by his Parish. As to the poetry of his New-fangled Stanza, I wish they would write the octave or the Spenser ; we have no other legitimate measure of that kind. He is right in defending *Pope* against the bastard Pelicans of the poetical winter day, who add insult to their Parricide by sucking the blood of the parent of English *real* poetry—poetry without fault,—and then spurning the bosoms which fed them.

TO THE LORD KINNAIRD *   *Venice, May 26th, 1819*

MY DEAR KINNAIRD,—I saw in the papers the attack you mention, which is blackguard enough, but what you ought naturally to have expected as the consequence of having endeavoured to do a good action, by discovering a bad one. You remember the Scotch proverb " The Redder aye gets the worst lick o' the fray ", so the next time that anyone is to be shot, pray, don't interrupt them ; it appeared to have equally displeased the gentleman missed, the gentleman missing, and the un-gentleman prosecuting, who has lavished upon you such gratuitous and absurd calumny. For my own part (so you were out of it) I feel no curiosity about the matter, unless to know whether Julia [Gramont ?] the Dalilah of that very bad shot (who missed a whole Coach and horses : we could have taught him better at Joe Manton's) was a good piece. I have no patience for the rest of their trash, and if you don't lose yours, the thing can do you no real harm, though it is hard enough to be sure, to be treated in such a manner for having wished to expose an assassin and discover a conspiracy.

It is my intention to leave Venice on Saturday next, perhaps you had better address to me " ferma in posta, Bologna ". I will do my best to meet you on my return, as I shall probably remain but a few days at Ravenna. I leave you your choice of time, place etc. as a few posts in or out of the way will make no difference. I mean to proceed to Ravenna and Rimini, and to stay a few days at Bologna on my way back again to Venice. You may be very sure that I shall have great pleasure in meeting you.

My departure would have taken place before, but our abortion has not yet let us out of our chamber at Ravenna, except once, when we fell ill again. I was still required to set out, but my instructions were a little confused, and though I am really very much in love, yet I see no great use in not adopting a little caution ; we had already terminated the *Essential* part of the business *four* continuous days previous to her setting out from V. (the whole affair was of a week) so that there is nothing very new before us.   I can't tell whether I was the involuntary cause of the miscarriage, but certes I was not the father of the foetus, for she was three months advanced before our first passade, and whether the Count was the parent or not I can't imagine ; perhaps he might ; they are but a year married, and she miscarried once before.

Pray let me have your news.   I have heard of your " campaigning at the King of Bohemy " as Jerry Sneak says of Major Sturgeon, and of Reggio, and Turin also.   I recollect seeing your charmer dance three years ago, but never saw her off the stage.   Believe me, my dear K., ever yours very truly and affectly.,

BYRON

TO JOHN MURRAY   *Bologna, June 7, 1819*

DEAR SIR,—Tell Mr. Hobhouse that I wrote to him a few days ago from Ferrara.   It will therefore be idle in him or you to wait for any further answers or returns of proofs from Venice, as I have directed that no English letters be sent after me. The publication can be proceeded in without, and I am already sick of your remarks, to which I think not the least attention ought to be paid.

Tell Mr. Hobhouse that, since I wrote to him, I had availed myself of my Ferrara letters, and found the society much younger and better there than at Venice.   I was very much pleased with the little the shortness of my stay permitted me to see of the Gonfaloniere Count Mosti, and his family and friends in general.

I have been picture-gazing this morning at the famous Domenichino and Guido, both of which are superlative.   I afterwards went to the beautiful Cimetery of Bologna, beyond the walls, and found, besides the superb Burial-ground, an original of a *Custode*, who reminded me of the grave-digger in

Hamlet. He has a collection of Capuchins' skulls, labelled on the forehead, and taking down one of them, said, " This was Brother Desiderio Berro, who died at forty—one of my best friends. I begged his head of his brethren after his decease, and they gave it me. I put it in lime and then boiled it. Here it is, teeth and all, in excellent preservation. He was the merriest, cleverest fellow I ever knew. Wherever he went, he brought joy; and when any one was melancholy, the sight of him was enough to make him cheerful again. He walked so actively, you might have taken him for a dancer—he joked— he laughed—oh! he was such a Frate as I never saw before, nor ever shall again! "

He told me that he had himself planted all the Cypresses in the Cimetery; that he had the greatest attachment to them and to his dead people; that since 1801 they had buried fifty three thousand persons. In showing some older monuments, there was that of a Roman girl of twenty, with a bust by Bernini. She was a Princess Barberini, dead two centuries ago : he said that, on opening her grave, they had found her hair complete, and " as yellow as gold ". Some of the epitaphs at Ferrara pleased me more than the more splendid monuments of Bologna ; for instance :—

> " Martini Luigi
>   Implora pace."

> " Lucrezia Picini
>   Implora eterna quiete."

Can any thing be more full of pathos? Those few words say all that can be said or sought : the dead had had enough of life ; all they wanted was rest, and this they " *implore* ". There is all the helplessness, and humble hope, and deathlike prayer, that can arise from the grave—" *implora pace* ". I hope, who- ever may survive me, and shall see me put in the foreigners' burying-ground at the Lido, within the fortress by the Adriatic, will see those two words, and no more, put over me. I trust they won't think of " pickling, and bringing me home to Clod or Blunderbuss Hall ". I am sure my bones would not rest in an English grave, or my clay mix with the earth of that country. I believe the thought would drive me mad on my deathbed,

could I suppose that any of my friends would be base enough
to convey my carcase back to your soil. I would not even feed
your worms, if I could help it.

So, as Shakespeare says of Mowbray, the banished Duke of
Norfolk, who died at Venice (see Richard II.), that he, after
fighting

> " Against black pagans, Turks, and Saracens,
> And toil'd with works of war, retir'd himself
> To Italy; and there, at *Venice*, gave
> His body to that *pleasant* country's earth,
> And his pure soul unto his Captain Christ,
> Under whose colours he had, fought so long."

Before I left Venice, I had returned to you your late, and
Mr. Hobhouse's, sheets of *Juan*. Don't wait for further answers
from me, but address yours to Venice, as usual. I know nothing
of my own movements; I may return there in a few days, or
not for some time. All this depends on circumstances. I left
Mr. Hoppner very well, as well as his son and Mrs. Hoppner.
My daughter Allegra was well too, and is growing pretty; her
hair is growing darker, and her eyes are blue. Her temper and
her ways, Mr. Hoppner says, are like mine, as well as her
features : she will make, in that case, a manageable young lady.

I never hear any thing of Ada, the little Electra of my
Mycenæ; the moral Clytemnestra is not very communicative
of her tidings, but there will come a day of reckoning, even if I
should not live to see it.

I have at least seen Romilly shivered who was one of the
assassins. When that felon, or lunatic (take your choice he
must be one and might be both), was doing his worst to uproot
my whole family tree, branch, and blossoms; when, after
taking my retainer, he went over to them; when he was
bringing desolation on my hearth and destruction on my
household Gods, did he think that, in less than three years, a
natural event—a severe domestic—but an expected and
common domestic calamity,—would lay his carcase in a cross
road, or stamp his name in a verdict of Lunacy? Did he (who
in his drivelling sexagenary dotage had not the courage to
survive his Nurse—for what else was a wife to him at his time
of life?)—reflect or consider what my feelings must have been,

when wife, and child, and sister, and name, and fame, and
country were to be my sacrifice on his legal altar—and this at
a moment when my health was declining, my fortune embarrassed, and my mind had been shaken by many kinds of
disappointment, while I was yet young and might have re-
formed what might be wrong in my conduct, and retrieved
what was perplexing in my affairs. But the wretch is in his
grave. I detested him living, and I will not affect to pity him
dead ; I still loathe him—as much as we can hate dust—but
that is nothing.

What a long letter I have scribbled !

Yours truly, B.

P.S.—Here, as in Greece, they strew flowers on the tombs.
I saw a quantity of rose-leaves, and entire roses, scattered over
the graves at Ferrara. It has the most pleasing effect you can
imagine.

TO RICHARD BELGRAVE HOPPNER † *Ravenna, June 20ᵗʰ 1819*

MY DEAR HOPPNER,—I wrote to you a week ago (particularly begging a line in answer by return of post) to request
you would send off Augustine with the two Grey saddle horses,
and the Carriage and Carriage horses, saddles, etc., to wait for
me at the *Pellegrino*—(the Inn there) in *Bologna*. To this letter
and one of the same purport to Mr. Scott, I have had no
answer, which makes me uneasy as I shall probably not return
to Venice for some time. I wished my English letters also to
be forwarded with Augustine to Bologna. If there was any
want of Money, Siri and Willhalm would equip him.

Pray write to me here (*Ravenna*) by next post ; it will reach
me in time, and do not let Augustine delay a moment for the
nonsense of that son of a bitch Edgecombe, who may probably
be the cause of his dawdling.

I wrote to you from Padua, and from Bologna, and since
from Ravenna. I find my situation very agreeable, but want
my horses very much, there being good riding in the environs.
I can fix no time for my return to Venice—it may be soon
or late—or not at all—it all depends on the *Dama* [Teresa

Guiccioli], whom I found very seriously in *bed* with a cough and spitting of blood, etc., all of which has subsided, and something else has recommenced. Her miscarriage has made her a good deal thinner ; and I found all the people here firmly persuaded that she would never recover ;—they were mistaken, however.

My letters were useful as far as I employed them ; and I like both the place and people, though I don't trouble the latter more than I can help. *She* manages very well, though the *local* is inconvenient (no *bolts* and be d—d to them) and we run great risks (were it not at sleeping hours—after dinner) and *no* place but the great Saloon of his own palace. So that if I come away with a Stiletto in my gizzard some fine afternoon, I shall not be astonished.

I can't make *him* out at all—he visits me frequently, and takes me out (like Whittington, the Lord Mayor) in a coach and *six* horses. The fact appears to be, that he is completely *governed* by her—for that matter, so am I. The people here don't know what to make of us, as he had the character of jealousy with all his wives—this is the third. He is the richest of the Ravennese, by their own account, but is not popular among them.

By the aid of a Priest, a Chambermaid, a young Negro-boy, and a female friend, we are enabled to carry on our un-lawful loves, as far as they can well go, though generally with some peril, especially as the female friend and priest are at present out of town for some days, so that some of the pre-cautions devolve upon the Maid and Negro.

Now do pray—send off Augustine—and carriage—and cattle to Bologna without fail or delay—or I shall lose my remaining Shred of senses.

Don't forget this. My coming—going—and every thing depends upon *her* entirely just as Mrs. Hoppner—(to whom I remit my reverences) said, in the true spirit of female prophecy.

You are but a shabby fellow not to have written before—and I am,

Truly yours, B.

P.S.—Address by return of Post to me—at *Ravenna*.

TO THE LORD KINNAIRD *   *Ravenna, July 5th, 1819*

MY DEAR KINNAIRD,—The G[uiccioli] has been very unwell (not ill enough though to induce any amatory abstinence, except that single day when the *Chat* awoke a little prematurely) and I persuaded *him* to have Aglietti from Venice. He came yesterday ; they have put on leeches, and prescribed a regimen, and say that she may be cured if she likes. Will she like ? I doubt her liking anything for very long, except one thing, and I presume she will soon arrive at varying even that, in which case I should be at liberty to repass the Po, and perhaps the Alps ; but as yet I can say nothing.

I had a letter from W. Webster the other day ; he is at Nantes Loire Nif, and I have half a mind to go back in search of *La Fanchette*, but I know nothing of the geography of the place. Where the devil is Nantes ? And what is Loire *Nif* ? A river, I suppose, an't it ?

La Geltruda is gone to Bologna, after pinching her left thigh one evening. I was never permitted to set eyes on her *not no more*. It is no fault of mine, her not coming to Faenza ; she did not set off till yesterday.

I have been exchanging visits with the Cardinal Legate who called on me to day. He is a fine old fellow, Malvasia by name, and has been rather loose in his youth, without being much tighter in his age. He and I took very kindly to each other.

How am I to get the books, and to leave yours ? Is the Bianchi to be visible, or my *Aunt* only ? Of course, you could not doubt the lady and still less your friend ; but I suppose, nevertheless, I shall see my aunt only. Well, it is hard, but I agree, only adding that my green carriage has lost much of its splendour and consequently I am shorn of one of the principal seductive qualities of an accomplished gentleman. I am, as I said, in perfect indecision, depending upon the *will* of a woman who has none, and on whom I never calculate for more than twelve hours. She will do as she pleases, and then so will I. A young Italian, married to a rich old Patrician, with only one man besides for a lover, is not likely to embarrass either with a long Constancy ; and in that case, you know, there could be no great harm in my beginning the world again, or giving it up for good.

Will you tell me where this *Nantes* is? I can't find it in the road book.

Addio. I am just going to take a canter into the pine forest with Ferdinando.

Yours ever and truly, B.

P.S.—I approve your intentions about the books and the *Sequins* also.

TO LADY BYRON   *Ravenna, July 20th 1819*

[Enclosing verses of a German poet]

I have received from Holstein (I believe) the annexed paper of the Baroness of Hohenhausen etc. and the inclosed letter of a Mr. Jacob (or Jacobssen) and as they " ardently wish it could reach you " I transmit it. You will smile, as I have done, at the importance which they attach to such things, and the effect which they conceive capable of being produced by composition, but the Germans are still a young and a romantic people, and live in an ideal world. Perhaps it may not offend you, however it may surprise, that the good people on the frontiers of Denmark have taken an interest in your domestic Affairs, which have now, I think, nearly made the tour of Europe, and been discussed in most of its languages, to as little purpose as in our own. If you like to retain the enclosed, you can do so, an indication to my Sister that you have received the letter will be a sufficient answer. I will not close this sheet without a few words more. Fletcher has complained to me of your declining to give his wife a character, on account of your " doubts of her veracity in some circumstances a short time before she left you ". If your doubts allude to her testimony on your case during the then discussion, you *must* or at least ought to be the best judge how far she spoke truth or not; *I* can only say that She never had directly or indirectly, through me or mine, the slightest inducement to the contrary, nor am I indeed perfectly aware of what her Evidence was, never having seen her nor communicated with her at that period or since. I presume that you will weigh well your justice before you deprive the woman of the means of obtaining her bread. No one can be more fully aware than I am of the utter inefficacy of any words of mine to you on this or on any other subject, but I have discharged my duty to Truth in stating the above, and now do yours.

The date of my letter, indeed my letter itself, may surprize you, but I left Venice in the beginning of June, and came down into Romagna; there is the famous forest of Boccaccio's Story and Dryden's fable hardby, the Adriatic not far distant, and the Sepulchre of Dante within the walls. I am just going to take a Canter (for I have resumed my Tartar habits since I left England) in the cool of the Evening, and in the shadow of the forest till the Ave Maria. I have got both my saddle and Carriage horses with me, and don't spare them, in the cooler part of the day. But I shall probably return to Venice in a short time. Ravenna itself preserves perhaps more of the old Italian manners than any City in Italy. It is out of the way of travellers and armies, and thus they have retained more of their originality. They make love a good deal, and assassinate a little. The department is governed by a Cardinal Legate (Alberoni was once legate here) to whom I have been presented and who told me some singular anecdotes of past times —of Alfieri etc. and others. I tried to discover for Leigh Hunt some traces of Francesca, but except her father Guido's tomb, and the mere notice of the fact in the Latin commentary of Benvenuto da Imola in M.S. in the library, I could discover nothing for him. He (Hunt) has made a sad mistake about " old Ravenna's *clear-shewn towers* and *bay* " the city lies so low that you must be close upon it before it is " shewn " at all, and the Sea had retired *four miles* at least, long before Francesca was born, and as far back as the Exarchs and Emperors. They tell me that at Rimini they know as little about her now—as they do here—so I have not gone there, it lies in the way to Rome, but I was at Rome in 1817. This is odd, for at Venice I found many traditions of the old Venetians, and at Ferrara a plentiful assortment of the House of Este, with the remains of the very Mirror, whose reflection cost at least a dozen lives, including those of Parisina and Ugo. I was wrong in placing those two naughty people in a garden. Parisina was a Malatesta of Rimini, and her daughter by Niccolo of Este was also put to death by some Italian Chief her husband in nearly the same manner as her mother. Her name was Ginevra. So that including the alliance of Francesca with Launcelot Malatesta of Rimini, that same Malatesta family appears to have been but indifferently fortunate in their matrimonial speculations——I have written to you thus much, because in writing to you at all I may as well write much as little. I have not heard of Ada for many months but they say " no news is good news " she must now be three years and almost eight months old. You must let her be taught Italian as soon as she can be taught any language but her own, and pray let her be musical, that is if She has a turn that way. I presume that Italian being a language of mine, will not prevent you from recollecting my request at the proper time.

I am etc.   B.

TO THE HON. AUGUSTA LEIGH *   *Ravenna, July 26th, 1819*

MY DEAREST AUGUSTA,—I am at too great a distance to scold you, but I *will* ask you whether *your* letter of the *1st* July *is an answer* to the letter I wrote you before I quitted Venice? What? is it come to *this*? Have you no memory? or no heart? You *had* both—and I *have* both—at least for *you*.

I write this presuming that you received *that* letter. Is it that you fear? Do not be afraid of the past ; the world has its own affairs without thinking of *ours* and you may write safely. If you do, address as usual to *Venice*. My house is not in St. Marc's but on the Grand Canal, within sight of the Rialto Bridge.

I do not like at all this pain in your side and always think of your mother's constitution. You must always be to me the first consideration in the world. Shall I come to *you*? or would a warm climate do you good? If so say the word, and I will provide you and your whole family (including that precious luggage your husband) with the means of making an agreeable journey. You need not fear about *me*. I am much altered and should be little trouble to you, nor would I give you more of my company than you like. I confess after three and a half— and *such years* ! and *such a year* as preceded those three years !— it would be a relief to me to see you again, and if it would be so to you I will come to you. Pray answer me, and recollect that I will do as you like in everything, even to returning to England, which is not the pleasantest of residences were *you* out of it.

I write from Ravenna. I came here on account of a Countess Guiccioli, a girl of twenty married to a very rich old man of sixty about a year ago. With her last winter I had a *liaison* according to the good old Italian custom. She miscarried in May and sent for me here, and here I have been these two months. She is pretty, a great coquette, extremely vain, excessively affected, clever enough, without the smallest principle, with a good deal of imagination and some passion. She had set her heart on carrying me off from Venice out of vanity, and succeeded, and having made herself the subject of general conversation has greatly contributed to her recovery. Her husband is one of the richest nobles of Ravenna, threescore years of age. This is his third wife. You may suppose what *esteem* I entertain for *her*. Perhaps it is about equal on both sides. I have my saddle-horses here and there is good riding in the forest. With these, and my carriage which is here also, and the sea, and my books, and the lady, the time passes. I am very fond of riding and always *was out* of England. But I hate your Hyde Park, and your turnpike roads, and must have forests, downs, or desarts to expatiate in. I detest *knowing* the road one is to go, and being interrupted by your damned finger-posts, or a blackguard roaring for twopence at a turnpike.

I send you a sonnet which this faithful lady had made for the nuptials of one of her relations in which she swears the most *alarming constancy* to her husband. Is not this good? You may suppose my *face* when she shewed it to me. I could not help laughing—one of *our* laughs. All this is very absurd, but you see that I have good morals at bottom.

She is an equestrian too, but a bore in her rides, for she can't guide her horse and he runs after mine, and tries to bite him, and then she begins screaming in a high hat and sky-blue riding habit, making a most absurd figure, and embarrassing me and both our grooms, who have the devil's own work to keep her from tumbling, or having her clothes torn off by the trees and thickets of the pine forest. I fell a little in love with her intimate friend, a certain Geltruda (that is *Gertrude*) who is very young and seems very well disposed to be perfidious; but alas! *her* husband is jealous, and the G. also detected me in an illicit squeezing of hands, the consequence of which was that the friend was whisked off to Bologna for a few days, and since her return I have never been able to see her but twice, with a dragon of a mother in law and a barbarian husband by her side, besides my own dear precious *Amica*, who hates all flirting but her own. But I have a priest who befriends me and the Gertrude says a good deal with her great black eyes, so that perhaps . . . but alas! I mean to give up these things altogether. I have now given you some account of my present state. The guide-book will tell you about Ravenna. I can't tell how long or short may be my stay. Write to me—love me —as ever

Yours most affectly B.

P.S.—*This* affair is *not* in the least expensive, being all in the wealthy line, but troublesome, for the lady is imperious, and exigeante. However there are hopes that we may quarrel. When we do you shall hear.

TO JOHN CAM HOBHOUSE †   *Ravenna, July 30th, 1819*

DEAR HOBHOUSE,—Your last letter was of the beginning of June. How is it with you?—are you slain by Major Cartwright? [1] or ill of a quinsey? or are you writing a pamphlet in rejoinder to Erskine? I understand that a tailor and you are amongst the most strenuous writers in favour of the *measures* taken by the reformers. I sometimes get a glimpse of your speeches with the names of the tavern and company, in a stray newspaper, "Galignani", or the "Lugano Gazette"; there is Mr. *Bicker*-stith, the man-midwife, and several other worthies of the like calibre; "there never was a set of more amicable officers", as Major Sturgeon says. Pray let me hear how you go on.

My sister writes to me that "Scrope looks ill and out of spirits", and has not his wonted air of prosperity, and that she fears his pursuits have not had all their former success. Is it even so? I suppose there is no knowing, and that the only

[1] Major Cartwright, a veteran supporter of parliamentary reform, had challenged Hobhouse, after a dispute arising out of the Westminster Election of 1819, in which Hobhouse was defeated.

way in which his friends will be apprized will be by some confounded thing or other happening to him. He has not written
to me since the winter, in last year's last month. What is he
about?

The Dougal Creature [1] has written to mention the pact with
Murray; if *it* (*i.e.*, D[on] J[uan]) fails, the sum is too much; if it
succeeds, it is too little by five hundred guineas in coin or ingots.
Donny Johnny will either succeed greatly, or tumble flatly;
there will be no medium—at least I think not. Galignani
announces " Mazeppa " as stamped, but I know nothing, and
hear nothing of it, nor of " Juan "; what is become of the
" Ode to Venice "? I am endeavouring here to get a transcript of Benevento da Imola's Latin commentary on Dante,
never yet stamped, quite " inedita ". They promise it me.

I have been swimming in the Adriatic, and cantering
through Boccaccio's Pinery; it is a fine forest, " so full of
pastime and prodigality ", and I have persuaded my contessa
to put a side-saddle upon a pony of her sposo's, and we ride
together—she in a hat shaped like Punch's and the merry
Mrs. Ford's of Windsor, and a sky-blue tiffany riding-habit,
like the ghost of Prologue's grandmother. I bought an English
horse of Capt. Fyler some time ago (which, with my others,
is here), and he is a famous leaper, and my amusement has been
to make her groom, on a huge coach-horse, follow me over
certain ditches and drain-lets, an operation in which he is
considerably incommoded by a pair of jack-boots, as well as
by the novelty of the undertaking. You would like the forest;
it reaches from here to Rimini.

I have been here these two months, and hitherto all hath
gone on well, with the usual *excerpta* of some " gelosie ", which
are the fault of the climate, and of the conjunction of two such
capricious people as the Guiccioli and the Inglese, but here
hath been no stabbing nor drugging of possets. The last
person assassinated here was the Commissary of Police, three
months ago; they *kilt* him from an alley one evening, but he
is recovering from the slugs with which they sprinkled him,
from an " Archibugia " that shot him round a corner, like the
Irishman's gun. He and Manzoni, who was stabbed dead
going to the theatre at Forli, not long before, are the only

---

[1] Douglas Kinnaird.

recent instances.   But it is the custom of the country, and not much worse than duelling, where one undertakes, at a certain personal risk of a more open nature, to get rid of a disagreeable person, who is injurious or inconvenient, and if such people become insupportable, what is to be done?   It is give and take, like everything else—you run the same risk, and they run the same risk; it has the same object with duelling, but adopts a different means.   As to the trash about *honour*, that is all stuff; a man offends, you want to kill him, this is amiable and natural, but *how*?   The natural mode is obvious, but the artificial varies according to education.

I am taking the generous side of the question, seeing I am much more exposed here to become the patient than the agent of such an experiment.   I know but one man whom I should be tempted to put to rest, and he is not an Italian nor in Italy, therefore I trust that he won't pass through Romagna during my sojourn, *because* 'gin he did, there is no saying what the fashionable facilities might induce a vindictive gentleman to meditate;   besides, there are injuries where the balance is so greatly against the offender, that you are not to risk life against his (excepting always the law, which is originally a convention), but to trample as [you] would on any other venomous animal.

To return to Dante (where you will find a pretty eulogy on revenge) : his tomb is within fifty yards of my " locanda ", the effigy and tombstone well preserved, but the outside is a mere modern cupola.

The house flanking this house, but divided by a street, is said to have been inhabited by him, but that is mere *say-so*, as far as I can make out;   it is old enough to have been inhabited by Honorius, for that matter.   The Polentani, his patrons, are buried in a church behind his grave, but there are no tidings nor tradition of Francesca, here or at Rimini, except the mere fact, which, to be sure, is a thumper, as they were actually killed in it.   Hunt made a devil of a mistake about—

" Old Ravenna's clear shewn towers and bay."

There has been no bay nor sea within five miles since long before the time of the Exarchs, and as to " *clear shewn* ", the town lies so low that you must be close upon it before it is seen at all, and then there is no comprehensive view unless you climb the steeple.

I was introduced to the Cardinal Legate, a fine old boy, and I might have known all the world, but I prefer a private life, and have lived almost entirely with my paramour, her husband, *his* son by a former marriage, and her father, with her confidante, " in white linen ", a very pretty woman, noble also as her friend, called Gertrude Vicari, who has, however, a jealous husband, " a strange Centaur ", as Gibbon calls a philosophical theologian.   But he is a profane historian.

I also fell in love with a promised bride, named Ursula—— something, one of the prettiest creatures I ever saw ; but her barbarous mother, suspecting her of smiling from a window upon me, has watched her ever since, and she won't be married till September so there be no hopes ; however, I am trying my best with a priest (*not* to marry me, you may believe) and others to bring about some-at.

A precious epistle of gossip this is.   But these are all I can say of " fatti miei ".   I have had the G—— (whom I came for) in any case.   And what more I can get I know not, but will try.   It is much better for beauty than Lombardy.   Canova is now in the Austrian states.

Ever, etc., very truly yours, B.

P.S. *July* 31*st*.—Considerable *lusinghe* that Ursula will be obtained, she being well-disposed.   Do you know what happened to Lord Kinnaird at Faenza?   When he went back to Milan, they stopped his carriage to search for the Bianchi (the dancer he keeps) thinking she had broke her engagement for the Fair of Smigaglia to return into Lombardy.   Lege, Dick, lege.   But it was not so.   She *is* dancing at the Fair.

An old woman at Rome, reading Boccaccio, exclaimed, " I wish to God that this was saying one's prayers ".

TO ALEXANDER SCOTT*   *Ravenna, July 31st, 1819*

DEAR SCOTTIN,[1]—You were right.   I *will* consider first. But the truth is I *do* like terra firma a little after the long

---

[1] With Alexander Scott and the Cavaliere Mongaldo (otherwise *Mengaldo*), " a gentleman of Bassano ", Byron had set out to swim from the Lido to Venice in 1818.   The Italian was outdistanced and gave up the contest.

absence from it. As to the G[uiccioli] she has not much to do with my resolution, as I have something besides her on my hands—and in my eye. But I shall say nothing more now, till I am more sure. There are better things in that line, in this part of the world, than at Venice. Besides, like the preserve of a manor, this part has not yet been shot over.

It would be very unpleasant to me that you should quit Venice without our meeting again. I would almost take a flight there again on purpose to see you rather than this should be, and arrange my concerns in person. Where do you think of going? How are the cows? You are wrong about H's letter. There was nothing in it to offend *her*—but me. For instance telling her that *she* would be the *planter*. That *she* was voluble—what is all this? If I had told her that she was called and thought an absurd woman (which I carefully avoided) there indeed I should have been thoroughly Hoppnerian. You may tell a man that he is thought libertine, profligate, a villain, but not that his nose wants blowing or that his neckcloth is ill tied. Suppose you were to say to that Coxcomb Mongaldo that he was dangerous, disaffected, a severe disciplinarian in his regiment, that he had ill used Carlotta Aglietti, that he had been guilty of atrocities in his retreat from *Moscow* (*Moscow* would sweeten him) he would affect but feel nothing. But if you told him that his father sold eggs not very fresh he would be wrath to a degree.

I do not know whether I make myself understood; but it is in the little nooks of character where your true tormentors play the mosquito and the gadfly, and where such fellows as M. and H. distil their little drop of venom. Now I do maintain that I have always avoided this, which is never necessary unless in cases where your fame or fortunes may be seriously attacked. I could have driven Hoppner mad had I ever told him a 10,000th part of the things that I knew and the buffone Cavaliere little less so. But I resisted the pettiness of repaying them in kind. In future I shall be less kind to them and you may tell Mongaldo so—a little tittle tattle boasting parvenu, who never could forgive one's beating him in his own narrow field as we did hollow besides in the wider one of waters. I wish you had heard the account he had left at Ferrara of the swimming match. *You* were sunk and omitted altogether, and *he* had passed the Rialto and was only beaten by me by some accident! We knew him to be a liar before but would think the complete drubbing we both gave him in the swimming match would have silenced him on that score. I could not help saying, on hearing it, to his friends, " this story is Mongaldo all over ".

I enclose a letter which I beg you to forward to Siri and W—. I wish them to remit the 23 francs to Genoa as I know not how.

I have as yet decided nothing, but have a general idea to quit Venice altogether, particularly if I can get this other girl. But in the meantime the establishment may remain as it is, except that I wish they enquire on what terms the landlords of the houses would take them back again supposing me to be so disposed. Edgecombe may have hint of my thoughts and Mr. Domville also. As to the " baron fottuto ", as he is not the only thing " fottuto " (by me) in his family, I overlook that for his wife's sake. What *can* he do unless I buy or sell with him?—And I don't mean to do either. If *she plants*—let her. " There are as good fish in the sea as ever came out of it." There is a Scotch proverb for you hot as haggis. By the way how many *t*'s are there in " fottuto "—one or two? " Fotuto "— eh? Continue to write. Remember me to Missiaglia and *Peppi*, and Marina, and all the Conversazioners. I regret to have missed Canova at Venice, having missed him also at Rome, and in London. Believe me ever and truly yours affectly

　　　　　　　　　　　　　　　　　　　　BYRON

TO JOHN MURRAY †　　　　　　*Ravenna, August 1, 1819*
　　　　　(Address your answer to Venice, however.)

DEAR SIR,—Don't be alarmed. You will see me defend myself gaily—that is, if I happen to be in Spirits; and by *Spirits*, I don't mean your meaning of the word, but the spirit of a bull-dog when pinched, or a bull when pinned—it is then that they make best sport—and as my Sensations under an attack are probably a happy compound of the united energies of those amiable animals, you may perhaps see what Marrall calls " rare sport ", and some good tossing and goring, in the course of the controversy. But I must be in the right cue first, and I doubt I am almost too far off to be in a sufficient fury for the purpose; and then I have effeminated and enervated myself with love and the summer in these last two months.

I wrote to Mr. Hobhouse the other day, and foretold that Juan would either fail entirely or succeed completely—there will be no medium: appearances are not favourable; but as you write the day after publication, it can hardly be decided what opinion will predominate. You seem in a fright, and doubtless with cause. Come what may, I never will flatter the million's canting in any shape: circumstances may or may not have placed me at times in a situation to lead the public opinion, but the public opinion never led, nor ever shall lead, me. I will not sit " on a degraded throne "; so pray put Messrs. Southey, or Sotheby, or Tom Moore, or Horace Twiss upon it—they will all of them be transported with their coronation.

You have bought Harlow's drawings of Margarita and me rather dear methinks; but since you desire the story of Margarita Cogni, you shall be told it, though it may be lengthy.

Her face is of the fine Venetian cast of the old Time, and her figure, though perhaps too tall, not less fine—taken altogether in the national dress.

In the summer of 1817, Hobhouse and myself were sauntering on horseback along the Brenta one evening, when, amongst a group of peasants, we remarked two girls as the prettiest we had seen for some time. About this period, there had been great distress in the country, and I had a little relieved some of the people. Generosity makes a great figure at very little cost in Venetian livres, and mine had probably been exaggerated—as an Englishman's. Whether they remarked us looking at them or no, I know not; but one of them called out to me in Venetian, " Why do not you, who relieve others, think of us also? " I turned round and answered her—" *Cara, tu sei troppo bella e giovane per aver' bisogno del' soccorso mio* ". She answered, " If you saw my hut and my food, you would not say so ". All this passed half jestingly, and I saw no more of her for some days.

A few evenings after, we met with these two girls again,
and they addressed us more seriously, assuring us of the truth
of their statement. They were cousins; Margarita married,
the other single. As I doubted still of the circumstances, I
took the business up in a different light, and made an appointment with them for the next evening. Hobhouse had taken a
fancy to the single lady, who was much shorter in stature, but
a very pretty girl also. They came attended by a third woman,
who was cursedly in the way, and Hobhouse's charmer took
fright (I don't mean at Hobhouse, but at not being married—
for here no woman will do anything under adultery), and flew
off; and mine made some bother—at the propositions, and
wished to consider of them. I told her, " if you really are in
want, I will relieve you without any conditions whatever, and
you may make love with me or no just as you please—*that* shall
make no difference; but if you are not in absolute necessity,
this is naturally a rendezvous, and I presumed that you understood this when you made the appointment ". She said that
she had no objection to make love with me, as she was married,
and all married women did it : but that her husband (a baker)
was somewhat ferocious, and would do her a mischief. In
short, in a few evenings we arranged our affairs, and for two
years, in the course of which I had more women than I can
count or recount, she was the only one who preserved over me
an ascendancy which was often disputed, and never impaired.
As she herself used to say publicly, " It don't matter, he may
have five hundred ; but he will always come back to me ".

The reasons of this were, firstly, her person—very dark,
tall, the Venetian face, very fine black eyes—and certain
other qualities which need not be mentioned. She was two
and twenty years old, and, never having had children, had not
spoilt her figure, nor anything else—which is, I assure you, a
great desideratum in a hot climate where they grow relaxed
and doughy, and flumpity a short time after breeding. She
was, besides, a thorough Venetian in her dialect, in her thoughts,
in her countenance, in every thing, with all their naïveté and
Pantaloon humour. Besides, she could neither read nor write,
and could not plague me with letters,—except twice that she
paid sixpence to a public scribe, under the piazza, to make a
letter for her, upon some occasion, when I was ill and could

not see her. In other respects she was somewhat fierce and *prepotente*, that is, overbearing, and used to walk in whenever it suited her, with no very great regard to time, place, nor persons; and if she found any women in her way, she knocked them down.

When I first knew her, I was in *relazione* (*liaison*) with la Signora Segati, who was silly enough one evening at Dolo, accompanied by some of her female friends, to threaten her; for the Gossips of the Villeggiatura had already found out, by the neighing of my horse one evening, that I used to " ride late in the night " to meet the Fornarina. Margarita threw back her veil (*fazziolo*), and replied in very explicit Venetian, " *You* are *not* his *wife*: *I* am *not* his *wife*: *you* are his *Donna*, and *I* am his *Donna*: *your* husband is a cuckold, and *mine* is another. For the rest, what *right* have you to reproach me? if he prefers what is mine to what is yours, is it my fault? if you wish to secure him, tie him to your petticoat-string; but do not think to speak to me without a reply, because you happen to be richer than I am." Having delivered this pretty piece of eloquence (which I translate as it was related to me by a bye-stander), she went on her way, leaving a numerous audience with Madame Segati, to ponder at her leisure on the dialogue between them.

When I came to Venice for the Winter, she followed. I never had any regular *liaison* with her, but whenever she came I never allowed any other connection to interfere with her; and as she found herself out to be a favourite, she came pretty often. But she had inordinate Self-love, and was not tolerant of other women, except of the Segati, who was, as she said, my regular *Amica*, so that I, being at that time somewhat promiscuous, there was great confusion and demolition of head-dresses and handkerchiefs; and sometimes my servants, in " redding the fray " between her and other feminine persons, received more knocks than acknowledgements for their peaceful endeavours. At the *Cavalchina*, the masqued ball on the last night of the Carnival, where all the World goes, she snatched off the mask of Madame Contarini, a lady noble by birth, and decent in conduct, for no other reason, but because she happened to be leaning on my arm. You may suppose what a cursed noise this made; but this is only one of her pranks.

At last she quarrelled with her husband, and one evening ran away to my house. I told her this would not do : she said she would lie in the street, but not go back to him ; that he beat her (the gentle tigress), spent her money, and scandalously neglected his Oven. As it was Midnight I let her stay, and next day there was no moving her at all. Her husband came, roaring and crying, and entreating her to come back :—*not* she ! He then applied to the Police, and they applied to me : I told them and her husband to *take* her ; I did not want her ; she had come, and I could not fling her out of the window ; but they might conduct her through that or the door if they chose it. She went before the Commissary, but was obliged to return with that *becco ettico* (" consumptive cuckold "), as she called the poor man, who had a Ptisick. In a few days she ran away again. After a precious piece of work, she fixed herself in my house, really and truly without my consent, but, owing to my indolence, and not being able to keep my countenance ; for if I began in a rage, she always finished by making me laugh with some Venetian pantaloonery or another ; and the Gipsy knew this well enough, as well as her other powers of persuasion, and exerted them with the usual tact and success of all She-things—high and low, they are all alike for that.

Madame Benzone also took her under her protection, and then her head turned. She was always in extremes, either crying or laughing ; and so fierce when angered, that she was the terror of men, women, and children—for she had the strength of an Amazon, with the temper of Medea. She was a fine animal, but quite untameable. *I* was the only person that could at all keep her in any order, and when she saw me really angry (which they tell me is rather a savage sight), she subsided. But she had a thousand fooleries : in her *fazziolo*, the dress of the lower orders, she looked beautiful ; but, alas ! she longed for a hat and feathers, and all I could say or do (and I said much) could not prevent this travestie. I put the first into the fire ; but I got tired of burning them, before she did of buying them, so that she made herself a figure—for they did not at all become her.

Then she would have her gowns with a *tail*—like a lady, forsooth : nothing would serve her but " *l' abito colla coua* ", or *cua*, (that is the Venetian for " *la Coda* ", the tail or train,) and

as her cursed pronunciation of the word made me laugh, there
was an end of all controversy, and she dragged this diabolical
tail after her every where.

In the meantime, she beat the women and stopped my
letters. I found her one day pondering over one : she used to
try to find out by their shape whether they were feminine or
no ; and she used to lament her ignorance, and actually studied
her Alphabet, on purpose (as she declared) to open all letters
addressed to me and read their contents.

I must not omit to do justice to her housekeeping qualities :
after she came into my house as *donna di governo*, the expences
were reduced to less than half, and every body did their duty
better—the apartments were kept in order, and every thing
and every body else, except herself.

That she had a sufficient regard for me in her wild way, I
had many reasons to believe. I will mention one. In the
autumn, one day, going to the Lido with my Gondoliers, we
were overtaken by a heavy Squall, and the Gondola put in
peril—hats blown away, boat filling, oar lost, tumbling sea,
thunder, rain in torrents, night coming, and wind increasing.
On our return, after a tight struggle, I found her on the open
steps of the Mocenigo palace, on the Grand Canal, with her
great black eyes flashing through her tears, and the long dark
hair, which was streaming drenched with rain over her brows
and breast. She was perfectly exposed to the storm ; and the
wind blowing her hair and dress about her tall thin figure, and
the lightning flashing round her, with the waves rolling at her
feet, made her look like Medea alighted from her chariot, or
the Sibyl of the tempest that was rolling around her, the only
living thing within hail at that moment except ourselves. On
seeing me safe, she did not wait to greet me, as might be expected, but calling out to me—*Ah! can' della Madonna, xe esto
il tempo per andar' al' Lido ?* (Ah ! Dog of the Virgin, is this a time
to go to Lido?) ran into the house, and solaced herself with
scolding the boatmen for not foreseeing the " *temporale* ". I
was told by the servants that she had only been prevented
from coming in a boat to look after me, by the refusal of all the
Gondoliers of the Canal to put out into the harbour in such a
moment : and that then she sate down on the steps in all the
thickest of the Squall, and would neither be removed nor

comforted. Her joy at seeing me again was moderately mixed with ferocity, and gave me the idea of a tigress over her recovered Cubs.

But her reign drew near a close. She became quite ungovernable some months after; and a concurrence of complaints, some true, and many false—" a favourite has no friend" —determined me to part with her. I told her quietly that she must return home, (she had acquired a sufficient provision for herself and mother, etc., in my service,) and She refused to quit the house. I was firm, and she went, threatening knives and revenge. I told her that I had seen knives drawn before her time, and that if she chose to begin, there was a knife, and fork also, at her service on the table, and that intimidation would not do. The next day, while I was at dinner, she walked in, (having broke open a glass door that led from the hall below to the staircase, by way of prologue,) and, advancing strait up to the table, snatched the knife from my hand, cutting me slightly in the thumb in the operation. Whether she meant to use this against herself or me, I know not—probably against neither—but Fletcher seized her by the arms, and disarmed her. I then called my boatmen, and desired them to get the Gondola ready, and conduct her to her own house again, seeing carefully that she did herself no mischief by the way. She seemed quite quiet, and walked down stairs. I resumed my dinner.

We heard a great noise : I went out, and met them on the staircase, carrying her up stairs. She had thrown herself into the Canal. That she intended to destroy herself, I do not believe; but when we consider the fear women and men who can't swim have of deep or even of shallow water, (and the Venetians in particular, though they live on the waves,) and that it was also night, and dark, and very cold, it shows that she had a devilish spirit of some sort within her. They had got her out without much difficulty or damage, excepting the salt water she had swallowed, and the wetting she had undergone.

I foresaw her intention to refix herself, and sent for a Surgeon, enquiring how many hours it would require to restore her from her agitation; and he named the time. I then said, " I give you that time, and more if you require it; but at the expiration of the prescribed period, if *She* does not leave the house, *I* will ".

All my people were consternated—they had always been frightened at her, and were now paralyzed : they wanted me to apply to the police, to guard myself, etc., etc., like a pack of sniveling servile boobies as they were. I did nothing of the kind, thinking that I might as well end that way as another; besides, I had been used to savage women, and knew their ways.

I had her sent home quietly after her recovery, and never saw her since, except twice at the opera, at a distance amongst the audience. She made many attempts to return, but no more violent ones. And this is the story of Margarita Cogni, as far as it belongs to me.

I forgot to mention that she was very devout, and would cross herself if she heard the prayer-time strike—sometimes when that ceremony did not appear to be much in unison with what she was then about.

She was quick in reply; as, for instance—One day when she had made me very angry with beating somebody or other, I called her a *Cow* (*Cow*, in Italian, is a sad affront and tanta-mount to the feminine of dog in English). I called her " *Vacca* ". She turned round, curtesied, and answered, " *Vacca tua*, *'Celenza*" (*i.e. Eccelenza*). " *Your* Cow, please your Excellency." In short, she was, as I said before, a very fine Animal, of considerable beauty and energy, with many good and several amusing qualities, but wild as a witch and fierce as a demon. She used to boast publicly of her ascendancy over me, con-trasting it with that of other women, and assigning for it sundry reasons, physical and moral, which did more credit to her person than her modesty. True it was, that they all tried to get her away, and no one succeeded till her own absurdity helped them. Whenever there was a competition, and some-times one would be shut in one room and one in another to prevent battle, she had generally the preference.

Yours very truly and affectionately, B.

P.S.—The Countess G[uiccioli] is much better than she was. I sent you, before leaving Venice, a letter containing the real original sketch which gave rise to the *Vampire*, etc. : did you get it?

TO JOHN MURRAY   *Bologna, August 12, 1819*

DEAR SIR,—I do not know how far I may be able to reply to your letter, for I am not very well to-day. Last night I went to the representation of Alfieri's *Mirra*,[1] the two last acts of which threw me into convulsions. I do not mean by that word a lady's hysterics, but the agony of reluctant tears, and the choaking shudder, which I do not often undergo for fiction. This is but the second time for anything under reality ; the first was on seeing Kean's Sir Giles Overreach. The worst was, that the " *dama* ", in whose box I was, went off in the same way, I really believe more from fright than any other sympathy—at least with the players : but she has been ill, and I have been ill, and we are all languid and pathetic this morning, with great expenditure of Sal Volatile. But, to return to your letter of the 23d of July.

You are right, Gifford is right, Crabbe is right, Hobhouse is right—you are all right, and I am all wrong ; but do, pray, let me have that pleasure. Cut me up root and branch ; quarter me in the *Quarterly* ; send round my *disjecti membra poetæ*, like those of the Levite's Concubine ; make me, if you will, a spectacle to men and angels ; but don't ask me to alter, for I can't :—I am obstinate and lazy—and there's the truth.

But, nevertheless, I will answer your friend C[ohen],[2] who objects to the quick succession of fun and gravity, as if in that case the gravity did not (in intention, at least) heighten the fun. His metaphor is, that " we are never scorched and drenched at the same time ". Blessings on his experience ! Ask him these questions about " scorching and drenching ". Did he never play at Cricket, or walk a mile in hot weather? Did he never spill a dish of tea over himself in handing the cup to his charmer, to the great shame of his nankeen breeches? Did he never swim in the sea at Noonday with the Sun in his eyes and on his head, which all the foam of Ocean could not cool? Did he never draw his foot out of a tub of too hot water, damning his eyes and his valet's? * * * * * Was he ever in a Turkish bath, that marble paradise of sherbet and Sodomy? Was he ever in a cauldron of boiling oil, like St. John? or in

---

[1] Alfieri's tragedy concerns a young woman smitten with passion for her father.
[2] Afterwards Sir Francis Palgrave.

the sulphureous waves of hell? (where he ought to be for his
" scorching and drenching at the same time "). Did he never
tumble into a river or lake, fishing, and sit in his wet cloathes
in the boat, or on the bank, afterwards " scorched and
drenched ", like a true sportsman? " Oh for breath to utter ! "
—but make him my compliments ; he is a clever fellow for
all that—a very clever fellow.

You ask me for the plan of Donny Johnny : I *have* no plan
—I *had* no plan ; but I had or have materials ; though if,
like Tony Lumpkin, I am " to be snubbed so when I am in
spirits ", the poem will be naught, and the poet turn serious
again. If it don't take, I will leave it off where it is, with all
due respect to the Public ; but if continued, it must be in my
own way. You might as well make Hamlet (or Diggory)
" act mad " in a strait waistcoat as trammel my buffoonery, if
I am to be a buffoon : their gestures and my thoughts would
only be pitiably absurd and ludicrously constrained. Why,
Man, the Soul of such writing is its licence ; at least the *liberty*
of that *licence*, if one likes—*not* that one should abuse it : it is
like trial by Jury and Peerage and the Habeas Corpus—a very
fine thing, but chiefly in the *reversion* ; because no one wishes to
be tried for the mere pleasure of proving his possession of the
privilege.

But a truce with these reflections. You are too earnest and
eager about a work never intended to be serious. Do you
suppose that I could have any intention but to giggle and make
giggle?—a playful satire, with as little poetry as could be helped,
was what I meant : and as to the indecency, do, pray, read in
Boswell what *Johnson*, the sullen moralist, says of *Prior* and
Paulo Purgante.

Will you get a favour done for me? *You* can, by your
Government friends, Croker, Canning, or my old Schoolfellow
Peel, and I can't. Here it is. Will you ask them to appoint
(*without salary or emolument*) a noble Italian [1] (whom I will name
afterwards) Consul or Vice-Consul for Ravenna? He is a
man of very large property,—noble, too ; but he wishes to
have a British protection, in case of changes. Ravenna is near
the sea. He wants *no emolument* whatever : that his office might

---

[1] Count Guiccioli, a secret Liberal, had solicited Byron's interest in obtaining
such employment.

be useful, I know; as I lately sent off from Ravenna to Trieste a poor devil of an English Sailor, who had remained there sick, sorry, and penniless (having been set ashore in 1814), from the want of any accredited agent able or willing to help him home-wards. Will you get this done? It will be the greatest favour to me. If you do, I will then send his name and condition, subject, of course, to rejection, if *not* approved when known.

I know that in the Levant you make consuls and Vice-Consuls, perpetually, of foreigners. This man is a Patrician, and has twelve thousand a year. His motive is a British protec-tion in case of new Invasions. Don't you think Croker would do it for us? To be sure, *my interest* is rare!! but, perhaps a brother-wit in the Tory line might do a good turn at the re-quest of so harmless and long absent a Whig, particularly as there is no *salary* nor *burthen* of any sort to be annexed to the office.

I can assure you, I should look upon it as a great obliga-tion; but, alas! that very circumstance may, very probably, operate to the contrary—indeed, it ought. But I have, at least, been an honest and an open enemy. Amongst your many splendid Government Connections, could not you, think you, get our Bibulus made a Consul? Or make me one, that I may make him my Vice. You may be assured that, in case of accidents in Italy, he would be no feeble adjunct—as you would think if you knew his property.

What is all this about Tom Moore? but why do I ask? since the state of my own affairs would not permit me to be of use to him, although they are greatly improved since 1816, and may, with some more luck and a little prudence, become quite Clear. It seems his Claimants are *American* merchants? *There* goes *Nemesis*! Moore abused America. It is always thus in the long run:—Time, the Avenger. You have seen every trampler down, in turn, from Buonaparte to the simplest individuals. You saw how some were avenged even upon my insignificance, and how in turn Romilly paid for his atrocity. It is an odd World; but the Watch has its mainspring, after all.

So the Prince has been repealing Lord Ed. Fitzgerald's forfeiture?[1] *Ecco un' Sonnetto!*

[1] Lord Edward Fitzgerald, the Irish rebel, had met his death, while resisting arrest, in 1798. His attainder was repealed in 1819.

To be the father of the fatherless,
To stretch the hand from the throne's height, and raise
  His offspring, who expired in other days
To make thy Sire's Sway by a kingdom less,—
This is to be a Monarch, and repress
  Envy into unutterable praise.
Dismiss thy Guard, and trust thee to such traits,
For who would lift a hand, except to bless?
Were it not easy, Sir, and is't not sweet
To make thyself beloved? and to be
Omnipotent by Mercy's means? for thus
Thy Sovereignty would grow but more complete,
A Despot thou, and yet thy people free,
And by the Heart, not Hand, enslaving us.

There, you dogs: there's a Sonnet for you: you won't have such as that in a hurry from Mr. Fitzgerald. You may publish it with my name, an ye wool. He deserves all praise, bad and good; it was a very noble piece of principality. Would you like an epigram—a translation?

If for silver, or for gold,
  You could melt ten thousand pimples
  Into half a dozen dimples,
Then your face we might behold,
  Looking, doubtless, much more smugly,
  Yet even then 'twould be damned ugly.

This was written on some Frenchwoman, by Rulhières, I believe. And so " good morrow t' ye, good Master lieutenant ".

Yours, BYRON

TO JOHN CAM HOBHOUSE   *Bologna, August 20th, 1819*

MY DEAR HOBHOUSE,—I have not lately had of your news, and shall not reproach you because I think that if you had good to send me, you would be the first. I wrote to you twice or thrice from Ravenna, and now I am at Bologna. Address to me, however, at Venice.

My time has been passed viciously and agreeably; at thirty-one so few years, months, days remain, that " Carpe diem " is not enough. I have been obliged to crop even the seconds, for who can trust *to-morrow?*—*to-morrow* quotha? to-hour, to-*minute*. I can not repent me (I try very often) so much of anything I have done, as of anything I have left undone. Alas ! I have been but idle, and have the prospect of an early decay, without having seized every available instant of our pleasurable years. This is a bitter thought, and it will be difficult for me ever to recover the despondency into which this idea naturally throws one. Philosophy would be in vain—let us try action.

In England I see and read of reform, " and there never were such troublesome times, especially for *constables* " ; they have wafered Mr. Birch of Stockport. There is much of Hunt and Harrison, and Sir Charles (Linsey) Woolsey but we hear nothing of you and Burdett? The " Venerable Cartwright ", too—why did you not shorten that fellow's longevity? I do assure you (though that lust for duelling of which you used to accuse me in the Stevens's Coffee-house has long subsided into a moderate desire of killing one's more personal enemies) that I would have Mantoned [1] old Cartwright most readily. I have no notion of an old fool like that drivelling defiance, and coughing a challenge at his youngers and his betters. " *Solder him up* ", as Francis said of his defunct wife.

And now what do you think of doing? I have two notions : one to visit England in the spring, the other to go to South America. Europe is grown decrepit ; besides, it is all the same thing over again ; those fellows are fresh as their world, and fierce as their earthquakes. Besides, I am enamoured of General Paer, who has proved that my grandfather spoke truth about the Patagonians, with his gigantic cavalry.

Would that the Dougal of Bishop's Castle would find a purchaser for Rochdale.

I would embark (with Fletcher as a breeding beast of burthen) and possess myself of the pinnacle of the Andes, or a spacious plain of unbounded extent in an eligible earthquake situation.

[1] Manton's was a famous shooting-gallery, frequented by Byron and his friends.

Will my wife always live? will her mother never die? is her father immortal? What are you about? married and settled in the country, I suppose by your silence.

Yours, B.

P.S.—I hear nothing of Don Juan but in two letters from Murray; the first very tremulous, the second in better spirits.

Of the fate of the " pome " I am quite uncertain, and do not anticipate much brilliancy from your silence. But I do not care. I am as sure as the Archbishop of Grenada that I never wrote better, and I wish you all better taste, but will not send you any pistoles.

TO JOHN CAM HOBHOUSE　　　　　*Bologna, August 23rd, 1819*

MY DEAR HOBHOUSE,—I have received a letter from Murray containing the " British Review's " eleventh article. Had you any conception of a man's tumbling into such a trap as Roberts [1] has done? Why it is precisely what he was wished to do. I have enclosed an epistle for publication with a queer signature (to Murray, who should keep the anonymous still about D. Juan) in answer to Roberts, which pray approve if you can. It is written in an evening and morning in haste, with ill-health and worse nerves. I am so bilious, that I nearly lose my head, and so nervous that I cry for nothing; at least to-day I burst into tears, all alone by myself, over a cistern of gold-fishes, which are not pathetic animals. I can assure you it is not Mr. Roberts, or any of his crew that can affect me; but I have been excited and agitated, and exhausted mentally and bodily all this summer, till I really sometimes begin to think not only " that I shall die at top first ", but that the moment is not very remote. I have had no particular cause of griefs, except the usual accompaniments of all unlawful passions.

I have to do with a woman rendered perfectly disinterested by her situation in life, and young and amiable and pretty; in short as good, and at least as attractive as anything of the sex can be, with all the advantages and disadvantages of being

[1] William Roberts, editor of the *British Review*, which had suggested that *Don Juan* could not be by Byron.

scarcely twenty years old, and only two out of her Romagnuolo convent at Faenza.

But I feel—and I feel it bitterly—that a man should not consume his life at the side and on the bosom of a woman, and a stranger; that even the recompense, and it is much, is not enough, and that this Cicisbean existence is to be condemned. But I have neither the strength of mind to break my chain, nor the insensibility which would deaden its weight. I cannot tell what will become of me—to leave, or to be left would at present drive me quite out of my senses; and yet to what have I conducted myself? I have, luckily, or unluckily, no ambition left; it would be better if I had, it would at least awake me; whereas at present I merely start in my sleep.

I think I wrote to you last week, but really (like Lord Grizzle) cannot positively tell.

Why don't you write? pray do—never mind " Don Juan ", let him tumble—and let me too—like Jack and Gill.

Write, and believe me—as long as I can keep my sanity, ever yours most truly and affect^ly,

B.

TO JOHN MURRAY   *Bologna, August 24, 1819*

DEAR SIR,—I wrote to you by last post, enclosing a buffooning letter for publication, addressed to the buffoon Roberts, who has thought proper to tie a cannister to his own tail. It was written off hand, and in the midst of circumstances not very favourable to facetiousness, so that there may, perhaps, be more bitterness than enough for that sort of small acid punch. You will tell me.

Keep the *anonymous,* in every case : it helps what fun there may be; but if the matter grows serious about *Don Juan,* and you feel *yourself* in a scrape, or *me* either, *own that I am the author. I* will never *shrink*; and if *you* do, I can always answer you in the question of Guatimozin to his minister—each being on his own coals.

I wish that I had been in better spirits, but I am out of sorts, out of nerves; and now and then (I begin to fear) out of my senses. All this Italy has done for me, and not England : I defy all of you, and your climate to boot, to make me mad.

But if ever I do really become a Bedlamite, and wear a strait waistcoat, let me be brought back among you; your people will then be proper compagny.

I assure you what I here say and feel has nothing to do with England, either in a literary or personal point of view. All my present pleasures or plagues are as Italian as the Opera. And after all, they are but trifles, for all this arises from my *dama's* being in the country for three days (at Capofiume); but as I could never live for but one human being at a time, (and, I assure you, *that one* has never been *myself*, as you may know by the consequences, for the *Selfish* are *successful* in life,) I feel alone and unhappy.

I have sent for my daughter from Venice, and I ride daily, and walk in a Garden, under a purple canopy of grapes, and sit by a fountain, and talk with the Gardener of his toils, which seem greater than Adam's, and with his wife, and with his Son's wife, who is the youngest of the party, and, I think, talks best of the three. Then I revisit the Campo Santo, and my old friend, the Sexton, has two—but *one* the prettiest daughter imaginable; and I amuse myself with contrasting her beautiful and innocent face of fifteen with the skulls with which he has peopled several cells, and particularly with that of one skull dated 1766, which was once covered (the tradition goes,) by the most lovely features of Bologna—noble and rich. When I look at these, and at this girl—when I think of what *they were*, and what *she* must be—why, then, my dear Murray, I won't shock you by saying what I think. It is little matter what becomes of us " bearded men ", but I don't like the notion of a beautiful woman's lasting less than a beautiful tree—than her own picture—her own shadow, which won't change so to the Sun as her face to the mirror. I must leave off, for my head aches consumedly: I have never been quite well since the night of the representation of Alfieri's *Mirra*, a fortnight ago.

Yours ever, B.

TO THE COUNTESS GUICCIOLI   *Bologna, August 25, 1819*

MY DEAR TERESA,—I have read this book in your garden; —my love, you were absent, or else I could not have read it.

It is a favourite book of yours, and the writer was a friend of mine. You will not understand these English words, and *others* will not understand them—which is the reason I have not scrawled them in Italian. But you will recognise the hand-writing of him who passionately loved you, and you will divine that, over a book which was yours, he could only think of love. In that word, beautiful in all languages, but most so in yours—*Amor mio*—is comprised my existence here and hereafter. I feel I exist here, and I fear that I shall exist hereafter,—to *what* purpose you will decide; my destiny rests with you, and you are a woman, seventeen years of age, and two out of a convent. I wish that you had stayed there, with all my heart,—or, at least, that I had never met you in your married state.

But all this is too late. I love you, and you love me,—at least, you *say so*, and *act* as if you *did* so, which last is a great consolation in all events. But *I* more than love you, and cannot cease to love you.

Think of me, sometimes, when the Alps and the ocean divide us,—but they never will, unless you *wish* it.

BYRON

TO CAPT. HAY *   *Venice, Sept. 1819*

My dear Hay,[1]—It is said that when Sir Isaac Newton delivered an opinion which any one chose to controvert, he never was at the pains to defend it, but contented himself with saying—" I believe, Sir, if you will be at the trouble of examin-ing my opinion, you will find that I have very good reason for it."—In making the assertion you allude to, I, too, have a most potent reason. Having been an eye and ear witness though an involuntary one, I ought to know what passed behind the curtain. There is nothing new under the sun, nay, under the moon neither. The mystical tradition of Apollo flaying his competitor is related by Diodorus Siculus with such praises of

---

[1] Captain John Hay, an acquaintance both of Byron and of Shelley, was involved with them and Trelawny in the scuffle which occurred at the gates of Pisa in 1822, when Sergeant-Major Masi claimed that he had been assaulted by the English party and afterwards stabbed by one of the Gambas' servants. This incident led to the Gambas' exile.

the musical skill of Marsyas, and with such imputations of trickery and cruelty on the God of Poetry, that it was probably an allegory, not so much of the chastisement merited by presumptuous ignorance as of the vindictive jealousy of *gens de plume*.—Damn the old sentimental serpent.—Lives there that being with wit enough to keep him from putrifying who doubts the rascality of the fellow?—

To my extreme mortification I grow wiser every day—though Venice be not exactly the place for turning Solomon in a hurry—if you come over to the city of the winged lion you will soon convince yourself of it . . . 3 o'clock A.M. Good morrow!

ever yours, Byron

TO JOHN CAM HOBHOUSE   *Venice, Oct. 3rd, 1819*

DEAR HOBHOUSE,—I wrote to Murray last week and begged him to reassure you of my health and sanity, as far as I know at present. At Bologna I was out of sorts in health and spirits. Here—I have health at least. My South American project, of which I believe I spoke to you (as you mention it)—was this. I perceived by the inclosed paragraphs that advantageous offers were—or are to be held out to settlers in the Venezuela territory. My affairs in England are nearly settled or in prospect of settlement; in Italy I have no debts, and I could leave it when I choose. The Anglo-Americans are a little too coarse for me, and their climate too cold, and I should prefer the others. I could soon grapple with the Spanish language. Ellice or others would get me letters to Bolivar and his government, and if men of little, or no property are encouraged there, surely with present income, and—if I could sell Rochdale —with some capital, I might be suffered as a landholder there, or at least a tenant, and if possible, and legal—a Citizen. I wish you would speak to *Perry* of the *M[orning] C[hronicle]*— who is their Gazetteer—about this, and ask like Jeremy Diddler—not for eighteen pence—but information on the subject. I assure you that I am very *serious* in the idea, and that the notion has been about me for a long time, as you will see by the worn state of the advertisement. I should go there with my natural daughter, Allegra,—now nearly three years old, and with me here,—and pitch my tent for good and all.

I am not tired of Italy, but a man must be a Cicisbeo and a Singer in duets, and a connoisseur of Operas—or nothing—here. I have made some progress in all these accomplishments, but I can't say that I don't feel the degradation. Better be an unskilful Planter, an awkward settler,—better be a hunter, or anything, than a flatterer of fiddlers, and fan carrier of a woman. I like women—God he knows—but the more their system here developes upon me, the worse it seems, after Turkey too; here the *polygamy* is all on the female side. I have been an intriguer, a husband, a whoremonger, and now I am a Cavalier Servente—by the holy! it is a strange sensation. After having belonged in my own and other countries to the intriguing, the married, and the keeping parts of the town,—to be sure an honest arrangement is the best, and I have had that too, and have—but they expect it to be for *life*, thereby, I presume, excluding longevity. But let us be serious, if possible.

You must not talk to me of England, that is out of the question. I had a house and lands, and a wife and child, and a name there—once—but all these things are transmuted or sequestered. Of the last, and best, ten years of my life, nearly six have been passed out of it. I feel no love for the soil after the treatment I received before leaving it for the last time, but I do not hate it enough to wish to take a part in its calamities, as on either side harm must be done before good can accrue; revolutions are not to be made with rosewater. My taste for revolution is abated, with my other passions.

Yet I want a country, and a home, and—if possible—a free one. I am not yet thirty-two years of age. I might still be a decent Citizen, and found a house, and a family as good—or better—than the former. I could at all events occupy myself rationally, my hopes are not high, nor my ambition extensive, and when tens of thousands of our countrymen are colonizing (like the Greeks of old in Sicily and Italy) from so many causes, does my notion seem visionary or irrational? There is no freedom in Europe—that's certain; it is besides a worn out portion of the globe. What I should be glad of is *information* as to the encouragement, the means required, and what is acceded, and what would be my probable reception. Perry —or Ellice or many merchants would be able to tell you this for me. I won't go there to travel, but to settle. Do not laugh at me; you will, but I assure you I am quite in earnest if the thing be practicable. I do not want to have anything to do with war projects, but to go there as a settler, and if as a citizen all the better, my own government would not, I think, refuse me permission, if they know their own interest; such fellows as I am are no desideratum for Sidmouth at present, I think. Address to me at Venice. I should of course come to Liverpool, or some town on your coast, to take my passage and receive my credentials. Believe me,

Ever yours most truly, BYRON

TO THE HON. DOUGLAS KINNAIRD† *Venice, Octr 26, 1819* [1]

MY DEAR DOUGLAS,—My late expenditure has arisen from living at a distance from Venice and being obliged to keep up two establishments, from frequent journeys and buying some furniture and books as well as a horse or two—and not from any renewal of the *Epicurean* system as you suspect.

I have been faithful to my honest liaison with Countess Guiccioli and I can assure you that she has never cost me directly or indirectly a sixpence, indeed the circumstances of herself and family render this no merit. I never offered her but one present—a broach of brilliants and she sent it back to me with her *own hair* in it (* * * * * * * but *that* is an Italian custom) and a note to say that she was not in the habit of receiving presents of that value, but hoped that I would not consider her sending it back as an affront, nor the value diminished by the enclosure. * * * * * * * * * * * * *

Why should you prevent Hanson from making a *peer* if he likes it. I think the " *garrotting* " would be by far the best parliamentary privilege I know of. Damn your delicacy. It is a low commercial quality and very unworthy a man who prefixes " honourable " to his nomenclature. If you say that I must sign the bonds, I suppose that I must, but it is very

[1] Wrongly dated as Oct. 26th, 1818, by Byron.

iniquitous to make me pay my debts—you have no idea of the pain it gives me.

Pray do three things, get my property out of the *funds*, get Rochdale sold, get me some information from Parry about *South* America, and 4thly ask Lady Noel not to live so very long. As to subscribing to Manchester—if I do that I will write a letter to Burdett for publication to accompany the Subscription which shall be more radical than anything yet rooted—but I feel lazy. I have thought of this for some time but, alas, the air of this cursed Italy enervates and disfranchises the thoughts of a man after nearly four years of respiration to say nothing of emission.

As to "Don Juan", confess, confess—you dog and be candid—that it is the sublime of *that there* sort of writing—it may be bawdy but is it not good English? It may be profligate but is it not *life*, is it not *the thing*? Could any man have written it who has not lived in the world?—and [f]ooled in a post-chaise?—in a hackney coach?—in a gondola?—against a wall?—in a court carriage?—in a vis à vis?—on a table?—and under it? I have written about a hundred stanzas of a third Canto, but it is a damned modest—the outcry has frighted me. I have such projects for the Don but the Cant is so much stronger than the *, nowadays, that the benefit of experience in a man who had well weighed the worth of both monosyllables must be lost to despairing posterity. After all what stuff this outcry is—Lalla Rookh and Little are more dangerous than my burlesque poem can be. Moore has been here, we got tipsy together and were very amicable; he is gone to Rome. I put my life (in M.S.) into his hands (not for publication), you or anybody else may see it at his return. It only comes up to 1816. He is a noble fellow and looks quite fresh and poetical, nine years (the age of a poem's education) my senior. He looks younger. This comes from marriage and being settled in the country. I want to go to South America— I have written to Hobhouse all about it. I wrote to my wife, three months ago, under cover to Murray. Has she got the letter—or is the letter got into Blackwood's Magazine?

You ask after my christmas pye. Remit it anyhow— *circulars* is the best. You are right about *income*—I must have it all. How the devil do I know that I may live a year or a month? I wish I knew, that I might regulate my spending in more ways than one. As it is one always thinks there is but a span. A man may as well break or be damned for a large sum as a small one. I should be loath to pay the devil or any other creditor more than six pence in the pound.

B.

TO RICHARD BELGRAVE HOPPNER† *October 29, 1819*

MY DEAR HOPPNER,—The Ferrara Story is of a piece with all the rest of the Venetian manufacture; you may judge. I only changed horses there since I wrote to you after my visit in June last. " *Convent* "—and " *carry off* " quotha!—and " *girl* "—I should like to know *who* has been carried off—except poor dear *me*. I have been more ravished myself than any body since the Trojan war; but as to the arrest and it's causes—one is as true as the other, and I can account for the invention of neither. I suppose it is some confusion of the tale of the F[ornarina]—and of Mᵉ Guiccioli—and half a dozen more—but it is useless to unravel the web, when one has only to brush it away.

I shall settle with Muster Edgecombe who looks very blue at your *in-decision*, and swears that he is the best arithmetician in Europe; and so I think also, for he makes out two and two to be five.

You may see me next week. I have a horse or two more (five in all) and I shall repossess myself of Lido, and I will rise earlier, and we will go and shake our livers over the beach as heretofore—if you like, and we will make the Adriatic roar again with our hatred of that now empty Oyster shell without it's pearl—the city of Venice.

Murray sent me a letter yesterday; the impostors have published *two* new *third* Cantos of *Don Juan*; the devil take the impudence of some blackguard bookseller or other there*for*.

Perhaps I did not make myself understood. He told me the sale had not been great—1200 out of 1500 quarto I believe (which is nothing after selling 13000 of *The Corsair* in one day) but that the " best judges, etc.", had said it was very fine, and clever, and particularly good English, and poetry, and all those

consolatory things which are not, however, worth a single copy
to a bookseller;—and as to the author—of course I am in a
damned passion at the bad taste of the times, and swear there
is nothing like posterity, who of course must know more of the
matter than their Grandfathers.

There has been an eleventh commandment to the women
not to read it—and what is still more extraordinary they seem
not to have broken it. But that can be of little import to them,
poor things, for the reading or non-reading a book will never
keep down a single petticoat;—but it is of import to Murray,
who will be in scandal for his aiding as publisher.

He is bold howsomedever—wanting two more cantos
against the winter. I think that he had better not, for by the
larkins! it will only make a new row for him.

Edgecombe is gone to Venice to-day to consign my chattels
to t'other fellow.

Count G[uiccioli] comes to Venice next week and I am
requested to consign his wife to him, which shall be done—
with all her linen.

What you say of the long evenings at the Mira, or Venice,
reminds me of what *Curran* said to Moore—" so—I hear—you
have married a pretty woman—and a very good creature too
—an excellent creature—pray—um—*how do you pass your
evenings ?* " it is a devil of a question that, and perhaps as easy
to answer with a wife as with a mistress ; but surely they are
longer than the nights. I am all for morality now, and shall
confine myself henceforward to the strictest adultery, which
you will please to recollect is all that that virtuous wife of mine
has left me.

If you go to Milan, pray leave at least a *Vice-Consul*—the
only Vice that will ever be wanting in Venice. D'Orville is a
good fellow. But you should go to England in the Spring with
me, and plant Mrs. Hoppner at Berne with her relations for a
few months.

I wish you had been here (at Venice I mean not the Mira)
when Moore was here ; we were very merry and tipsy—he
hated Venice by the way, and swore it was a sad place.

So—Madame Albrizzi's death is in danger, poor woman.
Saranzo is of course in the crazy recollection of their rancid
amours.

Moore told me that at Geneva they had made a devil of a story of the Fornaretta—" young lady seduced—subsequent abandonment—leap into the grand canal—her being in the hospital of *fous* in consequence ". I should like to know who was nearest being made "*fou*" and be damned to them. Don't you think me in the interesting character of a very ill used gentleman?

I hope your little boy is well. Allegrina is flourishing like a pome-granate blossom.

Yours ever, BYRON

TO LADY BYRON   [*Ravenna, December 31st 1819*]

Augusta can tell you all about me and mine if you think either worth the enquiry ;—But the object of my writing is to come—

It is this.—I saw Moore three months ago and gave to his care—a long Memoir written up to the Summer of 1816, of my life—which I had been writing since I left England.—It will not be published till after my death—and in fact it is a " Memoir " and not " confessions " I have omitted the most important and decisive events and passions of my existence not to compromise others.—But it is not so with the part you occupy—which is long and minute—and I could wish you to see, read—and mark any part or parts that do not appear to coincide with the truth.—The truth I have always stated—but there are two ways of looking at it—and your way may be not mine.—I have never revised the papers since they were written —You may read them—and mark what you please—I wish you [to] know what I think and say of you and yours.—You will find nothing to flatter you—nothing to lead you to the most remote supposition that we could ever have been—or be happy together.—But I do not choose to give to another generation statements which we cannot arise from the dust to prove or disprove—without letting you see fairly and fully what I look upon you to have been—and what I depict you as being.—If seeing this—you can detect what is false—or answer what is charged—do so—*your mark*—shall not be erased.

You will perhaps say *why* write my life?—Alas! I say so too—but they who have traduced it—and blasted it—and branded me—should know—that it is they—and not I—are the cause—It is no great pleasure to have lived—and less to live over again the details of existence—but the last becomes sometimes a necessity and even a duty.—

If you choose to see this you may—if you do not—you have at least had the option.

[Finished] January 1st—[1820].

TO RICHARD BELGRAVE HOPPNER   *Ravenna, Dec. 31, 1819*

MY DEAR HOPPNER,—Will you have the goodness to ask or cause to be asked of Siri and Willhalm, if they have not *three* sabres of mine in custody according to the enclosed note? if not, they must have lost two for they never sent them back.

And will you desire Missiaglia to subscribe for and send me the *Minerva*, a Paris paper, as well as *Galignani*.

I have been here this week, and was obliged to put on my armour and go the night after my arrival to the Marquis Cavalli's, where there were between two and three hundred of the best company I have seen in Italy,—more beauty, more youth, and more diamonds among the women than have been seen these fifty years in the Sea-Sodom. I never saw such a difference between two places of the same latitude, (or *p*latitude, it is all one,)—music, dancing, and play, all in the same *salle*. The G.'s object appeared to be to parade her foreign lover as much as possible, and, faith, if she seemed to glory in the Scandal, it was not for me to be ashamed of it. Nobody seemed surprised;—all the women, on the contrary, were, as it were, delighted with the excellent example. The Vice-legate, and all the other Vices, were as polite as could be;—and I, who had acted on the reserve, was fairly obliged to take the lady under my arm, and look as much like a Cicisbeo as I could on so short a notice,—to say nothing of the embarrass-ment of a cocked hat and sword, much more formidable to me than ever it will be to the enemy.

I write in great haste—do you answer as hastily. I can

understand nothing of all this; but it seems as if the G. had been presumed to be *planted*, and was determined to show that she was not,—*plantation*, in this hemisphere, being the greatest moral misfortune. But this is mere conjecture, for I know nothing about it—except that every body are very kind to her, and not discourteous to me. Fathers, and all relations, quite agreeable.

Yours ever and truly, B.

P.S.—Best respects to Mrs. H.

I would send the *compliments* of the season; but the season itself is so little complimentary with snow and rain that I wait for sunshine.

5

Teresa Guiccioli

January 1820 to July 1823

Byron's life in Ravenna was as placid and humdrum as his career in Venice had been feverish. He occupied rooms in the Guiccioli palace, was cordially received by Teresa's husband, " a very polite personage ", and in conjunction with Count Gamba, her father, and Pietro Gamba, her youthful and enthusiastic brother, played some part in revolutionary intrigues against the Austrian government. Then, during the summer of *1821*, the revolutionary movement was unmasked, and the Gambas banished from Ravenna. Byron, as in duty bound, followed them to Pisa, where he installed his cumbrous household at the Palazzo Lanfranchi. But the Tuscan authorities became suspicious: a scuffle in which Byron's servants were involved gave them the pretext that they needed: and, though they hesitated to meddle with a celebrated Englishman, his Italian friends were advised that they would do well to leave the city. Byron thereupon took a villa at Montenero near Leghorn, sent the Gambas on ahead, and removed thither himself during the early summer months of *1822*. Two deaths, which occurred in the course of that year, affected him profoundly. In April he learned that Allegra, his natural daughter, had died of fever at her convent: on June 8th Shelley was drowned while sailing in the Gulf of Spezzia. A few days before Shelley's death, Leigh Hunt, who had agreed to edit a paper which Byron and Shelley thought of founding, reached Italy with his wife and children. The Liberal was doomed to early extinction; and Leigh Hunt and his good-natured, but indolent and capricious, patron were very soon at variance. Byron was growing bored and restive, and at moments talked of emigrating to the New World and " buying a principality in one of the South American States—Chili or Peru ", when the news that a Whig committee had been formed in London to assist the Greek insurgents gave his imagination a fresh interest and his plans a new direction.

TO THE HON. DOUGLAS KINNAIRD * *January 2nd, 1820*

DEAR DOUGLAS,—In the present state of the funds and of the country, you will hardly wonder at my anxiety to be informed whether you have succeeded in investing the settled property elsewhere, or what has been done towards that object. I wrote to you twice lately to tell you that I had postponed my intention of return for some time. Neither the season nor the length of the journey would have suited my daughter's health after her illness.

You will do me a great favour in letting me know all about any steps that may have been or are to be taken. You do not write, nor like to receive, long letters ; so I will not trail this further. I read your speeches in Galignani. Is H. or is he not the author of " a trifling mistake ", or is the House mistaken and not H.? [1] I always said that I should " have to bail my old friend out of the round-house ", and so it seems. What will be the issue of it all? He has not written to me these four months. But it is no time to reproach his silence when he is in a scrape. Don't forget to let me know all about him.

Yours ever truly and [indecipherable], B.

P.S.—You may remit my half year to the usual address—Venice—in *circulars* as most universal.

TO JOHN MURRAY *Ravenna, February 21, 1820*

DEAR MURRAY,—The Bulldogs will be very agreeable : I have only those of this country, who, though good, and ready to fly at any thing, yet have not the tenacity of tooth and Stoicism in endurance of my canine fellow-citizens : then pray send them by the readiest conveyance—perhaps best by Sea. Mr. Kinnaird will disburse for them, and deduct from the amount on your application or on that of Captain Fyler.

I see the good old King is gone to his place : one can't

---

[1] During December 1819, Hobhouse's pamphlet, *A Trifling Mistake in Thomas Lord Erskine's Recent Preface*, was brought to the notice of the House of Commons and voted a breach of privilege. He was committed to Newgate, where he remained till February. At the next election he finally entered the House as one of the representatives for Westminster.

help being sorry, though blindness, and age, and insanity, are supposed to be drawbacks on human felicity; but I am not at all sure that the latter, at least, might not render him happier than any of his subjects.

I have no thoughts of coming to the Coronation, though I should like to see it, and though I have a right to be a puppet in it; but my division with Lady Byron, which has drawn an equinoctial line between me and mine in all other things, will operate in this also to prevent my being in the same procession.

By Saturday's post I sent you four packets, containing Cantos third and fourth of D[on] J[uan]; recollect that these two cantos reckon only as *one* with you and me, being, in fact, the third Canto cut into two, because I found it too long. Remember this, and don't imagine that there could be any other motive. The whole is about 225 Stanzas, more or less, and a lyric of 96 lines, so that they are no longer than the first *single* cantos: but the truth is, that I made the first too long, and should have cut those down also had I thought better. Instead of saying in future for so many cantos, say so many *Stanzas* or pages: it was Jacob Tonson's way, and certainly the best: it prevents mistakes. I might have sent you a dozen cantos of 40 Stanzas each,—those of *the Minstrel* (Beattie's) are no longer, —and ruined you at once, if you don't suffer as it is; but recollect you are not *pinned down* to anything you say in a letter, and that, calculating even these two cantos as *one* only (which they were and are to be reckoned), you are not bound by your offer: act as may seem fair to all parties.

I have finished my translation of the first Canto of the " *Morgante Maggiore* " of Pulci, which I will transcribe and send: it is the parent, not only of *Whistle-craft*,[1] but of all jocose Italian poetry. You must print it side by side with the original Italian, because I wish the reader to judge of the fidelity: it is stanza for stanza, and often line for line, if not word for word.

You ask me for a volume of manners, etc., on Italy: perhaps I am in the case to know more of them than most Englishmen, because I have lived among the natives, and in parts of the country where Englishmen never resided before (I

---

[1] John Hookham Frere's *Prospectus and Specimen of an intended National Work, by William and Robert Whistlecraft*, is said to have inspired Byron's *Beppo*. Frere was also a brilliant translator of Aristophanes.

speak of Romagna and this place particularly) ; but there are many reasons why I do not choose to touch in print on such a subject. I have lived in their houses and in the heart of their families, sometimes merely as " *amico di casa* ", and sometimes as " *Amico di cuore* " of the *Dama,* and in neither case do I feel myself authorized in making a book of them. Their moral is not your moral ; their life is not your life ; you would not understand it : it is not English, nor French, nor German, which you would all understand. The Conventual education, the Cavalier Servitude, the habits of thought and living are so entirely different, and the difference becomes so much more striking the more you live intimately with them, that I know not how to make you comprehend a people, who are at once temperate and profligate, serious in their character and buffoons in their amusements, capable of impressions and passions, which are at once *sudden* and *durable* (what you find in no other nation), and who actually have *no society* (what we would call so), as you may see by their Comedies : they have no real comedy, not even in Goldoni ; and that is because they have no Society to draw it from.

Their Conversazioni are not Society at all. They go to the theatre to talk, and into company to hold their tongues. The *women* sit in a circle, and the men gather into groupes, or they play at dreary *Faro* or " *Lotto reale* ", for small sums. Their Academie are Concerts like our own, with better music and more form. Their best things are the Carnival balls and masquerades, when every body runs mad for six weeks. After their dinners and suppers, they make extempore verses and buffoon one another ; but it is in a humour which you would not enter into, ye of the North.

In their houses it is better. I should know something of the matter, having had a pretty general experience among their women, from the fisherman's wife up to the *Nobil' Donna,* whom I serve. Their system has its rules, and its fitnesses, and decorums, so as to be reduced to a kind of discipline or game at hearts, which admits few deviations, unless you wish to lose it. They are extremely tenacious, and jealous as furies ; not permitting their lovers even to marry if they can help it, and keeping them always close to them in public as in private whenever they can. In short, they transfer marriage to adultery, and strike the *not* out of that commandment. The reason is, that they marry for their parents, and love for themselves. They exact fidelity from a lover as a debt of honour, while they pay the husband as a tradesman, that is, not at all. You hear a person's character, male or female, canvassed, not as depending on their conduct to their husbands or wives, but to their mistress or lover. And—and—that's all. If I wrote a quarto, I don't know that I could do more than amplify what I have here noted. It is to be observed that while they do all this, the greatest outward respect is to be paid to the husbands, not only by the ladies, but by their *Serventi*—particularly if the husband serves no one himself (which is not often the case, however) : so that you would often suppose them relations— the *Servente* making the figure of one adopted into the family. Sometimes the ladies run a little restive and elope, or divide, or make a scene ; but this is at starting, generally, when they know no better, or when they fall in love with a foreigner, or some such anomaly,—and is always reckoned unnecessary and extravagant.

You enquire after " Dante's prophecy " : I have not done more than six hundred lines, but will vaticinate at leisure.

Of the bust I know nothing. No Cameos or Seals are to be cut here or elsewhere that I know of, in any good style. Hobhouse should write himself to Thorwalsen : the bust was made and paid for three years ago.

Pray tell Mrs. Leigh to request Lady Byron to urge forward the transfer from the funds, which Hanson is opposing, because he has views of investment for some Client of his own, which I can't consent to. I wrote to Lady B. on business this post, addressed to the care of Mr. D. Kinnaird.

Somebody has sent me some American abuse of *Mazeppa* and " the Ode " : in future I will compliment nothing but Canada, and desert to the English.

By the king's death Mr. H[obhouse], I hear, will stand for Westminster : I shall be glad to hear of his standing any where except in the pillory, which, from the company he must have lately kept (I always except Burdett, and Douglas K., and the genteel part of the reformers), was perhaps to be apprehended. I was really glad to hear it was for libel instead of larceny ; for, though impossible in his own person, he might have been taken up by mistake for another at a meeting. All reflections on his present case and place are so *Nugatory*, that it would be useless to pursue the subject further. I am out of all patience to see my friends sacrifice themselves for a pack of black-guards, who disgust one with their Cause, although I have always been a friend to and a Voter for reform. If Hunt had addressed the language to me which he did to Mr. H. last election, I would not have descended to call out such a mis-creant who won't fight; but have passed my sword-stick through his body, like a dog's, and then thrown myself on my Peers, who would, I hope, have weighed the provocation : at any rate, it would have been as public a Service as Walworth's chastisement of Wat. Tyler. If we must have a tyrant, let him at least be a gentleman who has been bred to the business, and let us fall by the axe and not by the butcher's cleaver.

No one can be more sick of, or indifferent to, politics than I am, if they let me alone ; but if the time comes when a part must be taken one way or the other, I shall pause before I lend myself to the views of such ruffians, although I cannot but approve of a Constitutional amelioration of long abuses.

Lord George Gordon, and Wilkes, and Burdett, and Horne Tooke, were all men of education and courteous deportment : so is Hobhouse ; but as for these others, I am convinced that Robespierre was a Child, and Marat a Quaker in comparison of what they would be, could they throttle their way to power.

Yours ever, B.

TO JOHN CAM HOBHOUSE†   *Ravenna, March 3rd, 1820*

My dear Hobhouse,—I have paused thus long in replying to your letter not knowing well in what terms to write ; because though I approve of the object, yet, with the exception of Burdett and Doug. K. and one or two others, I dislike the companions of your labours as much as the place to which they have brought you.

I perceive by the papers that " ould Apias Kerkus " has not extricated you from the " puddle " into which your wit hath brought you. However, if this be but a prologue to a seat for Westminster I shall less regret your previous ordeal; but I am glad that I did not come to England, for it would not have pleased me to find on my own return from transportation my best friends in Newgate. " Did I ever—no I never ",—but I will say no more, all reflections being quite *Nugatory* on the occasion, still I admire your gallantry, and think you could not do otherwise, *having* written the pamphlet, but " *why bitch* Mr. Wild? " why write it? why lend yourself to Hunt and Cobbett, and the bones of Tom Paine? " Death and fiends ! " You used to be thought a prudent man, at least by me, whom you favoured with so much good counsel; but methinks you are waxed somewhat rash, at least in politics. However, the king is dead, so get out of Mr. Burn's apartments, and get into the House of Commons; and then abuse it as much as you please, and I'll come over and hear you. Seriously; I did not " laugh " as you supposed I would ; no more did Fletcher ; but we looked both as grave as if we had got to have been your bail, particularly that learned person who pounced upon the event in the course of spelling the Lugano Gazette.

So Scrope is gone [1]—down-*diddled*—as Doug. K. writes it, the said Doug. being like the man who, when he lost a friend, went to the Saint James's Coffee House and took a new one ; but to you and me the loss of Scrope is irreparable ; we could have better spared not only a " better man ", but the " best of men ". Gone to Bruges where he will get tipsy with Dutch beer and shoot himself the first foggy morning. Brummell at Calais ; Scrope at Bruges, Buonaparte at St. Helena, you in your new apartments, and I at Ravenna, only think ! so many great men ! There has been nothing like it since Themistocles at Magnesia, and Marius at Carthage.

But times change, and they are luckiest who get over their first rounds at the beginning of the battle.

The other day, February 25th, we plucked violets by the wayside *here*, at Ravenna ; and now, March 3rd, it is snowing for all the world as it may do in Cateaton St.

We have nothing new here but the Cardinal from Imola and the news of the berri-cide in France by a sadler ; I suppose the Duke had not paid his bill.

I shall let " dearest duck " waddle alone at the Corona-

[1] Scrope Davies had escaped from his creditors by leaving the country.

tion; a ceremony which I should like to see, and have a right to act Punch in; but the crown itself would not bribe me to return to England, unless business or actual urgency required it. I was very near coming, but that was because I had been very much " agitato " with some circumstances of a domestic description, here in Italy, and not from any love of the tight little Island.

Tell Doug. K. that I answered his last letter long ago, and enclosed in the letter an order peremptory to Spooney, to make me an Irish Absentee, according to Doug.'s own directions.

I like the security in Dublin houses, " an empty house on Ormond Quay ", but pray, are they insured in case of conflagration? Deliver me that, and let us be guaranteed, otherwise what becomes of my fee?

My Clytemnestra stipulated for the security of her jointure; it was delicately done, considering that the poor woman will only have ten thousand a year, more or less, for life, on the death of her mother.

I sent Murray two more cantos of Donny Johnny, but they are only to reckon as *one* in arithmetic, because they are but one long one, cut into *two*, whilk was expedient on account of tedium. So don't let him be charged for these two but as one. I sent him also a translation, close and rugged, of the first canto of the Morgante Maggiore, to be published with the original text, side by side, " cheek by jowl gome ", on account of the superlative merits of both. All these are to be corrected by you by way of solace during your probation.

William Bankes came to see me twice, once at Venice and he since came a second time from Bologna to Ravenna on purpose, so I took him to a Ball here, and presented him to all the Ostrogothic Nobility, and to the Dama whom I serve. I have settled into regular *serventismo*, and find it the happiest state of all, always excepting scarmentado's. I double a shawl with considerable alacrity; but have not yet arrived at the perfection of putting it on the right way; and I hand in and out, and know my post in a conversazione, and theatre; and play at cards as well as a man can do who of all the Italian pack can only distinguish " Asso " and " Re ", the rest for me are hieroglyphics. Luckily the play is limited to " Papetti ", that is pieces of four Pauls, somewhere in, or about two shillings.

I am in favour and respect with the Cardinal, and Vice-legato, and in decent intercourse with the Gonfaloniere and all the Nobilità of the middle ages. Nobody has been stabbed this winter, and few new liaisons formed—there is Sposa Fiorantina, a pretty girl yet in abeyance, but no one can decide yet who is to be her servante, most of the men being already adulterated, and she showing no preferences to any who are not. There is a certain Marchese who I think would run a chance if he did not take matters rather too phi[lo]sophically.

Syricci is here improvising away with great success * * *

B.

TO JOHN CAM HOBHOUSE†   *Ravenna, March 29th, 1820*

MY DEAR HOBHOUSE,—I congratulate you on your change of residence, which, I perceive by the papers, took place on the dissolution of king and parliament. The other day I sent (through Murray) a song for you—you dog—to pay you off for them there verses which you compounded in April 1816.

> " No more shall Mr. Murray
> Pace Piccadilly in a hurry,
> Nor Holmes with not a few grimaces
> Beg a few pounds for a few faces,
> Nor Douglas——"

but I won't go on, though you deserve it, but you see I forget nothing—but good.

I suppose I shall soon see your speeches again, and your determination " not to be saddled with wooden shoes as the Gazetteer says ", but do pray get into Parliament, and out of the company of all these fellows, except Burdett and Douglas Kinnaird, and don't be so very violent. I doubt that Thistlewood [1] will be a great help to the ministers in all the elections, but especially in the Westminster. What a set of desperate fools these Utican conspirators seem to have been. As if in London, after the disarming acts, or indeed at any time, a

---

[1] Thistlewood was one of the ringleaders of the " Cato Street Conspiracy ", to assassinate the whole Cabinet at a dinner-party at Lord Harrowby's house.

secret could have been kept among thirty or forty. And if they had killed poor Harrowby—in whose house I have been five hundred times, at dinners and parties; his wife is one of " the Exquisites "—and t'other fellows, what end would it have answered? " They understand these things better in France ", as Yorick says, but really, if these sort of awkward butchers are to get the upper hand, *I* for one will declare *off*. I have always been (*before* you were, as you well know) a well-wisher to, and voter for reform in parliament; but " such fellows as these, who will never go to the gallows with any credit ", such infamous scoundrels as Hunt and Cobbett, in short, the whole gang (always excepting you, B. and D.) disgust, and make one doubt of the virtue of any principle or politics which can be embraced by similar ragamuffins. I know that revolutions are not to be made with rose water, but though some blood may, and must be shed on such occasions, there is no reason it should be *clotted*; in short, the Radicals seem to be no better than Jack Cade or Wat Tyler, and to be dealt with accordingly.

I perceive you talk *Tacitus* to them sometimes; what do they make of it? It is a great comfort, however, to see you termed "*young Mr. Hobhouse* ", at least to me who am a year and a half younger, and had given up for these two years all further idea of being

> " Gentle and juvenile, curly and gay,
>   In the manner of Ackermann's dresses for May."

And now, my man—my parliament man I hope—what is become of Scrope? Is he at Bruges? or have you gone to " the St. James's coffee-house to take another "?

You will have been sadly plagued by this time with some new packets of poesy and prose for the press; but Murray was so pressing and in such a hurry for something for the *Season*, that I e'en sent him a cargo; otherwise I had got sulky about Juan, and did not mean to print any more, at least " *before term ends* ". You will see that I have taken up the *Pope* question (in prose) with a high hand, and *you* (when you can spare yourself from *Party* to Mankind) must help me. You know how often, under the Mira elms, and by the Adriatic on the Lido, we have discussed that question, and lamented the villainous cant which at present would decry him. It is my intention to give battle to the blackguards and try if the " little Nightingale " can't be heard again.

But at present you are on the hustings, or in the chair. Success go with you.

P.S.—Items of " Poeshie of the King your Master ". Sent last Moon.

Cantos of Don Juan—two. To reckon as one only, however, with Murray on account of their brevity.
First Canto of Morgante Maggiore translated.
Prophecy of Dante—*four short* Cantos.
Prose Observations on an article in B.d's Edin : Magazine.
Poeshie—Episode of Francesca of Rimini translated.

For all these matters you will request the honourable Dougal to arrange the elements with Mr. Murray. Tell the Dougal I answered him peremptorily in favour of the Irish Mortgage long ago, and *against* Spooney, and hope that he hath done the needful ; but yr. damned parliaments cut up all useful friendship.

[Note on the margin of the first sheet]
Ask Dougal to get Spooney's bill and try to bring Rochdale to the hammer. I want to buy an Annuity like.

TO RICHARD BELGRAVE HOPPNER*   *Ravenna,*
March 31st, 1820

DEAR HOPPNER,—Laziness has kept me from answering your letter. It is an inveterate vice, which grows stronger, and I feel it in my pen at this moment. . . . With regard to Mr. Gnoatto, I doubt that the Chevalier is too honest a man to make a good lawyer. Castelli is a bustling, sly, sharp Atornato, and will be more likely to make the rascal wince. But I mean to do thus,—that is to say, with your approbation. . . . You will inform Madame Mocenigo, that till Mr. Gnoatto's money is paid, I *shall deduct that sum* from her rent in

June, till she compels her Servant to pay it. She may make a cause of it, if she likes *so will I* and carry it through all the tribunals so as to give her as many years work of it, as she pleases. At the same time I will prosecute *him* also. I am not even sure that I will pay her *at all*, till she compels her Scoundrelly dependant to do me justice, which a word from *her* would do. All this you had better let *her* know as soon as can be.

By the way, I should like to have my *Gondola* sold, for what it will bring and do you carry the money to the account of expences. If Mother Mocenigo does as she ought to do, I may perhaps give up her house, and pay her rent into the bargain. If not, I'll pay nothing and we'll go to law—I *loves* a " lité." . . .

What you tell me of Mrs. Strephon is very amusing, but all private matters must be suppressed at present by the public plots, and so forth. I wonder what it will all end in. I should probably have gone to England for the Coronation, but for my wife—I don't wish to walk in such company under present circumstances. . . . Ravenna continues much the same as I described it—Conversazione all Lent, and much better even than any at Venice. There are small games at hazard—that is Faro—where nobody can point more than a shilling or two—other Card-tables—and as much talk and Coffee as you please. Everybody does and says what they please, and I do not recollect any disagreeable events, except being three times falsely accused of flirtation, and once being robbed of six sixpences by a nobleman of the city—a Count Bozzi. I did not suspect the illustrious delinquent, but the Countess Vitelloni and the Marquess Lovatelli told me of it directly, and also that it was a way he had—of filching money, when he saw it before him. But I did not ax him for the cash, but contented myself with telling him that if he did it again I should anticipate the law. . . . There is to be a theatre in April, and a fair, and an Opera, and another in June, besides the fine weather of Nature's giving, and the ride in the Forest of Pine. . . . Augustine overturned the carriage a fortnight ago, and smashed it, and himself and me, and Tita, and the horses, into a temporary hodge-podge. He pleaded against the horses, but it was his own bad driving. Nobody was hurt—a few slight bruises—the escape was tolerable—being between a river on one side and a steep bank on the other. I was luckily alone—Allegra

being with Madame Guiccioli. With my best respects to Mrs
Hoppner,

Believe me ever most truly yrs.

BYRON

P.S.—Could you give me an Item of what books remain at
Venice. I *don't* want them, but merely to know whether the
few that are not here are there, and were not lost by the way.
. . . I hope and trust you have got all your wine safe—and
that it is drinkable. . . .

Allegra is prettier I think, but as obstinate as a Mule, and
as ravenous as a Vulture. Health good to judge by the complexion, temper tolerable, but for vanity and pertinacity. She
thinks herself handsome, and will do as she pleases. . . .

TO RICHARD BELGRAVE HOPPNER   *Ravenna, April 22ᵈ 1820*

MY DEAR HOPPNER,—With regard to Gnoatto, I cannot
relent in favour of Madame Mocenigo, who protects a rascal
and retains him in her service. Suppose the case of your
Servant or mine, you having the same claim upon F[letche]r or
I upon your Tim, would either of us retain them an instant
unless they paid the debt? As " there is no force in the decrees
of Venice ", no Justice to be obtained from the tribunals,—
because even conviction does not compel payment, nor enforce
punishment,—you must excuse me when I repeat *that not one
farthing of the rent shall be paid*, till either Gnoatto pays me his
debt, or quits Madame Mocenigo's service. I will abide by
the consequences ; but I could wish that no time was lost in
apprizing her of the affair. You must not mind her relation
Seranzo's statement ; he may be a very good man, but he is
but a Venetian, which I take to be in the present age the
ne plus ultra of human abasement in all moral qualities whatsoever. I dislike differing from you in opinion ; but I have no
other course to take, and either Gnoatto pays me, or quits her
Service, or I will resist to the uttermost the liquidation of her
rent. I have nothing against her, nor for her ; I owe her neither
ill will, nor kindness ;—but if she protects a Scoundrel, and
there is no other redress, I will *make* some.

It has been and always will be the case where there is *no law*. Individuals must then right themselves. They have set the example " and it shall go hard but I will better the Instruction ". Two words from her would suffice to make the villain do his duty ; if they are not said, or if they have no effect, let him be dismissed ; if not, as I have said, so will I do.

I wrote last week to Siri to desire *Vincenzo* to be sent to take charge of the beds and Swords to this place by Sea. I am in no hurry for the books,—none whatever,—and don't want them.

Pray has not Mingaldo the Biography of living people? —it is not here, nor in your list. I am not at all sure that *he* has it either, but it may be possible.

Let Castelli go on to the last. I am determined to see Merryweather *out* in this business, just to discover what is or is not to be done in their tribunals, and if ever I cross him, as I have tried the law in vain, (since it has but convicted him and then done nothing in consequence)—I will try a shorter process with that personage.

About Allegra, I can only say to Claire—that I so totally disapprove of the mode of Children's treatment in their family,[1] that I should look upon the Child as going into a hospital. Is it not so? Have they *reared* one? Her health here has hitherto been *excellent*, and her temper not bad ; she is sometimes vain and obstinate, but always clean and cheerful, and as, in a year or two, I shall either send her to England, or put her in a Convent for education, these defects will be remedied as far as they can in human nature. But the Child shall not quit me again to perish of Starvation, and green fruit, or be taught to believe that there is no Deity. Whenever there is convenience of vicinity and access, her Mother can always have her with her ; otherwise no. It was so stipulated from the beginning.

The Girl is not so well off as with you, but far better than with them ; the fact is she is spoilt, being a great favourite with every body on account of the fairness of her skin, which shines among their dusky children like the milky way, but there is no comparison of her situation now, and that under Elise, or with them. She has grown considerably, is very clean, and

---

[1] The Shelleys.

lively. She has plenty of air and exercise at home, and she goes out daily with M⁵ Guiccioli in her carriage to the Corso. The paper is finished and so must the letter be.

Yours ever, B.

My best respects to Mrs. H. and the little boy—and Dorville.

TO THE HON. DOUGLAS KINNAIRD * *Ravenna, May 3rd, 1820*

MY DEAR DOUGLAS,—I have written to you twice lately, once enclosing a letter of Hanson's, and secondly a letter of Murray's. I shall therefore not trouble you now at great length on the subject of yours of the 18th ult?. It holds out no great inducements to visit England, which you say you yourself would like to quit.

I see the funds are improving. If they get high enough to enable us to sell out without loss, do so, and place the money any where or how rather than have it in the three per cents. I have already given my consent to complete the Mortgage for Ireland, if it can be done without a heavy loss, and so that the house property is ensured. I once more recommend *Rochdale* to your notice, the more so, that you will perceive that Hanson particularly alludes to it and to the proposal of accommodation made by the other party.

I have had no letter from Murray since the one I sent to you, with my opinions thereupon, and shall therefore not intrude upon the man of books for the present with my correspondence. I will just repeat that my *prose* (an Answer to the Galin. Magazine) is *not* for present publication, but I wish you to read it, because as how I think you will find it very smart in the invective line.

I sometimes think of making one among you (not among the radicals by the way) in the coming Autumn, *after the Coronation*, for I won't waddle with " dearest duck " ;[1] but really the encouragement you hold out is not very great, and I don't know how my finances may stand for an English visit unless a

---

[1] A day after leaving her husband in London, Lady Byron wrote him an affectionate letter, beginning " Dearest Duck ".

better interest of the settled property, or a sale of Rochdale, take place.

I have been obliged to be at expenses in changing my sea-residence for a land house, much as a Triton would on coming ashore. I have had to buy me a landau in lieu of a Conch or Gondola, to get me horses, to alter my tarpaulin liveries into terra firma fashions, and to leave nothing of the Sea about us but the crest on my carriage, a Mermaid, as you may remember. I have bought me furniture and new Saddles and all that from Milan, and chairs and tables from various parts of the Globe, at some cost and great trouble. However, I am still in respect-able cash, having no occasion to spend money except upon *myself* and *family*, which only consists of my daughter and servant.

Sir Humphrey Davy was here the other day, and much pleased with the *primitive Italian* character of the people, who like strangers because they see so few of them. He will tell you himself all about it being on his way to England.

I am glad to hear any good of any body, and particularly of our Hobhouse. Pray get in for Bishop's Castle, and let me hear from you, how you are and all that, and what you may have settled or *not* settled with Spooney, and Moray " the *dear*."

Yours ever and truly,   BYRON

TO THOMAS MOORE   *Ravenna, May 24, 1820*

I wrote to you a few days ago. There is also a letter of January last for you at Murray's, which will explain to you why I am here. Murray ought to have forwarded it long ago. I enclose you an epistle from a countrywoman of yours at Paris, which has moved my entrails. You will have the good-ness, perhaps, to enquire into the truth of her story, and I will help her as far as I can,—though not in the useless way she proposes. Her letter is evidently unstudied, and so natural, that the orthography is also in a state of nature.

Here is a poor creature, ill and solitary, who thinks, as a last resource, of translating you or me into French ! Was there ever such a notion? It seems to me the consummation of despair. Pray enquire, and let me know, and, if you could draw a bill on me *here* for a few hundred francs, at your banker's, I will duly honour it,—that is, if she is not an impostor. If not, let me know, that I may get something remitted by my banker Longhi, of Bologna, for I have no correspondence myself at Paris : but tell her she must not translate ;—if she does, it will be the height of ingratitude.

I had a letter (not of the same kind, but in French and flattery) from a Madame Sophie Gail, of Paris, whom I take to be the spouse of a Gallo-Greek of that name. Who is she ? and what is she ? and how came she to take an interest in my *poeshie* or its author? If you know her, tell her, with my compliments, that, as I only *read* French, I have not answered her letter, but would have done so in Italian, if I had not thought it would look like an affectation. I have just been scolding my monkey for tearing the seal of her letter, and spoiling a mock book, in which I put rose leaves. I had a civet-cat the other day, too ; but it ran away, after scratching my monkey's cheek, and I am in search of it still. It was the fiercest beast I ever saw, and like * * in the face and manner.

I have a world of things to say ; but, as they are not come to a *dénouement*, I don't care to begin their history till it is wound up. After you went, I had a fever, but got well again without bark. Sir Humphry Davy was here the other day, and liked Ravenna very much. He will tell you any thing you may wish to know about the place and your humble servitor.

Your apprehensions (arising from Scott's) were unfounded. There are *no damages* in this country, but there will probably be a separation between them, as her family, which is a principal one, by its connections, are very much against *him*, for the whole of his conduct ;—and he is old and obstinate, and she is young and a woman, determined to sacrifice every thing to her affections. I have given her the best advice, viz. to stay with him,—pointing out the state of a separated woman, (for the priests won't let lovers live openly together, unless the husband sanctions it,) and making the most exquisite moral reflections,—but to no purpose. She says, " I will stay with him, if he will let you remain with me. It is hard that I should be the only woman in Romagna who is not to have her *Amico* ; but, if not, I will not live with him ; and as for the consequences, love, etc., etc., etc."—you know how females reason on such occasions.

He says he has let it go on till he can do so no longer. But he wants her to stay, and dismiss me; for he doesn't like to pay back her dowry and to make an alimony. Her relations are rather for the separation, as they detest him,—indeed, so does every body. The populace and the women are, as usual, all for those who are in the wrong, viz. the lady and her lover. I should have retreated, but honour, and an erysipelas which has attacked her, prevent me,—to say nothing of love, for I love her most entirely, though not enough to persuade her to sacrifice every thing to a frenzy. " I see how it will end; she will be the sixteenth Mrs. Shuffleton."

My paper is finished, and so must this letter.

Yours ever, B.

P.S.—I regret that you have not completed the Italian Fudges. Pray, how come you to be still in Paris? Murray has four or five things of mine in hand—the new *Don Juan*, which his back-shop synod don't admire;—a translation of the first canto of Pulci's *Morgante Maggiore*, excellent;—a short ditto from Dante, not so much approved: the *Prophecy of Dante*, very grand and worthy, etc., etc., etc.:—a furious prose answer to Blackwood's " Observations on *Don Juan* ", with a savage Defence of Pope—likely to make a row. The opinions above I quote from Murray and his Utican senate;—you will form your own, when you see the things.

You will have no great chance of seeing me, for I begin to think I must finish in Italy. But, if you come my way, you shall have a tureen of macaroni. Pray tell me about yourself, and your intents.

My trustees are going to lend Earl Blessington sixty thousand pounds (at six per cent.) on a Dublin mortgage. Only think of my becoming an Irish absentee!

TO JOHN CAM HOBHOUSE *   *Ravenna, June 8th, 1820*

My dear Hobhouse,—You are right. The *prose* must not be published—at least the merely *personal part*; and how the portion on Pope may be divided I do not know. I wish you would ferret out at Whitton the " Hints from Horace ". I think it (the Pope part) might be appended to that Popean poem—for publication or no, as you decide. I care not a damn. Murray was in a violent hurry for poetry. I sent it— and now he is reluctant. I don't *pin* him ; I am quite equal upon the subject. I do not even require his own offers. About Don Juan—as I said before, you may lock up the whole— Dante and all—in your desk ; it is to me the same. The only thing that mattered was the " conscription "—lawyer Scout's object of respect—his fee. But I won't dispute about dirty elements in such matters, least of all with Murray. Anything disagreeable is his own fault. He bored me for something all the winter, and I sent him what I had. But I am not at all persuaded of the merits of aught but the translation from Pulci, which is verse for verse, and word for word, an't it? I am tired of scribbling, and nothing but the convenience of an occasional extra thousand pounds would have induced me to go on. But even that will not weigh with me, if it is to be cavilled upon. I don't know whether the *Danticles* [1] be good or no ; for my opinions on my poeshie are always those of the last person I hear speak about them. Murray's costivity is a bad sign of their merits, and your notion is probably the right one ; for my own part I don't understand a word of the whole four cantos, and was therefore lost in admiration of their sublimity.

Tell Dougal that by this post I expedite a *full and unconditional* consent to the Mortgage. He is sullen, but must cheer up. If I quarrel with my banker as well as the bookseller, it would be troppo.

It is quite unlikely that the poeshies should be popular ; but in case of non-publication you can take care of the M.S.S. They will do for a posthumous—someday or other. I can't promise to be in England in autumn. I don't much affect that paese.

You say the Po verses are fine. I thought so little of them that they lay by me a year uncopied. But they were written in *red-hot Earnest* ; and that makes them good.

The best news you could send me, would be the translation

[1] *The Prophecy of Dante.*

of Lady N., the adjustment and sale of Rochdale, the conclusion of the Irish Mortgage and, though last not least, your own *Succes* (as Madame D. had it) which will be ensured by " *delicaci* ". I have quite lost all personal interest about anything except money to supply my own indolent expences; and when I rouse up to appear to take an interest about anything, it is a temporary irritation like Galvanism upon Mutton. The life of an Epicurean, and the philosophy of one, are merely prevented by " that rash humour which my Mother gave me " that makes one restless and nervous, and can overthrow all tranquillity with a Sirocco. Surely you agree with me about the real *vacuum* of human pursuits, but one must face an object of attainment, not to rust in the Scabbard altogether.

Yrs. ever most truly, B.

TO THOMAS MOORE   *Ravenna, July 13, 1820*

To remove or increase your Irish anxiety about my being " in a wisp ", I answer your letter forthwith; premising that, as I am a " *Will* of the wisp ", I may chance to flit out of it. But, first, a word on the Memoir; [1]—I have no objection, nay, I would rather that *one* correct copy was taken and deposited in honourable hands, in case of accidents happening to the original; for you know that I have none, and have never even *re*-read, nor, indeed, *read* at all what is there written; I only know that I wrote it with the fullest intention to be " faithful and true " in my narrative, but *not* impartial—no, by the Lord! I can't pretend to be that, while I feel. But I wish to give every body concerned the opportunity to contradict or correct me.

I have no objection to any proper person seeing what is there written,—seeing it was written, like every thing else, for the purpose of being read, however much many writings may fail in arriving at that object.

With regard to " the wisp ", the Pope has pronounced *their*

---

[1] Byron's autobiographical manuscript, afterwards destroyed by Byron's executors, had been handed to Moore, to dispose of as he pleased, at Venice during the autumn of 1819.

separation. The decree came yesterday from Babylon,—it was *she* and *her friends* who demanded it, on the grounds of her husband's (the noble Count Cavalier's) extraordinary usage. *He* opposed it with all his might because of the alimony, which has been assigned, with all her goods, chattels, carriage, etc., to be restored by him. In Italy they can't divorce. He insisted on her giving me up, and he would forgive every thing,—even the adultery, which he swears that he can prove by " famous witnesses ". But, in this country, the very courts hold such proofs in abhorrence, the Italians being as much more delicate in public than the English, as they are more passionate in private.

The friends and relatives, who are numerous and powerful, reply to him—" *You*, yourself, are either fool or knave,—fool, if you did not see the consequences of the approximation of these two young persons,—knave, if you connive at it. Take your choice,—but don't break out (after twelve months of the closest intimacy, under your own eyes and positive sanction) with a scandal, which can only make you ridiculous and her unhappy."

He swore that he thought our intercourse was purely amicable, and that *I* was more partial to him than to her, till melancholy testimony proved the contrary. To this they answer, that " Will of *this* wisp " was not an unknown person, and that " *clamosa Fama* " had not proclaimed the purity of my morals ;—that *her* brother, a year ago, wrote from Rome to warn him that his wife would infallibly be led astray by this *ignis fatuus*, unless he took proper measures, all of which he neglected to take, etc., etc.

Now he says that he encouraged my return to Ravenna, to see " *in quanti piedi di acqua siamo* ", and he has found enough to drown him in. In short,

> " Ce ne fut pas le tout ; sa femme se plaignit—
>   Procès—La parenté se joint en excuse et dit
> Que du *Docteur* venoit tout le mauvais ménage ;
> Que cet homme étoit fou, que sa femme étoit sage.
>   On fit casser le mariage."

It is best to let the women alone, in the way of conflict, for they are sure to win against the field. She returns to her father's house, and I can only see her under great restrictions—such is the custom of the country. The relations behave very well :— I offered any settlement, but they refused to accept it, and swear she *shan't* live with G[uiccioli] (as he has tried to prove her faithless), but that he shall maintain her ; and, in fact, a judgment to this effect came yesterday. I am, of course, in an awkward situation enough.

I have heard no more of the carabiniers who protested against my liveries. They are not popular, those same soldiers, and, in a small row, the other night, one was slain, another wounded, and divers put to flight, by some of the Romagnuole youth, who are dexterous, and somewhat liberal of the knife. The perpetrators are not discovered, but I hope and believe that none of my ragamuffins were in it, though they are somewhat savage, and secretly armed, like most of the inhabitants. It is their way, and saves sometimes a good deal of litigation.

There is a revolution at Naples. If so, it will probably leave a card at Ravenna in its way to Lombardy.

Your publishers seem to have used you like mine. M. has shuffled, and almost insinuated that my last productions are *dull*. Dull, sir !—damme, dull ! I believe he is right. He begs for the completion of my tragedy of *Marino Faliero*, none of which is yet gone to England. The fifth act is nearly completed, but it is dreadfully long—40 sheets of long paper of 4 pages each—about 150 when printed ; but " so full of pastime and prodigality " that I think it will do.

Pray send and publish your *Pome* upon me ; and don't be afraid of praising me too highly. I shall pocket my blushes.

" Not actionable ! "—*Chantre d'enfer!*—by * * that's " a speech ", and I won't put up with it. A pretty title to give a man for doubting if there be any such place !

So my Gail is gone—and Miss Mahony won't take money. I am very glad of it—I like to be generous, free of expense. But beg her not to translate me.

Oh, pray tell Galignani that I shall send him a screed of doctrine if he don't be more punctual. Somebody *regularly detains two*, and sometimes *four*, of his Messengers by the way. Do, pray, entreat him to be more precise. News are worth money in this remote kingdom of the Ostrogoths.

Pray, reply. I should like much to share some of your

Champagne and La Fitte, but I am too Italian for Paris in general. Make Murray send my letter to you—it is full of *epigrams*.

Yours, etc.

TO THE HON. DOUGLAS KINNAIRD*   *Ravenna, July 20th, 1820*
11 o'clock at night

DEAR DOUGLAS,—Some weeks ago you will have received my consent to the Mortgage to be lent to Ld Blessington. What have you done upon it? My half year's fee from the funds, where is it? Messrs. Hanson write that the Rochdale Cause has been heard. Is it decided? I shall be glad to hear on these and other points at your imperial leisure.

There is a Revolution at Naples, and one is expected throughout Italy daily. I have completed (but have to copy out) a tragedy in five acts, on Marino Faliero Doge of Venice. The fever has attacked me again but slightly. I caught it riding in the forest, part of which is agueish and marshy.

Madame Guiccioli has been separated from her husband who has been sentenced (by the Pope) to pay her twelve hundred crowns a year of alimony, a handsome allowance for a lone woman in these parts—almost three hundred pounds sterling a year, and worth about a thousand in England. The story is a long one. He wanted to bully, and failed with both lady and gentleman. They say here that he will have me taken off, it is the custom. There were two [perished last] week, a priest and a factor, one by a political club, and the other by a private hand, for revenge; nobody fights, but they pop at you from behind trees, and put a knife into you in company, or in turning a corner, while you are blowing your nose. He may do as he pleases; I only recommend him not to miss, for if such a thing is attempted, and fails, he shan't have another opportunity; " Sauce for the Goose is sauce for the Gander ". It would be easy to know the quarter whence it came, and I would pistol him on the spot on my return from the escape. I have taken no precautions, (which indeed would be useless) except taking my pistols when I ride out in the woods every evening. You know I used to be a pretty good shot, and that if the rogues missed, that I should probably hit.

All these fooleries are what the people of the place say (who detest him by the way) and, whether true or not, I shan't stir a step out of my way; a man's life is not worth holding on such a tenure as the fear of such fellows, and what must be will, if it be decreed but not otherwise.

While I am in *the very act of writing* to you, my Steward Lega has come to tell me that this moment, a quarter of an hour past, a brigadier of the Gens d'armes has been shot in the thigh (I heard the pistol and thought it was my servants cleaning my own and firing them first) by no one knows who; all we know is that they had a quarrel with the populace two weeks ago, who warned them and had already wounded two before.

They had also a squabble (the Gens d'armes) with my servants about the lace of my liveries as resembling their uniforms, but they were reduced to order by the decision of the police in favour of the liveries.

I hope none of my ragamuffins have been in this matter.

Here is a state of society for you! It is like the middle ages. Grand uncertainty, but very dramatic.

Yours ever, B.

P.S.—all *fact* I assure you. It is moonlight. A fortnight ago a similar thing happened to these soldiers, but they were only [wounded] (two of them) with knives. One lost his hat in the scuffle.

TO JOHN MURRAY   *Ravenna, July 22ⁿᵈ 1820*

DEAR MURRAY,—The tragedy is finished, but when it will be copied is more than can be reckoned upon. We are here upon the eve of evolutions and revolutions. Naples is revolutionized, and the ferment is among the Romagnuoles, by far the bravest and most original of the present Italians, though still half savage. Buonaparte said the troops from Romagna were the best of his Italic corps, and I believe it. The Nea-

politans are not worth a curse, and will be beaten if it comes to
fighting : the rest of Italy, I think, might stand. The Cardinal
is at his wits' end ; it is true that he had not far to go. Some
papal towns on the Neapolitan frontier have already revolted.
Here there are as yet but the sparks of the volcano ; but the
ground is hot, and the air sultry. Three assassinations last
week here and at Faenza—an anti-liberal priest, a factor, and
a trooper last night,—I heard the pistol-shot that brought him
down within a short distance of my own door. There had
been quarrels between the troops and people of some duration :
this is the third soldier wounded within the last month. There
is a great commotion in people's minds, which will lead to
nobody knows what—a row probably. There are secret
Societies all over the country as in Germany, who cut off those
obnoxious to them, like the Free tribunals, be they high or low ;
and then it becomes impossible to discover or punish the
assassins—their measures are taken so well.

You ask me about the books. *Jerusalem* is the best ; *Anas-
tasius* good, but no more written by a Greek than by a Hebrew ;
the *Diary of an Invalid* good and true, bating a few mistakes about
Serventismo, which no foreigner can understand or really know
without residing years in the country. I read that part (translated that is) to some of the ladies in the way of knowing how
far it was accurate, and they laughed, particularly at the part
where he says that " they must not have children by their
lover ". " Assuredly " (was the answer), " we don't pretend
to say that it is right ; but *men* cannot conceive the repugnance
that a *woman* has to have children *except by the man she loves* ".
They have been known even to obtain abortions when it was
by the *other*, but that is rare. I know one instance, however,
of a woman making herself miscarry, because she wanted to
meet her lover (they were in two different cities) in the lying-in
month (hers was or should have been in October). She was a
very pretty woman—young and clever—and brought on by it
a malady which she has not recovered to this day : however,
she met her *Amico* by it at the proper time. It is but fair to say
that he had dissuaded her from this piece of amatory atrocity,
and was very angry when he knew that she had committed it ;
but the " it was for your sake, to meet you at the time, which
could not have been otherwise accomplished ", applied to his

Self love, disarmed him ; and they set about supplying the loss.

I have had a little touch of fever again ; but it has receded. The heat is 85 in the shade.

I remember what you say of the Queen : it happened in Lady Ox——'s boudoir or dressing room, if I recollect rightly ; but it was not her Majesty's fault, though very laughable at the time : a minute sooner, she might have stumbled on something still more awkward. How the *Porcelain* came there I cannot conceive, and remember asking Lady O. afterwards, who laid the blame on the Servants. I think the Queen will win—I wish she may : she was always very civil to me. You must not trust Italian witnesses : nobody believes them in their own courts ; why should you ? For 50 or 100 Sequins you may have any testimony you please, and the Judge into the bargain.

Yours ever, B.

Pray forward my letter of January to Mr. Moore.

TO THE COUNTESS GUICCIOLI *   *Ravenna, August 7th, 1820*

MY LOVE + + +" Forget what has happened ", you say—a fine forgetfulness—but what then did happen ? The woman is as ugly as an ogre—a thing of Lega's [1]—not very young—not of bad reputation—not adorned with the slightest quality that might arouse a caprice. But you have condescended to be jealous—which I shall not so easily forget, as you so *generously* forgive yourself. It is a very naughty *O* : I feel it.

Allegrina has already spoiled your present—breaking one of the little carriages. Her fever is a little better ; I shall not go to my " fair country " of *NO*—unless you are jealous of filthy maids—in which case I shall.

I think you should neither accept nor refuse Guiccioli's proposal without thinking it over. Perhaps one could do this —reply—that he should *assign you 2000 scudi* after his death —and in return you would be prepared to give up 400 of the 1200 decreed by the most just of all Popes. Freedom would be a

---

[1] Antonio Lega Zambelli, Byron's Secretary at Ravenna.

great thing no doubt—with that head of yours—but 400 scudi is a respectable sum in this country—and not to be given up without any compensation. For the rest—you can trust me— I will make you independent of everyone—at least during my lifetime. But you are made angry with the mere idea—and want to be independent on your own and to write "*Cantate*" in lengthy epistles in the style of Santa Chiara—the convent where you were said to be always in a rage.[1]

I am reading the second volume of the proposal of that classic cuckold Perticari.[2]—It may be well-written—in a style worthy of Santa Chiara and the *trecento*—but it would be more à propos if the Count, instead of proving that *Dante* was the greatest of men (which no one at present wishes to deny, as he is now all the fashion), could prove to his contemporaries that his father-in-law Monti [3] is not the most vile and infamous of men ; it is such a dishonour to talent itself that a man of ability ought to blush to belong to the same century as that Judas of Parnassus.

This seems to have become a peroration, or at least would be in English, but my thoughts fail me when I must express myself in the effeminate words of the language of musicians. I am in a rage this evening—as you were in the convent.—I kiss and embrace you 100000000 . . . times. Love me.

P.S.—There is a certain O—I feel it in the note itself— and very much yes—Greet both the G[amba]s—I value their good graces. That blessed villa is being got ready—as quickly as possible on account of the two little girls—Allegra —and *you*.

---

[1] Byron wrote " rabbiosa " (in a rage), which Teresa has attempted to change into " studiosa " (studious).

[2] Count Giulio Perticari (1790–1822), the son-in-law of the poet Vincenzo Monti, whose wife was notoriously unfaithful to him, was one of the defenders of the classicists, against the new-fangled romantics. The work referred to is " Dell' amor patrio di Dante " (1820).

[3] The reference is to Monti's political unreliability. He was also, like his son-in-law, unfortunate in his matrimonial relations, a fact on which Byron commented in his *Prophecy of Dante*, in lines omitted in the earlier editions of Byron's Poems, but quoted by Moore :

> " The prostitution of his Muse and wife,
> Both beautiful, and both by him debased,
> Shall salt his bread and give him means of life."

TO THE HON. AUGUSTA LEIGH　　*Ravenna, August 19ᵗʰ 1820*

My DEAREST AUGUSTA,—I always loved you better than any earthly existence, and I always shall unless I go mad. And if I did *not* so love you—still I would not persecute or oppress any one wittingly—especially for debts, of which I know the *agony by experience.* Of Colonel Leigh's bond, I really have forgotten all particulars, except that it was *not* of *my wishing.* And I never would nor ever will be *pressed* into the *Gang of his creditors.* I would *not take the money* if he had it. You may judge if I would dun him having it not ——

Whatever measure I can take for his extrication will be taken. Only tell me how—for I am ignorant, and far away. *Who does* and *who can* accuse *you* of " interested views " ? I think people must have gone into Bedlam such things appear to me so very incomprehensible. Pray explain——

yors ever and truly　BYRON.

TO JOHN MURRAY　　　　*Ravenna, September 7, 1820*

DEAR MURRAY,—In correcting the proofs you must refer to the *Manuscript,* because there are in it *various readings.* Pray attend to this, and choose what Gifford thinks best. Let me know what he thinks of the whole.

You speak of Lady Noel's illness : she is not of those who die :—the amiable only do ; and those whose death would *do good* live. Whenever she is pleased to return, it may be presumed that she will take her " *divining rod* " along with her ; it may be of use to her at home, as well as to the " *rich man* " of the Evangelists.

Pray do not let the papers paragraph me back to England : they may say what they please—any loathsome abuse—but that. Contradict it.

My last letters will have taught you to expect an explosion here : it was primed and loaded, but they hesitated to fire the train. One of the Cities shirked from the league. I cannot write more at large for a thousand reasons. Our " *puir hill folk* " offered to strike, and to raise the first banner. But

Bologna paused—and now 'tis Autumn, and the season half
over. " Oh Jerusalem, Jerusalem ! " the Huns are on the Po ;
but if once they pass it on their march to Naples, all Italy will
rise behind them : the Dogs—the Wolves—may they perish
like the Host of Sennacherib ! If you want to publish the
Prophecy of Dante, you never will have a better time.

Thanks for books—but as yet no *Monastery* of Walter Scott's,
the ONLY book except *Edinburgh* and *Quarterly* which I desire
to see. Why do you send me so much *trash* upon Italy—such
tears, etc., which I know *must be false* ? Matthews is good—
very good : all the rest are like Sotheby's " *Good* ", or like
Sotheby himself, that old rotten Medlar of Rhyme. The
Queen—how is it ? prospers She ?

TO RICHARD BELGRAVE HOPPNER   *Ravenna, Sept. 10th 1820*

MY DEAR HOPPNER,—*Ecco* Advocate Fossati's letter. No
paper has nor will be signed. Pray *draw* on me for the Napoleons,
for I have no mode of remitting them otherwise ; Missiaglia
would empower some one here to receive them for you, as it
is not a *piazza bancale*.

I regret that you have such a bad opinion of Shiloh ; [1]
you used to have a good one. Surely he has talent and honour,
but is crazy against religion and morality. His tragedy is sad
work ; but the subject renders it so. His *Islam* had much
poetry. You seem lately to have got some notion against
him.

Clare writes me the most insolent letters about Allegra ;
see what a man gets by taking care of natural children !
Were it not for the poor little child's sake, I am almost tempted
to send her back to her atheistical mother, but that would be
too bad ; you cannot conceive the excess of her insolence, and
I know not why, for I have been at great care and expense,—
taking a house in the country on purpose for her. She has *two*
maids and every possible attention. If Clare thinks that she
shall ever interfere with the child's morals or education, she
mistakes ; she never shall. The girl shall be a Christian and

---

[1] Shelley.

a married woman, if possible.   As to seeing her, she may see her—under proper restrictions ; but she is not to throw every thing into confusion with her Bedlam behaviour.   To express it delicately, I think Madame Clare is a damned bitch.   What think you ?

Yours ever and truly, B.

TO THE HON. DOUGLAS KINNAIRD *   *Ravenna,*
September 17th, 1820

DEAR DOUGLAS,—I got your letter—why, man ! what are ye aboot?   What makes you so careful of your paper?   Is it for the sake of contrast?   This is the Paper Age.   The Golden, the Silver and the Iron ages are long since past, the two former *never to return* !   We are now happily arrived at the *Age of Rags.* The *He*-mans [1] and *She*-mans of our literature are as plenty as blackberries as we of the North say.   They have made a *litter*-ature of literature, which at this moment is more extensively spread ; but 'tis grown shallow, it seems, in proportion to its diffusion.   Our age is in everything an affected age, and where affectation prevails the *fair* sex—or rather the *blue*—are always strongly tinctured with it.   A little learning may be swelled to an enormous size by artifice.   Madam de Stael, I grant, is a clever woman ; but all the other *madams* are no Staels.   The philosophical petticoats of our times surpass even those of the age of Elizabeth who pretended to cultivate an acquaintance with the classics.   Roger Asham tells us that, going to wait on Lady Jane Grey at her father's house in Leicestershire, he found her reading Plato's works in the Greek, while the rest of the family were hunting in the park.   Possibly the lady had no objection to be interrupted in her studies—*she* was *hunting* for applause.   I shall be at them one of these days—there is nothing like ridicule, the only weapon that the English climate cannot rust.

I have to acknowledge the receipt of sundry books which at present I have no inclination to anatomize—they are rather

[1] Felicia Dorothea Hemans, authoress of *Domestic Affections, and other Poems*, etc.

stale. But why do you send anything to the Foreign Office—
that den of thieves? Your friend with his young spouse arrived
safely in this place. He has just remitted your letter of introduction. I shall invade him in the cause of [indecipherable]—
out of envy—as Lucifer looked at Adam and Eve.

Sta sempre umilissimo servitore   BIRON

TO RICHARD BELGRAVE HOPPNER   *Ravenna, 8ʰʳᵉ· 1º· 1820*

MY DEAR HOPPNER,—Your letters and papers came very
safely, though slowly, missing one post.

The Shiloh story is true no doubt,[1] though Elise is but a sort
of *Queen's evidence.* You remember how eager she was to return
to them, and then she goes away and abuses them. Of the
facts, however, there can be little doubt ; it is just like them.
You may be sure that I keep your counsel.

I have not remitted the 30 Napoleons (or *what* was it?), till
I hear that Missiaglia has received his safely, when I shall do
so by the like channel.

What you say of the Queen's affair is very just and true ;
but the event seems not very easy to anticipate.

I enclose an epistle from Shiloh.

Yours ever and truly, BYRON

TO THE HON. AUGUSTA LEIGH *   *Ravenna, 8ʰʳᵉ 1820*

MY DEAREST AUGUSTA,—I suppose by this time that you
will be out of your fidget, and that the dilatory Hanson will
have set Colonel L[eigh] at rest upon the subject of the bond,
etc.

Ada's picture is very like her mother—I mean the prints,
for I have not received the picture, neither has Murray sent it,
I presume. She seems stout of her age, which is five years on
the 10th. of 10ᵇʳᵉ,—is it not so ? It is almost as long since I
have seen her, all but a month. What day of January was it,

---

[1] Elise Foggi, a Swiss nursemaid dismissed by the Shelleys, had spread stories
to their discredit, alleging that Claire Clairmont had had an intrigue with Shelley,
and that he had consigned their child to the Foundlings' Hospital.

when Lady B. marched upon Kirkby? which was the Signal of war. Sir Walter Scott says in the beginning of *the Abbot*, that " every *five* years we find ourselves another and yet the same, with a change of views and no less of the light in which we regard them ; a change of motives as well as of actions." This I presume applies still more to those who have past their *five* years in foreign countries, for my part I suppose that I am *two* others, for it seems that some fool has been betting that he saw me in London the other day in a *Curricle*. If he said a *Canoe*, it would have been much more likely. And *you*? What have *your* " five years " done?—made your house like a Lying-in Hospital ;—there never was such a creature, except a rabbit, for increase and multiplication. In short we are five years older in fact, and I at least *ten* in appearance. The Lady B——, I suppose, retains her old starch obstinacy, with a deeper dash of Sternness from the dint of time, and the effort it has cost her to be " magnanimous ", as they called her mischief-making. People accused somebody of painting her in " Donna *Inez* " ; did it strike you so? I can't say it did me, there might be something of her in the outline ; but the Spaniard was only a silly woman, and the other is a cut-and-dry, made-up character, which is another matter.

Time and Events will one day or the other revenge her past conduct, without any interference of mine.

So—Joe Murray is gathered to his Masters ; as you say, the very Ghosts have died with him. Newstead and he went almost together, and now the B's must carve them out another inheritance. If Ada had been a Son, I do not think that I should have parted with it after all ; but I dislike George B[yro]n for his behaviour in 1816, and I am unacquainted with the others who may be in the line of the title, and, being myself abroad, and at feud with the whole of the Noels, and with most of the B's except yourself, of course these concurring with other and pressing circumstances, rendered the disposal of the Abbey necessary and not improper. Somebody said the other day that " Lady Noel had been ill " ; she is too troublesome an old woman ever to die while her death can do any good, but, if she ever does march, it is to be presumed that she will take her " water-divining rod " with her ; it may be a useful twig to her, and the devil too, when she gets home again.

I can say little to you of Italy, except that it is a very distracted State.

In England the Queen has been bountiful to the Scandalmongers. She has got the Noel batch of Counsellors, it seems (except Romilly—who cut his throat) ; you see what *those* sort of fellows *are*, and how they prey on a cause of this kind, like crows on carrion. Her Majesty's innocence is probably something like another person's guilt. However she has been an ill-used woman ; that's the truth on't, and, in the nature of things, the woman ought to get the better. They generally do, whether they ought or not.

I did not come over,—for fifty reasons,—and amongst others, that I do not think it a very creditable thing to be one of the Judges even, upon such matters.

I have got a flourishing family, (besides my daughter Allegra) ; here are two Cats, six dogs, a badger, a falcon, a tame Crow, and a Monkey. The fox died, and a Civet Cat ran away. With the exception of an occasional civil war about provisions, they agree to admiration, and do not make more noise than a well-behaved Nursery.

I have also eight horses,—four carriage, and four saddle,— and go prancing away daily, at present up to the middle in mire, for here have been the Autumnal rains, and drenched every thing, amongst others myself yesterday. I got soaked through, cloak and all, and the horse through his skin, I believe.

I have now written to you a long family letter.[1]

Ever yours, B.

TO JOHN MURRAY *Ravenna, 8bre 6, 1820*

DEAR Mʸ,—You will have now received all the acts, corrected, of the *M[arino] F[aliero]*. What you say of the " Bet of 100 guineas ", made by some one who says that he saw me last week, reminds me of what happened in 1810. You can easily ascertain the fact, and it is an odd one.

In the latter end of 1811, I met one evening at the Alfred my old School and form-fellow, (for we were within two of each other—*he* the higher, though both very near the top of our

[1] Here a line has been cut out.

remove,) *Peel*, the Irish Secretary. He told me that, in 1810, he met me, as he thought, in St. James's Street, but we passed without speaking. He mentioned this, and it was denied as impossible, I being then in Turkey. A day or two after, he pointed out to his brother a person on the opposite side of the way ; " there ", said he, " is the man whom I took for Byron " : his brother instantly answered, " why, it *is* Byron, and no one else ". But this is not all : I was *seen* by somebody to *write down my name* amongst the Enquirers after the King's health, then attacked by insanity. Now, at this very period, as nearly as I could make out, I was ill of a *strong fever* at Patras, caught in the marshes near Olympia, from the *Malaria*. If I had died there, this would have been a new Ghost Story for you. You can easily make out the accuracy of this from Peel himself, who told it in detail. I suppose you will be of the opinion of Lucretius, who (denies the immortality of the Soul, but) asserts that from the " flying off of the Surfaces of bodies perpetually, these surfaces or cases, like the Coats of an onion, are sometimes seen entire when they are separated from it, so that the shapes and shadows of both the dead and absent are frequently beheld ".

But if they are, are their coats and waistcoats also seen ? I do not disbelieve that we may be *two* by some unconscious process, to a certain sign ; but which of these two I happen at present to be, I leave you to decide. I only hope that *t'other me* behaves like a Gemman.

I wish you would get Peel asked how far I am accurate in my recollection of what he told me ; for I don't like to say such things without authority.

I am not sure that I was *not spoken* with ; but this also you can ascertain. I have written to you such lots that I stop.

Yours, B.

P.S.—Send me the proofs of the " *Hints from H., etc.*".

P.S.—Last year (in June, 1819), I met at Count Mosti's, at Ferrara, an Italian who asked me " if I knew Lord Byron ? " I told him *no* (no one knows himself, *you* know) : " then ", says he, " I do ; I met him at Naples the other day ". I pulled out my card and asked him if that was the way he spelt his name : and he answered, *yes*. I suspect that it was a blackguard Navy Surgeon, named *Bury* or *Berry*, who attended a young travelling

Madman about, named Graham, and passed himself for a Lord at the Posthouses : he was a vulgar dog—quite of the Cockpit order—and a precious representative I must have had of him, if it was even so ; but I don't know. He passed himself off as a Gentleman, and squired about a Countess Zinnani (of this place), then at Venice, an ugly battered woman, of bad morals even for Italy.

TO JOHN MURRAY   *Ravenna, 9ᵇʳᵉ 4°, 1820*

I have received from Mr. Galignani the enclosed letters, duplicates and receipts, which will explain themselves. As the poems are your property by purchase, right, and justice, *all matters of publication*, etc., etc., *are for you to decide upon*. I know not how far my compliance with Mr. G.'s request might be legal, and I doubt that it would not be honest. In case you choose to arrange with him, I enclose the permits to *you*, and in so doing I wash my hands of the business altogether. I sign them merely to enable you to exert the power you justly possess more properly. I will have nothing to do with it further, except, in my answer to Mr. Galignani, to state that the letters, etc., etc., are sent to you, and the causes thereof.

If you can check those foreign Pirates, do ; if not, put the permissive papers in the fire : *I* can have no view nor object whatever, but to secure to you your property.

Yours, BYRON

P.S.—There will be shortly " *the Devil to pay* " *here* ; and, as there is no saying that I may not form an *Item in his bill*, I shall not now write at greater length : *you* have *not answered* my late letters ; and you have acted foolishly, as you will find out some day.

P.S.—I have read part of the *Quarterly* just arrived : Mr. Bowles shall be answered ; he is not *quite* correct in his statement about *E[nglish] B[ards] and S[cotch] R[eviewers]*. They support Pope, I see, in the *Quarterly*. Let them continue to do so : it is a Sin, and a Shame, and a *damnation* to think that *Pope!!* should require it—but he does. Those miserable mountebanks of the day, the poets, disgrace themselves and deny God, in running down Pope, the most *faultless* of Poets, and almost of men.

The *Edinburgh* praises Jack Keats or Ketch, or whatever his names are : why, his is the * of Poetry—something like the pleasure an Italian fiddler extracted out of being suspended daily by a Street Walker in Drury Lane.   This went on for some weeks : at last the Girl went to get a pint of Gin—met another, chatted too long, and Cornelli was *hanged outright before she returned.*   Such like is the trash they praise, and such will be the end of the *outstretched* poesy of this miserable Self-polluter of the human mind.

W. Scott's *Monastery* just arrived : many thanks for that Grand Desideratum of the last six months.

P.S.—You have cut up old Edgeworth, it seems, amongst you.   You are right : he was a bore.   I met the whole batch— Mr., Mrs., and Miss—at a blue breakfast of Lady Davy's in Blue Square ; and he proved but bad, in taste and tact and decent breeding.   He began by saying that *Parr* (Dr. Parr) had attacked him, and that he (the father of Miss E.) had *cut him up* in his answer.   Now, Parr would have annihilated him ; and if he had not, why tell *us* (a long story) *who* wanted to break- fast ?   I saw them different times in different parties, and I thought him a very tiresome coarse old Irish half-and-half Gentleman, and her a pleasant reserved old woman—* * * * * * * * * * *

TO JOHN MURRAY   *R[avenn]a, 9bre 9°, 1820*

DEAR MORAY,—The talent you approve of is an amiable one and as you say might prove " a national Service ", but unfor- tunately I must be angry with a man before I draw his real portrait ; and I can't deal in " *generals* ", so that I trust never to have provocation enough to make a *Gallery.*   If " *the* person " had not by many little dirty sneaking traits provoked it, I should have been silent, though I *had observed* him.   Here follows an alteration.   Put—

> Devil with *such* delight in damning,
> That if at the resurrection
> Unto him the free selection
> Of his future could be given,
> 'Twould be rather Hell than Heaven.

That is to say, if these two new lines do not too much lengthen out and weaken the amiability of the original thought and expression.   You have a discretionary power about showing : I should think that Croker and D'Israeli would not disrelish a sight of these light little humorous things, and may be indulged now and then.

D'Israeli wrote the article on Spence : I know him by the mark in his mouth.   I am glad that the *Quarterly* has had so much Classical honesty as to insert it : it is good and true.

Hobhouse writes me a facetious letter about my *indolence* and love of Slumber.   It becomes him : he is in active life ; he writes pamphlets against Canning, to which he does not put his name ; he gets into Newgate and into Parliament—both honourable places of refuge ; and he " greatly daring dines " at all the taverns (why don't he set up a *tap* room at once), and then writes to quiz my laziness.

Why, I do like one or two vices, to be sure ; but I can back a horse and fire a pistol " without winking or blinking " like Major Sturgeon ; I have fed at times for two months together on *sheer biscuit and water* (without metaphor) ; I can get over seventy or eighty miles a day *riding* post upon [?] of all sorts, and *swim five* at a Stretch, taking a *piece* before and after, as at Venice, in 1818, or at least I *could do*, and have done it ONCE, and I never was ten minutes in my life over a *solitary* dinner.

Now, my friend Hobhouse, when we were wayfaring men, used to complain grievously of hard beds and sharp insects, while I slept like a top, and to awaken me with his swearing at them : he used to damn his dinners daily, both quality and cookery and quantity, and reproach me for a sort of " brutal " indifference, as he called it, to these particulars ; and now he writes me facetious sneerings because I *do not* get up early in a morning, when there is no occasion—if there were, *he* knows that I was always *out* of bed before him, though it is true that my ablutions detained me longer in dressing than his noble contempt of that " oriental scrupulosity " permitted.

Then he is still sore about " *the ballad* "—he ! ! why, he lampooned me at Brighton, in 1808, about Jackson the boxer and bold Webster, etc. : in 1809, he turned the death of my friend E^d *Long* into ridicule and rhyme, because his name was susceptible of a *pun* ; and, although he saw that I was distressed at it, before I left England in 1816, he wrote rhymes upon *D. Kinnaird, you,* and *myself*; and at Venice he parodied the lines " Though the day of my destiny's over " in a comfortable quizzing way : and now he harps on my ballad about his election ! Pray tell him all this, for I will have no underhand work with my " old Cronies ". If he can deny the facts, let him. I maintain that he is more *carnivorously* and *carnally sensual* than I am, though I am bad enough too for that matter ; but not in eating and haranguing at the Crown and Anchor, where I never was but twice—and those were at " Whore's Hops " when I was a younker in my teens ; and, Egad, I think them the most respectable meetings of the two. But he is a little wroth that I would not come over to the *Queen's* trial : *lazy,* quotha ! it is so true that he should be ashamed of asserting it. He counsels me not to " get into a Scrape " ; but, as Beau Clincher says, " How melancholy are Newgate reflections ! " To be sure, his advice is worth following ; for experience teacheth : he has been in a dozen within these last two years. *I pronounce me the more temperate of the two.*

Have you gotten *The Hints* yet ?

I know Henry Matthews : he is the image, to the very voice, of his brother Charles, only darker : his *laugh* his in particular. The first time I ever met him was in Scrope Davies's rooms after his brother's death, and I nearly dropped, thinking that it was his Ghost. I have also dined with him in his rooms at King's College. Hobhouse once purposed a similar memoir ; but I am afraid that the letters of Charles's correspondence with me (which are at Whitton with my other papers) would hardly do for the public : for our lives were not over strict, and our letters somewhat lax upon most subjects.

His Superiority over all his contemporaries was quite indisputable and acknowledged : none of us ever thought of being *at all near* Matthews ; and yet there were some high men of his standing—Bankes, Bob Milnes, Hobhouse, Bailey, and many others—without numbering the *mere Academical* men, of whom we hear little out of the University, and whom he beat *hollow* on *their own* Ground.

His gaining the Downing Fellowship was the completest thing of the kind ever known. He carried off both declamation prizes : in short, he did whatever he chose. He was three or four years my Senior, but I lived a good deal with him latterly, and with his friends. He wrote to me the very day of his death (I believe), or at least a day before, if not the very day. He meant to have stood for the University Membership. He was a very odd and humourous fellow besides, and spared nobody : for instance, walking out in Newstead Garden, he stopped at Boatswain's monument inscribed " Here lies Boatswain, a Dog ", etc., and then observing a *blank* marble tablet on the other side, " So (says he) there is room for another friend, and I propose that the Inscription be ' Here lies H—bh—se, a Pig '," etc. You may as well not let *this* transpire to the worthy member, lest he regard neither his dead friend nor his living one, with his wonted Suavity.

Rose's *lines* must be at his own option : *I* can have no objection to their publication. Pray salute him from me.

Mr. Keats, whose poetry you enquire after, appears to me what I have already said : such writing is a sort of mental masturbation—* * * * * * * * his *Imagination*. I don't mean he is *indecent*, but viciously soliciting his own ideas into a state, which is neither poetry nor any thing else but a Bedlam vision produced by raw pork and opium. Barry Cornwall would write well, if he would let himself. Croly is superior to many, but seems to think himself inferior to Nobody.

Last week I sent you a correspondence with Galignani, and some documents on your property. You have now, I think, an opportunity of *checking*, or at least *limiting*, those *French re-publications*. You may let all your authors publish what they please *against me* or *mine* : a publisher is not, and cannot be, responsible for all the works that issue from his printer's.

The " White Lady of Avenel " is not quite so good as a *real well-authenticated* (" Donna bianca ") *White Lady* of *Colalto*, or spectre in the Marca Trivigiana, who has been repeatedly seen : there is a man (a huntsman) now alive who saw her also. Hoppner could tell you all about her, and so can Rose perhaps. I myself have *no doubt* of the fact, historical and spectral. She always appeared on particular occasions, before the deaths of the family, etc., etc. I heard Me Benzoni say, that she knew a Gentleman who had seen her cross his room at Colalto Castle. Hoppner saw and spoke with the Huntsman who met her at the Chase, and never *hunted* afterwards. She was a Girl attendant, who, one day dressing the hair of a Countess Colalto, was seen by her mistress to smile upon her husband in the Glass.   The Countess had her shut up in the wall at the Castle, like Constance de Beverley.   Ever after, she haunted them and all the Colaltos.   She is described as very beautiful and fair.   It is well authenticated.

Yours, B.

TO THE HON. AUGUSTA LEIGH   *Ravenna, 9ᵇʳᵉ 18ᵗʰ 1820*

MY DEAREST AUGUSTA,—You will I hope have received a discreetly long letter from me—not long ago,—Murray has just written that *Waite* [1]—is dead—poor fellow—he and Blake—both deceased—what *is* to become of our hair and teeth.— The hair is less to be minded—any body can cut hair—though not so well—but the *mouth* is a still more serious concern.——

Has he no Successor?—pray tell me the next best—for what am I to do for brushes and powder?——And then the *Children* —only think—what will become of their jaws? Such men ought to be immortal—and not your stupid heroes—orators and poets.——

I am really so sorry—that I can't think of anything else just now.—Besides I liked him with all his Coxcombry.——

Let me know what we are all to do,—and to whom we can have recourse without damage for our cleaning—scaling and powder.—

How do you get on with your affairs?—and how does every body get on.——

How is all your rabbit-warren of a family? I gave you an account of mine by last letter.—The Child Allegra is well— but the Monkey has got a cough—and the tame Crow has lately suffered from the head ache.——Fletcher has been bled for a Stitch—and looks flourishing again——

Pray write—excuse this short scrawl—

yours ever   B

P.S.—Recollect about Waite's Successor—why he was only *married* the other day—and now I don't wonder so much that the poor man died of it.——

---

[1] Waite was a fashionable dentist, resident at 2 Old Burlington Street; Blake, an equally renowned barber.

TO JOHN MURRAY   *Ravenna, 9bre 19, 1820*

DEAR MURRAY,—What you said of the late Charles Skinner Matthews has set me to my recollections; but I have not been able to turn up any thing which would do for the purposed Memoir of his brother,—even if he had previously done enough during his life to sanction the introduction of anecdotes so merely personal. He was, however, a very extraordinary man, and would have been a great one. No one ever succeeded in a more surpassing degree than he did as far as he went. He was indolent, too; but whenever he stripped, he overthrew all antagonists. His conquests will be found registered at Cambridge, particularly his *Downing* one, which was hotly and highly contested, and yet easily *won*. Hobhouse was his most intimate friend, and can tell you more of him than any man. William Bankes also a great deal. I myself recollect more of his oddities than of his academical qualities, for we lived most together at a very idle period of *my* life. When I went up to Trinity, in 1805, at the age of seventeen and a half, I was miserable and untoward to a degree. I was wretched at leaving Harrow, to which I had become attached during the two last years of my stay there; wretched at going to Cambridge instead of Oxford (there were no rooms vacant at Christchurch); wretched from some private domestic circumstances of different kinds, and consequently about as unsocial as a wolf taken from the troop. So that, although I knew Matthews, and met him often *then* at Bankes's, (who was my collegiate pastor, and master, and patron,) and at Rhode's, Milnes's, Price's, Dick's, Macnamara's, Farrell's, Gally Knight's, and others of that *set* of contemporaries, yet I was neither intimate with him nor with any one else, except my old schoolfellow Edward Long (with whom I used to pass the day in riding and swimming), and William Bankes, who was good-naturedly tolerant of my ferocities.

It was not till 1807, after I had been upwards of a year away from Cambridge, to which I had returned again to *reside* for my degree, that I became one of Matthews's familiars, by means of Hobhouse, who, after hating me for two years, because I wore a *white hat*, and a *grey* coat, and rode a *grey* horse (as he says himself), took me into his good graces because I had written some poetry. I had always lived a good deal, and got drunk occasionally, in their company—but now we became really friends in a morning. Matthews, however, was not at this period resident in College. I met *him* chiefly in London, and at uncertain periods at Cambridge. Hobhouse, in the mean time, did great things : he founded the Cambridge " Whig Club " (which he seems to have forgotten), and the " Amicable Society ", which was dissolved in consequence of the members constantly quarrelling, and made himself very popular with " us youth ", and no less formidable to all tutors, professors, and heads of Colleges. William Bankes was gone ; while he stayed, he ruled the roast—or rather the *roasting*— and was father of all mischiefs.

Matthews and I, meeting in London, and elsewhere became great cronies. He was not good tempered—nor am I— but with a little tact his temper was manageable, and I thought him so superior a man, that I was willing to sacrifice something to his humours, which were often, at the same time, amusing and provoking. What became of his *papers* (and he certainly had many), at the time of his death, was never known. I mention this by the way, fearing to skip it over, and *as he wrote* remarkably well, both in Latin and English. We went down to Newstead together, where I had got a famous cellar, and *Monks*' dresses from a masquerade warehouse. We were a company of some seven or eight, with an occasional neighbour or so for visiters, and used to sit up late in our friars' dresses, drinking burgundy, claret, champagne, and what not, out of the *skull-cup*, and all sorts of glasses, and buffooning all round the house, in our conventual garments. Matthews always denominated me " the Abbot ", and never called me by any other name in his good humours, to the day of his death. The harmony of these our symposia was somewhat interrupted, a few days after our assembling, by Matthews's threatening to throw Hobhouse out of a *window*, in consequence of I know not what commerce of jokes ending in this epigram. Hobhouse came to me and said, that " his respect and regard for me as host would not permit him to call out any of my guests, and that he should go to town next morning ". He did. It was in vain that I represented to him that the window was not high, and that the turf under it was particularly soft. Away he went.

Matthews and myself had travelled down from London together, talking all the way incessantly upon one single topic. When we got to Loughborough, I know not what chasm had made us diverge for a moment to some other subject, at which he was indignant. " Come," said he, " don't let us break through—let us go on as we began, to our journey's end " ; and so he continued, and was as entertaining as ever to the very end. He had previously occupied, during my year's absence from Cambridge, my rooms in Trinity, with the furniture ; and Jones, the tutor, in his odd way, had said, on putting him in, " Mr. Matthews, I recommend to your attention not to damage any of the moveables, for Lord Byron, Sir, is a young man of *tumultuous passions* ". Matthews was delighted with this ; and whenever anybody came to visit him, begged them to handle the very door with caution ; and used to repeat Jones's admonition in his tone and manner. There was a large mirror in the room, on which he remarked, " that he thought his friends were grown uncommonly assiduous in coming to *see him*, but he soon discovered that they only came to *see themselves* ". Jones's phrase of " *tumultuous passions* ", and the whole scene, had put him into such good humour, that I verily believe that I owed to it a portion of his good graces.

When at Newstead, somebody by accident rubbed against one of his white silk stockings, one day before dinner ; of course the gentleman apologised. " Sir," answered Matthews, " it may be all very well for you, who have a great many silk stockings, to dirty other people's ; but to me, who have only this *one pair*, which I have put on in honour of the Abbot here, no apology can compensate for such carelessness ; besides, the expense of washing." He had the same sort of droll sardonic way about every thing. A wild Irishman, named Farrell, one evening began to say something at a large supper at Cambridge, Matthews roared out " Silence ! " and then, pointing to Farrell, cried out, in the words of the oracle, " *Orson is endowed with reason* ". You may easily suppose that Orson lost what reason he had acquired, on hearing this compliment. When Hobhouse published his volume of poems, the *Miscellany* (which Matthews *would* call the " *Miss-sell-any* "), all that could be drawn from him was, that the preface was " extremely like *Walsh* ". Hobhouse thought this at first a compliment ; but we never could make out what it was, for all we know of *Walsh* is his Ode to King William, and Pope's epithet of " *knowing Walsh* ". When the Newstead party broke up for London, Hobhouse and Matthews, who were the greatest friends possible, agreed, for a whim, to *walk together* to town. They quarrelled by the way, and actually walked the latter half of the journey, occasionally passing and repassing, without speaking. When Matthews had got to Highgate, he had spent all his money but three-pence halfpenny, and determined to spend that also in a pint of beer, which I believe he was drinking before a public-house, as Hobhouse passed him (still without speaking) for the last time on their route. They were reconciled in London again.

One of Matthews's passions was " the fancy " ; and he sparred uncommonly well. But he always got beaten in rows, or combats with the bare fist. In swimming, too, he swam well ; but with *effort* and *labour*, and *too high* out of the water ; so that Scrope Davies and myself, of whom he was therein somewhat emulous, always told him that he would be drowned if ever he came to a difficult pass in the water. He was so ; but surely Scrope and myself would have been most heartily glad that

> " the Dean had lived,
> And our prediction proved a lie ".

His head was uncommonly handsome, very like what *Pope's* was in his youth.

His voice, and laugh, and features, are strongly resembled by his brother Henry's, if Henry be *he* of *King's College*. His passion for boxing was so great, that he actually wanted me to match him with Dogherty (whom I had backed and made the match for against Tom Belcher), and I saw them spar together at my own lodgings with the gloves on. As he was bent upon it, I would have backed Dogherty to please him, but the match went off. It was of course to have been a private fight, in a private room.

On one occasion, being too late to go home and dress, he was equipped by a friend (Mr. Baillie, I believe,) in a mag-nificently fashionable and somewhat exaggerated shirt and neckcloth. He proceeded to the Opera, and took his station in

Fop's Alley. During the interval between the opera and the ballet, an acquaintance took his station by him and saluted him : " Come round," said Matthews, " come round ".— " Why should I come round? " said the other ; " you have only to turn your head—I am close by you."—" That is exactly what I cannot do," said Matthews ; " don't you see the state I am in? " pointing to his buckram shirt collar and inflexible cravat,—and there he stood with his head always in the same perpendicular position during the whole spectacle.

One evening, after dining together, as we were going to the Opera, I happened to have a spare Opera ticket (as subscriber to a box), and presented it to Matthews. " Now, sir," said he to Hobhouse afterwards, " this I call *courteous* in the Abbot—another man would never have thought that I might do better with half a guinea than throw it to a door-keeper ;— but here is a man not only asks me to dinner, but gives me a ticket for the theatre." These were only his oddities, for no man was more liberal, or more honourable in all his doings and dealings, than Matthews. He gave Hobhouse and me, before we set out for Constantinople, a most splendid entertain- ment, to which we did ample justice. One of his fancies was dining at all sorts of out-of-the-way places. Somebody popped upon him in I know not what coffee-house in the Strand—and what do you think was the attraction? Why, that he paid a shilling (I think) to *dine with his hat on*. This he called his " *hat* house ", and used to boast of the comfort of being covered at meal times.

When Sir Henry Smith was expelled from Cambridge for a row with a tradesman named " Hiron ", Matthews solaced himself with shouting under Hiron's windows every evening,

> " Ah me ! what perils do environ
> The man who meddles with *hot Hirons* ".

He was also of that band of profane scoffers who, under the auspices of [Bankes], used to rouse Lort Mansel (late Bishop of Bristol) from his slumbers in the lodge of Trinity ; and when he appeared at the window foaming with wrath, and crying out, " I know you, gentlemen, I know you ! " were wont to reply, " We beseech thee to hear us, good *Lort* ! "—" Good *Lort* deliver us ! " (Lort was his Christian name.) As he was very free in his speculations upon all kinds of subjects, although by no means either dissolute or intemperate in his conduct, and as I was no less independent, our conversation and correspondence used to alarm our friend Hobhouse to a considerable degree.

You must be almost tired of my packets, which will have cost a mint of postage.

Salute Gifford and all my friends.

Yours, B.

TO THE HON. DOUGLAS KINNAIRD † *Ravenna, 9ᵇʳᵉ 22nd, 1820*

My dear Douglas,—You ask me to *make* Hanson *make Claughton* pay *me*. I would willingly know how I am to make Hanson do that or any thing else at this distance of time and place? If you intimate to him that what is taken out of Claughton's pocket will go into his own, in diminution of his " bill of pains and penalties ", he may perhaps condescend to do his duty. It is useless for me to say more. I have written, and written, and *you* have spoken. I suppose he will end by having his own way, and a pretty way it is.

The affairs of this part of Italy are simplifying; the liberals have delayed till it is too late for them to do anything to the purpose. If the scoundrels of Troppau decide on a massacre (as is probable) the Barbarians will march in by one frontier, and the Neapolitans by the other. They have *both asked* permission of his Holiness so to do, which is equivalent to asking a man's permission to give him a kick on the a—se; if he grants it, it is a sign he can't return it.

The worst of all is, that this devoted country will become, for the six thousandth time, since God made man in his own image, the seat of war. I recollect Spain in 1809, and the Morea and part of Greece in 1810–1811, when Veli Pacha was on his way to combat the Russians (the Turkish armies make their *own country* like an enemy's on a march), and a small stretch also of my own county of Nottingham under the Luddites, when we were burning the frames, and sometimes the manufactories, so that I have a tolerable idea of what may ensue. Here all is suspicion and terrorism, bullying, arming, and disarming; the priests scared, the people gloomy, and the merchants *buying* up corn to *supply the armies*. I am so pleased with the last piece of Italic patriotism, that I have underlined it for your remark; it is just as if our Hampshire farmers should prepare magazines for any two continental scoundrels, who could land and fight it out in New Forest.

I come in for my share of the *vigorous* system of the day. They have taken it into their heads that I am popular (which no one ever was in Italy but an opera singer, or ever will be till the resurrection of Romulus), and are trying by all kinds of petty vexations to disgust and make me retire. This I should hardly believe, it seems so absurd, if some of their priests did not avow it. They try to fix squabbles upon my servants, to involve me in scrapes (no difficult matter), and lastly they (the governing party) menace to shut Madame Guiccioli up in a *convent*. The last piece of policy springs from two motives; the one because her *family* are suspected of liberal principles, and the second because mine (although I do not preach them) are known, and were known when it was far less reputable to be a friend to liberty than it is now.

If I am proud of some of the poetry, I am much prouder of some of my predictions; they are as good as Fitzgerald's, the Literary Fund seer, and Murray's post poet.

If they should succeed in putting this poor girl into a convent for doing that with me which all the other countesses of Italy have done with everybody for these 1000 years, of course I would accede to a retreat on my part, rather than a prison on hers, for the former only is what they *really* want. She is, as women are apt to be by opposition, sufficiently heroic and obstinate; but as both these qualities may only tend the more to put her in monastic durance, I am at a loss what to do. I have seen the correspondence of half a dozen bigots on the subject, and perceive that they have set about it, merely as an indirect way of attacking part of her relations, and myself. You may imagine that I am, as usual, in warm water with this affair in prospect.

As for public affairs they look no better. [word torn out], parties have dawdled till it is too late. I question if they could get together twelve thousand men of their own, *now*. And some months ago it was different.

Pray write.   Remember me to Hobhouse, and believe me ever

Yours most truly, B.

P.S.—The police at present is under the Germans, or rather the Austrians, who do not merit the name of Germans, who open all letters it is supposed.   I have no objection, so that they see how I hate and utterly despise and detest those *Hun brutes*, and all they can do in their temporary wickedness, for Time and Opinion, and the vengeance of a roused-up people will at length manure Italy with their carcases, it may not be for one year, or two, or ten, but it *will* be, and so that it *could be* sooner, I know not what a man ought *not* to do, but their antagonists are no great shakes.   The Spaniards are the boys after all.

TO JOHN MURRAY   *Ravenna, D^{ecr} 9th 1820*

DEAR MURRAY,—I intended to have written to you at some length by this post, but as the Military Commandant is now lying dead in my house, on Fletcher's bed, I have other things to think of.

He was shot at 8 o'clock this evening about two hundred paces from our door.   I was putting on my great coat to pay a visit to the Countess G., when I heard a shot, and on going into the hall, found all my servants on the balcony exclaiming that " a Man was murdered ".   As it is the custom here to let people fight it through, they wanted to hinder me from going out ; but I ran down into the Street :   Tita, the bravest of them, followed me ;   and we made our way to the Commandant, who was lying on his back, with five wounds, of which three in the body—one in the heart.   There were about him Diego, his Adjutant, crying like a Child ;   a priest howling ;   a surgeon who dared not touch him ;   two or three confused and frightened soldiers ;   one or two of the boldest of the mob ;   and the Street dark as pitch, with the people flying in all directions.   As Diego could only cry and wring his hands, and the Priest could only pray, and nobody seemed able or willing to do anything except exclaim, shake and stare, I made my servant and one of the mob take up the body ;   sent off Diego crying to the Cardinal,

the Soldiers for the Guard ; and had the Commandant conveyed up Stairs to my own quarters. But he was quite gone. I
made the surgeon examine him, and examined him myself.
He had bled inwardly, and very little external blood was
apparent. One of the slugs had gone quite through—all but
the skin : I felt it myself. Two more shots in the body, one
in a finger, and another in the arm. His face not at all disfigured : he seems asleep, but is growing livid. The assassin
has not been taken ; but the gun was found—a gun filed down
to half the barrel.

He said nothing but *O Dio!* and *O Gesu* two or three times.

The house was filled at last with soldiers, officers, police,
and military ; but they are clearing away—all but the sentinels,
and the body is to be removed tomorrow. It seems that, if I
had not had him taken into my house, he might have lain in
the Streets till morning ; as here nobody meddles with such
things, for fear of the consequences—either of public suspicion,
or private revenge on the part of the slayers. They may do as
they please : I shall never be deterred from a duty of humanity
by all the assassins of Italy, and that is a wide word.

He was a brave officer, but an unpopular man. The whole
town is in confusion.

You may judge better of things here by this detail, than by
anything which I could add on the Subject : communicate this
letter to Hobhouse and Douglas K^d, and believe me

Yours ever truly, B.

P.S.—The poor Man's wife is not yet aware of his death :
they are to break it to her in the morning.

The Lieutenant, who is watching the body, is smoking
with the greatest *sangfroid* : a strange people.

TO LADY BYRON *Ravenna, [Thursday], 10bre 28th 1820*

I acknowledge your note which is on the whole satisfactory
—the style a little harsh—but that was to be expected—it
would have been too great a peace-offering after nearly five
years—to have been gracious in the manner, as well as in the
matter.—Yet you might have been so—for communications

between *us*—are like " Dialogues of the Dead "—or " letters between this world and the next ". You have alluded to the "*past*" and I to the future.—As to Augusta—she knows as little of my request, as of your answer—Whatever She is or may have been—*you* have never had reason to complain of her—on the contrary—you are not aware of the obligations under which you have been to her.—Her life and mine—and yours and mine—were two things perfectly distinct from each other—when one ceased the other began—and now both are closed.

You must be aware of the reasons of my bequest in favour of Augusta and her Children which are the restrictions I am under by the Settlement, which death would make yours—at least the available portion.

I wrote to you on the 8th or ninth inst, I think.—Things here are fast coming to a Crisis.— — — War may be considered as nearly inevitable—though the King of N[aples] is gone to Congress, that will scarcely hinder it—the people are so excited, you must not mind what the English fools say of Italy—they know nothing—they go gaping from Rome to Florence and so on—which is like seeing England—in Saint James's Street.— — —

I live with the people and amongst them—and know them —and you may rely upon my not deceiving you, though I may myself. If you mean ever to extricate the Settlement from the funds now is the time to make the trustees act—while Stocks are yet up—and peace not actually broken. Pray attend to this—

Yours BYRON

P.S.—Excuse haste—I have scribbled in great quickness,— and do not attribute it to ill-humour—but to matters which are on hand—and which must be attended to—I am really obliged by your attention to my request.— — — You could not have sent me any thing half so acceptable but I have *burnt* your note that you may be under no restraint but your internal feeling.— It is a comfort to me *now*—beyond all comforts ; that A— and her children will be thought of—after I am nothing ; but five years ago—it would have been something more? why did you *then keep silence?* I told you that I was going *long*—and going *far* (not so *far* as I intended—for I meant to have gone to

Turkey and am not sure that I shall not finish with it—but *longer* than I meant to have made of existence—at least at that time—) and two words about her or hers would have been to me—like vengeance or freedom to an Italian—i.e. the " Ne plus ultra " of gratifications—She and two others were the only things I ever really loved—I may say it now—for we are young no longer.——

TO THOMAS MOORE   *Ravenna, January 2, 1821*

Your entering into my project for the *Memoir*, is pleasant to me. But I doubt (contrary to me my dear Mad^e Mac F * * ,[1] whom I always loved, and always shall—not only because I really *did* feel attached to her *personally*, but because she and about a dozen others of that sex were all who stuck by me in the grand conflict of 1815)—but I doubt, I say, whether the *Memoir* could appear in my lifetime;—and, indeed, I had rather it did not; for a man always *looks dead* after his Life has appeared, and I should certes not survive the appearance of mine. The first part I cannot consent to alter, even although Madame de S[tael]'s opinion of B. C. and my remarks upon Lady C.'s beauty (which is surely great, and I suppose that I have said so—at least, I ought) should go down to our grandchildren in unsophisticated nakedness.

As to Madame de S[tael], I am by no means bound to be her beadsman—she was always more civil to me in person than during my absence. Our dear defunct friend, Monk Lewis, who was too great a bore ever to lie, assured me upon his tiresome word of honour, that at Florence, the said Madame de S[tael] was open-*mouthed* against me; and when asked, in *Switzerland*, *why* she had changed her opinion, replied, with laudable sincerity, that I had named her in a sonnet with Voltaire, Rousseau, etc. and that she could not help it through decency. Now, I have not forgotten this, but I have been generous,—as mine acquaintance, the late Captain Whitby, of the navy, used to say to his seamen (when " married to the gunner's daughter ")—" two dozen and let you off easy ". The " two dozen " were with the cat-o'-nine tails;—the " let you off easy " was rather his own opinion than that of the patient.

My acquaintance with these terms and practices arises from my having been much conversant with ships of war and naval heroes in the year of my voyages in the Mediterranean. Whitby was in the gallant action off Lissa in 1811. He was brave, but a disciplinarian. When he left his frigate, he left a *parrot*, which was taught by the crew the following sounds— (it must be remarked that Captain Whitby was the image of

[1] Presumably Madame de Flahaut, the former Miss Mercer Elphinstone.

Fawcett the actor, in voice, face, and figure, and that he squinted).

The Parrot loquitur.

" Whitby ! Whitby ! funny eye ! funny eye ! two dozen, and let you off easy. Oh you——— ! "

Now, if Madame de B. has a parrot, it had better be taught a French parody of the same sounds.

With regard to our purposed Journal, I will call it what you please, but it should be a newspaper, to make it *pay*. We can call it " The Harp ", if you like—or any thing.

I feel exactly as you do about our " art ", but it comes over me in a kind of rage every now and then, like * * * *, and then, if I don't write to empty my mind, I go mad. As to that regular, uninterrupted love of writing, which you describe in your friend, I do not understand it. I feel it as a torture, which I must get rid of, but never as a pleasure. On the contrary, I think composition a great pain.

I wish you to think seriously of the Journal scheme—for I am as serious as one can be, in this world, about any thing. As to matters here, they are high and mighty—but not for paper. It is much about the state of things betwixt Cain and Abel. There is, in fact, no law or government at all; and it is wonderful how well things go on without them. Excepting a few occasional murders, (every body killing whomsoever he pleases, and being killed, in turn, by a friend, or relative, of the defunct,) there is as quiet a society and as merry a Carnival as can be met with in a tour through Europe. There is nothing like habit in these things.

I shall remain here till May or June, and, unless " honour comes unlooked for ", we may perhaps meet, in France or England, within the year.

Yours, etc.

Of course, I cannot explain to you existing circumstances, as they open all letters.

Will you set me right about your curst *Champs Elysées?*— are they " *és* " or " *ées* " for the adjective? I know nothing of French, being all Italian. Though I can read and under-stand French, I never attempt to speak it; for I hate it. From the second part of the Memoirs cut what you please.

550

EXTRACTS FROM A DIARY
JANUARY 4–FEBRUARY 27, 1821

Ravenna, January 4, 1821

"A SUDDEN thought strikes me." Let me begin a Journal once more. The last I kept was in Switzerland, in record of a tour made in the Bernese Alps, which I made to send to my sister in 1816, and I suppose that she has it still, for she wrote to me that she was pleased with it. Another, and longer, I kept in 1813–1814, which I gave to Thomas Moore in the same year.

This morning I gat me up late, as usual—weather bad— bad as England—worse. The snow of last week melting to the sirocco of to-day, so that there were two damned things at once. Could not even get to ride on horseback in the forest. Stayed at home all the morning—looked at the fire—wondered when the post would come. Post came at the Ave Maria, instead of half-past one o'clock, as it ought. Galignani's *Messengers*, six in number—a letter from Faenza, but none from England. Very sulky in consequence (for there ought to have been letters), and ate in consequence a copious dinner ; for when I am vexed, it makes me swallow quicker—but drank very little.

I was out of spirits—read the papers—thought what *fame* was, on reading, in a case of murder, that " Mr. Wych, grocer, at Tunbridge, sold some bacon, flour, cheese, and, it is believed, some plums, to some gipsy woman accused. He had on his counter (I quote faithfully) a *book*, the Life of *Pamela*, which he was *tearing* for *waste* paper, etc., etc. In the cheese was found, etc., and a *leaf* of *Pamela wrapt round the bacon*." What would Richardson, the vainest and luckiest of *living* authors (*i.e.* while alive)—he who, with Aaron Hill, used to prophesy and chuckle over the presumed fall of Fielding (the *prose* Homer of human nature) and of Pope (the most beautiful of poets)—what would he have said, could he have traced his pages from their place on the French prince's toilets (see Boswell's Johnson) to the grocer's counter and the gipsy-murderess's bacon ! ! !

What would he have said? What can any body say, save what Solomon said long before us? After all, it is but passing from one counter to another, from the bookseller's to the other tradesman's—grocer or pastry-cook. For my part, I have met with most poetry upon trunks; so that I am apt to consider the trunk-maker as the sexton of authorship.

Wrote five letters in about half an hour, short and savage, to all my rascally correspondents. Carriage came. Heard the news of three murders at Faenza and Forli—a carabinier, a smuggler, and an attorney—all last night. The two first in a quarrel, the latter by premeditation.

Three weeks ago—almost a month—the 7th it was—I picked up the commandant, mortally wounded, out of the street; he died in my house; assassins unknown, but presumed political. His brethren wrote from Rome last night to thank me for having assisted him in his last moments. Poor fellow! it was a pity; he was a good soldier, but imprudent. It was eight in the evening when they killed him. We heard the shot; my servants and I ran out, and found him expiring, with five wounds, two whereof mortal—by slugs they seemed. I examined him, but did not go to the dissection next morning.

Carriage at 8 or so—went to visit La Contessa G[uiccioli]— found her playing on the piano-forte—talked till ten, when the Count, her father, and the no less Count, her brother, came in from the theatre. Play, they said, Alfieri's *Fileppo*—well received.

Two days ago the King of Naples passed through Bologna on his way to congress. My servant Luigi brought the news. I had sent him to Bologna for a lamp. How will it end? Time will show.

Came home at eleven, or rather before. If the road and weather are comfortable, mean to ride to-morrow. High time —almost a week at this work—snow, sirocco, one day—frost and snow the other—sad climate for Italy. But the two seasons, last and present, are extraordinary. Read a Life of Leonardo da Vinci by Rossi [? Bossi]—ruminated—wrote this much, and will go to bed.

January 5, 1821

Rose late—dull and drooping—the weather dripping and dense. Snow on the ground, and sirocco above in the sky, like yesterday. Roads up to the horse's belly, so that riding (at least for pleasure) is not very feasible. Added a postscript to my letter to Murray. Read the conclusion, for the fiftieth time

(I have read all W. Scott's novels at least fifty times), of the third series of *Tales of my Landlord*—grand work—Scotch Fielding, as well as great English poet—wonderful man! I long to get drunk with him.

Dined *versus* six o' the clock. Forgot that there was a plum-pudding, (I have added, lately, *eating* to my " family of vices ",) and had dined before I knew it. Drank half a bottle of some sort of spirits—probably spirits of wine ; for what they call brandy, rum, etc., etc., here is nothing but spirits of wine, coloured accordingly. Did *not* eat two apples, which were placed by way of dessert. Fed the two cats, the hawk, and the tame (but *not tamed*) crow. Read Mitford's *History of Greece*—Xenophon's *Retreat of the Ten Thousand*. Up to this present moment writing, 6 minutes before eight o' the clock—French hours, not Italian.

Hear the carriage—order pistols and great coat, as usual—necessary articles. Weather cold—carriage open, and inhabitants somewhat savage—rather treacherous and highly inflamed by politics. Fine fellows, though,—good materials for a nation. Out of chaos God made a world, and out of high passions comes a people.

Clock strikes—going out to make love. Somewhat perilous, but not disagreeable. Memorandum—a new screen put up to-day. It is rather antique, but will do with a little repair.

Thaw continues—hopeful that riding may be practicable to-morrow. Sent the papers to All[1].—grand events coming.

11 o' the clock and nine minutes. Visited La Contessa G[uiccioli] *nata* G[hisleri] G[amba]. Found her beginning my letter of answer to the thanks of Alessio del Pinto of Rome for assisting his brother the late Commandant in his last moments, as I had begged her to pen my reply for the purer Italian, I being an ultra-montane, little skilled in the set phrase of Tuscany. Cut short the letter—finish it another day. Talked of Italy, patriotism, Alfieri, Madame Albany, and other branches of learning. Also Sallust's *Conspiracy of Catiline*, and the *War of Jugurtha*. At 9 came in her brother, Il Conte Pietro—at 10, her father, Conte Ruggiero.

Talked of various modes of warfare—of the Hungarian and Highland modes of broad-sword exercise, in both whereof I was once a moderate " master of fence ". Settled that the

R. will break out on the 7th or 8th of March, in which appointment I should trust, had it not been settled that it was to have
broken out in October, 1820. But those Bolognese shirked the
Romagnuoles.

" It is all one to Ranger." One must not be particular, but
take rebellion when it lies in the way. Come home—read the
Ten Thousand again, and will go to bed.

Mem.—Ordered Fletcher (at four o'clock this afternoon)
to copy out seven or eight apophthegms of Bacon, in which I
have detected such blunders as a schoolboy might detect rather
than commit. Such are the sages ! What must they be, when
such as I can stumble on their mistakes or misstatements?   I
will go to bed, for I find that I grow cynical.

January 6, 1821

Mist—thaw—slop—rain. No stirring out on horseback.
Read Spence's *Anecdotes*. Pope a fine fellow—always thought
him so. Corrected blunders in *nine* apophthegms of Bacon—
all historical—and read Mitford's *Greece*. Wrote an epigram.
Turned to a passage in Guinguené—ditto in Lord Holland's
Lope de Vega. Wrote a note on *Don Juan*.

At eight went out to visit. Heard a little music—like
music. Talked with Count Pietro G[amba] of the Italian
comedian Vestris, who is now at Rome—have seen him often
act in Venice—a good actor—very.   Somewhat of a mannerist ;
but excellent in broad comedy, as well as in the sentimental
pathetic. He has made me frequently laugh and cry, neither
of which is now a very easy matter—at least, for a player to
produce in me.

Thought of the state of women under the ancient Greeks
—convenient enough. Present state a remnant of the barbarism of the chivalric and feudal ages—artificial and un-
natural. They ought to mind home—and be well fed and
clothed—but not mixed in society. Well educated, too, in
religion—but to read neither poetry nor politics—nothing but
books of piety and cookery. Music—drawing—dancing—also
a little gardening and ploughing now and then. I have seen
them mending the roads in Epirus with good success. Why not,
as well as haymaking and milking?

Came home, and read Mitford again, and played with my

mastiff—gave him his supper. Made another reading to the epigram, but the turn the same. To-night at the theatre, there being a prince on his throne in the last scene of the comedy,— the audience laughed, and asked him for a *Constitution*. This shows the state of the public mind here, as well as the assassinations. It won't do. There must be an universal republic,— and there ought to be.

The crow is lame of a leg—wonder how it happened— some fool trod upon his toe, I suppose. The falcon pretty brisk —the cats large and noisy—the monkeys I have not looked to since the cold weather, as they suffer by being brought up. Horses must be gay—get a ride as soon as weather serves. Deuced muggy still—an Italian winter is a sad thing, but all the other seasons are charming.

What is the reason that I have been, all my lifetime, more or less *ennuyé*? and that, if any thing, I am rather less so now than I was at twenty, as far as my recollection serves? I do not know how to answer this, but presume that it is constitutional,—as well as the waking in low spirits, which I have invariably done for many years. Temperance and exercise, which I have practised at times, and for a long time together vigorously and violently, made little or no difference. Violent passions did;—when under their immediate influence—it is odd, but—I was in agitated, but *not* in depressed, spirits.

A dose of salts has the effect of a temporary inebriation, like light champagne, upon me. But wine and spirits make me sullen and savage to ferocity—silent, however, and retiring, and not quarrelsome, if not spoken to. Swimming also raises my spirits,—but in general they are low, and get daily lower. That is *hopeless*; for I do not think I am so much *ennuyé* as I was at nineteen. The proof is, that then I must game, or drink, or be in motion of some kind, or I was miserable. At present, I can mope in quietness; and like being alone better than any company—except the lady's whom I serve. But I feel a something, which makes me think that, if I ever reach near to old age, like Swift, " I shall die at top " first. Only I do not dread idiotism or madness so much as he did. On the contrary, I think some quieter stages of both must be preferable to much of what men think the possession of their senses.

January 7, 1821, Sunday

Still rain—mist—snow—drizzle—and all the incalculable combinations of a climate where heat and cold struggle for mastery. Read Spence, and turned over Roscoe, to find a passage I have not found. Read the fourth vol. of W. Scott's second series of *Tales of my Landlord*. Dined. Read the *Lugano Gazette*. Read—I forget what. At eight went to conversazione. Found there the Countess Geltrude, Betti V. and her husband, and others. Pretty black-eyed woman that—*only* nineteen—same age as Teresa, who is prettier, though.

The Count Pietro G[amba] took me aside to say that the Patriots have had notice from Forli (twenty miles off) that to-night the government and its party mean to strike a stroke—that the Cardinal here has had orders to make several arrests immediately, and that, in consequence, the Liberals are arming, and have posted patroles in the streets, to sound the alarm and give notice to fight for it.

He asked me " what should be done? " I answered, " Fight for it, rather than be taken in detail "; and offered, if any of them are in immediate apprehension of arrest, to receive them in my house (which is defensible), and to defend them, with my servants and themselves (we have arms and ammunition), as long as we can,—or to try to get them away under cloud of night. On going home, I offered him the pistols which I had about me—but he refused, but said he would come off to me in case of accidents.

It wants half an hour of midnight, and rains;—as Gibbet says, " a fine night for their enterprise—dark as hell, and blows like the devil ". If the row don't happen *now*, it must soon. I thought that their system of shooting people would soon produce a re-action—and now it seems coming. I will do what I can in the way of combat, though a little out of exercise. The cause is a good one.

Turned over and over half a score of books for the passage in question, and can't find it. Expect to hear the drum and the musquetry momently (for they swear to resist, and are right,)—but I hear nothing, as yet, save the plash of the rain and the gusts of the wind at intervals. Don't like to go to bed, because I hate to be waked, and would rather sit up for the row, if there is to be one.

Mended the fire—have got the arms—and a book or two, which I shall turn over. I know little of their numbers, but think the Carbonari strong enough to beat the troops, even here. With twenty men this house might be defended for twenty-four hours against any force to be brought against it, *now* in this place, for the same time; and, in such a time, the country would have notice, and would rise,—if ever they *will* rise, of which there is some doubt. In the mean time, I may as well read as do any thing else, being alone.

January 8, 1821, Monday

Rose, and found Count P. G. in my apartments. Sent away the servant. Told me that, according to the best information, the Government had not issued orders for the arrests apprehended; that the attack in Forli had not taken place (as expected) by the *Sanfedisti*—the opponents of the *Carbonari* or Liberals—and that, as yet, they are still in apprehension only. Asked me for some arms of a better sort, which I gave him. Settled that, in case of a row, the Liberals were to assemble *here* (with me), and that he had given the word to Vincenzo G. and others of the *Chiefs* for that purpose. He himself and father are going to the chase in the forest; but V. G. is to come to me, and an express to be sent off to him, P. G., if any thing occurs, Concerted operations. They are to seize—but no matter.

I advised them to attack in detail, and in different parties, in different *places* (though at the *same* time), so as to divide the attention of the troops, who, though few, yet being disciplined, would beat any body of people (not trained) in a regular fight— unless dispersed in small parties, and distracted with different assaults. Offered to let them assemble here if they choose. It is a strongish post—narrow street, commanded from within— and tenable walls.

Dined. Tried on a new coat. Letter to Murray, with corrections of Bacon's *Apophthegms* and an epigram—the *latter not* for publication. At eight went to Teresa, Countess G. At nine and a half came in Il Conte P. and Count P. G. Talked of a certain proclamation lately issued. Count R. G. had been with * * (the * *), to sound him about the arrests. He, * *, is a *trimmer*, and deals, at present, his cards with both hands. If he don't mind, they'll be full. * * pretends (*I* doubt him —*they* don't,—we shall see) that there is no such order, and seems staggered by the immense exertions of the Neapolitans, and the fierce spirit of the Liberals here. The truth is, that * * cares for little but his place (which is a good one), and wishes to play pretty with both parties. He has changed his mind thirty times these last three moons, to my knowledge, for he corresponds with me. But he is not a bloody fellow—only an avaricious one.

It seems that, just at this moment (as Lydia Languish says), " there will be no elopement after all ". I wish that I had known as much last night—or, rather, this morning—I should have gone to bed two hours earlier. And yet I ought not to complain ; for, though it is a sirocco, and heavy rain, I have not *yawned* for these two days.

Came home—read *History of Greece*—before dinner had read Walter Scott's *Rob Roy*. Wrote address to the letter in answer to Alessio del Pinto, who has thanked me for helping his brother (the late Commandant, murdered here last month) in his last moments. Have told him I only did a duty of humanity —as is true. The brother lives at Rome.

Mended the fire with some *sgobole* (a Romagnuole word), and gave the falcon some water. Drank some Seltzer-water. Mem.—received to-day a print, or etching, of the story of Ugolino, by an Italian painter—different, of course, from Sir Joshua Reynolds's, and I think (as far as recollection goes) *no worse*, for Reynolds's is not good in history. Tore a button in my new coat.

I wonder what figure these Italians will make in a regular row. I sometimes think that, like the Irishman's gun (somebody had sold him a crooked one), they will only do for " shooting round a corner " ; at least, this sort of shooting has been the late tenor of their exploits. And yet there are materials in this people, and a noble energy, if well directed. But who is to direct them? No matter. Out of such times heroes spring. Difficulties are the hotbeds of high spirits, and Freedom the mother of the few virtues incident to human nature.

Tuesday, January 9, 1821

Rose—the day fine. Ordered the horses; but Lega (my *secretary*, an Italianism for steward or chief servant) coming to tell me that the painter had finished the work in fresco for the room he has been employed on lately, I went to see it before I set out. The painter has not copied badly the prints from Titian, etc., considering all things.

Dined. Read Johnson's *Vanity of Human Wishes*,—all the examples and mode of giving them sublime, as well as the latter part, with the exception of an occasional couplet. I do not so much admire the opening. I remember an observation of Sharpe's, (the *Conversationist*, as he was called in London, and a very clever man,) that the first line of this poem was superfluous, and that Pope (the best of poets, *I* think,) would have begun at once, only changing the punctuation—

" Survey mankind from China to Peru ".

The former line, " Let observation ", etc., is certainly heavy and useless. But 'tis a grand poem—and *so true!*—true as the 10th of Juvenal himself. The lapse of ages *changes* all things— time—language—the earth—the bounds of the sea—the stars of the sky, and every thing " about, around, and underneath " man, *except man himself*, who has always been, and always will be, an unlucky rascal. The infinite variety of lives conduct but to death, and the infinity of wishes lead but to disappointment. All the discoveries which have yet been made have multiplied little but existence. An extirpated disease is succeeded by some new pestilence; and a discovered world has brought little to the old one, except the p— first and freedom afterwards —the *latter* a fine thing, particularly as they gave it to Europe in exchange for slavery. But it is doubtful whether " the Sovereigns " would not think the *first* the best present of the two to their subjects.

At eight went out—heard some news. They say the King of Naples has declared by couriers from Florence, to the *Powers* (as they call now those wretches with crowns), that his Constitution was compulsive, etc., etc., and that the Austrian barbarians are placed again on *war* pay, and will march. Let them—" they come like sacrifices in their trim ", the hounds of hell! Let it still be a hope to see their bones piled like those of the human dogs at Morat, in Switzerland, which I have seen.

Heard some music. At nine the usual visitors—news, *war*, or rumours of war. Consulted with P. G., etc., etc. They mean to *insurrect* here, and are to honour me with a call thereupon. I shall not fall back; though I don't think them in force or heart sufficient to make much of it. But, *onward!*— it is now the time to act, and what signifies *self*, if a single spark of that which would be worthy of the past can be bequeathed unquenchedly to the future? It is not one man, nor a million, but the *spirit* of liberty which must be spread. The waves which dash upon the shore are, one by one, broken, but yet the *ocean* conquers, nevertheless. It overwhelms the Armada, it wears the rock, and, if the *Neptunians* are to be believed, it has not only destroyed, but made a world. In like manner, whatever the sacrifice of individuals, the great cause will gather strength, sweep down what is rugged, and fertilise (for *sea-weed* is *manure*) what is cultivable. And so, the mere selfish calculation ought never to be made on such occasions; and, at present, it shall not be computed by me. I was never a good arithmetician of chances, and shall not commence now.

January 10, 1821

Day fine—rained only in the morning. Looked over accounts. Read Campbell's *Poets*—marked errors of Tom (the author) for correction. Dined—went out—music—Tyrolese air, with variations. Sustained the cause of the original simple air against the variations of the Italian school.

Politics somewhat tempestuous, and cloudier daily. To-morrow being foreign post-day, probably something more will be known.

Came home—read. Corrected Tom Campbell's slips of the pen. A good work, though—style affected—but his defence of Pope is glorious. To be sure, it is his *own cause* too,— but no matter, it is very good, and does him great credit.

Midnight

I have been turning over different *Lives* of the Poets. I rarely read their works, unless an occasional flight over the

classical ones, Pope, Dryden, Johnson, Gray, and those who
approach them nearest (I leave the *rant* of the rest to the *cant*
of the day), and—I had made several reflections, but I feel
sleepy, and may as well go to bed.

January 11, 1821

Read the letters. Corrected the tragedy and the *Hints from
Horace*. Dined, and got into better spirits. Went out—returned
—finished letters, five in number. Read *Poets*, and an anecdote
in Spence.

All¹. writes to me that the Pope, and Duke of Tuscany, and
King of Sardinia, have also been called to Congress; but the
Pope will only deal there by proxy. So the interests of millions
are in the hands of about twenty coxcombs, at a place called
Leibach !

I should almost regret that my own affairs went well, when
those of nations are in peril. If the interests of mankind could
be essentially bettered (particularly of these oppressed Italians),
I should not so much mind my own " sma peculiar ". God
grant us all better times, or more philosophy !

In reading, I have just chanced upon an expression of Tom
Campbell's ;—speaking of Collins, he says that " no reader
cares any more about the *characteristic manners* of his Eclogues
than about the authenticity of the tale of Troy ". 'Tis false—
we *do* care about " the authenticity of the tale of Troy ". I
have stood upon that plain *daily*, for more than a month in
1810 ; and if any thing diminished my pleasure, it was that the
blackguard Bryant had impugned its veracity. It is true I read
Homer Travestied (the first twelve books), because Hobhouse
and others bored me with their learned localities, and I love
quizzing. But I still venerated the grand original as the truth
of *history* (in the material *facts*) and of *place*. Otherwise, it
would have given me no delight. Who will persuade me,
when I reclined upon a mighty tomb, that it did not contain a
hero?—its very magnitude proved this. Men do not labour
over the ignoble and petty dead—and why should not the
dead be *Homer's* dead? The secret of Tom Campbell's defence
of *inaccuracy* in costume and description is, that his *Gertrude*, etc.,
has no more locality in common with Pennsylvania than with
Penmanmaur. It is notoriously full of grossly false scenery, as

all Americans declare, though they praise parts of the poem.
It is thus that self-love for ever creeps out, like a snake, to sting
anything which happens, even accidentally, to stumble upon it.

January 12, 1821

The weather still so humid and impracticable, that London,
in its most oppressive fogs, were a summer-bower to this mist
and sirocco, which has now lasted (but with one day's interval),
chequered with snow or heavy rain only, since the 30th of
December, 1820. It is so far lucky that I have a literary turn ;
—but it is very tiresome not to be able to stir out, in comfort,
on any horse but Pegasus, for so many days. The roads are
even worse than the weather, by the long splashing, and the
heavy soil, and the growth of the waters.

Read the Poets—English, that is to say—out of Campbell's
edition. There is a good deal of taffeta in some of Tom's
prefatory phrases, but his work is good as a whole. I like him
best, though, in his own poetry.

Murray writes that they want to act the Tragedy of *Marino
Faliero*—more fools they, it was written for the closet. I have
protested against this piece of usurpation, (which, it seems, is
legal for managers over any printed work, against the author's
will) and I hope they will not attempt it. Why don't they bring
out some of the numberless aspirants for theatrical celebrity,
now encumbering their shelves, instead of lugging me out of
the library? I have written a fierce protest against any such
attempt ; but I still would hope that it will not be necessary,
and that they will see, at once, that it is not intended for the
stage. It is too regular—the time, twenty-four hours—the
change of place not frequent—nothing *melo*-dramatic—no
surprises, no starts, nor trap-doors, nor opportunities " for
tossing their heads and kicking their heels "—and no *love*—
the grand ingredient of a modern play.

I have found out the seal cut on Murray's letter. It is
meant for Walter Scott—or *Sir* Walter—he is the first poet
knighted since Sir Richard Blackmore. But it does not do him
justice. Scott's—particularly when he recites—is a very
intelligent countenance, and this seal says nothing.

Scott is certainly the most wonderful writer of the day.

His novels are a new literature in themselves, and his poetry as good as any—if not better (only on an erroneous system)—and only ceased to be so popular, because the vulgar learned were tired of hearing " Aristides called the Just ", and Scott the Best, and ostracised him.

I like him, too, for his manliness of character, for the extreme pleasantness of his conversation, and his good-nature towards myself, personally. May he prosper !—for he deserves it. I know no reading to which I fall with such alacrity as a work of W. Scott's. I shall give the seal, with his bust on it, to Madame la Comtesse G[uiccioli] this evening, who will be curious to have the effigies of a man so celebrated.

How strange are my thoughts !—The reading of the song of Milton, " Sabrina fair " has brought back upon me—I know not how or why—the happiest, perhaps, days of my life (always excepting, here and there, a Harrow holiday in the two latter summers of my stay there) when living at Cambridge with Edward Noel Long, afterwards of the Guards,—who, after having served honourably in the expedition to Copenhagen (of which two or three thousand scoundrels yet survive in plight and pay), was drowned early in 1809, on his passage to Lisbon with his regiment in the *St. George* transport, which was run foul of in the night by another transport. We were rival swimmers—fond of riding—reading—and of conviviality. We had been at Harrow together ; but—*there*, at least—his was a less boisterous spirit than mine. I was always cricketing—rebelling—fighting—*rowing* (from *row*, not *boat*-rowing, a different practice), and in all manner of mischiefs ; while he was more sedate and polished. At Cambridge—both of Trinity—my spirit rather softened, or his roughened, for we became very great friends. The description of Sabrina's seat reminds me of our rival feats in *diving*. Though Cam's is not a very translucent wave, it was fourteen feet deep, where we used to dive for, and pick up—having thrown them in on purpose—plates, eggs, and even shillings. I remember, in particular, there was the stump of a tree (at least ten or twelve feet deep) in the bed of the river, in a spot where we bathed most commonly, round which I used to cling, and " wonder how the devil I came there ".

Our evenings we passed in music (he was musical, and

played on more than one instrument, flute and violoncello), in which I was audience; and I think that our chief beverage was soda-water. In the day we rode, bathed, and lounged, reading occasionally. I remember our buying, with vast alacrity, Moore's new quarto (in 1806), and reading it together in the evenings.

We only passed the summer together;—Long had gone into the Guards during the year I passed in Notts, away from college. *His* friendship, and a violent, though *pure*, love and passion—which held me at the same period—were the then romance of the most romantic period of my life.

* * * * * * *

I remember that, in the spring of 1809, Hobhouse laughed at my being distressed at Long's death, and amused himself with making epigrams upon his name, which was susceptible of a pun—*Long, short*, etc. But three years after, he had ample leisure to repent it, when our mutual friend, and his, Hobhouse's, particular friend, Charles Matthews, was drowned also, and he himself was as much affected by a similar calamity. But *I* did not pay him back in puns and epigrams, for I valued Matthews too much myself to do so; and, even if I had not, I should have respected his griefs.

Long's father wrote to me to write his son's epitaph. I promised—but I had not the heart to complete it. He was such a good amiable being as rarely remains long in this world; with talent and accomplishments, too, to make him the more regretted. Yet, although a cheerful companion, he had strange melancholy thoughts sometimes. I remember once that we were going to his uncle's, I think—I went to accompany him to the door merely, in some Upper or Lower Grosvenor or Brook Street, I forget which, but it was in a street leading out of some square,—he told me that, the night before, he " had taken up a pistol—not knowing or examining whether it was loaded or no—and had snapped it at his head, leaving it to chance whether it might not be charged ". The letter, too, which he wrote me on leaving college to join the Guards, was as melancholy in its tenour as it could well be on such an occasion. But he showed nothing of this in his deportment, being mild and gentle;—and yet with much turn for the ludicrous in his disposition. We were both much attached to

Harrow, and sometimes made excursions there together from London to revive our schoolboy recollections.

Midnight

Read the Italian translation by Guido Sorelli of the German Grillparzer—a devil of a name, to be sure, for posterity; but they *must* learn to pronounce it. With all the allowance for a *translation,* and above all, an *Italian* translation (they are the very worst of translators, except from the Classics—Annibale Caro, for instance—and *there,* the bastardy of their language helps them, as, by way of *looking legitimate,* they ape their father's tongue) ;—but with every allowance for such a disadvantage, the tragedy of *Sappho* is superb and sublime! There is no denying it. The man has done a great thing in writing that play. And *who is he?* I know him not; but *ages will.* 'Tis a high intellect.

I must premise, however, that I have read *nothing* of Adolph Müllner's (the author of *Guilt*), and much less of Goethe and Schiller, and Wieland, than I could wish. I only know them through the medium of English, French, and Italian translations. Of the *real* language I know absolutely nothing,— except oaths learned from postillions and officers in a squabble! I can *swear* in German potently, when I like—" Sacrament— *Verfluchter—Hundsfott* "—and so forth; but I have little else of their energetic conversation.

I like, however, their women, (I was once *so desperately* in love with a German woman, Constance,) and all that I have read, translated, of their writings, and all that I have seen on the Rhine of their country and people—all, except the Austrians, whom I abhor, loathe, and—I cannot find words for my hate of them, and should be sorry to find deeds correspondent to my hate; for I abhor cruelty more than I abhor the Austrians—except on an impulse, and then I am savage— but not deliberately so.

Grillparzer is grand—antique—*not so simple* as the ancients, but very simple for a modern—too Madame de Stael*ish,* now and then—but altogether a great and goodly writer.

January 13, 1821, Saturday

Sketched the outline and Drams. Pers. of an intended tragedy of Sardanapalus, which I have for some time meditated. Took the names from Diodorus Siculus, (I know the history of Sardanapalus, and have known it since I was twelve years old,) and read over a passage in the ninth vol. octavo, of Mitford's *Greece*, where he rather vindicates the memory of this last of the Assyrians.

Dined—news come—the *Powers* mean to war with the peoples. The intelligence seems positive—let it be so—they will be beaten in the end. The king-times are fast finishing. There will be blood shed like water, and tears like mist; but the peoples will conquer in the end. I shall not live to see it, but I foresee it.

I carried Teresa the Italian translation of Grillparzer's *Sappho*, which she promises to read. She quarrelled with me, because I said that love was *not the loftiest* theme for true tragedy; and, having the advantage of her native language, and natural female eloquence, she overcame my fewer arguments. I believe she was right. I must put more love into *Sardanapalus* than I intended. I speak, of course, *if* the times will allow me leisure. That *if* will hardly be a peace-maker.

January 14, 1821

Turned over Seneca's tragedies. Wrote the opening lines of the intended tragedy of *Sardanapalus*. Rode out some miles into the forest. Misty and rainy. Returned—dined—wrote some more of my tragedy.

Read Diodorus Siculus—turned over Seneca, and some other books. Wrote some more of the tragedy. Took a glass of grog. After having ridden hard in rainy weather, and scribbled, and scribbled again, the spirits (at least mine) need a little exhilaration, and I don't like laudanum now as I used to do. So I have mixed a glass of strong waters and single waters, which I shall now proceed to empty. Therefore and thereunto I conclude this day's diary.

The effect of all wines and spirits upon me is, however, strange. It *settles*, but it makes me gloomy—gloomy at the very moment of their effect, and not gay hardly ever. But it composes for a time, though sullenly.

January 15, 1821

Weather fine. Received visit. Rode out into the forest— fired pistols. Returned home—dined—dipped into a volume of Mitford's *Greece*—wrote part of a scene of *Sardanapalus*. Went out—heard some music—heard some politics. More ministers from the other Italian powers gone to Congress. War seems certain—in that case, it will be a savage one. Talked over various important matters with one of the initiated. At ten and half returned home.

I have just thought of something odd. In the year 1814, Moore (" the poet ", *par excellence*, and he deserves it) and I were going together, in the same carriage, to dine with Earl Grey, the *Capo Politico* of the remaining Whigs. Murray, the magnificent (the illustrious publisher of that name), had just sent me a Java gazette—I know not why, or wherefore. Pulling it out, by way of curiosity, we found it to contain a dispute (the said Java gazette) on Moore's merits and mine. I think, if I had been there, that I could have saved them the trouble of disputing on the subject. But, there is *fame* for you at six and twenty! Alexander had conquered India at the same age; but I doubt if he was disputed about, or his conquests compared with those of Indian Bacchus, at Java.

It was a great fame to be named with Moore; greater to be compared with him; greatest—*pleasure*, at least—to be *with* him; and, surely, an odd coincidence, that we should be dining together while they were quarrelling about us beyond the equinoctial line.

Well, the same evening, I met Lawrence the painter, and heard one of Lord Grey's daughters (a fine, tall, spirit-looking girl, with much of the *patrician thoroughbred look* of her father, which I dote upon) play on the harp, so modestly and ingenuously, that she *looked music*. Well, I would rather have had my talk with Lawrence (who talked delightfully) and heard the girl, than have had all the fame of Moore and me put together.

The only pleasure of fame is that it paves the way to pleasure; and the more intellectual our pleasure, the better for the pleasure and for us too. It was, however, agreeable to have heard our fame before dinner, and a girl's harp after.

January 16, 1821

Read — rode — fired pistols — returned — dined — wrote —visited—heard music—talked nonsense—and went home.

Wrote part of a Tragedy—advanced in Act 1st with " all deliberate speed ". Bought a blanket. The weather is still muggy as a London May—mist, mizzle, the air replete with Scotticisms, which, though fine in the descriptions of Ossian, are somewhat tiresome in real, prosaic perspective. Politics still mysterious.

January 17, 1821

Rode i' the forest—fired pistols—dined. Arrived a packet of books from England and Lombardy—English, Italian, French, and Latin. Read till eight—went out.

January 18, 1821

To-day, the post arriving late, did not ride. Read letters— only two gazettes instead of twelve now due. Made Lega write to that negligent Galignani, and added a postscript. Dined.

At eight proposed to go out. Lega came in with a letter about a bill *unpaid* at Venice, which I thought paid months ago. I flew into a paroxysm of rage, which almost made me faint. I have not been well ever since. I deserve it for being such a fool—but it *was* provoking—a set of scoundrels ! It is, however, but five and twenty pounds.

January 19, 1821

Rode. Winter's wind somewhat more unkind than ingratitude itself, though Shakspeare says otherwise. At least, I am so much more accustomed to meet with ingratitude than the north wind, that I thought the latter the sharper of the two. I had met with both in the course of the twenty-four hours, so could judge.

Thought of a plan of education for my daughter Allegra, who ought to begin soon with her studies. Wrote a letter— afterwards a postscript. Rather in low spirits—certainly hippish—liver touched—will take a dose of salts.

I have been reading the Life, by himself and daughter, of Mr. R. L. Edgeworth, the father of *the* Miss Edgeworth.[1] It is altogether a great name. In 1813, I recollect to have met them in the fashionable world of London (of which I then formed an item, a fraction, the segment of a circle, the unit of a million, the nothing of something) in the assemblies of the hour, and at a breakfast of Sir Humphry and Lady Davy's, to which I was invited for the nonce. I had been the lion of 1812 : Miss Edge-

[1] Maria Edgeworth, the celebrated moralist and fashionable woman of letters.

worth and Madame de Stael, with " the Cossack ", towards the end of 1813, were the exhibitions of the succeeding year.

I thought Edgeworth a fine old fellow, of a clarety, elderly, red complexion, but active, brisk, and endless. He was seventy, but did not look fifty—no, nor forty-eight even. I had seen poor Fitzpatrick not very long before—a man of pleasure, wit, eloquence, all things. He tottered—but still talked like a gentleman, though feebly. Edgeworth bounced about, and talked loud and long ; but he seemed neither weakly nor decrepit, and hardly old.

He began by telling " that he had given Dr. Parr a dressing, who had taken him for an Irish bogtrotter ", etc., etc. Now I, who know Dr. Parr, and who know (*not* by experience—for I never should have presumed so far as to contend with him— but by hearing him *with* others, and *of* others) that it is not so easy a matter to " dress him ", thought Mr. Edgeworth an assertor of what was not true. He could not have stood before Parr for an instant. For the rest, he seemed intelligent, vehe- ment, vivacious, and full of life. He bids fair for a hundred years.

He was not much admired in London, and I remember a " ryghte merrie " and conceited jest which was rife among the gallants of the day,—viz. a paper had been presented for the *recall of Mrs. Siddons to the stage*, (she having lately taken leave, to the loss of ages,—for nothing ever was, or can be, like her,) to which all men had been called to subscribe. Whereupon Thomas Moore, of profane and poetical memory, did propose that a similar paper should be *sub*scribed and *circum*scribed " for the recall of Mr. Edgeworth to Ireland ".

The fact was—every body cared more about *her*. She was a nice little unassuming " Jeannie Deans-looking body ", as we Scotch say—and, if not handsome, certainly not ill-looking. Her conversation was as quiet as herself. One would never have guessed she could write *her name* ; whereas her father talked, *not* as if he could write nothing else, but as if nothing else was worth writing.

As for Mrs. Edgeworth, I forget—except that I think she was the youngest of the party. Altogether, they were an excellent cage of the kind ; and succeeded for two months, till the landing of Madame de Stael.

To turn from them to their works, I admire them ; but

they excite no feeling, and they leave no love—except for some Irish steward or postillion. However, the impression of intellect and prudence is profound—and may be useful.

January 21, 1821

Rode—fired pistols. Read from Grimm's *Correspondence*. Dined—went out—heard music—returned—wrote a letter to the Lord Chamberlain to request him to prevent the theatres from representing the Doge, which the Italian papers say that they are going to act. This is pretty work—what! without asking my consent, and even in opposition to it!

January 21, 1821

Fine, clear, frosty day—that is to say, an Italian frost, for their winters hardly get beyond snow; for which reason nobody knows how to skate (or skait)—a Dutch and English accomplishment. Rode out, as usual, and fired pistols. Good shooting—broke four common, and rather small, bottles, in four shots, at fourteen paces, with a common pair of pistols and indifferent powder. Almost as good *wafering* or shooting—considering the difference of powder and pistol,—as when, in 1809, 1810, 1811, 1812, 1813, 1814, it was my luck to split walking-sticks, wafers, half-crowns, shillings, and even the *eye* of a walking-stick, at twelve paces, with a single bullet—and all by *eye* and calulation; for my hand is not steady, and apt to change with the very weather. To the prowess which I here note, Joe Manton and others can bear testimony; for the former taught, and the latter has seen me do, these feats.

Dined—visited—came home—read. Remarked on an anecdote in Grimm's *Correspondence*, which says that " Regnard et la plûpart des poëtes comiques étaient gens bilieux et mélancoliques; et que M. de Voltaire, qui est très gai, n'a jamais fait que des tragédies—et que la comédie gaie est le seul genre où il n'ait point réussi. C'est que celui qui rit et celui qui fait rire sont deux hommes fort différens."—Vol. VI.

At this moment I feel as bilious as the best comic writer of them all, even as Regnard himself, the next to Molière, who has written some of the best comedies in any language, and who is supposed to have committed suicide,) and am not in spirits to continue my proposed tragedy of *Sardanapalus*, which I have, for some days, ceased to compose.

To-morrow is my birth-day—that is to say, at twelve o' the clock, midnight, *i.e.* in twelve minutes, I shall have completed thirty and three years of age ! ! !—and I go to my bed with a heaviness of heart at having lived so long, and to so little purpose.

It is three minutes past twelve.—" 'Tis the middle of the night by the castle clock ", and I am now thirty-three !

> " Eheu, fugaces, Posthume, Posthume,
>   Labuntur anni " ;—

but I don't regret them so much for what I have done, as for what I *might* have done.

> Through life's road, so dim and dirty,
> I have dragged to three-and-thirty.
> What have these years left to me?
> Nothing—except thirty-three.

January 22, 1821

1821.
Here lies
interred in the Eternity
of the Past,
from whence there is no
Resurrection
for the Days—Whatever there may be
for the Dust—
the Thirty-Third Year
of an ill-spent Life,
Which, after
a lingering disease of many months
sunk into a lethargy,
and expired,
January 22d, 1821, A. D.
Leaving a successor
Inconsolable
for the very loss which
occasioned its
Existence.

January 23, 1821

Fine day. Read — rode — fired pistols, and returned. Dined — read. Went out at eight — made the usual visit. Heard of nothing but war,—" the cry is still, They come ". The Carbonari seem to have no plan—nothing fixed among themselves, how, when, or what to do. In that case, they will make nothing of this project, so often postponed, and never put in action.

Came home, and gave some necessary orders, in case of circumstances requiring a change of place. I shall act according to what may seem proper, when I hear decidedly what the Barbarians mean to do. At present, they are building a bridge of boats over the Po, which looks very warlike. A few days will probably show. I think of retiring towards Ancona, nearer the northern frontier; that is to say, if Teresa and her father are obliged to retire, which is most likely, as all the family are Liberals. If not, I shall stay. But my movements will depend upon the lady's wishes—for myself, it is much the same.

I am somewhat puzzled what to do with my little daughter, and my effects, which are of some quantity and value,—and neither of them do in the seat of war, where I think of going. But there is an elderly lady who will take charge of *her*, and T[eresa] says that the Marchese C. will undertake to hold the chattels in safe keeping. Half the city are getting their affairs in marching trim. A pretty Carnival ! The blackguards might as well have waited till Lent.

January 24, 1821

Returned—met some masques in the Corso—*Vive la bagatelle!*—the Germans are on the Po, the Barbarians at the gate, and their masters in council at Leybach (or whatever the eructation of the sound may syllable into a human pronunciation), and lo ! they dance and sing and make merry, " for to-morrow they may die ". Who can say that the Arlequins are not right? Like the Lady Baussiere, and my old friend Burton —I " rode on ".

Dined—(damn this pen !)—beef tough—there is no beef in Italy worth a curse; unless a man could eat an old ox with the hide on, singed in the sun.

The principal persons in the events which may occur in a

few days are gone out on a *shooting party*. If it were like a
" *highland* hunting ", a pretext of the chase for a grand re-union
of counsellors and chiefs, it would be all very well. But it is
nothing more or less than a real snivelling, popping, small-
shot, water-hen waste of powder, ammunition, and shot, for
their own special amusement : a rare set of fellows for " a man
to risk his neck with ", as " Marishall Wells " says in the
Black Dwarf.

If they gather,—" whilk is to be doubted ",—they will not
muster a thousand men. The reason of this is, that the populace
are not interested,—only the higher and middle orders. I wish
that the peasantry *were*; they are a fine savage race of two-
legged leopards. But the Bolognese won't—the Romagnuoles
can't without them. Or, if they try—what then? They will
try, and man can do no more—and, if he *would* but try his
utmost, much might be done. The Dutch, for instance, against
the Spaniards—*then* the tyrants of Europe, since, the slaves,
and, lately, the freedmen.

The year 1820 was not a fortunate one for the individual
me, whatever it may be for the nations. I lost a lawsuit, after
two decisions in my favour. The project of lending money on
an Irish mortgage was finally rejected by my wife's trustee
after a year's hope and trouble. The Rochdale lawsuit had
endured fifteen years, and always prospered till I married ;
since which, every thing has gone wrong—with me at least.

In the same year, 1820, the Countess T[eresa] G[uiccioli]
nata G[hisleri] G[amba], in despite of all I said and did to
prevent it, *would* separate from her husband, Il Cavalier Com-
mendatore G[amba], etc., etc., etc., and all on the account of
" P. P. clerk of this parish ". The other little petty vexations
of the year—overturns in carriages—the murder of people
before one's door, and dying in one's beds—the cramp in
swimming—colics—indigestions and bilious attacks, etc., etc.,
etc.—   " Many small articles make up a sum,
           And hey ho for Caleb Quotem, oh ! "

January 25, 1821

Received a letter from Lord S[idney] O[sborne], state
secretary of the Seven Islands—a fine fellow—clever—dished

in England five years ago, and came abroad to retrench and to renew. He wrote from Ancona, in his way back to Corfu, on some matters of our own. He is son of the late Duke of L[eeds] by a second marriage. He wants me to go to Corfu. Why not?—perhaps I may, next spring.

Answered Murray's letter—read—lounged. Scrawled this additional page of life's log-book. One day more is over of it and of me :—but " which is best, life or death, the gods only know ", as Socrates said to his judges, on the breaking up of the tribunal. Two thousand years since that sage's declaration of ignorance have not enlightened us more upon this important point ; for, according to the Christian dispensation, no one can know whether he is *sure* of salvation—even the most righteous—since a single slip of faith may throw him on his back, like a skaiter, while gliding smoothly to his paradise. Now, therefore, whatever the certainty of faith in the facts may be, the certainty of the individual as to his· happiness or misery is no greater than it was under Jupiter.

It has been said that the immortality of the soul is a *grand peut-être*—but still it is a *grand* one. Every body clings to it— the stupidest, and dullest, and wickedest of human bipeds is still persuaded that he is immortal.

January 26, 1821

Fine day—a few mares' tails portending change, but the sky clear, upon the whole. Rode—fired pistols—good shooting. Coming back, met an old man. Charity—purchased a shilling's worth of salvation. If that was to be bought, I have given more to my fellow-creatures in this life—sometimes for *vice*, but, if not more *often*, at least more *considerably*, for virtue— than I now possess. I never in my life gave a mistress so much as I have sometimes given a poor man in honest distress ; but no matter. The scoundrels who have all along persecuted me (with the help of * * who has crowned their efforts) will triumph ;—and, when justice is done to me, it will be when this hand that writes is as cold as the hearts which have stung me.

Returning, on the bridge near the mill, met an old woman. I asked her age—she said " *Tre croci* ". I asked my groom (though myself a decent Italian) what the devil *her* three crosses meant. He said, ninety years, and that she had five years more to boot!! I repeated the same three times—not to mistake—ninety-five years!!!—and she was yet rather active—heard my question, for she answered it—*saw* me, for she advanced towards me; and did not appear at all decrepit, though certainly touched with years. Told her to come to-morrow, and will examine her myself. I love phenomena. If she *is* ninety-five years old, she must recollect the Cardinal Alberoni, who was legate here.

On dismounting, found Lieutenant E. just arrived from Faenza. Invited him to dine with me to-morrow. Did *not* invite him for to-day, because there was a small *turbot*, (Friday, fast regularly and religiously,) which I wanted to eat all myself. Ate it.

Went out—found T. as usual—music. The gentlemen, who make revolutions and are gone on a shooting, are not yet returned. They don't return till Sunday—that is to say, they have been out for five days, buffooning, while the interests of a whole country are at stake, and even they themselves compromised.

It is a difficult part to play amongst such a set of assassins and blockheads—but, when the scum is skimmed off, or has boiled over, good may come of it. If this country could but be freed, what would be too great for the accomplishment of that desire? for the extinction of that Sigh of Ages? Let us hope. They have hoped these thousand years. The very revolvement of the chances may bring it—it is upon the dice.

If the Neapolitans have but a single Massaniello amongst them, they will beat the bloody butchers of the crown and sabre. Holland, in worse circumstances, beat the Spains and Philips; America beat the English; Greece beat Xerxes; and France beat Europe, till she took a tyrant; South America beats her old vultures out of their nest; and, if these men are but firm in themselves, there is nothing to shake them from without.

January 28, 1821

Lugano Gazette did not come. Letters from Venice. It appears that the Austrian brutes have seized my three or four pounds of English powder. The scoundrels!—I hope to pay them in *ball* for that powder. Rode out till twilight.

Pondered the subjects of four tragedies to be written (life and circumstances permitting), to wit, Sardanapalus, already begun ; Cain, a metaphysical subject, something in the style of Manfred, but in five *acts*, perhaps, with the chorus ; Francesca of Rimini, in five acts ; and I am not sure that I would not try Tiberius. I think that I could extract a something, of *my* tragic, at least, out of the gloomy sequestration and old age of the tyrant—and even out of his sojourn at Caprea—by softening the *details*, and exhibiting the despair which must have led to those very vicious pleasures. For none but a powerful and gloomy mind overthrown would have had recourse to such solitary horrors,—being also, at the same time, *old*, and the master of the world.

Memoranda.

What is Poetry?—The feeling of a Former world and Future.

Thought Second.

Why, at the very height of desire and human pleasure,—worldly, social, amorous, ambitious, or even avaricious,—does there mingle a certain sense of doubt and sorrow—a fear of what is to come—a doubt of what *is*—a retrospect to the past, leading to a prognostication of the future? (The best of Prophets of the future is the Past.) Why is this, or these?—I know not, except that on a pinnacle we are most susceptible of giddiness, and that we never fear falling except from a precipice —the higher, the more awful, and the more sublime ; and, therefore, I am not sure that Fear is not a pleasurable sensation ; at least, *Hope* is ; and *what Hope* is there without a deep leaven of Fear? and what sensation is so delightful as Hope? and, if it were not for Hope, where would the Future be?—in hell. It is useless to say *where* the Present is, for most of us know ; and as for the Past, *what* predominates in memory?—*Hope baffled.* Ergo, in all human affairs, it is Hope—Hope—Hope. I allow sixteen minutes, though I never counted them, to any given or supposed possession. From whatever place we commence, we know where it all must end. And yet, what good is there in knowing it? It does not make men better or wiser. During the greatest horrors of the greatest plagues, (Athens and Florence, for example—see Thucydides and Machiavelli,) men were more cruel and profligate than ever. It is all a mystery. I feel most things, but I know nothing, except

— — — — — — — —
— — — — — — — —
— — — — — — — —[1]

Thought for a Speech of Lucifer, in the Tragedy of Cain :—
Were *Death* an *evil*, would *I* let thee *live*?
Fool ! live as I live—as thy father lives,
And thy son's sons shall live for evermore.

Past Midnight.　　One o' the clock

I have been reading Frederick Schlegel (brother to the other of the name) till now, and I can make out nothing. He evidently shows a great power of words, but there is nothing to be taken hold of. He is like Hazlitt, in English, who *talks pimples*—a red and white corruption rising up (in little imitation of mountains upon maps), but containing nothing, and discharging nothing, except their own humours.

I dislike him the worse, (that is, Schlegel,) because he always seems upon the verge of meaning ; and, lo, he goes down like sunset, or melts like a rainbow, leaving a rather rich confusion,—to which, however, the above comparisons do too much honour.

Continuing to read Mr. Frederick Schlegel. He is not such a fool as I took him for, that is to say, when he speaks of the North. But still he speaks of things *all over the world* with a kind of authority that a philosopher would disdain, and a man of common sense, feeling, and knowledge of his own ignorance, would be ashamed of. The man is evidently wanting to make an impression, like his brother,—or like George in the Vicar of Wakefield, who found out that all the good things had been said already on the right side, and therefore " dressed up some paradoxes " upon the wrong side—ingenious, but false, as he himself says—to which " the learned world said nothing, nothing at all, sir ". The " learned world ", however, *has* said something to the brothers Schlegel.

It is high time to think of something else. What they say of the antiquities of the North is best.

[1] " Thus marked, with impatient strokes of the pen, by himself in the original." Moore.

January 29, 1821

Yesterday, the woman of ninety-five years of age was with me. She said her eldest son (if now alive) would have been seventy. She is thin—short, but active—hears, and sees, and talks incessantly. Several teeth left—all in the lower jaw, and single front teeth. She is very deeply wrinkled, and has a sort of scattered grey beard over her chin, at least as long as my mustachios. Her head, in fact, resembles the drawing in crayons of Pope the poet's mother, which is in some editions of his works.

I forgot to ask her if she remembered Alberoni (legate here), but will ask her next time. Gave her a louis—ordered her a new suit of clothes, and put her upon a weekly pension. Till now, she had worked at gathering wood and pine-nuts in the forest—pretty work at ninety-five years old! She had a dozen children, of whom some are alive. Her name is Maria Montanari.

Met a company of the sect (a kind of Liberal Club) called the *Americani* in the forest, all armed, and singing, with all their might, in Romagnuole—" *Sem* tutti soldat' per la liberta " (" we are all soldiers for liberty "). They cheered me as I passed—I returned their salute, and rode on. This may show the spirit of Italy at present.

My to-day's journal consists of what I omitted yesterday. To-day was much as usual. Have rather a better opinion of the writings of the Schlegels than I had four-and-twenty hours ago ; and will amend it still further, if possible.

They say that the Piedmontese have at length arisen—*ça ira!*

Read Schlegel. Of Dante he says, " that at no time has the greatest and most national of all Italian poets ever been much the favourite of his countrymen ". 'Tis false! There have been more editors and commentators (and imitators, ultimately) of Dante than of all their poets put together. *Not* a favourite! Why, they talk Dante—write Dante—and think and dream Dante at this moment (1821) to an excess, which would be ridiculous, but that he deserves it.

In the same style this German talks of gondolas on the Arno—a precious fellow to dare to speak of Italy!

He says also that Dante's chief defect is a want, in a word, of gentle feelings. Of gentle feelings!—and Francesca of Rimini—and the father's feelings in Ugolino—and Beatrice—and " La Pia ! " Why, there is gentleness in Dante beyond all gentleness, when he is tender. It is true that, treating of the Christian Hades, or Hell, there is not much scope or site for gentleness—but who *but* Dante could have introduced any " gentleness " at all into *Hell*? Is there any in Milton's? No—and Dante's Heaven is all love, and glory and majesty.

One o'clock

I have found out, however, where the German is right—it is about the *Vicar of Wakefield*. " Of all romances in miniature (and, perhaps, this is the best shape in which Romance can appear) the *Vicar of Wakefield* is, I think, the most exquisite ". He *thinks!*—he might be sure. But it is very well for a Schlegel. I feel sleepy, and may as well get me to bed. To-morrow there will be fine weather.

" Trust on, and think to-morrow will repay."

January 30, 1821

The Count P[ietro] G[amba] this evening (by commission from the Ci.) transmitted to me the new *words* for the next six months. * * * and * * *. The new sacred word is * * *—the reply * * *—the rejoinder * * *. The former word (now changed) was * * *—there is also * * *—* * *. Things seem fast coming to a crisis—*ça ira!*

We talked over various matters of moment and movement. These I omit ;—if they come to any thing, they will speak for themselves. After these, we spoke of Kosciusko. Count R. G. told me that he has seen the Polish officers in the Italian war burst into tears on hearing his name.

Something must be up in Piedmont—all the letters and papers are stopped. Nobody knows anything, and the Germans are concentrating near Mantua. Of the decision of Leybach nothing is known. This state of things cannot last long. The ferment in men's minds at present cannot be conceived without seeing it.

January 31, 1821

For several days I have not written any thing except a few answers to letters. In momentary expectation of an explosion of some kind, it is not easy to settle down to the desk for the higher kinds of composition. I *could* do it, to be sure, for, last summer, I wrote my drama in the very bustle of Madame la Contessa G[uiccioli]'s divorce, and all its process of accompaniments. At the same time, I also had the news of the loss of an important lawsuit in England. But these were only private and personal business; the present is of a different nature.

I suppose it is this, but have some suspicion that it may be laziness, which prevents me from writing; especially as Rochefoucalt says that " laziness often masters them all "— speaking of the *passions*. If this were true, it could hardly be said that " idleness is the root of all evil ", since this is supposed to spring from the passions only : *ergo*, that which masters all the passions (laziness, to wit) would in so much be a good. Who knows?

Midnight

I have been reading Grimm's *Correspondence*. He repeats frequently, in speaking of a poet, or a man of genius in any department, even in music, (Grétry, for instance,) that he must have *une ame qui se tourmente, un esprit violent*. How far this may be true, I know not; but if it were, I should be a poet " *per excellenza* "; for I have always had *une ame*, which not only tormented itself but every body else in contact with it; and an *esprit violent*, which has almost left me without any *esprit* at all. As to defining what a poet *should* be, it is not worth while, for what are *they* worth? what have they done?

Grimm, however, is an excellent critic and literary historian. His *Correspondence* forms the annals of the literary part of that age of France, with much of her politics, and still more of her " way of life ". He is as valuable, and far more entertaining than Muratori or Tiraboschi—I had almost said, than Ginguené— but there we should pause. However, 'tis a great man in its line.

Monsieur St. Lambert has,

" Et lorsqu' à ses regards la lumière est ravie,
    Il n'a plus, en mourant, à perdre que la vie ".

580

This is, word for word, Thomson's

" And dying, all we can resign is breath ",

without the smallest acknowledgment from the Lorrainer of a poet. M. St. Lambert is dead as a man, and (for any thing I know to the contrary) damned, as a poet, by this time. However, his *Seasons* have good things, and, it may be, some of his own.

February 2, 1821

I have been considering what can be the reason why I always wake, at a certain hour in the morning, and always in very bad spirits—I may say, in actual despair and despondency, in all respects—even of that which pleased me over night. In about an hour or two, this goes off, and I compose either to sleep again, or, at least, to quiet. In England, five years ago, I had the same kind of hypochondria, but accompanied with so violent a thirst that I have drank as many as fifteen bottles of soda-water in one night, after going to bed, and been still thirsty—calculating, however, some lost from the bursting out and effervescence and overflowing of the soda-water, in drawing the corks, or striking off the necks of the bottles from mere thirsty impatience. At present, I have *not* the thirst; but the depression of spirits is no less violent.

I read in Edgeworth's *Memoirs* of something similar (except that his thirst expended itself on *small beer*) in the case of Sir F. B. Delaval;—but then he was, at least, twenty years older. What is it?—liver? In England, Le Man (the apothecary) cured me of the thirst in three days, and it had lasted as many years. I suppose that it is all hypochondria.

What I feel most growing upon me are laziness, and a disrelish more powerful than indifference. If I rouse, it is into fury. I presume that I shall end (if not earlier by accident, or some such termination), like Swift—" dying at top ". I confess I do not contemplate this with so much horror as he apparently did for some years before it happened. But Swift had hardly *begun life* at the very period (thirty-three) when I feel quite an *old sort* of feel.

Oh! there is an organ playing in the street—a waltz, too! I must leave off to listen. They are playing a waltz which I have heard ten thousand times at the balls in London, between 1812 and 1815. Music is a strange thing.

February 5, 1821

At last, " the kiln's in a low ". The Germans are ordered to march, and Italy is, for the ten thousandth time to become a field of battle. Last night the news came.

This afternoon—Count P. G. came to me to consult upon divers matters. We rode out together. They have sent off to the C. for orders. To-morrow the decision ought to arrive, and then something will be done. Returned—dined—read— went out—talked over matters. Made a purchase of some arms for the new enrolled Americani, who are all on tiptoe to march. Gave order for some *harness* and portmanteaus necessary for the horses.

Read some of Bowles's dispute about Pope, with all the replies and rejoinders. Perceive that my name has been lugged into the controversy, but have not time to state what I know of the subject. On some " piping day of peace " it is probable that I may resume it.

February 9, 1821

Before dinner wrote a little ; also, before I rode out, Count P. G. called upon me, to let me know the result of the meeting of the Ci. at F. and at B. * * returned late last night. Every thing was combined under the idea that the Barbarians would pass the Po on the 15th inst. Instead of this, from some previous information or otherwise, they have hastened their march and actually passed two days ago ; so that all that can be done at present in Romagna is, to stand on the alert and wait for the advance of the Neapolitans. Every thing was ready, and the Neapolitans had sent on their own instructions and intentions, all calculated for the *tenth* and *eleventh*, on which days a general rising was to take place, under the supposition that the Barbarians could not advance before the 15th.

As it is, they have but fifty or sixty thousand troops, a number with which they might as well attempt to conquer the world as secure Italy in its present state. The artillery marches *last*, and alone, and there is an idea of an attempt to cut part of them off. All this will much depend upon the first steps of the

Neapolitans. *Here,* the public spirit is excellent, provided it be kept up. This will be seen by the event.

It is probable that Italy will be delivered from the Barbarians if the Neapolitans will but stand firm, and are united among themselves. *Here* they appear so.

February 10, 1821

Day passed as usual—nothing new. Barbarians still in march—not well equipped, and, of course, not well received on their route. There is some talk of a commotion at Paris.

Rode out between four and six—finished my letter to Murray on Bowles's pamphlets—added postscript. Passed the evening as usual—out till eleven—and subsequently at home.

February 11, 1821

Wrote—had a copy taken of an extract from Petrarch's Letters, with reference to the conspiracy of the Doge, Marino Faliero, containing the poet's opinion of the matter. Heard a heavy firing of cannon towards Comacchio—the Barbarians rejoicing for their principal pig's birthday, which is to-morrow—or Saint day—I forget which. Received a ticket for the first ball to-morrow. Shall not go to the first, but intend going to the second, as also to the Veglioni.

February 13, 1821

To-day read a little in Louis B.'s *Hollande,* but have written nothing since the completion of the letter on the Pope controversy. Politics are quite misty for the present. The Barbarians still upon their march. It is not easy to divine what the Italians will now do.

Was elected yesterday *Socio* of the Carnival Ball Society. This is the fifth carnival that I have passed. In the four former, I racketed a good deal. In the present, I have been as sober as Lady Grace herself.

February 14, 1821

Much as usual. Wrote, before riding out, part of a scene of *Sardanapalus.* The first act nearly finished. The rest of the day and evening as before—partly without, in conversazione—partly at home.

Heard the particulars of the late fray at Russi, a town not far from this. It is exactly the fact of Roméo and Giulietta— *not* Roméo, as the Barbarian writes it. Two families of *Contadini* (peasants) are at feud. At a ball, the younger part of the families forget their quarrel, and dance together. An old man of one of them enters, and reproves the young men for dancing with the females of the opposite family. The male relatives of the latter resent this. Both parties rush home and arm themselves. They meet directly, by moonlight, in the public way, and fight it out. Three are killed on the spot, and six wounded, most of them dangerously,—pretty well for two families, methinks—and all *fact*, of the last week. Another assassination has taken place at Cesenna—in all about *forty* in Romagna within the last three months. These people retain much of the middle ages.

February 15, 1821

Last night finished the first act of *Sardanapalus*. To-night, or to-morrow, I ought to answer letters.

February 16, 1821

Last night Il Conte P. G. sent a man with a bag full of bayonets, some muskets, and some hundreds of cartridges to my house, without apprizing me, though I had seen him not half an hour before. About ten days ago, when there was to be a rising here, the Liberals and my brethren C¹. asked me to purchase some arms for a certain few of our ragamuffins. I did so immediately, and ordered ammunition, etc., and they were armed accordingly. Well—the rising is prevented by the Barbarians marching a week sooner than appointed; and an *order* is issued, and in force, by the Government, " that all persons having arms concealed, etc., etc., shall be liable to, etc., etc."—and what do my friends, the patriots, do two days afterwards? Why, they throw back upon my hands, and into my house, these very arms (without a word of warning previously) with which I had furnished them at their own request, and at my own peril and expense.

It was lucky that Lega was at home to receive them. If any of the servants had (except Tita and F. and Lega) they would have betrayed it immediately. In the mean time, if they are denounced or discovered, I shall be in a scrape.

At nine went out—at eleven returned. Beat the crow for
stealing the falcon's victuals. Read *Tales of my Landlord*—
wrote a letter—and mixed a moderate beaker of water with
other ingredients.

February 18, 1821

The news are that the Neapolitans have broken a bridge,
and slain four pontifical carabiniers, whilk carabiniers wished to
oppose. Besides the disrespect to neutrality, it is a pity that the
first blood shed in this German quarrel should be Italian.
However, the war seems begun in good earnest : for, if the
Neapolitans kill the Pope's carabiniers, they will not be more
delicate towards the Barbarians. If it be even so, in a short
time " there will be news o' thae craws ", as Mrs. Alison Wilson
says of Jenny Blane's " unco cockernony " in the *Tales of my
Landlord*.

In turning over Grimm's *Correspondence* to-day, I found a
thought of Tom Moore's in a song of Maupertuis to a female
Laplander

" Et tous les lieux
Où sont ses yeux,
Font la zone brûlante ".

This is Moore's,

" And those eyes make my climate, wherever I roam."

But I am sure that Moore never saw it ; for this was published
in Grimm's *Correspondence*, in 1813, and I knew Moore's by heart
in 1812.   There is also another, but an antithetical coincidence—

" Le soleil luit,
Des jours sans nuit
Bientôt il nous destine ;
Mais ces longs jours
Seront trop courts,
Passés près de Christine ".

This is the *thought reversed*, of the last stanza of the ballad on
Charlotte Lynes, given in Miss Seward's *Memoirs of Darwin*,
which is pretty—I quote from memory of these last fifteen
years.

" For my first night I'd go
To those regions of snow,
Where the sun for six months never shines ;
And think, even then,
He too soon came again,
To disturb me with fair Charlotte Lynes."

To-day I have had no communication with my Carbonari
cronies ; but, in the mean time, my lower apartments are full
of their bayonets, fusils, cartridges, and what not. I suppose
that they consider me as a depôt, to be sacrificed, in case of
accidents. It is no great matter, supposing that Italy could be
liberated, who or what is sacrificed. It is a grand object—
the very *poetry* of politics. Only think—a free Italy ! ! ! Why,
there has been nothing like it since the days of Augustus. I
reckon the times of Cæsar (Julius) free ; because the com-
motions left every body a side to take, and the parties were
pretty equal at the set out. But, afterwards, it was all prætorian
and legionary business—and since !—we shall see, or, at least,
some will see, what card will turn up. It is best to hope, even
of the hopeless. The Dutch did more than these fellows have
to do, in the Seventy Years' War.

February 19, 1821

Came home *solus*—very high wind—lightning—moonshine
—solitary stragglers muffled in cloaks—women in masks—
white houses—clouds hurrying over the sky, like spilt milk
blown out of the pail—altogether very poetical. It is still
blowing hard—the tiles flying, and the house rocking—rain
splashing—lightning flashing—quite a fine Swiss Alpine evening, and the sea roaring in the distance.

Visited—conversazione. All the women frightened by the
squall : they *won't* go to the masquerade because it lightens—
the pious reason !

Still blowing away. A. has sent me some news to-day.
The war approaches nearer and nearer. Oh those scoundrel
sovereigns ! Let us but see them beaten—let the Neapolitans
but have the pluck of the Dutch of old, or the Spaniards of
now, or of the German Protestants, the Scotch Presbyterians,
the Swiss under Tell, or the Greeks under Themistocles—*all*
small and solitary nations (except the Spaniards and German

Lutherans), and there is yet a resurrection for Italy, and a hope for the world.

February 20, 1821

The news of the day are, that the Neapolitans are full of energy. The public spirit *here* is certainly well kept up. The *Americani* (a patriotic society here, an under branch of the *Carbonari*) give a dinner in *the Forest* in a few days, and have invited me, as one of the C¹. It is to be in *the Forest* of Boccacio's and Dryden's " Huntsman's Ghost " ; and, even if I had not the same political feelings, (to say nothing of my old convivial turn, which every now and then revives,) I would go as a poet, or, at least, as a lover of poetry. I shall expect to see the spectre of " Ostasio degli Onesti " (Dryden has turned him into Guido Cavalcanti—an essentially different person, as may be found in Dante) come " thundering for his prey in the midst of the festival ". At any rate, whether he does or no, I will get as tipsy and patriotic as possible.

Within these few days I have read, but not written.

February 21, 1821

As usual, rode—visited, etc. Business begins to thicken. The Pope has printed a declaration against the patriots, who, he says, meditate a rising. The consequence of all this will be, that, in a fortnight, the whole country will be up. The proclamation is not yet published, but printed, ready for distribution. * * sent me a copy privately—a sign that he does not know what to think. When he wants to be well with the patriots, he sends to me some civil message or other.

For my own part, it seems to me, that nothing but the most decided success of the Barbarians can prevent a general and immediate rise of the whole nation.

February 23, 1821

Almost ditto with yesterday—rode, etc.—visited—wrote nothing—read Roman History.

Had a curious letter from a fellow, who informs me that the Barbarians are ill-disposed towards me. He is probably a spy, or an impostor. But be it so, even as he says. They cannot bestow their hostility on one who loathes and execrates them more than I do, or who will oppose their views with more zeal, when the opportunity offers.

February 24, 1821

Rode, etc., as usual. The secret intelligence arrived this morning from the frontier to the C^i. is as bad as possible. The *plan* has missed—the Chiefs are betrayed, military, as well as civil—and the Neapolitans not only have *not* moved, but have declared to the P. government, and to the Barbarians, that they know nothing of the matter ! ! !

Thus the world goes ; and thus the Italians are always lost for lack of union among themselves. What is to be done *here*, between the two fires, and cut off from the N^n. frontier, is not decided. My opinion was,—better to rise than be taken in detail ; but how it will be settled now, I cannot tell. Messengers are despatched to the delegates of the other cities to learn their resolutions.

I always had an idea that it would be *bungled*; but was willing to hope, and am so still. Whatever I can do by money, means, or person, I will venture freely for their freedom ; and have so repeated to them (some of the Chiefs here) half an hour ago. I have two thousand five hundred scudi, better than five hundred pounds, in the house, which I offered to begin with.

February 25, 1821

Came home—my head aches—plenty of news, but too tiresome to set down. I have neither read nor written, nor thought, but led a purely animal life all day. I mean to try to write a page or two before I go to bed. But, as Squire Sullen says, " My head aches consumedly : Scrub, bring me a dram ! " Drank some Imola wine, and some punch !

Log-book continued

February 27, 1821

I have been a day without continuing the log, because I could not find a blank book. At length I recollected this.

Rode, etc.—wrote down an additional stanza for the 5th canto of *D[on J[uan]* which I had composed in bed this morning. Visited *l'Amica*. We are invited, on the night of the

Veglione (next Dominica) with the Marchesa Clelia Cavalli
and the Countess Spinelli Rasponi. I promised to go. Last
night there was a row at the ball, of which I am a *socio*. The
Vice-legate had the imprudent insolence to introduce *three* of
his servants in masque—*without tickets*, too! and in spite of
remonstrances. The consequence was, that the young men of
the ball took it up, and were near throwing the Vice-legate out
of the window. His servants, seeing the scene, withdrew, and
he after them. His reverence Monsignore ought to know, that
these are not times for the predominance of priests over
decorum. Two minutes more, two steps further, and the whole
city would have been in arms, and the government driven out
of it.

Such is the spirit of the day, and these fellows appear not
to perceive it. As far as the simple fact went, the young men
were right, servants being prohibited always at these festivals.

Yesterday wrote two notes on the " Bowles and Pope "
controversy, and sent them off to Murray by the post. The
old woman whom I relieved in the forest (she is ninety-four
years of age) brought me two bunches of violets. *Nam vita
gaudet mortua floribus.* I was much pleased with the present.
An English woman would have presented a pair of worsted
stockings, at least, in the month of February. Both excellent
things; but the former are more elegant. The present, at
this season, reminds one of Gray's stanza, omitted from his
elegy :—

> " Here scatter'd oft, the *earliest* of the year,
>   By hands unseen, are showers of violets found ;
> The red-breast loves to build and warble here,
>   And little footsteps lightly print the ground ".

As fine a stanza as any in his elegy. I wonder that he could
have the heart to omit it.

Last night I suffered horribly—from an indigestion, I
believe. I *never* sup—that is, never at home. But, last night,
I was prevailed upon by the Countess Gamba's persuasion, and
the strenuous example of her brother, to swallow, at supper, a
quantity of boiled cockles, and to dilute them, *not* reluctantly,
with some Imola wine. When I came home, apprehensive
of the consequences, I swallowed three or four glasses of spirits,

which men (the venders) call brandy, rum, or hollands, but
which gods would entitle spirits of wine, coloured or sugared.
All was pretty well till I got to bed, when I became somewhat
swollen, and considerably vertiginous.   I got out, and mixing
some soda-powders, drank them off.   This brought on temporary relief.   I returned to bed ; but grew sick and sorry once
and again.   Took more soda-water.   At last I fell into a dreary
sleep.   Woke, and was ill all day, till I had galloped a few miles.
Query—was it the cockles, or what I took to correct them, that
caused the commotion?   I think both.   I remarked in my illness the complete inertion, inaction, and destruction of my
chief mental faculties.   I tried to rouse them, and yet could not
—and this is the *Soul! ! !*   I should believe that it was married
to the body, if they did not sympathise so much with each
other.   If the one rose, when the other fell, it would be a sign
that they longed for the natural state of divorce.   But as it is,
they seem to draw together like post-horses.

Let us hope the best—it is the grand possession.

TO THE HON. DOUGLAS KINNAIRD *   *Ravenna,*
                                              February 1st, 1821

DEAR DOUGLAS,—Murray's offer is not a liberal one, nor in
proportion to what he offered for Ld. W[aldegrave]'s trash of
memoirs ; Lord Orford's may and must be better—he was a
truly clever fellow.   Besides it was my intention to deal with
Mr. M. for the *whole*, and not in parts.   Murray has certainly
shuffled a little with me of late ; when Galignani wrote to offer
me in an indirect manner to purchase the *Copyright in France* of
my works I *enclosed his letters with the instrument signed* to Murray,
desiring him to *make use of them for himself only*, as I thought it
fair that *he* should have the advantage.   He never wrote for
three months, even to acknowledge, far less to thank me, but after
repeated letters of mine he at last owns that he had the letters
and offered the *instruments* to Galignani—for " a reasonable
sum ".   In this he only did as I meant him to do, but it was not
very liberal [*erased* : a dirty trick] to say nothing about it till it
was wrung from him.   I can name no sum for the *whole* of the

poems.   I have been five years out of England ; things may be altered, the sale of books different, my writings less popular. What can I say ?   You must be in the way of judging better than I can by a little enquiry or by consulting with mutual friends.   Had it been five years ago (when I was in my zenith) I certainly would not have taken three thousand guineas for the *whole* of the M.S.S. now in his hands ; and I speak of the very lowest.   But still I will not swerve from any agreement *you* may make with him.   With *me* he always avoids the subject, and always has done whenever he could.

With Mr. Hanson I shall henceforward be *two*.   I sent my answer to him enclosed to *you* the other day ; and I beg you to advise him that from henceforward there is an end to all *personal* friendship between him and me, and that the sooner we close our professional connection also the better.   Of course I desire a mortgage, but this their last piece of rascality makes me despair.   You may give my compliments to Mr. Bland and tell him that I have no *personal* pique against him, for I do not even know him ; but if the funds ever fail and I lose my property in them it is through *him* and his formalities and by all that is dear to man I will *blow his brains out* and take what fortune may afterwards send me.   I am perfectly serious, and pray tell him so, for as I have said so will I do.   I address this to Pall Mall, anticipating your return.

yours ever and most truly, BYRON

P.S.—I had heard through your brother the other day something of what you tell me about the boy.   But you know by experience that I never interfere in any matters with the women or children of my friends.   It is the only quiet course.

P.P.S.—I write to desire you to interfere to oppose any representation of " the Doge ", and have written ditto to Mr. Murray.

TO JOHN CAM HOBHOUSE*   *Ravenna, Fy. 22nd, 1821*

MY DEAR HOBHOUSE,—Why the devil don't you write? Are you out of humour?   And why?   I am not, and shall therefore favour you with one epistle and two requests.   The first is to make a short note to a letter I have written to Murray for publication (in any Magazine or in the Examiner) on the remarks of a diplomatic puppy called Turner who, having *failed* in swimming the Hellespont, says that Elkenhead and I succeeded because the *current* was in our favour ! ! From the *European* side was it so? Were we not obliged to *swim up* against it to pass at all?

My next request is that you will be personally polite—and request Douglas K. to be so—to Mr. Curioni (an Opera Singer) and Madame Taruscelli, a Venetian fair (the same that Kinnaird wanted to be introduced to and was refused) who will arrive in London early in March from Barcelona for the Opera. I am sure that you would like the Lady's society vastly, and oblige her by yours ; she is an old friend of mine, and very pretty. She has written to me the enclosed epistle [1] which will explain her. Now an't I a good fellow? I am not like those Venetian fellows who, when their own liaisons are over with a piece, would prevent all others from partaking of the public property, as they did by Kinnaird and *would* have done by me ; but I introduced myself, being piqued by their " Dog in a Manger " behaviour.

As to politics, I enclose you the Pope's proclamation. Of course, I cannot write at length, all letters being opened. The Germans are within hail of the Neapolitans by this time. They will get their gruel. They marched ten days sooner than expected, which prevented a general rising. But they are in a situation that, if they do not win their first battle, they will have all Italy upon them. They are damned rascals and deserve it. It is, however, hard upon the poor Pope—in his old age to have all this row in his neighbourhood.

Yours ever and truly, B.

TO THE HON. DOUGLAS KINNAIRD *   *Ravenna, Fy. 26th, 1821*

MY DEAR DOUGLAS,—You have seen, or will soon see, a greater number of your circular billets than usual from my

---

[1] In the enclosed letter, Signora Taruscelli, who addresses Byron as " Amico piu che carissimo ", besides announcing her projected visit to London and asking for letters of introduction, remarks that she is " always in enamoured of, and always faithful to Curioni " and blesses the day when she left Venice. She understands that the delights of Ravenna still occupy all her friend's attention. " So much constancy in Byron ? "

quarter; and that you may not suppose me more extravagant than usual I will let you know the reason. In the present confusion, and approaching convulsion, of all these countries, Mr. Ghigi (my banker here) has taken a fancy to your notes, and is continually giving me *cash* for them, which cash is still in my strong box, and not more of it spent than usual. I believe that Ghigi is speculating upon grain etc. on account of the war, or that he finds your notes *better paper* than the country bills of exchange. This is all I know, and the reason of this apparent extravagance of mine.

I have a favour to ask you. Curioni, the Opera Singer, will arrive in England from Barcelona in March. He is accompanied by the Signora Arpalice Taruscelli of Venice, a very pretty woman, and an old acquaintance of mine. They have written to me for letters. Will you call upon them? and introduce them to such of the theatrical people and Editors— Perry etc.—as may be useful to them? You may perhaps *not* have to repent of it; for she is very pretty, and no less gallant, and grateful for any attention. You will find them out by enquiring at the Opera House. I have lately written to you on various matters. On politics I can say nothing; but you will hear strange things soon probably. The confusion is as great as it can well be. I am going to put my daughter into a convent, and for myself I shall take what fortune is pleased to send; you may imagine what sort of scene Italy is likely to present in a row.

If you can do anything by way of purchase or mortgage to lay my money out on while the funds are high, let me know. Hanson's rascality throws me into despair. You will have received my message *for* him, which I beg of you to repeat. I am anxious to have done with him. Could we not purchase or find an English mortgage? In the course of time land must get up again, and now might be the time to buy. As I want no *mansion house* nor ornamental grounds—nothing but *rental* land—what think you? I shall be guided by your opinion in all such matters; but if the funds fail I will blow Bland's brains out.

Yours ever and truly, B.

P.S.—I answered you about Murray.

TO JOHN MURRAY   *Ravenna, Marzo, 1821*

DEAR MORAY,—In my packet of the 12th Instant, in the last sheet (*not* the *half* sheet), last page, *omit* the sentence which (defining, or attempting to define, what and who are gentlemanly) begins, " I should say at least in life, that most military men have it, and few naval; that several men of rank have it, and few lawyers," etc., etc. I say, omit the whole of that Sentence, because, like the " Cosmogony, or Creation of the World," in the *Vicar of Wakefield*, it is not much to the purpose.

In the Sentence above, too, almost at the top of the same page, after the words " that there ever was, or can be, an Aristocracy of poets," add and insert these words—" I do not mean that they should write in the Style of the Song by a person of Quality, or *parle Euphuism*; but there is a *Nobility* of thought and expression to be found no less in Shakespeare, Pope, and Burns, than in Dante, Alfieri, etc., etc.," and so on. Or, if you please, perhaps you had better omit the whole of the latter digression on the *vulgar* poets, and insert only as far as the end of the Sentence upon Pope's Homer, where I prefer it to Cowper's, and quote Dr. Clarke in favour of its accuracy.

Upon all these points, take an opinion—take the Sense (or nonsense) of your learned visitants, and act thereby. I am very tractable—in PROSE.

Whether I have made out the case for Pope, I know not; but I am very sure that I have been zealous in the attempt. If it comes to the proofs, we shall beat the Blackguards. I will show more *imagery* in twenty lines of Pope than in any equal length of quotation in English poesy, and that in places where they least expect it: for instance, in his lines on *Sporus*,—now, do just *read* them over—the subject is of no consequence (whether it be Satire or Epic)—we are talking of *poetry* and *imagery* from *Nature and Art*. Now, mark the images separately and arithmetically :—

1. The thing of *Silk*.
2. *Curd* of *Ass's* milk.
3. The *Butterfly*.
4. The *Wheel*.

5. Bug with gilded wings.
6. *Painted* Child of dirt.
7. Whose *Buzz*.
8. Well-bred *Spaniels*.
9. *Shallow streams run dimpling.*
10. *Florid impotence.*
11. *Prompter.   Puppet squeaks.*
12. *The Ear of Eve.*
13. *Familiar toad.*
14. *Half-froth, half-venom, spits* himself abroad.
15. *Fop* at the *toilet.*
16. *Flatterer* at the *board.*
17. *Amphibious thing.*
18. Now *trips a lady.*
19. Now *struts a Lord.*
20. A *Cherub's face.*
21. A *reptile* all the rest.
22. The *Rabbins.*
23. Pride that *licks the dust.*

" Beauty that shocks you, parts that none will trust,
  Wit that can creep, and *Pride* that *licks* the *dust*."

Now, is there a line of all the passage without the most
forcible imagery (for his purpose)?   Look at the *variety*, at the
poetry, of the passage—at the *imagination* : there is hardly a line
from which a *painting* might not be made, and *is*.   But this is
nothing in comparison with his higher passages in the *Essay
on Man*, and many of his other poems, serious and comic.
There never was such an unjust outcry in this world as that
which these Scoundrels are trying against Pope.
   In the letter to you upon Bowles, etc., insert *these* which
follow (*under* the place, as a Note, where I am speaking
of Dyer's " Grongar Hill ", and the use of *artificial* imagery
in illustrating *Nature*) :—" Corneille's celebrated lines on
Fortune—

" ' Et comme elle a l'éclat du *Verre*,
        Elle en a la fragilité '—

are a further instance of the noble use which may be made of
artificial imagery, and quite equal to any taken from Nature."

Ask Mr. Gifford if, in the 5ᵗʰ act of *The Doge*,[1] you could not contrive (where the Sentence of the *Veil* is past) to insert the following lines in Marino Faliero's answer :—

But let it be so. It will be in vain :
The Veil which blackens o'er this blighted name,
And hides, or seems to hide, these lineaments,
Shall draw more Gazers than the thousand portraits
Which glitter round it in their painted trappings,
Your delegated Slaves—the people's tyrants.

Which will be best ? " painted trappings ", or " pictured purple ", or " pictured trappings ", or " painted purple " ? Perpend, and let me know.

I have not had any letter from you, which I am anxious for, to know whether you have received my letters and packets, the letter on Bowles's Pope, etc., etc. Let me hear from you.

Yours truly, B.

P.S.—Upon *public* matters here I say little : You will all hear soon enough of a general row throughout Italy. There never was a more foolish step than the Expedition to N. by these fellows.

I wish you to propose to *Holmes*, the miniature painter, to come out to me this spring. I will pay his expences, and any sum in reason. I wish him to take my daughter's picture (who is in a convent) and the Countess G.'s, and the head of a peasant Girl, which latter would make a study for Raphael. It is a complete *peasant* face, but an *Italian* peasant's, and quite in the Raphael Fornarina style. Her figure is tall, but rather large, and not at all comparable to her face, which is really superb. She is not seventeen, and I am anxious to have her likeness while it lasts. Madame G. is also very handsome, but it is quite in a different style—completely blonde and fair— very uncommon in Italy : yet not an *English* fairness, but more like a Swede or a Norwegian. Her figure, too, particularly the bust, is uncommonly good. It must be *Holmes* : I like him because he takes such inveterate likenesses. There is a war here ; but a solitary traveller, with little baggage, and nothing

---

[1] *Marino Faliero, a Tragedy*, finished July 1820, was published at the end of the year, together with the *Prophecy of Dante*.

to do with politics, has nothing to fear.   Pack him up in the diligence.   Don't forget.

TO THE HON. DOUGLAS KINNAIRD*   *Ra. March 23rd, 1821*

My dear Douglas,—I shall consent to nothing of the kind. Our good friends must have the goodness to " bide a wee ". One of three events must occur :—Lady Noel will die—or Lady B.—or myself.   In the first case they will be paid out of the incoming : in the second my property will be so far liberated (the offspring being a daughter) as to leave a surplus to cover more than any outstanding present debts : in the third, my executors will of course see their claims liquidated.   But as to my parting at this present with a thousand guineas—I wonder if you take me for an Atheist, to make me so unchristian a proposition.   It is true that I have reduced my expences in *that* line ; but I have had others to encounter.   On getting to dry land, I have had to buy carriages, and some new horses, and to furnish my house, for here you find only walls, *no furnished* apartments—it is not the custom.   Besides, though I do not subscribe to liquidate the sum of two thousand pounds for a man of twenty thousand a year, nor write me down a contributor to the English radical societies, yet wherever I find a poor man suffering for his opinions—and there are many such in this country—I always let him have a shilling out of a guinea. You speak with some facetiousness of the *Hans*—etc.   Wait till the play is played out.   Whatever happens, no tyrant nor tyranny nor barbarian army shall make me change my tone or thoughts or notions, or alter anything but my temper.   I say so *now*, as I said so then—now that they are at their butcher-work, as before when they were merely preparing for it.

As to Murray, I presume that you forwarded my letter. I acquiesce in what you say about the arrangement with him, but not at all in the appropriation of the fee.   Let me see it in circulars, and then I will tell you whether I will pay them away or no.   You must have a very bad opinion of my principles to hint at such a thing.   If you pay them anything, pay them the interest, provided it is not above a hundred and fifty pounds.

You persuaded me to give those bonds and now you see the consequence. It would have been better to have stood a suit out. At the worst, Rochdale will always in any case bring enough to cover the bonds, and they may seize and sell it for anything I care. I have had more trouble than profit with it. As to Lady Noel, what you say of her declining health would be very well to any one else; but the way to be immortal (I mean *not* to die at all) is to have me for your heir. I recommend you to put me in your will; and you will see that (as long as *I* live at least) you will never even catch cold.

I have written to you twice or thrice lately—and so on. I could give you some curious and interesting details on things here; but they open all letters, and I have no wish to gratify any curiosity, except that of my friends and gossips. Some day or other when we meet (if we meet) I will make your hair stand on end, and Hobhouse's wig (does he wear one still) start from its frame, and leave him under *bare poles*. There is one thing I wish particularly to propose to you patriots; and yet it can't be, without this letter went in a balloon—and, as Moleda [?] says, " *thaut's* impossible ". Let me hear from you —and as good news as you can send in that agreeable soft conciliatory style of yours——

TO RICHARD BELGRAVE HOPPNER   *Ravenna, April 3, 1821*

Thanks for the translation. I have sent you some books, which I do not know whether you have read or no—you need not return them, in any case. I enclose you also a letter from Pisa. I have neither spared trouble nor expense in the care of the child; and as she was now four years old complete, and quite above the control of the servants—and as a *man* living without any woman at the head of his house cannot much attend to a nursery—I had no resource but to place her for a time (at a high pension too) in the convent of Bagna-Cavalli (twelve miles off), where the air is good, and where she will, at least, have her learning advanced, and her morals and religion inculcated. I had also another reason;—things were and are in such a state here, that I had no reason to look upon my own personal safety as particularly insurable; and I thought the infant best out of harm's way, for the present.

It is also fit that I should add that I by no means intended, nor intend, to give a *natural* child an *English* education, because with the disadvantages of her birth, her after settlement would be doubly difficult. Abroad, with a fair foreign education and a portion of five or six thousand pounds, she might and may marry very respectably. In England such a dowry would be a pittance, while elsewhere it is a fortune. It is, besides, my wish that she should be a Roman Catholic, which I look upon as the best religion, as it is assuredly the oldest of the various branches of Christianity. I have now explained my notions as to the *place* where she now is—it is the best I could find for the present; but I have no prejudices in its favour.

I do not speak of politics, because it seems a hopeless subject, as long as those scoundrels are to be permitted to bully states out of their independence. Believe me,
Yours ever and truly.

P.S.—There is a report here of a change in France; but with what truth is not yet known.

P.S.—My respects to Mrs. H. I *have* the " best opinion " of her countrywomen;[1] and at my time of life, (three and thirty, 22d January, 1821,) that is to say, after the life I have led, a *good* opinion is the only rational one which a man should entertain of the whole sex—up to *thirty*, the worst possible opinion a man can have of them in *general*, the better for himself. Afterwards, it is a matter of no importance to *them*, nor to him either, *what opinion* he entertains—his day is over, or, at least, should be.

You see how sober I am become.

TO THE HON. DOUGLAS KINNAIRD*   *Ra. April 26th, 1821*

MY DEAR DOUGLAS,—" The Mystery is resolved " as Mrs. Malaprop says. You were not taken in—but I was. However, I cannot laugh at the joke for sundry reasons—some of them personal. If ever we meet, I can tell you a few things which

[1] Mrs. Hoppner was of Swiss origin.

may perhaps amuse you for a moment. In the meantime I have been disappointed, and you are amused without me. So that there is no loss to you at least.

I have received your letters, all very kind and sensible—nobody like you for business. But I cannot part with more of the produce than the 150—for the present. As for Claughton, why don't he pay? I wrote to desire that he might be proceeded with weeks ago. I hear from Mrs. L[eigh] that Lady N[oel] *has been* " dangerously ill " ; but it should seem by *her* letter that she is now getting dangerously well again. Your letter seems more dubious. Your approval of *the B.'s Letter* is gratifying. I shall be glad to hear as much on the part of the general reader. I did not mean you to be " *profuse* " with Murray. On the contrary, I shall thank you to be *active* ; for I will not treat with him except through *you* or Hobhouse. *Judge* for yourself, according to the appearance of the impression made by the M.S.S. on their publication, or consult any honest men who understand such matters, and I will abide by your decision. Murray complains to me that you are *brusque* with him. For that matter, so you are at times with most people ; and I see no reason for any exception in his favour. I gave in about the D. Juans because you all seemed to think them heavy. You see I was tractable ; but, if you had taken the other line, I should have been as acquiescent in your decision.

I do not know how far your new Opera Acquaintances may answer your expectation ; but any civility to them will be an addition to the many you have conferred on your *trusting* client —and affectionate friend.

B.

P.S.—What's that you say about " *Yolk of Egg for the hair* " ? The receipt—the receipt immediately. Does *the Letter take*? Love to Hobhouse.

Why should Rogers take the " Venerable " ill? He was sixty-three years, eleven months and fourteen days old when I first knew him ten years ago come next November. I meant him a compliment. As for his age, I have seen the certificate from Bow Church dated " 1747—October 10th. Baptized Samuel son of Peter Rogers, Scrivener, Furnivals Inn ". He and Dryden and Chaucer are the oldest upon record to have written so well at that advanced period. His age is a credit to him. I wonder what you mean.

Don't forget the " recipe ". . . .

TO PERCY BYSSHE SHELLEY   *Ravenna, April 26, 1821*

The child continues doing well, and the accounts are regular and favourable. It is gratifying to me that you and Mrs. Shelley do not disapprove of the step which I have taken, which is merely temporary.

I am very sorry to hear what you say of Keats—is it *actually* true? I did not think criticism had been so killing. Though I differ from you essentially in your estimate of his performances, I so much abhor all unnecessary pain, that I would rather he had been seated on the highest peak of Parnassus than have perished in such a manner. Poor fellow! though with such inordinate self-love he would probably have not been very happy. I read the review of *Endymion* in the *Quarterly*. It was severe,—but surely not so severe as many reviews in that and other journals upon others.

I recollect the effect on me of the *Edinburgh* on my first poem; it was rage, and resistance, and redress—but not despondency nor despair. I grant that those are not amiable feelings; but, in this world of bustle and broil, and especially in the career of writing, a man should calculate upon his powers of *resistance* before he goes into the arena.

" Expect not life from pain nor danger free,
    Nor deem the doom of man reversed for thee."

You know my opinion of *that second-hand* school of poetry. You also know my high opinion of your own poetry,—because it is of *no* school. I read *Cenci*—but, besides that I think the *subject* essentially *un*dramatic, I am not an admirer of our old dramatists *as models*. I deny that the English have hitherto had a drama at all. Your *Cenci*, however, was a work of power, and poetry. As to *my* drama, pray revenge yourself upon it, by being as free as I have been with yours.

I have not yet got your *Prometheus*, which I long to see. I have heard nothing of mine, and do not know that it is yet published. I have published a pamphlet on the Pope controversy, which you will not like. Had I known that Keats was dead—or that he was alive and so sensitive—I should have omitted some remarks upon his poetry, to which I was provoked by his *attack* upon *Pope*, and my disapprobation of *his own* style of writing.

You want me to undertake a great poem—I have not the inclination nor the power. As I grow older, the indifference—*not* to life, for we love it by instinct—but to the stimuli of life, increases. Besides, this late failure of the Italians has latterly disappointed me for many reasons,—some public, some personal. My respects to Mrs. S.

Yours ever, B.

P.S.—Could not you and I contrive to meet this summer? Could not you take a run here *alone*?

TO THOMAS MOORE   *Ravenna, April 28, 1821*

You cannot have been more disappointed than myself, nor so much deceived. I have been so at some personal risk also, which is not yet done away with. However, no time nor circumstances shall alter my tone nor my feelings of indignation against tyranny triumphant. The present business has been as much a work of treachery as of cowardice,—though both may have done their part. If ever you and I meet again, I will have a talk with you upon the subject. At present, for obvious reasons, I can write but little, as all letters are opened. In *mine* they shall always find *my* sentiments, but nothing that can lead to the oppression of others.

You will please to recollect that the Neapolitans are now nowhere more execrated than in Italy, and not blame a whole people for the vices of a province. That would be like condemning Great Britain because they plunder wrecks in Cornwall.

And now let us be literary;—a sad falling off, but it is always a consolation. If " Othello's occupation be gone ", let us take to the next best; and, if we cannot contribute to make mankind more free and wise, we may amuse ourselves and those who like it. What are you writing? I have been scribbling at intervals, and Murray will be publishing about now.

Lady Noel has, as you say, been dangerously ill; but it may console you to learn that she is dangerously well again.

I have written a sheet or two more of Memoranda for you; and I kept a little Journal for about a month or two, till I had filled the paper-book. I then left it off, as things grew busy, and, afterwards, too gloomy to set down without a painful feeling. This I should be glad to send you, if I had an opportunity; but a volume, however small, don't go well by such posts as exist in this Inquisition of a country.

I have no news. As a very pretty woman said to me a few nights ago, with the tears in her eyes, as she sat at the harpsichord, " Alas! the Italians must now return to making operas ". I fear *that* and maccaroni are their forte, and " motley their only wear ". However, there are some high spirits among them still. Pray write.

And believe me, etc.

"MY DICTIONARY," MAY, 1821—DETACHED THOUGHTS, OCTOBER 15, 1821–MAY 18, 1822

Ravenna, May 1st 1821

AMONGST various journals, memoranda, diaries, etc., which I have kept in the course of my living, I began one about three months ago, and carried it on till I had filled one paper-book (thinnish), and two sheets or so of another. I then left off, partly because I thought we should have some business here, and I had furbished up my arms, and got my apparatus ready for taking a turn with the Patriots, having my drawers full of their proclamations, oaths, and resolutions, and my lower rooms of their hidden weapons of most calibres; and partly because I had filled my paper book. But the Neapolitans have betrayed themselves and all the World, and those who would have given their blood for Italy can now only give her their tears.

Some day or other, if dust holds together, I have been enough in the Secret (at least in this part of the country) to cast perhaps some little light upon the atrocious treachery which has replunged Italy into Barbarism. At present I have neither the time nor the temper. However, the *real* Italians are *not* to blame—merely the scoundrels at the *Heel of the Boot*, which the *Hun* now wears, and will trample them to ashes with for their Servility.

I have risked myself with the others *here*, and how far I may or may not be compromised is a problem at this moment : some of them like " Craigengelt " would " tell all and more than all to save themselves " ; but, come what may, the cause was a glorious one, though it reads at present as if the Greeks had run away from Xerxes.

Happy the few who have only to reproach themselves with believing that these rascals were less *rascaille* than they proved. *Here* in Romagna the efforts were necessarily limited to preparations and good intentions, until the Germans were fairly engaged in *equal* warfare, as we are upon their very frontiers without a single fort, or hill, nearer than San Marino. Whether " Hell will be paved with " those " good intentions ", I know not ; but there will probably be good store of Neapolitans to walk upon the pavement, whatever may be its composition. Slabs of lava from their mountain, with the bodies of their own damned Souls for cement, would be the fittest causeway for Satan's *Corso*.

But what shall I write? another Journal? I think not. Anything that comes uppermost—and call it " my Dictionary ".

MY DICTIONARY

Augustus.—I have often been puzzled with his character. Was he a great Man? Assuredly. But not one of *my* great men. I have always looked upon Sylla as the greatest Character in History, for laying down his power at the moment when it was

" too great to keep or to resign ",

and thus despising them all. As to the retention of his power by Augustus, the thing was already settled. If he had given it up, the Commonwealth was gone, the republic was long past all resuscitation. Had Brutus and Cassius gained the battle of Philippi, it would not have restored the republic—its days ended with the Gracchi, the rest was a mere struggle of parties. You might as well cure a Consumption, restore a broken egg, as revive a state so long a prey to every uppermost Soldier as Rome had long been.

As for a despotism, if Augustus could have been sure that all his Successors would have been like himself (I mean *not* as *Octavius*, but Augustus), or Napoleon would have insured the world that *none* of his Successors would have been like himself, the antient or modern World might have gone on like the Empire of China—in a state of lethargic prosperity.

Suppose, for instance, that, instead of Tiberius and Caligula, Augustus had been immediately succeeded by Nerva, Trajan, the Antonines, or even by Titus and his father, what a difference in our estimate of himself? So far from gaining by the *contrast*, I think that one half of our dislike arises from his having been heired by Tiberius, and one half of Julius Cæsar's fame from his having had his empire consolidated by Augustus.

Suppose that there had been *no Octavius*, and Tiberius had " jumped the life " between, and at once succeeded Julius? And yet it is difficult to say whether hereditary right, or popular choice, produce the worse Sovereigns. The Roman Consuls make a goodly show, but then they only reigned for a year, and were under a sort of personal obligation to distinguish themselves. It is still more difficult to say which form of Government is the *worst*—all are so bad. As for democracy, it is the worst of the whole; for what is (*in fact*) democracy? an Aristocracy of Blackguards.

ABERDEEN—OLD AND NEW, OR THE AULDTOUN AND NEWTOUN

For several years of my earliest childhood I was in that City, but have never revisited it since I was ten years old. I was sent at five years old, or earlier, to a School kept by a Mr. *Bowers*, who was called " *Bodsy* Bowers " by reason of his dapperness. It was a School for both sexes. I learned little there, except to repeat by rote the first lesson of Monosyllables —" God made man, let us love him "—by hearing it often repeated, without acquiring a letter. Whenever proof was made of my progress at home, I repeated these words with the most rapid fluency; but on turning over a new leaf, I continued to repeat them, so that the narrow boundaries of my first year's accomplishments were detected, my ears boxed (which they did not deserve, seeing that it was by *ear* only that I had acquired my letters), and my intellects consigned to a new preceptor. He was a very decent, clever, little Clergyman, named Ross, afterwards Minister of one of the Kirks (*East* I think). Under *him* I made an astonishing progress, and I recollect to this day his mild manners and good-natured pains-taking.

The moment I could read, my grand passion was *history*; and why, I know not, but I was particularly taken with the battle near the Lake Regillus in the Roman History, put into my hands the first.

Four years ago, when standing on the heights of Tusculum, and looking down upon the little round Lake, that was once Regillus, and which dots the immense expanse below, I remembered my young enthusiasm and my old instructor.

Afterwards I had a very serious, saturnine, but kind young man, named Paterson, for a Tutor: he was the son of my Shoemaker, but a good Scholar, as is common with the Scotch. He was a rigid Presbyterian also. With him I began Latin in Ruddiman's Grammar, and continued till I went to the " Grammar School " (*Scotice* " Schule "—*Aberdonice* " Squeel "), where I threaded all the Classes to the *fourth*, when I was recalled to England (where I had been hatched) by the demise of my Uncle.

I acquired this handwriting, which I can hardly read myself, under the fair copies of Mr. Duncan of the same city. I don't think that he would plume himself upon my progress. However, I wrote much better then than I have ever done since. Haste and agitation of one kind or another have quite spoilt as pretty a scrawl as ever scratched over a frank.

The Grammar School might consist of a hundred and fifty of all ages under age. It was divided into five classes, taught by four masters, the Chief teaching the fifth and fourth himself, as in England the fifth, sixth forms, and Monitors are heard by the Head Masters.

DETACHED THOUGHTS

Octr 15th 1821

I have been thinking over the other day on the various comparisons, good or evil, which I have seen published of myself in different journals English and foreign. This was suggested to me by accidentally turning over a foreign one lately; for I have made it a rule latterly never to *search* for anything of the kind, but not to avoid the perusal if presented by Chance.

To begin then—I have seen myself compared personally or poetically, in English, French, *German* (*as* interpreted to me), Italian, and Portuguese, within these nine years, to Rousseau— Göethe—Young—Aretino—Timon of Athens—" An Alabaster Vase lighted up within "—Satan—Shakespeare—Buonaparte — Tiberius — Aeschylus — Sophocles — Euripides — Harlequin—The Clown—Sternhold and Hopkins—to the Phantasmagoria—to Henry the 8th—to Chenies—to Mirabeau—to young R. Dallas (the Schoolboy)—to Michael Angelo—to Raphael—to a *petit maître*—to Diogenes—to Childe Harold— to Lara—to the Count in Beppo—to Milton—to Pope—to Dryden—to Burns—to Savage—to Chatterton—to " oft have I heard of thee my Lord Biron " in Shakespeare—to Churchill the poet—to Kean the Actor—to Alfieri, etc., etc., etc. The likeness to Alfieri was asserted very seriously by an Italian, who had known him in his younger days : it of course related merely to our apparent personal dispositions. He did not assert it to *me* (for we were not then good friends), but in society.

The Object of so many contradictory comparisons must probably be like something different from them all ; but what *that* is, is more than *I* know, or any body else.

My Mother, before I was twenty, would have it that I was like Rousseau, and Madame de Staël used to say so too in 1813, and the *Edin^h Review* has something of the sort in its critique on the 4th Canto of *Ch^e Ha^d*. I can't see any point of resemblance : he wrote prose, I verse : he was of the people, I of the Aristocracy : he was a philosopher, I am none : he published his first work at forty, I mine at eighteen : his first essay brought him universal applause, mine the contrary : he married his housekeeper, I could not keep house with my wife : he thought all the world in a plot against *him*, my little world seems to think *me* in a plot against it, if I may judge by their abuse in print and coterie : he liked Botany, I like flowers, and herbs, and trees, but know nothing of their pedigrees : he wrote Music, I limit my knowledge of it to what I catch by *Ear*—I never could learn any thing by *study*, not even a language, it was all by rote and ear and memory : he had a bad memory, I *had* at least an excellent one (ask Hodgson the poet, a good judge, for he has an astonishing one) : he wrote with hesitation and care, I with rapidity and rarely with pains : *he* could never ride nor swim " nor was cunning of fence ", *I* am an excellent swimmer, a decent though not at all a dashing rider (having staved in a rib at eighteen in the course of scampering), and was sufficient of fence—particularly of the Highland broad-sword ; not a bad boxer when I could keep my temper, which was difficult, but which I strove to do ever since I knocked down Mr. Purling and put his knee-pan out (with the gloves on) in Angelo's and Jackson's rooms in 1806 during the sparring ; and I was besides a very fair cricketer—one of the Harrow Eleven when we play[ed] against Eton in 1805. Besides, Rousseau's way of life, his country, his manners, his whole character, were so very different, that I am at a loss to conceive how such a comparison could have arisen, as it has done three several times, and all in rather a remarkable manner. I forgot to say, that *he* was also short-sighted, and that hitherto my eyes have been the contrary to such a degree, that, in the largest theatre of Bologna, I distinguished and read some busts and inscriptions painted near the stage, from a box so distant, and so *darkly* lighted, that none of the company (composed of young and very bright-eyed people—some of them in the same box) could make out a letter, and thought it was a trick, though I had never been in that theatre before.

Altogether, I think myself justified in thinking the comparison not well founded. I don't say this out of pique, for Rousseau was a great man, and the thing if true were flattering enough ; but I have no idea of being pleased with a chimera.

I

When I met old Courtenay, the Orator, at Rogers the poet's in 1811–1812, I was much taken with the portly remains of his fine figure, and the still acute quickness of his conversation. It was *he* who silenced Flood in the English House by a crushing reply to a hasty debût of the rival of Grattan in Ireland. I asked Courtenay (for I like to trace motives), if he had not some personal provocation ; for the acrimony of his answer seemed to me (as I had read it) to involve it. Courtenay said " he had—that when in Ireland (being an Irishman) at the *bar* of the Irish house of Commons that Flood had made a personal and unfair attack upon *himself*, who, not being a member of that house, could not defend himself ; and that some years afterwards, the opportunity of retort offering in the English Parliament, he could not resist it ". He certainly repaid F. with interest, for Flood never made any figure, and only a speech or two afterwards in the E. H. of Commons. I must except, however, his speech on Reform in 1790, which " Fox called the best he ever heard upon that Subject ".

2

When Fox was asked what he thought the best speech he had ever heard, he replied " Sheridan's on the Impeachment of Hastings in the house of Commons " (*not* that in Westminster Hall). When asked what he thought of his *own* speech on the breaking out of the War? he replied " that was a damned good speech too ".—From Lᵈ Holland.

3

When Sheridan made his famous speech already alluded to, Fox advised him to speak it over again in Westminster Hall on the trial, as nothing better *could* be made of the subject ; but Sheridan made his new speech as different as possible, and, according to the best Judges, very inferior to the former, notwithstanding the laboured panegyric of Burke upon his *Colleague.*—Lᵈ H.

4

Burke spoilt his own speaking afterwards by an imitation of Sheridan's in Westminster Hall : this Speech he called always " the grand desideratum, which was neither poetry nor eloquence, but something *better* than both ".

5

I have never heard any one who fulfilled my Ideal of an Orator. Grattan would have been near it but for his Harlequin delivery. Pitt I never heard. Fox but once, and then he struck me as a debater, which to me seems as different from an Orator as an Improvisatore or a versifier from a poet. Grey is great, but it is not oratory. Canning is sometimes very like one. Windham I did not admire, though all the world did : it seemed such sophistry. Whitbread was the Demosthenes of bad taste and vulgar vehemence, but strong and English. Holland is impressive from sense and sincerity. Lord Lansdowne good, but still a debater only. Grenville I like vastly, if he would prune his speeches down to an hour's delivery. Burdett is sweet and silvery as Belial himself, and *I* think the greatest favourite in Pandemonium ; at least I always heard the Country Gentlemen and the ministerial devilry praise his *speeches* upstairs, and run down from Bellamy's when he was upon his legs. I heard Bob. Milnes make his *second* speech : it made no impression. I like Ward—studied, but keen, and sometimes eloquent. Peel, my School and form-fellow (we sate within two of each other) strange to say I have never heard, though I often wished to do so ; but, from what I remember of him at Harrow, he *is*, or *should* be, amongst the best of them. Now, I do *not* admire Mr. Wilberforce's speaking ; it is nothing but a flow of *words*—" words, words alone ".

I doubt greatly if the English *have* any eloquence, properly so called, and am inclined to think that the Irish *had* a great deal, and that the French *will* have, and have had in Mirabeau. Lord Chatham and Burke are the nearest approaches to Orators in England. I don't know what Erskine may have been at the *bar*, but in the house I wish him at the Bar once more. Lauderdale is shrill, and Scotch, and acute. Of Brougham I shall say nothing, as I have a personal feeling of dislike to the man.

But amongst all these—good, bad, and indifferent—I never heard the speech which was not too long for the auditors, and not very intelligible except here and there. The whole thing is a grand deception, and as tedious and tiresome as may be to those who must be often present. I heard Sheridan only once, and that briefly; but I liked his voice, his manner, and his wit: he is the only one of them I ever wished to hear at greater length. In society I have met him frequently: he was superb! He had a sort of liking for me, and never attacked me —at least to my face, and he did every body else—high names, and wits, and orators, some of them poets also. I have seen [him] cut up Whitbread, quiz Me de Stael, annihilate Colman, and do little less by some others (whose names as friends I set not down), of good fame and abilities. Poor fellow! he got drunk very thoroughly and very soon. It occasionally fell to my lot to convoy him home—no sinecure, for he was so tipsy that I was obliged to put on his cock'd hat for him: to be sure it tumbled off again, and I was not myself so sober as to be able to pick it up again.

6

There was something odd about Sheridan. One day at a dinner he was slightly praising that pert pretender and im-postor, Lyttelton (The Parliament puppy, still alive, I believe). I took the liberty of differing from him: he turned round upon me, and said, " Is that your real opinion? " I confirmed it. Then said he, " Fortified by this concurrence, I beg leave to say that it in fact is also *my* opinion, and that he is a person whom I do absolutely and utterly despise, abhor, and detest ". He then launched out into a description of his despicable qualities, at some length, and with his usual wit, and evidently in earnest (for he hated Lyttelton). His former compliment had been drawn out by some preceding one, just as its reverse was by my hinting that it was unmerited.

7

One day I saw him take up his own " Monody on Garrick ". He lighted upon the dedication to the Dowager Lady Spencer: on seeing it he flew into a rage, and exclaimed " that it must be a forgery—that he had never dedicated anything of his to such a d—d canting b—h ", etc., etc., etc.; and so went on for half an hour abusing his own dedication, or at least the object of it. If all writers were equally sincere, it would be ludicrous.

8

He told me that, on the night of the grand success of his *S[chool] for S[candal]*, he was knocked down and put into the watch house for making a row in the Street, and being found intoxicated by the watchmen.

9

Latterly, when found drunk one night in the kennel, and asked his *Name* by the Watchmen, he answered " *Wilberforce* ".

The last time I met him was, I think, at Sir Gilbert Elliot's, where he was as quick as ever. No, it was not the last time : the last time was at Douglas K^(d's). I have met him in all places and parties—at Whitehall with the Melbournes, at the Marquis of Tavistock's, at Robins the Auctioneer's, at Sir Humphrey Davy's, at Sam Rogers's, in short, in most kinds of company, and always found him very convivial and delightful.

10

Sheridan's liking for me (whether he was not mystifying me I do not know ; but Lady C^e L. and others told me he said the same both before and after he knew me) was founded upon *English Bards and S. Reviewers*. He told me that he did not care about poetry (or about mine—at least, any but *that* poem of mine), but he was sure, from *that* and other symptoms, I should make an Orator, if I would but take to speaking, and grow a parliament man. He never ceased harping upon this to me, to the last ; and I remember my old tutor Dr. Drury had the same notion when I was a *boy* : but it never was my turn of inclination to try. I spoke once or twice as all young peers do, as a kind of introduction into public life ; but dissipation, shyness, haughty and reserved opinions, together with the short time I lived in England—after my majority (only about five years in all)—prevented me from resuming the experiment. As far as it went, it was not discouraging—particularly my *first* speech (I spoke three or four times in all) ; but just after it my poem of *C^e H^d* was published, and nobody ever thought about my *prose* afterwards : nor indeed did I ; it became to me a secondary and neglected object, though I sometimes wonder to myself *if* I should have succeeded?

11

The Impression of Parliament upon me was that it's members are not formidable as *Speakers*, but very much so as an *audience*; because in so numerous a body there may be little Eloquence (after all there were but *two* thorough Orators in all Antiquity, and I suspect still *fewer* in modern times), but must be a leaven of thought and good sense sufficient to make them *know* what is right, though they can't express it nobly.

12

Horne Tooke and Roscoe both are said to have declared, that they left Parliament with a higher opinion of its aggregate integrity and abilities than that with which they had entered it. The general amount of both in most parliaments is probably about the same, as also the number of *Speakers* and their *talent*. I except *Orators*, of course, because *they* are things of Ages and not of Septennial or triennial reunions.

Neither house ever struck me with more awe or respect than the same number of Turks in a Divan, or of Methodists in a barn would have done. Whatever diffidence or nervousness I felt (and I felt both in a great degree) arose from the number rather than the quality of the assemblage, and the thought rather of the *public without* than the persons within—knowing (as all know) that Cicero himself, and probably the Messiah, could never have alter'd the vote of a single Lord of the Bedchamber or Bishop.

I thought *our* house dull, but the other animating enough upon great days.

12 [so repeated by Byron]

Sheridan dying was requested to undergo " an Operation " : he replied that he had already submitted to *two*, which were enough for one man's life time. Being asked what they were, he answered, " having his hair cut, and sitting for his picture ".

13

Whenever an American requests to see me (which is *not* unfrequently), I comply : 1^{stly}, because I respect a people who acquired their freedom by firmness without excess ; and

2ndly, because these trans-atlantic visits, " few and far between ", make me feel as if talking with Posterity from the other
side of the Styx. In a century or two, the new English and
Spanish Atlantides will be masters of the old Countries in all
probability, as Greece and Europe overcame their Mother
Asia in the older, or earlier ages as they are called.

14

Sheridan was one day offered a bet by M. G. Lewis. " I
will bet you, Mr. Sheridan, a very large sum : I will bet you
what you *owe me* as Manager, for my ' Castle Spectre '." " I
never make *large bets*," said Sheridan : " but I will lay you a
very small one ; I will bet you *what it is* WORTH ! "

15

Lewis, though a kind man, hated Sheridan ; and we had
some words upon that score when in Switzerland in 1816.
Lewis afterwards sent me the following epigram upon Sheridan
from Saint Maurice :—

> " For worst abuse of finest parts
> Was Misophil begotten ;
> There might indeed be *blacker* hearts,
> But none could be more *rotten* ".

16

Lewis at Oatlands was observed one morning to have his
eyes red, and his air sentimental : being asked why? replied,
" that when people said any thing *kind* to him, it affected him
deeply ; and just now the Duchess has said something *so* kind
to me that . . ." here " tears began to flow " again. " Never
mind, Lewis," said Col. Armstrong to him, " never mind, don't
cry. *She could not mean it.*"

17

Lewis was a good man, a clever man, but a bore, a damned
bore, one may say. My only revenge or consolation used to be,
setting him by the ears with some vivacious person who hated
Bores, especially Me de Stael, or Hobhouse, for example. But
I liked Lewis : he was a Jewel of a Man had he been better set.

I don't mean *personally*, but less *tiresome*; for he was tedious, as well as contradictory, to every thing and every body.

Being short-sighted, when we used to ride out together near the Brenta in the twilight in Summer, he made me go *before* to pilot him. I am absent at times, especially towards evening; and the consequence of this pilotage was some narrow escapes to the Monk on horseback. Once I led him *into* a ditch, over which I had passed as usual forgetting to warn my convoy. Once I led him nearly into the river, instead of *on* the *moveable* bridge which *in*commodes passengers; and twice did we both run against the diligence, which, being heavy and slow, did communicate less damage than it received in its leaders, who were *terrassé*'d by the charge. Thrice did I lose him in the gray of the Gloaming, and was obliged to bring to to his distant signals of distance and distress. All the time he went on talking without intermission, for he was a man of many words.

Poor fellow, he died, a martyr to his new riches, of a second visit to Jamaica—

" I'll give the lands of Deloraine
  Dark Musgrave were alive again ! "

that is

I would give many a Sugar Cane
Monk Lewis were alive again !

18

Lewis said to me, " Why do you talk *Venetian* " (such as I could talk, not very fine to be sure) " to the Venetians? and not the usual Italian? " I answered, partly from habit, and partly to be understood, if possible. " It may be so," said Lewis, " but it sounds to me like talking with a *brogue* to an *Irishman*."

19

Baillie (commonly called Long Baillie, a very clever man, but odd), complained in riding to our friend Scrope B. Davies, " that he had a *stitch* in his side ". " I don't wonder at it " (said Scrope) " for you ride *like* a *tailor*." Whoever had seen B. on horseback, with his very tall figure on a small nag, would not deny the justice of the repartée.

20

In 1808, Scrope and myself being at Supper at Steevens's (I think Hobhouse was there too) after the Opera, young Goulburne (of the Blues and of the Blue-viad) came in full of the praises of his horse, Grimaldi, who had just won a race at Newmarket. " Did he win easy? " said Scrope. " Sir," replied Goulburne, " he did not even condescend to *puff* at coming in." " No " (said Scrope), " and so *you puff for* him."

21

Captain Wallace, a notorious character of that day, and *then* intimate with most of the more dissipated young men of the day, asked me one night at the Gaming table, where I thought *his Soul* would be found after death? I answered him, " In *Silver Hell* " (a cant name for a second rate Gambling house).

22

When the Honble J. W. Ward quitted the Whigs, he facetiously demanded, at Sir James Macintosh's table, in the presence of Mad^e de Staël, Malthus, and a large and goodly company of all parties and countries, " what it would take to *re-whig him,* as he thought of turning again ". " Before you can be *re-whigged*" (said I), " I am afraid you must be *re-Warded.*" This pun has been attributed to others : they are welcome to it ; but it was mine notwithstanding, as a numerous company and Ward himself doth know. I believe Luttrel versified it afterwards to put into the *M. Chronicle*—at least the late Lady Melbourne told me so. Ward took it good-humouredly at the time.

23

When Sheridan was on his death-bed, Rogers aided him with purse and person : this was particularly kind in Rogers, who always spoke ill of Sheridan (to me at least) ; but indeed he does that of every-body to any body. Rogers is the reverse of the line

" The *best good man* with the *worst natured* Muse ",
being

" The *worst* good man with the *best* natured Muse ".

His Muse being all Sentiment and Sago and Sugar, while he himself is a venomous talker. I say " *worst good* man " because he is (perhaps) a *good* man—at least he does good now and then, as well he may, to purchase himself a shilling's worth of Salvation for his Slanders. They are so *little* too—small talk, and old Womanny ; and he is malignant too, and envious, and—he be damned !

24

Curran ! Curran's the Man who struck me most. Such Imagination ! There never was any thing like it, that ever I saw or heard of. His *published* life, his published speeches, give you *no* idea of the Man—none at all. He was a *Machine* of Imagination, as some one said that Piron was an " Epigrammatic Machine ".

I did not see a great deal of Curran—only in 1813 ; but I met him at home (for he used to call on me), and in society, at Mac'Intosh's, Holland House, etc., etc., etc., and he was wonderful, even to me, who had seen many remarkable men of the time.

25

A young American, named Coolidge, called on me not many months ago : he was intelligent, very handsome, and not more than twenty years old according to appearances. A little romantic, but that sits well upon youth, and mighty fond of poesy as may be suspected from his approaching me in my cavern. He brought me a message from an old Servant of my family (Joe Murray), and told me that *he* (Mr. Coolidge) had obtained a copy of my bust from Thorwal[d]sen at Rome, to send to America. I confess I was more flattered by this young enthusiasm of a solitary trans-atlantic traveller, than if they had decreed me a Statue in the Paris Pantheon (I have seen Emperors and demagogues cast down from their pedestals even in my own time, and Grattan's name razed from the Street called after him in Dublin) I say that I was more flattered by it, because it was *single, un-political,* and was without motive or ostentation—the pure and warm feeling of a boy for the poet he admired. It must have been expensive though. *I* would not pay the price of a Thorwaldsen bust for any human head and shoulders, except Napoleon's, or my children's, or

some " *absurd Womankind's* " as Monkbarns calls them, or my
Sister's. If asked, *why* then I sate for my own—answer, that it
was at the request particular of J. C. Hobhouse, Esqre, and for
no one else. A *picture* is a different matter—every body sits
for their picture; but a bust looks like putting up pretensions
to permanency, and smacks something of a hankering for *public*
fame rather than private remembrance.

26

One of the cleverest men I ever knew in Conversation was
Scrope Beardmore Davies. Hobhouse is also very good in that
line, though it is of less consequence to a man who has other
ways of showing his talents than in company. Scrope was
always ready, and often witty : Hobhouse is witty, but not
always so ready, being more diffident.

27

A drunken man ran against Hobhouse in the Street. A
companion of the Drunkard, not much less so, cried out to
Hobhouse, " *An't* you ashamed to run against a drunken man?
couldn't you see that he was *drunk*? " " Damn him " (answered
Hobhouse) " isn't *he* ashamed to run against *me*? couldn't he
see that *I* was *sober*? "

28

When Brummell was obliged (by that affair of poor Meyler,
who thence acquired the name of " Dick the Dandy-killer "—
it was about money and debt and all that) to retire to France,
he knew no French ; and having obtained a Grammar for the
purposes of Study, our friend Scrope Davies was asked what
progress Brummell had made in French, to which he re-
sponded, " that B. had been stopped like Buonaparte in
Russia by the *Elements* ". I have put this pun into " Beppo ",
which is " a fair exchange and no robbery " ; for Scrope made
his fortune at several dinners (as he owned himself), by repeating occasionally as his own some of the buffooneries with
which I had encountered him in the Morning.

29

I liked the Dandies ; they were always very civil to *me*,
though in general they disliked literary people, and persecuted

and mystified Me de Staël, Lewis, Horace Twiss, and the like, damnably. They persuaded Me de Staël that Alvanley [1] had a hundred thousand a year, etc., etc., till she praised him to his *face* for his *beauty*! and made a set at him for Albertine (*Libertine*, as Brummell baptized her, though the poor Girl was and is as correct as maid or wife can be, and very amiable withal), and a hundred fooleries besides.

The truth is, that, though I gave up the business early, I had a tinge of Dandyism in my minority, and probably retained enough of it, to conciliate the great ones; at four and twenty. I had gamed, and drank, and taken my degrees in most dissipations; and having no pedantry, and not being overbearing, we ran quietly together. I knew them all more or less, and they made me a Member of Watier's (a superb Club at that time), being, I take it, the only literary man (except *two others*, both men of the world, M. and S.) in it.

Our Masquerade was a grand one; so was the Dandy Ball, too, at the Argyle, but *that* (the latter) was given by the four Chiefs, B., M., A., and P., if I err not.

30

I was a Member of the Alfred too, being elected while in Greece. It was pleasant—a little too sober and literary, and bored with Sotheby and Sir Francis D'Ivernois! but one met Peel, and Ward, and Valentia, and many other pleasant or known people; and was upon the whole a decent resource on a rainy day, in a dearth of parties, or parliament, or an empty season.

31

I belonged, or belong, to the following Clubs or Societies :— to the Alfred, to the Cocoa tree, to Watier's, to the Union, to Racket's (at Brighton), to the Pugilistic, to the Owls or " Fly by Night ", to the *Cambridge* Whig Club, to the Harrow Club, Cambridge, and to one or two private Clubs, to the Hampden political Club, and to the Italian Carbonari, etc., etc., etc., " though last *not least* ". I got into all these, and never stood for any other—at least to my own knowledge. I declined being proposed to several others; though pressed to stand Candidate.

---

[1] Lord Alvanley was a renowned dandy and wit, but notably ill-favoured : see Dighton's caricature " Going to White's ".

32

If the papers lie not (which they generally do), Demetrius Zograffo of Athens is at the head of the Athenian part of the present Greek Insurrection. He was my Servant in 1809, 1810, 1811, 1812, at different intervals in those years (for I left him in Greece when I went to Constantinople), and accompanied me to England in 1811. He returned to Greece, Spring 1812. He was a clever, but not *apparently* an enterprizing, man ; but Circumstances make men. His two sons (*then* infants) were named Miltiades and Alcibiades. May the Omen be happy !

33

I have a notion that Gamblers are as happy as most people, being always *excited*. Women, wine, fame, the table, even Ambition, *sate* now and then ; but every turn of the card, and cast of the dice, keeps the Gamester alive : besides one can Game ten times longer than one can do any thing else.

I was very fond of it when young, that is to say, of " Hazard " ; for I hate all *Card* Games, even Faro. When Macco (or whatever they spell it) was introduced, I gave up the whole thing ; for I loved and missed the *rattle* and *dash* of the box and dice, and the glorious uncertainty, not only of good luck or bad luck, but of *any luck at all*, as one had sometimes to throw *often* to decide at all.

I have thrown as many as fourteen mains running, and carried off all the cash upon the table occasionally ; but I had no coolness or judgement or calculation. It was the *delight* of the thing that pleased me. Upon the whole, I left off in time without being much a winner or loser. Since one and twenty years of age, I played but little, and then never above a hundred or two, or three.

34

As far as Fame goes (that is to say *living* Fame) I have had my share—perhaps, indeed, *certainly* more than my *deserts*. Some odd instances have occurred to my own experience of the wild and strange places, to which a name may penetrate, and where it may impress. Two years ago (almost three, being in August or July 1819), I received at Ravenna a letter

in *English* verse from *Drontheim* in Norway, written by a
Norwegian, and full of the usual compliments, etc., etc. It is
still somewhere amongst my papers. In the same month, I
received an invitation into *Holstein* from a Mr. Jacobsen (I
think), of Hamburgh ; also (by the same medium), a translation of Medora's song in the " Corsair " by a Westphalian
Baroness (not " Thunderton-tronck "), with some original
verses of hers (very pretty and Klopstock-ish), and a prose translation annexed to them, on the subject of my wife. As they
concerned *her* more than me, I sent them to her together with
Mr. J.'s letter. It was odd enough to receive an invitation to
pass the *summer* in *Holstein*, while in *Italy*, from people I never
knew. The letter was addressed to Venice. Mr. J. talked to
me of the " wild roses growing in the Holstein summer " :
why then did the Cimbri and Teutones emigrate?

What a strange thing is life and man? Were I to present
myself at the door of the house, where my daughter now is, the
door would be shut in my face, unless (as is not impossible) I
knocked down the porter ; and if I had gone in that year (and
perhaps now) to Drontheim (the furthest town in Norway),
or into Holstein, I should have been received with open arms
into the mansions of Stranger and foreigners, attached to me
by no tie but that of mind and rumour.

As far as *Fame* goes, I have had my share : it has indeed
been leavened by other human contingencies, and this in a
greater degree than has occurred to most literary men of a
decent rank in life ; but on the whole I take it that such equi-
poise is the condition of humanity.

I doubt sometimes whether, after all, a quiet and unagitated
life would have suited me : yet I sometimes long for it. My
earliest dreams (as most boys' dreams are) were martial ; but
a little later they were all for *love* and retirement, till the hopeless attachment to M. C. began, and continued (though sedul-
ously concealed) *very* early in my teens ; and so upwards for a
time. *This* threw me out again " alone on a wide, wide sea ".

In the year 1804, I recollect meeting my Sister at General
Harcourt's in Portland Place. I was then *one* thing, and *as*
she had always till then found me. When we met again in
1805 (she told me since), that my temper and disposition were
so completely altered, that I was hardly to be recognized. I

was not then sensible of the change, but I can believe it, and account for it.

35

A private play being got up at Cambridge, a Mr. *Tulk*, greatly to the inconvenience of Actors and audience, declined his part on a sudden, so that it was necessary to make an apology to the Company.   In doing this, Hobhouse (indignant like all the rest at this inopportune caprice of the Seceder) stated to the audience " that in consequence of *a* Mr. Tulk having unexpectedly thrown up his part, they must request their indulgence, etc., etc."   Next day, the furious Tulk demanded of Hobhouse, " did you, Sir, or did you not use *that* expression? " " Sir," (said Hobhouse) " I *did* or *did not* use that expression." " Perhaps " (said Scrope Davies, who was present), " you object to the *indefinite article*, and prefer being entitled *the Mr. Tulk?* "   *The* Tulk eyed Scrope indignantly ; but aware, probably, that the said Scrope, besides being a profane Jester, had the misfortune to be a very good shot, and had already fought two or three duels, he retired without further objections to either article, except a conditional menace—*if* he should ascertain that an intention, etc., etc., etc.

36

I have been called in as Mediator or Second at least twenty times in violent quarrels, and have always contrived to settle the business without compromising the honour of the parties, or leading them to mortal consequences ; and this too sometimes in very difficult and delicate circumstances, and having to deal with very hot and haughty Spirits—Irishmen, Gamesters, Guardsmen, Captains and Cornets of horse, and the like.   This was of course in my youth, when I lived in hot-headed company.   I have had to carry challenges from Gentlemen to Noblemen, from Captains to Captains, from lawyers to Counsellors, and once from a Clergyman to an officer in the Life-guards.   It may seem strange, but I found the latter by far the most difficult

" . . . to compose
The bloody duel without blows ".

The business being about a woman.   I must add too that I never saw a *woman* behave so ill, like a cold-blooded heartless whore as she was; but very handsome for all that. A certain Susan C. was she called. I never saw her but once, and that was to induce her but to say two words (which in no degree compromised herself), and which would have had the effect of saving a priest or a Lieutenant of Cavalry. She would *not* say them, and neither N. or myself (the Son of Sir E. N. and a friend of one of the parties) could prevail upon her to say them, though both of us used to deal in some sort with Womankind. At last I managed to quiet the combatants without her talisman, and, I believe, to her great disappointment. She was the d—st b—h that I ever saw, and I have seen a great many. Though my Clergyman was sure to lose either his life or his living, he was as warlike as the Bishop of Beauvais, and would hardly be pacified: but then he was in love, and that is a martial passion.

37

[Scrawled out by Byron]

38

Somebody asked Schlegel (the Dousterswivel of Madame de Stael) " whether he did not think *Canova* a great Sculptor? " "Ah! " replied the modest Prussian, " did you ever see *my bust* by *Tiecke?* "

39

At Venice, in the year 1817, an order came from Vienna for the Archbishop to go in State to Saint Mark's in his Carriage and four horses, which is much the same as commanding the Lord Mayor of London to proceed through Temple Bar in his Barge.

40

When I met Hudson Lowe, the Jailor, at Lord Holland's, before he sailed for Saint Helena, the discourse turned on the battle of Waterloo. I asked him whether the dispositions of Napoleon were those of a great General: he answered disparageingly, " that they were very *simple* ". I had always thought that a degree of Simplicity was an ingredient of Greatness.

41

I was much struck with the simplicity of Grattan's manners in private life: they were odd, but they were natural. Curran used to take him off bowing to the very ground, and " thanking God that he had no peculiarities of gesture or appearance ", in a way irresistibly ludicrous. And Rogers used to call him " a Sentimental Harlequin "; but Rogers back-bites every body; and Curran, who used to quiz his great friend Godwin to his very face, would hardly respect a fair mark of mimicry in another. To be sure, Curran *was* admirable! To hear his description of the examination of an Irish witness, was next to hearing his own speeches: the latter I never heard, but I have the former.

42

I have heard that, when Grattan made his first speech in the English Commons, it was for some minutes doubtful whether to laugh at or cheer him. The debût of his predecessor, Flood, had been a complete failure, under nearly similar circumstances. But when the ministerial part of our Senators had watched Pitt (their thermometer) for their cue, and saw him nod repeatedly his stately nod of approbation, they took the hint from their huntsman, and broke out into the most rapturous cheers. Grattan's speech indeed deserved them: it was a *chef d'œuvre*. I did not hear *that* speech of his (being then at Harrow), but heard most of his others on the same question; also that on the war of 1815. I differed from his opinion on the latter question, but coincided in the general admiration of his eloquence.

43

At the Opposition Meeting of the peers in 1812 at Lord Grenville's, when Lᵈ Grey and he read to us the correspondence upon Moira's negociation, I sate next to the present Duke of Grafton. When it was over, I turned to him, and said, " What is to be done next? " " Wake the Duke of Norfolk " (who was snoring near us) replied he, " I don't think the Negociators have left anything else for us to do this turn."

44

In the debate, or rather discussion, afterwards in the House of Lords upon that very question, I sate immediately behind Lord Moira, who was extremely annoyed at G.'s speech upon the subject, and while G. was speaking, turned round to me repeatedly, and asked me whether I agreed with him? It was an awkward question to me who had not heard both sides. Moira kept repeating to me, " it was *not so*, it was so and so, etc." I did not know very well what to think, but I sympathized with the acuteness of his feelings upon the subject.

45

Lord Eldon affects an Imitation of two very different Chancellors, Thurlow and Loughborough, and can indulge in an oath now and then. On one of the debates on the Catholic question, when we were either equal or within one (I forget which), I had been sent for in great haste to a Ball, which I quitted, I confess, somewhat reluctantly, to emancipate five Millions of people. I came in late, and did not go immediately into the body of the house, but stood just behind the Woolsack. Eldon turned round, and, catching my eye, immediately said to a peer (who had come to him for a few minutes on the Woolsack, as is the custom of his friends), " Damn them! they'll have it now, by G—d! The vote that is just come in will give it them."

46

When I came of age, some delays on account of some birth and marriage certificates from Cornwall occasioned me not to take my seat for several weeks. When these were over, and I had taken the Oaths, the Chancellor apologized to me for the delay, observing " that these forms were a part of his *duty* ". I begged of him to make no apology, and added (as he certainly had shown no violent hurry) " Your Lordship was exactly like ' Tom Thumb ' (which was then being acted), You did your *duty*, and you did *no more* ".

47

In a certain Capital abroad, the Minister's Secretary (the Minister being then absent) was piqued that I did not call upon him. When I was going away, Mr. W., an acquaintance of mine, applied to him for my passport, which was sent, but at the same time accompanied by a formal note from the Secretary stating " that at *Mr. W.'s request* he had granted, etc.", and in such a manner as appeared to *hint* that it was only to oblige *Mr. W.* that he had given me that which in fact he had no right to refuse to Any-body. I wrote to him the following answer :—" Lord B. presents his Compliments to L., and is extremely obliged to *Mr. W.* for the passport ".

48

There was a Madman of the name of Battersby, that frequented Steevens's and the Prince of Wales's Coffee-houses, about the time when I was leading a loose life about town, before I was of age. One night he came up to some hapless Stranger, whose coat was not to his liking, and said, " Pray, Sir, did the tailor cut your coat in that fashion, or the rats gnaw it? "

49

The following is (I believe) better known. A beau (*dandies* were not then christened) came into the P. of W.'s, and exclaimed, " Waiter, bring me a glass of Madeira Negus with a Jelly, and rub my plate with a Chalotte ". This in a very soft tone of voice. A Lieutenant of the Navy, who sate in the next box, immediately roared out the following rough parody : " Waiter, bring me a glass of d—d stiff Grog, and rub my a—e with a brick-bat."

50

Sotheby is a good man, rhymes well (if not wisely), but is a bore. He seizes you by the button. One night of a route at Mrs. Hope's, he had fastened upon me (something about Agamemnon, or Orestes, or some of his plays), notwithstanding my symptoms of manifest distress (for I was in love, and had just nicked a minute, when neither mothers, nor husbands, nor rivals, nor gossips, were near my then idol, who was beautiful as the Statues of the Gallery where we stood at the time)— Sotheby I say had seized upon me by the button and the heartstrings, and spared neither. W. Spencer, who likes fun, and don't dislike mischief, saw my case, and coming up to us both, took me by the hand, and pathetically bade me farewell : " for," said he, " I see it is all over with you ". Sotheby then went away. " Sic me servavit Apollo."

51

It is singular how soon we lose the impression of what ceases to be *constantly* before us. A year impairs, a lustre obliterates. There is little distinct left without an *effort* of memory : *then* indeed the lights are rekindled for a moment; but who can be sure that Imagination is not the torch-bearer? Let any man try at the end of *ten* years to bring before him the features, or the mind, or the sayings, or the habits, of his best friend, or his *greatest* man (I mean his favourite—his Buonaparte, his this, that or 'tother), and he will be surprized at the extreme confusion of his ideas. I speak confidently on this point, having always past for one who had a good, aye, an excellent memory. I except indeed our recollections of Womankind : there is no forgetting *them* (and be d—d to them) any more than any other remarkable Era, such as " the revolution ", or " the plague ", or " the Invasion ", or " the Comet ", or " the War " of such and such an Epoch—being the favourite dates of Mankind, who have so many *blessings* in their lot, that they never make their Calendars from them, being too common. For instance, you see " the great drought ", " the Thames frozen over ", " the Seven years war broke out ", the E. or F. or S. " Revolution commenced ", " The Lisbon Earthquake ", " the Lima Earthquake ", " The Earthquake of Calabria ", the " Plague of London ", " Ditto of Constantinople ", " the Sweating Sickness ", " The Yellow fever of Philadelphia ", etc., etc., etc.; but you don't see " the abundant harvest ", " the fine Summer ", " the long peace ", " the wealthy speculation ", the " wreckless voyage ", recorded so emphatically? By the way, there has been a *thirty years war,* and a *Seventy years war* : was there ever a *Seventy or a thirty years Peace*? Or was there ever even a *day's Universal* peace, except perhaps in China, where they have found out the miserable happiness of a stationary and unwarlike mediocrity? And is all this, because Nature is niggard or savage? or Mankind ungrateful? Let philosophers decide. I am none.

52

In the year 1814, as Moore and I were going to dine with Lord Grey in P. Square, I pulled out a " Java Gazette " (which

Murray had sent to me), in which there was a controversy on our respective merits as poets. It was amusing enough that we should be proceeding peaceably on the same table, while they were squabbling about us in the Indian Seas (to be sure, the paper was dated six months before), and filling columns with Batavian Criticism. But this is fame, I presume.

53

In general, I do not draw well with literary men : not that I dislike them, but I never know what to say to them after I have praised their last publication. There are several exceptions, to be sure ; but then they have either been men of the world, such as Scott, and Moore, etc., or visionaries out of it, such as Shelley, etc. : but your literary every day man and I never went well in company—especially your foreigner, whom I never could abide. Except Giordani, and—and—and—(I really can't name any other) I do not remember a man amongst them, whom I ever wished to see twice, except perhaps Mezzophanti, who is a Monster of Languages, the Briareus of parts of Speech, a walking Polyglott and more, who ought to have existed at the time of the tower of Babel as universal Interpreter. He is indeed a Marvel—unassuming also : I tried him in all the tongues of which I knew a single oath (or adjuration to the Gods against Postboys, Lawyers, Tartars, boatmen, Sailors, pilots, Gondoliers, Muleteers, Camel-drivers, Vetturini, Postmasters, post-horses, post-houses, post-everything), and Egad ! he astounded me even to my English.

54

Three Swedes came to Bologna, knowing no tongue but Swedish. The inhabitants in despair presented them to Mezzophanti. Mezzophanti (though a great Linguist) knew no more Swedish than the Inhabitants. But in two days, by dint of dictionary, he talked with them fluently and freely, so that they were astonished, and every body else, at his acquisition of another tongue in forty eight hours. I had this anecdote first from Me Albrizzi, and afterwards confirmed by *himself*—and he is not a boaster.

55

I sometimes wish that I had studied languages with more attention : those which I know, even the classical (Greek and Latin, in the usual proportion of a sixth form boy), and a smattering of modern Greek, the Armenian and Arabic Alphabets, a few Turkish and Albanian phrases, oaths, or requests, Italian tolerably, Spanish less than tolerably, French to read with ease but speak with difficulty—or rather not at all—all have been acquired by ear or eye, and never by anything like Study. Like " Edie Ochiltree ", " I never dowed to bide a hard turn o' wark in my life ".

To be sure, I set in zealously for the Armenian and Arabic, but I fell in love with some absurd womankind both times, before I had overcome the Characters ; and at Malta and Venice left the profitable Orientalists for—for—(no matter what), notwithstanding that my master, the Padre Pasquale Aucher (for whom, by the way, I compiled the major part of two Armenian and English Grammars), assured me " that the terrestrial Paradise had been certainly in *Armenia* ". I went seeking it—God knows where—did I find it? Umph! Now and then, for a minute or two.

56

Of Actors, Cooke was the most natural, Kemble the most supernatural, Kean a medium between the two, but Mrs. Siddons worth them all put together, of those whom I remember to have seen in England.

57

I have seen Sheridan weep two or three times : it may be that he was maudlin ; but this only renders it more impressive, for who would see—

" From Marlborough's eyes the tears of dotage flow,
And Swift expire a driveller and a show? "

Once I saw him cry at Robins's, the Auctioneer's, after a splendid dinner full of great names and high Spirits. I had the honour of sitting next to Sheridan. The occasion of his tears was some observation or other upon the subject of the sturdiness of the Whigs in resisting Office, and keeping to their principles. Sheridan turned round—" Sir, it is easy for my Lord G., or Earl G., or Marquis B., or Lᵈ H., with thousands upon thousands a year—some of it either *presently* derived or *inherited* in Sinecures or acquisitions from the public money—to boast of their patriotism, and keep aloof from temptation ; but they do not know from what temptations those have kept aloof, who had equal pride—at least equal talents, and not unequal passions, and nevertheless knew not in the course of their lives what it was to have a shilling of their own ". And in saying this he wept.

58

I have more than once heard Sheridan say, that he never " had a shilling of his own " : to be sure, he contrived to extract a good many of other people's.

In 1815, I had occasion to visit my Lawyer in Chancery Lane : he was with Sheridan. After mutual greetings, etc., Sheridan retired first. Before recurring to my own business, I could not help enquiring *that* of S. " Oh " (replied the Attorneo), " the usual thing—to stave off an action from his Wine-Merchant, my Client." " Well " (said I), " and what do you mean to do? " " Nothing at all for the present ", said he : " would you have us proceed against old Sherry? What would be the use of it? " And here he began laughing, and going over Sheridan's good gifts of Conversation. Now, from personal experience, I can vouch that my Attorneo is by no means the tenderest of men, or particularly accessible to any kind of impression out of the Statute or record. And yet Sheridan, in half an hour, had found the way to soften and seduce him in such a manner, that I almost think he would have thrown his Client (an honest man with all the laws and some justice on his side) out of the window, had he come in at the moment. Such was Sheridan ! He could soften an Attorney ! There has been nothing like it since the days of Orpheus.

59

When the Bailiffs (for I have seen most kinds of life) came upon me in 1815, to seize my chattels (being a peer of parliament my person was beyond him), being curious (as is my

habit), I first asked him " what Extents elsewhere he had for
Government? " upon which he showed me one upon *one house
only* for *seventy thousand pounds!* Next I asked him, if he had
nothing for Sheridan? " Oh, Sheridan," said he : " aye, I
have this " (pulling out a pocket-book, etc.). " But, my L.,
I have been in Mr. Sheridan's house a twelve-month at a
time : a civil gentleman—knows how to deal with *us*, etc.,
etc., etc." Our own business was then discussed, which was
none of the easiest for me at that time. But the Man was civil,
and, (what I valued more), communicative. I had met many
of his brethren years before in affairs of my friends (commoners,
that is), but this was the first (or second) on my own account.
A civil Man, feed accordingly : probably he anticipated as
much.

60

No man would live his life over again, is an old and true
saying, which all can resolve for themselves. At the same time,
there are probably *moments* in most men's lives, which they
would live over the rest of life to *regain?* Else, why do we live
at all? Because Hope recurs to Memory, both false ; but—
but—but—but—and this *but* drags on till—What? I do not
know, and who does? " He that died o' Wednesday." By
the way, there is a poor devil to be shot tomorrow here
(Ravenna) for murder. He hath eaten half a Turkey for his
dinner, besides fruit and pudding ; and he refuses to confess?
Shall I go to see him exhale? No. And why? Because it is
to take place at *Nine*. Now, could I *save* him, or a fly even
from the same catastrophe, I would out-match years ; but as I
cannot, I will not get up earlier to see another man shot, than I
would to run the same risk in person. Besides, I have seen more
men than one die that death (and other deaths) before to-day.

It is not cruelty which actuates mankind, but excitement,
on such occasions ; at least, I suppose so. It is detestable to
take life in that way, unless it be to preserve two lives.

61

Old Edgeworth, the fourth or fifth Mrs. Edgeworth, and
the Miss Edgeworth were in London, 1813. Miss Edgeworth
liked, Mrs. Edgeworth not disliked, old Edgeworth a bore—

the worst of bores—a boisterous Bore. I met them in society once at a breakfast of Sir H. D.'s. Old Edgeworth came in late, boasting that he had given " Dr. Parr a dressing the night before " (no such easy matter by the way). I thought *her* pleasant. They all abused Anna Seward's memory.

62

When on the road, they heard of *her* brother's, and *his* Son's, death. What was to be done? Their *London* Apparel was all ordered and made! So they sunk his death for the six weeks of their Sojourn, and went into mourning on their way back to Ireland. *Fact!*

63

While the Colony were in London, there was a book, with a Subscription for the " recall of Mrs. Siddons to the Stage ", going about for signatures. Moore moved for a similar sub-scription for the " recall of *Mr. Edgeworth to Ireland!* "

64

Sir Humphrey Davy told me, that the Scene of the French Valet and Irish postboy in " Ennui " was taken from *his* verbal description to the Edgeworths in Edgeworthtown of a similar fact on the road occurring to himself. So much the better— being *life*.

65

When I was fifteen years of age, it happened that in a Cavern in Derbyshire I had to cross in a boat (in which two people only could lie down) a stream which flows under a rock, with the rock so close upon the water, as to admit the boat only to be pushed on by a ferry-man (a sort of Charon), who wades at the stern stooping all the time. The Companion of my transit was M. A. C[haworth], with whom I had been long in love, and never told it, though *she* had discovered it without. I recollect my sensations, but cannot describe them—and it is as well.

We were a party—a Mr. W., two Miss W.'s, Mr. and Mrs. Cl—ke, Miss M., and *my* M. A. C. Alas! why do I say *My?* Our Union would have healed feuds, in which blood had been shed by our fathers ; it would have joined lands, broad and rich ;

it would have joined at least *one* heart, and two persons not ill-matched in years (she is two years my elder) ; and—and—and—what has been the result? *She* has married a man older than herself, been wretched, and separated. I have married, and am separated : and yet *We* are *not* united.

66

One of my notions, different from those of my contemporaries, is, that the present is not a high age of English Poetry : there are *more* poets (soi-disant) than ever there were, and proportionally *less* poetry.

This *thesis* I have maintained for some years, but, strange to say, it meeteth not with favour from my brethren of the Shell. Even Moore shakes his head, and firmly believes that it is the grand Era of British Poesy.

67

When I belonged to the D[rury] L[ane] Committee, and was one of the S. C. of Management, the number of plays upon the shelves were about *five* hundred. Conceiving that amongst these there must be *some* of merit, in person and by proxy I caused an investigation. I do not think that, of those which I saw, there was one which could be conscientiously tolerated. There never were such things as most of them.

Mathurin [1] was very kindly recommended to me by Walter Scott, to whom I had recourse ; firstly, in the hope that he would do something for us himself; and secondly, in my despair, that he would point out to us any young (or old) writer of promise. Mathurin sent his Bertram, and a letter *without* his address, so that at first I could give him no answer. When I at last hit upon his residence, I sent him a favourable answer, and something more substantial. His play succeeded, but I was at that time absent from England.

I tried Coleridge, too ; but he had nothing feasible in hand at the time. Mr. Sotheby obligingly offered *all* his tragedies, and I pledged myself; and, notwithstanding many squabbles with my Committe[e]d Brethren, did get " Ivan " accepted, read, and the parts distributed. But lo ! in the very heart of

---

[1] The Rev. Charles Robert Maturin, author of *Bertram, or The Castle of Aldobrand, Manuel*, etc., etc. : a dramatist admired by Walter Scott.

the matter, upon some *tepid*-ness on the part of Kean, or warmth on that of the Authour, Sotheby withdrew his play.

Sir J. B. Burgess did also present four tragedies and a farce, and I moved Green-room and S. Committee; but they would not.

Then the Scenes I had to go through! The authours, and the authoresses, the Milliners, the wild Irishmen, the people from Brighton, from Blackwall, from Chatham, from Cheltenham, from Dublin, from Dundee, who came in upon me! To all of whom it was proper to give a civil answer, and a hearing, and a reading. Mrs. Glover's father, an Irish dancing-Master of Sixty years, called upon me to request to play " *Archer* ", drest in silk stockings on a frosty morning, to show his legs (which were certainly good and Irish for his age, and had been still better). Miss Emma Somebody, with a play entitled the " Bandit of Bohemia ", or some such title or production. Mr. O'Higgins, then resident at Richmond, with an Irish tragedy, in which the unities could not fail to be observed, for the protagonist was chained by the leg to a pillar during the chief part of the performance. He was a wild man, of a salvage [*sic*] appearance; and the difficulty of *not* laughing at him was only to be got over by reflecting upon the probable consequences of such cachinnation.

As I am really a civil and polite person, and *do* hate giving pain, when it can be avoided, I sent them up to Douglas Kinnaird, who is a man of business, and sufficiently ready with a negative, and left them to settle with him. And, as at the beginning of next year, I went abroad, I have since been little aware of the progress of the theatres.

68

Players are said to be an impracticable people. They are so. But I managed to steer clear of any disputes with them, and, excepting one debate with the Elder Byrne about Miss Smith's Pas de (Something—I forget the technicals), I do not remember any litigation of my own. I used to protect Miss Smith, because she was like Lady Jane Harley in the face; and likenesses go a great way with me. Indeed, in general, I left such things to my more bustling colleagues, who used to reprove me seriously for not being able to take such things in hand without buffooning with the Histrions, and throwing things into confusion by treating light matters with levity.

69

Then the Committee!—then the Sub-Committee! We were but few, and never agreed! There was Peter Moore who contradicted Kinnaird, and Kinnaird who contradicted everybody: then our two managers, Rae and Dibdin, and our Secretary, Ward! And yet we were all very zealous and in earnest to do good, and so forth. Hobhouse furnished us with prologues to our revived Old English plays, but was not pleased with me for complimenting him as " the *Upton* " of our theatre (Mr. Upton is or was the poet who writes the songs for Astley's), and almost gave up prologuizing in consequence.

70

In the Pantomime of 1815–16, there was a Representation of the Masquerade of 1814, given by " us Youth " of Watier's Club to Wellington and Co. Douglas Kinnaird, and one or two others with myself, put on Masques, and went *on* the Stage amongst the " οἱ πολλοί ", to see the effect of a theatre from the Stage. It is very grand. Douglas danced among the figuranti, too ; and they were puzzled to find out who we were, as being more than their number. It was odd enough that D. K. and I should have been both at the *real* Masquerade, and afterwards in the Mimic one of the same on the stage of D. L. Theatre.

71

When I was a youth, I was reckoned a good actor. Besides " Harrow Speeches " (in which I shone) I enacted " Penruddock " in the " Wheel of Fortune ", and " Tristram Fickle " in Allingham's farce of " the Weathercock ", for three nights (the duration of our compact), in some private theatricals at Southwell in 1806, with great applause. The occasional prologue for our volunteer play was also of my composition. The other performers were young ladies and gentlemen of the neighbourhood ; and the whole went off with great effect upon our good-natured audience.

72

When I first went up to College, it was a new and a heavy hearted scene for me. Firstly, I so much disliked leaving Harrow, that, though it was time (I being seventeen), it broke my very rest for the last quarter with counting the days that remained. I always *hated* Harrow till the last year and half, but then I liked it. Secondly, I wished to go to Oxford and not to Cambridge. Thirdly, I was so completely alone in this new world, that it half broke my Spirits. My companions were not unsocial, but the contrary—lively, hospitable, of rank, and fortune, and gay far beyond my gaiety. I mingled with, and dined and supped, etc., with them; but, I know not how, it was one of the deadliest and heaviest feelings of my life to feel that I was no longer a boy. From that moment I began to grow old in my own esteem; and in my esteem age is not estimable. I took my gradations in the vices with great promptitude, but they were not to my taste; for my early passions, though violent in the extreme, were concentrated, and hated division or spreading abroad. I could have left or lost the world with or for that which I loved; but, though my temperament was naturally burning, I could not share in the common place libertinism of the place and time without disgust. And yet this very disgust, and my heart thrown back upon itself, threw me into excesses perhaps more fatal than those from which I shrunk, as fixing upon one (at a time) the passions, which, spread amongst many, would have hurt only myself.

73

People have wondered at the Melancholy which runs through my writings. Others have wondered at my personal gaiety; but I recollect once, after an hour, in which I had been sincerely and particularly gay, and rather brilliant, in company, my wife replying to me when I said (upon her remarking my high spirits) " and yet, Bell, I have been called and mis-called Melancholy—you must have seen how falsely, frequently ". " No, B.," (she answered) " it is not so : at *heart* you are the most melancholy of mankind, and often when apparently gayest."

74

If I could explain at length the *real* causes which have contributed to increase this perhaps *natural* temperament of mine,
this Melancholy which hath made me a bye-word, nobody
would wonder ; but this is impossible without doing much mischief.   I do not know what other men's lives have been, but I
cannot conceive anything more strange than some of the earlier
parts of mine.   I have written my memoirs, but omitted *all*
the really *consequential* and *important* parts, from deference to the
dead, to the living, and to those who must be both.

75

I sometimes think that I should have written the *whole* as a
lesson, but it might have proved a *lesson* to be *learnt* rather than
avoided; for passion is a whirlpool, which is not to be viewed
nearly without attraction from its Vortex.

76

I must not go on with these reflections, or I shall be letting
out some secret or other to paralyze posterity.

77

One night, Scrope Davies at a gaming house (before I was
of age), being tipsy as he usually was at the Midnight hour,
and having lost monies, was in vain intreated by his friends,
one degree less intoxicated than himself, to come or go home.
In despair, he was left to himself, and to the demons of the dice-
box.   Next day, being visited, about two of the Clock, by some
friends just risen with a severe headache and empty pockets
(who had left him losing at four or five in the morning), he was
found in a sound sleep, without a night-cap, and not particularly encumbered with bed-cloathes : a Chamber-pot stood
by his bed-side, *brim-full* of —— *Bank Notes !* all won, God knows
how, and crammed, Scrope knew not where ; but *there* they
were, all good legitimate notes, and to the amount of some
thousand pounds.

78

At Brighthelmstone (I love orthography at length), in the
year 1808, Hobhouse, Scrope Davies, Major Cooper, and my-

self, having dined together with Lord Delvin, Count (I forget the french Emigrant nomenclature) and others, did about the middle of the night (we *four*) proceed to a house of Gambling, being then *amongst us* possest of about *twenty guineas* of ready cash, with which we had to maintain as many of your whorson horses and servants, besides house-hold and whore-hold expenditure. We had, I say, twenty guineas or so, and we lost them, returning home in bad humour. Cooper went home. Scrope and Hobhouse and I (it being high Summer), did firstly strip and plunge into the Sea, whence, after half an hour's swimming of those of us (Scrope and I) who could swim, we emerged in our dressing-gowns to discuss a bottle or two of Champaigne and Hock (according to choice) at our quarters. In course of this discussion, words arose; Scrope seized H. by the throat; H. seized a knife in self-defence, and stabbed Scrope in the shoulder to avoid being throttled. Scrope fell bathed in blood and wine—for the *bottle* fell with him, being infinitely intoxicated with Gaming, Sea-bathing at two in the morning, and Supplementary Champaigne. The skirmish had past before I had time or thought to interfere. Of course I lectured against gambling—

" Pugnare Thracum est ",

and then examined Scrope's wound, which proved to be a gash long and broad, but not deep nor dangerous. Scrope was furious : first he wanted to fight, then to go away in a post-chaise, and then to *shoot* himself, which latter intention I offered to forward, provided that he did not use *my pistols*, which, in case of suicide, would become a deo-dand to the King. At length, with many oaths and some difficulty, he was gotten to bed. In the morning, Cool reflection and a Surgeon came, and, by dint of loss of blood, and sticking plaister, the quarrel (which Scrope had begun), was healed as well as the wound, and we were all friends as for years before and after.

79

My first dash into poetry was as early as 1800. It was the ebullition of a passion for my first Cousin Margaret Parker (daughter and grand-daughter of the two Admirals Parker), one of the most beautiful of evanescent beings. I have long forgotten the verses, but it would be difficult for me to forget her. Her dark eyes! her long eye-lashes! her completely Greek cast of face and figure! I was then about twelve—She rather older, perhaps a year. She died about a year or two afterwards, in consequence of a fall which injured her spine and induced consumption. Her Sister, Augusta (by some thought still more beautiful), died of the same malady; and it was indeed in attending her that Margaret met with the accident, which occasioned her own death. My Sister told me that, when she went to see her shortly before her death, upon accidentally mentioning my name, Margaret coloured through the paleness of mortality to the eyes, to the great astonishment of my Sister, who (residing with her Grandmother, Lady Holderness) saw at that time but little of me for family reasons, knew nothing of our attachment, nor could conceive why my name should affect her at such a time. I knew nothing of her illness (being at Harrow and in the country), till she was gone.

Some years after, I made an attempt at an Elegy. A very dull one. I do not recollect scarcely any thing equal to the *transparent* beauty of my cousin, or to the sweetness of her temper, during the short period of our intimacy. She looked as if she had been made out of a rainbow—all beauty and peace.

My passion had its usual effects upon me: I could not sleep, could not eat; I could not rest; and although I had reason to know that she loved me, it was the torture of my life to think of the time which must elapse before we could meet again—being usually about *twelve hours* of separation! But I was a fool then, and am not much wiser now.

80

My passions were developed very early—so early, that few would believe me, if I were to state the period, and the facts which accompanied it. Perhaps this was one of the reasons which caused the anticipated melancholy of my thoughts—having anticipated life.

My earlier poems are the thoughts of one at least ten years older than the age at which they were written: I don't mean for their solidity, but their Experience. The two first Cantos of C^e H^d were completed at twenty two, and they are written as if by a man older than I shall probably ever be.

[81 omitted by Byron]

82

Upon Parnassus, going to the fountain of Delphi (Castri), in 1809, I saw a flight of twelve Eagles (Hobhouse says they are Vultures—at least in conversation), and I seized the Omen. On the day before, I composed the lines to Parnassus (in Childe Harold), and, on beholding the birds, had a hope that Apollo had accepted my homage. I have at least had the name and fame of a Poet during the poetical period of life (from twenty to thirty) : whether it will last is another matter ; but I *have been* a votary of the Deity and the place, and am grateful for what he has done in my behalf, leaving the future in his hands as I left the past.

83

Like Sylla, I have always believed that all things depend upon Fortune, and nothing upon ourselves. I am not aware of any one thought or action worthy of being called good to myself or others, which is not to be attributed to the Good Goddess, Fortune !

84

Two or three years ago, I thought of going to one of the Americas, English or Spanish. But the accounts sent from England, in consequence of my enquiries, discouraged me. After all, I believe most countries, properly balanced, are equal to *a Stranger* (by no means to the *native*, though). I remembered General Ludlow's domal inscription :—

" Omne solum forti patria "—

And sate down free in a country of Slavery for many centuries. But there is *no* freedom, even for *Masters*, in the midst of slaves : it makes my blood boil to see the thing. I sometimes wish that I was the Owner of Africa, to do at once, what Wilberforce will do in time, viz.—sweep Slavery from her desarts, and look on upon the first dance of their Freedom.

As to *political* slavery—so general—it is man's own fault ; if they *will* be slaves, let them ! Yet it is but " a word and a blow ". See how England formerly, France, Spain, Portugal,

America, Switzerland, freed themselves! There is no one instance of a *long* contest, in which *men* did not triumph over Systems. If Tyranny misses her *first* spring, she is cowardly as the tiger, and retires to be hunted.

85

An Italian (the younger Count Ruota), writing from Ravenna to his friend at Rome in 1820, says of me, by way of compliment, " that in society no one would take me for an Englishman, though he believes that I *am* English at bottom— my manners were so different ". This he meant as a grand eulogy, and I accept it as such. The letter was shown to me this year by the Correspondent, Count P. G., or by his Sister.

86

I have been a reviewer. In " the Monthly Review " I wrote some articles, which were inserted. This was in the latter part of 1811. In 1807, in a Magazine called " Monthly Literary Recreations ", I reviewed Wordsworth's trash of that time. Excepting these, I cannot accuse myself of anonymous Criticism (that I recollect), though I have been *offered* more than one review in our principal Journals.

87

Till I was eighteen years old (odd as it may seem), I had never read a review. But, while at Harrow, my general information was so great on modern topics, as to induce a suspicion that I could only collect so much information from *reviews*, because I was never *seen* reading, but always idle and in mischief, or at play. The truth is that I read eating, read in bed, read when no one else reads; and had read all sorts of reading since I was five years old, and yet never *met* with a review, which is the only reason that I know of why I should not have read them. But it is true; for I remember when Hunter and Curzon, in 1804, told me this opinion at Harrow, I made them laugh by my ludicrous astonishment in asking them, " *what is* a review? " To be sure, they were then less common. In three years more, I was better acquainted with that same, but the first I ever read was in 1806–7.

88

At School, I was (as I have said) remarked for the extent and readiness of my *general* information; but in all other respects idle; capable of great sudden exertions (such as thirty or forty Greek Hexameters—of course with such prosody as it pleased God), but of few continuous drudgeries. My qualities were much more oratorical and martial, than poetical; and Dr. D., my grand patron (our head-master), had a great notion that I should turn out an Orator, from my fluency, my turbulence, my voice, my copiousness of declamation, and my action. I remember that my first declamation astonished him into some unwonted (for he was economical of such), and sudden compliments, before the declaimers at our first rehearsal. My first Harrow verses (that is, English as exercises), a translation of a chorus from the Prometheus of Aeschylus, were received by him but cooly: no one had the least notion that I should subside into poesy.

89

Peel, the Orator and Statesman ("that was, or is, or is to be "), was my form fellow, and we were both at the top of our remove (a public School Phrase). We were on good terms, but his brother was my intimate friend. There were always great hopes of Peel amongst us all—Masters and Scholars, and he has not disappointed them. As a Scholar, he was greatly my superior: as a declaimer, and Actor, I was reckoned at least his equal. As a school boy *out* of school, I was always *in* scrapes, and *he never*; and *in School* he *always* knew his lesson, and I rarely; but when I knew it, I knew it nearly as well. In general information, history, etc., etc., I think I was *his* Superior, as also of most boys of my standing.

89 [twice]

The prodigy of our School days was George Sinclair (son of Sir John): he made exercises for half the School (*literally*), verses at will, and themes without it. When in the Shell, he made exercises for his Uncle, Dudley Macdonald (a dunce who could only play upon the flute), in the sixth. He was a friend of mine, and in the same remove, and used at times to beg me to let him do my exercise—a request always most readily accorded, upon a pinch, or when I wanted to do something else, which was usually once an hour. On the other hand, he was pacific, and I savage; so I fought for him, or thrashed others for him, or thrashed himself to make him thrash others, whom it was necessary, as a point of honour and stature, that he should so chastise. Or, we talked politics, for he was a great politician, and were very good friends. I have some of his letters, written to me from School, still.

90

Clayton was another School Monster of learning, and talent, and hope; but what has become of him I do not know: he was certainly a Genius.

91

My School friendships were with *me passions* (for I was always violent), but I do not know that there is one which has endured (to be sure, some have been cut short by death) till now. That with Lord Clare began one of the earliest and lasted longest, being only interrupted by distance, that I know of. I never hear the word " *Clare* " without a beating of the heart even *now*, and I write it with the feelings of 1803-4-5 ad infinitum.

92

In 1812, at Middelton (Lord Jersey's), amongst a goodly company of Lords, Ladies, and wits, etc., there was poor old Vice Leach, the lawyer, attempting to play off the fine gentleman. His first exhibition—an attempt on horseback, I think, to escort the women—God knows where, in the month of November, ended in a fit of the Lumbago—as Lord Ogleby says, " a grievous enemy to Gallantry and address "—and if he could but have heard Lady Jersey quizzing him (as I did) next day for the *cause* of his malady, I don't think that he would have turned a " Squire of dames " in a hurry again. He seemed to me the greatest fool (in that line) I ever saw. This was the last I saw of old Vice Leach, except in town, where he was creeping into assemblies, and trying to look young and gentlemanly.

93

Erskine too! Erskine was there—good, but intolerable. He jested, he talked, he did every thing admirably, but then he *would* be applauded for the same thing twice over: he would read his own verses, his own paragraphs, and tell his own story, again and again—and then " the trial by Jury!!! " I almost wished it abolished, for I sate next him at dinner. As I had read his published speeches, there was no occasion to repeat them to me.

Chester (the fox hunter), surnamed " *Cheeks Chester* ", and I sweated the Claret, being the only two who did so. Cheeks, who loves his bottle, and had no notion of meeting with a " bon vivant " in a scribbler, in making my eulogy to somebody one evening, summed it up in—" By G—d, he *drinks like a Man!* "

94

Nobody drank, however, but Cheeks and I. To be sure, there was little occasion, for we swept off what was on the table (a most splendid board, as may be supposed, at Jersey's) very sufficiently. However, we carried our liquor discreetly, like " the Baron of Bradwardine ".

95

If I had to live over again, I do not know what I would change in my life, unless it were *for not to have lived at all.* All history and experience, and the rest, teaches us that the good and evil are pretty equally balanced in this existence, and that what is most to be desired is an easy passage out of it.

What can it give us but *years*? and those have little of good but their ending.

96

Of the Immortality of the Soul, it appears to me that there can be little doubt, if we attend for a moment to the action of Mind. It is in perpetual activity. I used to doubt of it, but reflection has taught me better. It acts also so very independent of body: in dreams for instance incoherently and madly, I grant you; but still it is *Mind*, and much more *Mind* than when we are awake. Now, that *this* should not act *separately*, as well as jointly, who can pronounce? The Stoics, Epictetus and Marcus Aurelius, call the present state " a Soul which drags a Carcase ": a heavy chain, to be sure; but all chains, being material, may be shaken off.

How far our future life will be individual, or, rather, how far it will at all resemble our *present* existence, is another question ; but that the *Mind* is *eternal*, seems as probable as that the body is not so. Of course, I have ventured upon the question without recurring to Revelation, which, however, is at least as rational a solution of it as any other.

A *material* resurrection seems strange, and even absurd, except for purposes of punishment ; and all punishment, which is to *revenge* rather than *correct*, must be *morally wrong*. And *when* the *World is at an end*, what moral or warning purpose *can* eternal tortures answer? Human passions have probably disfigured the divine doctrines here, but the whole thing is inscrutable. It is useless to tell me *not* to *reason*, but to *believe*. You might as well tell a man not to wake but *sleep*. And then to *bully* with torments ! and all that ! I cannot help thinking that the *menace* of Hell makes as many devils, as the severe penal codes of inhuman humanity make villains.

Man is born *passionate* of body, but with an innate though secret tendency to the love of Good in his Mainspring of Mind. But God help us all ! It is at present a sad jar of atoms.

97

Matter is eternal, always changing, but reproduced, and, as far as we can comprehend Eternity, Eternal ; and why not *Mind*? Why should not the Mind act with and upon the Universe? as portions of it act upon and with the congregated dust called Mankind? See, how one man acts upon himself and others, or upon multitudes? The same Agency, in a higher and purer degree, may act upon the Stars, etc., ad infinitum.

98

I have often been inclined to Materialism in philosophy but could never bear its introduction into *Christianity*, which appears to me essentially founded upon the *Soul*. For this reason, Priestley's Christian Materialism always struck me as deadly. Believe the resurrection of the body, if you will, but *not without* a Soul. The devil's in it, if, after having had a Soul (as surely the *Mind*, or whatever you call it, *is*) in this world, we must part with it in the next, even for an Immortal Materiality. I own my partiality for *Spirit*.

99

I am always most religious upon a sun-shiny day; as if there was some association between an internal approach to greater light and purity, and the kindler of this dark lanthorn of our eternal existence.

100

The Night is also a religious concern; and even more so, when I viewed the Moon and Stars through Herschell's telescope, and saw that they were worlds.

101

If, according to some speculations, you could prove the World many thousand years older than the Mosaic Chronology, or if you could knock up Adam and Eve and the Apple and Serpent, still what is to be put up in their stead? or how is the difficulty removed? Things must have had a beginning, and what matters it *when* or *how*?

I sometimes think that *Man* may be the relic of some higher material being, wrecked in a former world, and degenerated in the hardships and struggle through Chaos into Conformity— or something like it; as we see Laplanders, Esquimaux, etc., inferior in the present state, as the Elements become more inexorable. But even then this higher pre-Adamite supposititious Creation must have had an Origin and a *Creator*; for a *Creator* is a more natural imagination than a fortuitous concourse of atoms. All things remount to a fountain, though they may flow to an Ocean.

102

What a strange thing is the propagation of life! A bubble of Seed which may be spilt in a whore's lap—or in the orgasm of a voluptuous dream—might (for aught we know) have formed a Caesar or a Buonaparte: there is nothing remarkable recorded of their Sires, that I know of.

103

Lord Kames has said (if I misquote not), " that a power to call up agreeable ideas at will would be something greater for mortals than all the boons of a fairy tale ".

I have found increasing upon me (without sufficient cause at times) the depression of Spirits (with few intervals), which I have some reason to believe constitutional or inherited.

104

Plutarch says, in his life of Lysander, that Aristotle observes, " that in general great Geniuses are of a melancholy turn, and instances Socrates, Plato, and Hercules (or Heracleitus), as examples, and Lysander, though not *while* young, yet as inclined to it when approaching towards age ".   Whether I am a Genius or not, I have been called such by my friends as well as enemies, and in more countries and languages than one, and also within a no very long period of existence.   Of my Genius, I can say nothing, but of my melancholy, that it is " increasing and ought to be diminished "—but how?

105

I take it that most men are so at bottom, but that it is only remarked in the remarkable.   The Duchesse de Broglie, in reply to a remark of mine on the errors of clever people, said, " that they were not *worse* than others, only being more in view, more noted, especially in all that could reduce them to the rest, or raise the rest to them ".   In 1816, this was.

106

In fact (I suppose that), if the follies of fools were all set down like those of the wise, the wise (who seem at present only a better sort of fools), would appear almost intelligent.

107

I have met George Colman occasionally, and thought him extremely pleasant and convivial.   Sheridan's humour, or rather wit, was always saturnine, and sometimes savage : he never laughed (at least that *I* saw, and I watched him), but Colman did.   I have got very drunk with them both ; but, if I had to *choose*, and could not have both at a time, I should say, " let me begin the evening with Sheridan, and finish it with Colman ".   Sheridan for dinner—Colman for Supper. Sheridan for Claret or port ; but Colman for every thing, from the Madeira and Champaigne at dinner—the Claret with a *layer* of *port* between the Glasses—up to the Punch of the Night, and down to the Grog or Gin and water of day-break. All these I have threaded with both the same. Sheridan was a Grenadier Company of Life-Guards, but Colman a whole regiment—of *light Infantry*, to be sure, but still a *regiment*.

108

Alcibiades is said to have been "successful in all his battles"; but *what* battles? Name them! If you mention Caesar, or Annibal, or Napoleon, you at once rush upon Pharsalia, Munda, Alesia, Cannae, Thrasimene, Trebia, Lodi, Marengo, Jena, Austerlitz, Friedland, Wagram, Moskwa; but it is less easy to pitch upon the victories of Alcibiades, though they may be named too—though not so readily as the Leuctra and Mantinea of Epaminondas, the Marathon of Miltiades, the Salamis of Themistocles, and the Thermopylae of Leonidas.

Yet upon the whole it may be doubted, whether there be a name of Antiquity, which comes down with such a general charm as that of *Alcibiades*. *Why?* I cannot answer: who can?

109

The vanity of Victories is considerable. Of all who fell at Waterloo or Trafalgar, ask any man in company to *name you ten off hand*: they will stick at Nelson; the other will survive himself. *Nelson was* a hero: the other is a mere Corporal, dividing with Prussians and Spaniards the luck, which he never deserved. He even—but I hate the fool, and will be silent.

110

The Miscreant Wellington is the Cub of Fortune, but she will never lick him into shape: if he lives, he will be beaten— that's certain. Victory was never before wasted upon such an unprofitable soil, as this dunghill of Tyranny, whence nothing springs but Viper's eggs.

111

I remember seeing Blucher in the London Assemblies, and never saw anything of his age less venerable. With the voice and manners of a recruiting Sergeant, he pretended to the honours of a hero; just as if a stone could be worshipped, because a Man had stumbled over it.

112

There is nothing left for Mankind but a Republic, and I think that there are hopes of such. The two Americas (South and North) have it; Spain and Portugal approach it; all thirst for it. Oh Washington!

113

Pisa, Novr 5th 1821

" There is a strange coincidence sometimes in the little things of this world, Sancho ", says Sterne in a letter (if I mistake not); and so I have often found it.

Page 128, article 91, of this collection of scattered things, I had alluded to my friend Lord Clare in terms such as my feelings suggested. About a week or two afterwards, I met him on the road between Imola and Bologna, after not having met for seven or eight years. He was abroad in 1814, and came home just as I set out in 1816.

This meeting annihilated for a moment all the years between the present time and the days of *Harrow*. It was a new and inexplicable feeling, like rising from the grave, to me. Clare, too, was much agitated—*more* in appearance than even myself; for I could feel his heart beat to his fingers' ends, unless, indeed, it was the pulse of my own which made me think so. He told me that I should find a note from him, left at Bologna. I did. We were obliged to part for our different journeys—he for Rome, I for Pisa; but with the promise to meet again in Spring. We were but five minutes together, and in the public road; but I hardly recollect an hour of my existence which could be weighed against them. He had heard that I was coming on, and had left his letter for me at B., because the people with whom he was travelling could not wait longer.

Of all I have ever known, he has always been the least altered in every thing from the excellent qualities and kind affections which attached me to him so strongly at School. I should hardly have thought it possible for Society (or the World as it is called), to leave a being with so little of the leaven of bad passions. I do not speak from personal experience only, but from all I have ever heard of him from others during absence and distance.

114

I met with Rogers at Bologna : staid a day there, crossed the Appennines with him. He remained at Florence ; I went on to Pisa—8ᵇʳᵉ 29, 30ᵗʰ etc., 1821.

115

I re-visited the Florence Gallery, etc. My former impressions were confirmed ; but there were too many visitors there, to allow me to *feel* any thing properly. When we were (about thirty or forty) all stuffed into the Cabinet of Gems, and knick-knackeries, in a corner of one of the Galleries, I told R. that it " felt like being in the Watch-house ". I left him to make his obeisances to some of his acquaintances, and strolled on alone—the only few minutes I could snatch of any feeling for the works around me. I do not mean to apply this to a *tête à tête* scrutiny with Rogers, who has an excellent taste and deep feeling for the Arts (indeed much more of both than I can possess ; for of the *former* I have not much) ; but to the crowd of jostling starers and travelling talkers around me.

I heard one bold Briton declare to the woman on his arm, looking at the Venus of Titian, " Well, now, this is really very fine indeed ",—an observation, which, like that of the landlord in Joseph Andrews " on the certainty of death ", was (as the landlord's wife observed), " extremely true ".

In the Pitti palace, I did not omit Goldsmith's prescription for a Connoisseur, viz : " that the pictures would have been better, if the painter had taken more pains, and to praise the works of Pietro Perugino ".

116

I have lately been reading Fielding over again. They talk of Radicalism, Jacobinism, etc., in England (I am told), but they should turn over the pages of " Jonathan Wild the Great ". The inequality of conditions, and the littleness of the great, were never set forth in stronger terms ; and his contempt for Conquerors and the like is such, that, had he lived *now*, he would have been denounced in " the Courier " as the grand

Mouth-piece and Factionary of the revolutionists. And yet I never recollect to have heard this turn of Fielding's mind noticed, though it is obvious in every page.

117

The following dialogue passed between me and a very pretty peasant Girl (Rosa Benini, married to Domenico Ovioli, or Oviuoli, the Vetturino) at Ravenna.

Rosa. " *What* is the Pope? "

I. " Don't *you* know? "

Rosa. " No, I don't know. What or who is he? Is he a *Saint*? "

I. " He is an old man."

Rosa. " What nonsense to make such a fuss about an old man. Have you ever seen him? "

I. " Yes, at Rome."

Rosa. " You English don't obey the Pope ? "

I. " No, we don't ; but you do."

Rosa. " I don't know what I believe, but the priests talk about him. I am sure I did not know what he was."

This dialogue I have translated nearly verbatim, and I don't think that I have either added to or taken away from it. The speaker was under eighteen, and an old acquaintance of mine. It struck me as odd that I should have to instruct her *who* the Pope was : I think they might have found it out without me by this time. The fact is indisputable, and occurred but a few weeks ago, before I left Ravenna.

Pisa, Novr 6th 1821

118

I

Oh ! talk not to me of a name great in story
The days of our Youth are the days of our Glory,
And the myrtle and ivy of sweet two and twenty
Are worth all your laurels though ever so plenty.

2

What are garlands and crowns to the brow that is wrinkled?
'Tis but as a dead flower with May-dew besprinkled :
Then away with all such from the head that is hoary,
What care I for the wreaths that can *only* give Glory?

3

Oh! Fame! if I e'er took delight in thy praises,
'Twas less for the sake of thy high-sounding phrases,
Than to see the bright eyes of the dear One discover
She thought that I was not unworthy to love her.

4

There chiefly I sought thee, *there* only I found thee;
Her Glance was the best of the rays that surround thee,
When it sparkled o'er aught that was bright in my story,
I knew it was love, and I felt it was Glory.

I composed these stanzas (except the fourth added now) a
few days ago, on the road from Florence to Pisa.

Pisa, Nov^r *6th 1821*

119

My daughter Ada, on her recent birthday the other day
(the 10th of December 1821), completed her sixth year. Since
she was a Month old, or rather better, I have not seen her. But
I hear that she is a fine child, with a violent temper.

I have been thinking of an odd circumstance. My daughter,
my wife, my half sister, my mother, my sister's mother, my
natural daughter, and myself, are or were all *only* children.
My sister's Mother (Lady Conyers) had only my half *sister*
by that second marriage (herself too an only child), and my
father had only me (an only child) by his second marriage
with my Mother (an only child too). Such a complication of
only children, all tending to *one family*, is singular enough, and
looks like fatality almost. But the fiercest Animals have the
rarest numbers in their litters, as Lions, tigers, and even
Elephants which are mild in comparison.

120

May 18th 1822

I have not taken up this sort of Journal for many months:
shall I continue it? "Chi lo sa?"

I have written little this year, but a good deal last (1821).
Five plays in all (two yet unpublished), some Cantos, etc. I
have begun one or two things since, but under some discourage-
ment, or rather indignation at the brutality of the attacks, which

I hear (for I have seen but few of them) have been multiplied in every direction against me and my recent writings. But the English dishonour themselves more than me by such conduct. It is strange, but the Germans say that I am more popular in Germany by far than in England, and I have heard the Americans say as much of America. The French, too, have printed a considerable number of translations—in prose ! with good success ; but *their* predilection (if it exists) depends, I suspect, upon their belief that I have no great passion for England or the English. It would be singular if I had ; however, I wish them no harm.

121[1]

TO THOMAS MOORE   *May 14, 1821*

If any part of the letter to Bowles has (unintentionally, as far as I remember the contents) vexed you, you are fully avenged ; for I see by an Italian paper that, notwithstanding all my remonstrances through all my friends (and yourself among the rest), the managers persisted in attempting the tragedy,[2] and that it has been " unanimously hissed ! ! " This is the consolatory phrase of the Milan paper, (which detests me cordially, and abuses me, on all occasions, as a Liberal,) with the addition, that *I* " brought the play out " of my own good will.

All this is vexatious enough, and seems a sort of dramatic Calvinism—predestined damnation, without a sinner's own fault. I took all the pains poor mortal could to prevent this inevitable catastrophe—partly by appeals of all kinds, up to the Lord Chamberlain, and partly to the fellows themselves. But, as remonstrance was vain, complaint is useless. I do not understand it—for Murray's letter of the 24th, and all his preceding ones, gave me the strongest hopes that there would be no representation. As yet, I know nothing but the fact, which I presume to be true, as the date is Paris, and the 30th.

---

[1] Here the manuscript ends.

[2] *Marino Faliero*, in spite of an injunction obtained by John Murray's solicitor against the actor Robert William Elliston, was " dragged on to the stage " at the Surrey Theatre during Easter 1821. It proved less unsuccessful there than first reports suggested.

They must have been in a *hell* of a hurry for this damnation, since I did not even know that it was published; and, without its being first published, the histrions could not have got hold of it. Any one might have seen, at a glance, that it was utterly impracticable for the stage; and this little accident will by no means enhance its merit in the closet.

Well, patience is a virtue, and, I suppose, practice will make it perfect. Since last year (spring, that is) I have lost a lawsuit, of great importance, on Rochdale collieries—have occasioned a divorce—have had my poesy disparaged by Murray and the critics—my fortune refused to be placed on an advantageous settlement (in Ireland) by the trustees;—my life threatened last month (they put about a paper here to excite an attempt at my assassination, on account of politics, and a notion which the priests disseminated that I was in a league against the Germans,)—and, finally, my mother-in-law recovered last fortnight, and my play was damned last week! These are like "the eight-and-twenty misfortunes of Harlequin". But they must be borne. If I give in, it shall be after keeping up a spirit at least. I should not have cared so much about it, if our southern neighbours had not bungled us all out of freedom for these five hundred years to come.

Did you know John Keats? They say that he was killed by a review of him in the *Quarterly*—if he be dead, which I really don't know. I don't understand that *yielding* sensitiveness. What I feel (as at this present) is an immense rage for eight-and-forty hours, and then, as usual—unless this time it should last longer. I must get on horseback to quiet me.

Yours, etc.

Francis I. wrote, after the battle of Pavia, "All is lost except our honour". A hissed author may reverse it— "*Nothing* is lost, except our honour". But the horses are waiting, and the paper full. I wrote last week to you.

TO THE HON. AUGUSTA LEIGH *Ravenna, June 22d. 1821*

MY DEAREST A.,—What was I to write about? I live in a different world. You knew from others that I was in tolerable plight, and all that.   However write I will since you desire it. I have put my daughter in a convent for the present to begin her accomplishments by reading, to which she had a learned aversion, but the arrangement is merely temporary till I can settle some plan for her; if I return to England, it is likely that she will accompany me—if not—I sometimes think of Switzerland, and sometimes of the Italian Conventual education; I shall hear both sides (for I have Swiss Friends—through Mr. Hoppner the Consul General, he is connected by marriage with that country) and choose what seems most rational.   My menagerie—(which you enquire after) has had some vacancies by the elopement of one cat, the decease of two monkies and a crow, by indigestion—but it is still a flourishing and somewhat obstreperous establishment.

You may suppose that I was sufficiently provoked by Elliston's behaviour, the more so as the foreign Journals, the Austrian ones at least (who detest me for my politics) had misrepresented the whole thing.   The moment I knew the real facts from England, I made these Italical Gentry contradict themselves and tell the truth—the former they are used to— the latter was a sad trial to them, but they did it, however, by dint of Mr. Hoppner's and my own remonstrances.

Tell Murray that I enclosed him a month ago (on the 2d.) another play, which I presume that he has received (as I ensured it at the post Office) *you* must help him to decypher it, for I sent the only copy, and you can better make out my *griffonnage*;   tell him it *must* be printed (aye and published too) immediately, and copied out, for I do not choose to have only that *one* copy.

Will you for the hundredth time apply to Lady B. about the *funds*, they are now *high*, and I could sell out to a great advantage.   Don't forget this, that cursed connection crosses at every turn my fortunes, my feelings and my fame.   I had no wish to nourish my detestation of her and her family, but they pursue, like an Evil Genius.   I send you an Elegy upon Lady Noel's *recovery*—(made too [here about fourteen lines of the autograph are cut off] the parish register—I will reserve my tears for the demise of Lady Noel, but the old —— will live forever because she is so amiable and useful.

Yours ever and [illegible.], B

P.S.—Let me know about Holmes. Oh La !—is he as great a mountebank as ever?

TO JOHN CAM HOBHOUSE *Ravenna, July 6th, 1821*

My dear H.,—I have written by this post to Murray to omit the stanza to which you object.[1] In case he should forget, you can jog his memory. I have also agreed to a request of Madame Guiccioli's *not* to continue that poem further. She had read the French translation, and thinks it a detestable production. This will not seem strange even in Italian morality, because women all over the world always retain their freemasonry, and as that consists in the illusion of the sentiment which constitutes their sole empire (all owing to chivalry and the Goths—the Greeks knew better), all works which refer to the *comedy* of the passions, and laugh at sentimentalism, of course are proscribed by the whole *sect*. I never knew a woman who did not admire Rousseau, and hate Gil Blas, and de Grammont and the like, for the same reason. And I never met with a woman, English or foreign, who did not do as much by D[on] J[uan]. As I am docile, I yielded, and promised to confine myself to the " highflying of Buttons ", —(you remember Pope's phrase)—for the time to come. You will be very glad of this, as an earlier opponent of that poem's publication.

I only read your Canningippic in the papers, but even there it was worthy of anything since those against Anthony.

You must not give letters to me ; I have taken an oath against being civil ever since —— but you will see my reason in the last note to Marino Faliero.

I have sent to England a tragedy a month ago, and I am in the *fifth* act of another. Murray has not acknowledged its arrival. I must one day break with that gentleman, if he is not the civiler.

Of Burdett's affair I cannot judge, so I made an epigram

[1] " By the way, do not cut at poor Queeney in your Don Juan about Semiramis and her Courser courier. She would feel it very much I assure you." Hobhouse to Byron, June 19th, 1821.

on it, which I sent to Douglas K^d. By the way, now the *funds
are up, stir him* up, and the bloody trustees. It would give me
pleasure to see some of you, that I might gossip over the late
revolt (or rather revol*ting*) transactions of these parts. Things
are far from quiet even now. Have you seen my " Elegy on
the recovery of Lady Noel "?

> " Behold the blessings of a lucky lot !
> My play is damned—and Lady Noel *not*."

Do you know that your bust was sent to England (viâ
Livorno) months ago?

Let me hear from or of you.   Yours, B.

P.S.—Fletcher is turned money-lender, and puts out money
(*here*) at 20 per cent. Query, will he get it again? *Who*
knows?

TO RICHARD BELGRAVE HOPPNER   *Ravenna, July 23, 1821*

This country being in a state of proscription, and all my
friends exiled or arrested—the whole family of Gamba obliged
to go to Florence for the present—the father and son for politics
—(and the Guiccioli, because menaced with a *convent*, as her
father is *not* here,) I have determined to remove to Switzerland,
and they also. Indeed, my life here is not supposed to be
particularly safe—but that has been the case for this twelve-
month past, and is therefore not the primary consideration.

I have written by this post to Mr. Hentsch, junior, the
banker of Geneva, to provide (if possible) a house for me, and
another for Gamba's family, (the father, son, and daughter,)
on the *Jura* side of the lake of Geneva, furnished, and with
stabling (for *me* at least) for eight horses. I shall bring Allegra
with me. Could you assist me or Hentsch in his researches?
The Gambas are at Florence, but have authorised me to treat
for them. You know, or do not know, that they are great
patriots—and both—but the son in particular—very fine
fellows. *This* I know, for I have seen them lately in very
awkward situations—*not* pecuniary, but personal—and they
behaved like heroes, neither yielding nor retracting.

You have no idea what a state of oppression this country is in—they arrested above a thousand of high and low throughout Romagna—banished some and confined others, without *trial, process*, or even *accusation!!* Every body says they would have done the same by me if they dared proceed openly. My motive, however, for remaining, is because *every one* of my acquaintance, to the amount of hundreds almost, have been exiled.

Will you do what you can in looking out for a couple of houses *furnished*, and conferring with Hentsch for us? We care nothing about society, and are only anxious for a temporary and tranquil asylum and individual freedom.

Believe me, etc.

P.S.—Can you give me an idea of the comparative expenses of Switzerland and Italy? which I have forgotten. I speak merely of those of decent *living, horses*, etc., and not of luxuries or high living. Do *not*, however, decide any thing positively till I have your answer, as I can then know how to think upon these topics of transmigration, etc., etc., etc.

TO THE HON. DOUGLAS KINNAIRD* *July 24th* [14th?] *1821*

My DEAR DOUGLAS,—You perhaps did right in not forwarding the letter, which was none of the tenderest. Open, and read it, and forward it not. You must excuse my impatience about the funds. You *forget* that you must have a further power of attorney to sell out ; and, in the intervals of a courier's expedition, the funds may fall, or the courier may fall, or—what can I say? I should approve of the Exchequer bills.

So my lady has been civil—that's news—and new. However, it is her child's interest, and as such no great stretch of politeness.

With regard to M., you will please to recollect that I never meant any *comparison*. I sent his letter to show you his way of thinking. Mine is this. I believe M[urray] to be a good man with a personal regard for me. But a bargain is in its very essence a *hostile* transaction. If I were to come to you, Douglas, and say " lend me five hundred pounds ", you would either do it, or give a good reason why you would not.   But if I come and say " Douglas, I have a carriage and horses, or a library or what you will.   Give me five hundred pounds for them ", you first enquire if they are worth it.   And, even if they are, do not all men try to abate the price of all they buy ?   I contend that a bargain, even between brethren, is a declaration of war.   Now this must be much more so in a man like M. whose business is nothing but a perpetual speculation on what will or will not succeed, and can have no steady returns, being a matter of opinion.   I have no doubt that he would lend or give—freely —what he would refuse for value received in M.S.S.   So do not think as hardly of him.   I do not know myself to what he alludes, nor do I wish to know.   Your manner is quick, as is the case with all men of any vivacity ;   and *he* might feel perhaps a turn of the lip, or a short reply, which Hobhouse would only make a long letter about, and I should only keep in mind for six months, and then pay you off in your own coin on a fit opportunity.   Now there are resources which the great M. has not.   Neither is he on that equality of feeling with you (as doubtless neither in cash) which can admit of that agreeable give and take, which you and I and all of our Chorus have long reciprocated.   It is different with me.   A publisher becomes identified almost with his authors, and can say anything, or hear anything.

And now there approacheth new barter.   By this post is forwarded (with the returned proofs of " Sardanapalus ") the tragedy M.S.S. of " the two Foscari " in five acts.   When you have read both and formed your opinion, I leave to you the discretionary power of poundage and pence.   Perhaps it were as well to publish them first and settle afterwards according to success—if there be any.   You will perceive that I have kept aloof from the Stage as before.   By the time you receive this the Coronation will have subsided and you may have leisure to think of such things.

I write out of spirits ;   for they have been banishing (without trial) half the inhabitants—and many of my friends amongst them—of this country, as politicians.   I hope that this will find you in good humour.

Yours—B.

TO JOHN MURRAY R^a *July* 30th *1821*

DEAR SIR,—Enclosed is the best account of the Doge Faliero, which was only sent to me from an old MSS. the other day. Get it translated, and append it as a note to the next edition. You will perhaps be pleased to see that my conceptions of his character were correct, though I regret not having met with this extract before. You will perceive that he himself said exactly what he is made to say, about the Bishop of Treviso. You will see also that he spoke very little, and those only words " of rage and disdain ", *after* his arrest, which is the case in the play, except when he breaks out at the close of Act fifth. But his speech to the Conspirators is better in the MSS. than in the play : I wish that I had met with it in time. Do not forget this note, with a translation.

In a former note to the Juans, speaking of Voltaire, I have quoted his famous " Zaire, tu pleures ", which is an error ; it should be " Zaire, *vous pleurez* " ; recollect this ; and recollect also that your *want* of *recollection* has permitted you to publish the note on the Kelso traveller, which *I had positively desired you not*, for proof of which I refer you to my letters. I presume that you are able to lay your hand upon these letters, as you are accused publicly, in a pamphlet, of showing them about. I wait your acknowledgement of the packets containing *The Foscaris*, notes, etc., etc. : now your Coronation is over, perhaps you will find time. I have also written to Mr. Kinnaird, to say that I expect the two tragedies to be published speedily, and to inform him that I am willing to make any abatement, on your statement of loss liable to be incurred by publishing at an improper season.

I am so busy here about these poor proscribed exiles, who are scattered about, and with trying to get some of them recalled, that I have hardly time or patience to write a short preface, which will be proper for the two plays. However, I will make it out, on receiving the next proofs.

Yours ever and truly, B.

P.S.—Please to append the letter about *the Hellespont* as a note to your next opportunity of the verses on Leander, etc., etc., etc., in *Childe Harold*. Don't forget it amidst your multitudinous avocations, which I think of celebrating in a dithy-rambic ode to Albemarle Street.

Are you aware that Shelley has written an elegy on Keats, and accuses the *Quarterly* of killing him?

> " Who killed John Keats? "
> " I," says the Quarterly,
> So savage and Tartarly;
> " 'Twas one of my feats."

> " Who shot the arrow? "
> " The poet-priest Milman
> (So ready to kill man),
> Or Southey or Barrow."

You know very well that I did not approve of Keats's poetry, or principles of poetry, or of his abuse of Pope; but, as he is dead, omit *all* that is said *about him* in any *MSS.* of mine, or publication. His *Hyperion* is a fine monument, and will keep his name. I do not envy the man who wrote the article: your review people have no more right to kill than any other foot pads. However, he who would die of an article in a review would probably have died of something else equally trivial. The same thing nearly happened to Kirke White, who afterwards died of a consumption.

TO JOHN MURRAY   *R^a August 23^d 1821*

DEAR SIR,—Enclosed are the two acts corrected. With regard to the charges about the Shipwreck,—I think that I told both you and Mr. Hobhouse, years ago, that [there] was not a *single circumstance* of it *not* taken from *fact*; not, indeed, from any *single* shipwreck, but all from *actual* facts of different wrecks. Almost all *Don Juan* is *real* life, either my own, or from people I knew. By the way, much of the description of the *furniture*, in Canto 3^d, is taken from *Tully's Tripoli* (pray *note this*), and the rest from my own observation. Remember, I never meant to conceal this at all, and have only not stated it, because *Don Juan* had no preface nor name to it. If you think it worth while to make this statement, do so, in your own way. *I* laugh at such charges, convinced that no writer ever borrowed less, or made his materials more his own. Much is coincidence : for instance, Lady Morgan (in a really *excellent* book, I assure you, on Italy) calls Venice an *Ocean Rome* ; I have the very same expression in *Foscari*, and yet *you* know that the play was written months ago, and sent to England. The *Italy* I received only on the 16th in^{st}.

Your friend, like the public, is not aware, that my dramatic simplicity is *studiously* Greek, and must continue so : *no* reform ever succeeded at first. I admire the old English dramatists ; but this is quite another field, and has nothing to do with theirs. I want to make a *regular* English drama, no matter whether for the Stage or not, which is not my object,—but a *mental theatre*.

Yours ever, B.

Is the bust arrived?
P.S.—*Can't* accept your courteous offer.

> For Orford and for Waldegrave
> You give much more than me you *gave* ;
> Which is not fairly to behave
>> My Murray !

> Because if a live dog, 'tis said,
> Be worth a Lion fairly sped,
> A *live lord* must be worth *two* dead,
>> My Murray !

> And if, as the opinion goes,
> Verse hath a better sale than prose—
> Certes, I should have more than those,
>> My Murray !

> But now this sheet is nearly crammed,
> So, if *you will*, *I* shan't be shammed,
> And if you *won't*,—*you* may be damned,
>> My Murray !

These matters must be arranged with Mr. Douglas K. He is my trustee, and a man of honour. To him you can state all your mercantile reasons, which you might not like to state

to me personally, such as " heavy season "—" flat public "—
" don't go off "—" Lordship writes too much "—" won't
take advice "—" declining popularity "—" deductions for
the trade "—" make very little "—" generally lose by him "—
" pirated edition "—" foreign edition "—" severe criticisms ",
etc., with other hints and howls for an oration, which I leave
Douglas, who is an orator, to answer.

You can also state them more freely to a third person, as
between you and me they could only produce some smart
postscripts, which would not adorn our mutual archives.

I am sorry for the Queen, and that's more than you are.

TO THE HON. DOUGLAS KINNAIRD *   *Ra. August 23rd 1821*

My dear Douglas,—I have received the enclosed proposal
from Mr Murray which I can *not* accept. He offers me for *all*
the sum he once offered for *two* cantos of D. Juan. I will
accept nothing of the kind unless he advances very considerably, and unless the things have completely failed. This *you*
can inform yourself of, and act accordingly. With regard to
what his friend says of " *Simplicity* ",[1] I study to be so. It is
an experiment whether the English *Closet* or *mental* theatre
will or will not bear a *regular* drama instead of the melo-drama.
Murray's offer falls short by *one half* of the fair proposal, all
things considered. However I leave you a free discretion and
will ratify any agreement of *yours*, confident that it will be honest
and loyal to both parties.

                              Yours ever and truly, B.

[1] Preserved with this letter is a letter to Byron from John Murray, offering
a thousand guineas for " the Two Tragedies " (which will make " a handsome
and interesting volume ") and the same sum for the Third, Fourth, and Fifth
Cantos of *Don Juan*. Murray also quotes from a letter he has received from William
Gifford, to whom " two Acts of ' the Foscari ' " have been submitted: " Never
mind his plays not being stage-worthy : in these times it signifies not much—
but he has the true dramatic turn, and fails only in his plots. If he could but
get a little into the bustle of our old dramatists, absurd as it sometimes was, it
would do : otherwise he must die a martyr to his simplicity or singleness. . . .
After all [Gifford concludes] he is a wonderful creature—if I had him, I would
keep him up carefully, and shew him only on high days and holy days."

P.S.—Enclosed is a letter from Miss Boyce.[1] She was a transient piece of mine ; but I owe her little on that score, * * * * *. Advance the poor creature some money and *deduct* it from your books quoad banker for me.

[On a separate half-sheet]

Allow me to remind you that up to 1819 *all* the *offers* came from *our* part, and *not* from Murray's. *He* offered for the third Canto of Cᵉ H. *twelve hundred* and then came up to two thousand. For the 4th he gave at once two thousand five hundred ; and both yourself and Hᵉ and your brother thought that I might have obtained more. If *we* are *down* in the scribbling world, say so *at once*, and I will withdraw from the Arena without a word further. Excuse my ignorance, which comes from my foreign residence.

As I am about it, take one more quotation from your *own* letters : " I think that Murray ought to offer you *more* than *any other bookseller*. Now it is my belief that he bids you *less*. You may be *sure* that I have *good authority* for *what I say* ", etc. etc. etc. Now, my dear Dougal, these are your own words, and after them *what can* " *I say* " ?, when not *three months* after you write to me something sounding very like the reverse of your former expressions so recently transmitted?

TO OCTAVIUS GILCHRIST *   *Ravenna, September 5th, 1821*

SIR,[2]—I have to acknowledge the arrival of yr. three pamphlets " from the author " whom I thank very sincerely for the attention. The tone which Mr. Bowles has taken in this controversy has been so different with the different parties, that we are perhaps none of us fair personal judges of the subject. Long before I had seen Mr. B's answers to myself,

[1] Writing from No. 5 Church Hill, St. Pancras, Byron's petitioner, who signs herself " the wretched but *unchanged* Susan Boyce ", speaks of the misery she has endured " for the last 3 years in consequence of my so cruelly being turned from my situation at Drury Lane ". She begs Byron to repeat his former kindnesses and " save *me* and my *poor Boy* from perishing. I am at the Haymarket Theatre for £2 per week : it was the *only* vacant situation. . . ." For further light on Susan Boyce, see " *To Lord Byron* ", by George Paston and Peter Quennell.
[2] Octavius Graḥam Gilchrist, a poetical grocer of Stamford, had attempted to " rescue Pope from the rancorous persecution of his editor, the Rev. Mr. Bowles ".

or the last pamphlet of the three which you have sent to me,
I had written an answer to his attack upon yourself, which
perhaps you may have seen (or at any rate may see if you
think it worth the trouble) at Mr. Murray's. . . . As it was
somewhat savage, on reading Mr. Bowles's mild reply to me,
I suppressed its publication, recollecting also that you were
perfectly competent to your own defence, and might probably
look upon my interference as impertinent. . . . I have not
read Mr. Bowles's " Sequel " to which your third pamphlet
refers.   Mr. Bowles has certainly not set *you* an example of
forbearance in *controversy* ; but in *society* he really is what I have
described him, but as we are all mad upon some subject or
other, and the only reason why it does not appear in *all* is that
their insane chord has not been struck upon, our Editor seems
to have been touched upon the score of Pope, and for that
reason it is a thousand pities that he ever meddled with him.
By the way, to refer to myself, I think you might as well have
omitted the mention of Don Juan and Beppo and Little etc. as
more indecent than the " Imitation from Horace " of Pope,
for two reasons—firstly they are *not so* indecent by any means,
as for example,

> " And if a tight young girl will serve the turn
>   In arrant pride continues still to *churn* "

or

> " What pushed poor Q—— on the imperial whore
>   T'was but to be where Charles had been before."

and in the next place, as I had been fighting Pope's battles as
well as I could, it was rather hard in an *ally* to bring in an
" odious comparison " at the expence of his auxiliary.   However this is a trifle, and if Pope's moral reputation can be still
further elevated at the expence of mine, I will yield it as
freely, as I have always admired him sincerely—much more
indeed than you yourself in all probability, for *I* do not think
him inferior to Milton—although to state such an opinion
publicly in the present day would be equivalent to saying that
I do not think Shakespeare without the grossest of faults, which
is another heterodox notion of my entertainment.   Indeed I look
upon a proper appreciation of Pope as a touchstone of taste,

and the present question as not only whether Pope is or is not in the first rank of our literature, but whether *that* literature shall or shall not relapse into the Barbarism from which it has scarcely emerged for above a century and a half. I do not deny the natural powers of Mind of the courtier dramatists, but I think that their service as a *standard* is doing irreparable mischief. It is also a great error to suppose the *present* a *high* age of English poetry—it is equivalent to the age of *Statius* or *Silius Italicus* except that instead of imitating the Virgils of our language they are " trying back " (to use a hunting phrase) upon the Ennius's and Lucilius's who had better have remained in their obscurity. Those poor idiots of the Lakes, too, are diluting our literature as much as they can. In short, all of us more or less (except Campbell and Rogers) have much to answer for, and I don't see any remedy. But I am wandering from the subject—which is to thank you for your present and to beg you to believe me your obliged and very faithl. serv*,

BYRON

Is it not odd that hitherto Pope has been edited only by *priests*? Warburton—Warton—Bowles?—at least I know no others.

P.S.—I saw Mr. Mawman the other day ;—he tells me that the Booksellers have engaged Roscoe to edite Pope, and I think the choice is a very judicious one. Roscoe has all the elegance and classical turn of mind requisite to do Pope justice. Hitherto he has only been edited by his enemies or by Warburton who was a polemical parson and as fit to edite Poetry as Pope to preach in Gloucester Cathedral. The Attorney-bishop did him no good, and Warton and Bowles have done him harm. Mr. Murray tells me that Roscoe is requested (by the publishers) to keep the controversy with Mr. Bowles etc. quite out of sight and not to allude to it at all. This is the *quietest* way, but whether it is the best I know not. I suppose it is. . . . Mr. Mawman seemed indignant at Bowles's edition which he said " was a treachery to his employers who had paid him to edite Pope—and not to blame him ". He wondered that I had not put this more strongly in my letter. But how was I to know it? . . . It seemed to me inconceivable that they could publish such an edition without being aware of its *tendency*—and thus tacitly approving it with their " Imprimatur ". . . .

TO JOHN MURRAY   *Ravenna, September 12th 1821*

DEAR SIR,—By Tuesday's post, I forwarded, in three packets, the drama of " *Cain* ", in three acts, of which I request the acknowledgement when arrived. To the last speech of *Eve*, in the last act (*i.e.* where she curses Cain), add these three lines to the concluding one—

> May the Grass wither from thy foot ! the Woods
> Deny thee shelter ! Earth a home ! the Dust
> A Grave ! the Sun his light ! and Heaven her God !

There's as pretty a piece of Imprecation for you, when joined to the lines already sent, as you may wish to meet with in the course of your business. But don't forget the addition of the above three lines, which are clinchers to Eve's speech.

Let me know what Gifford thinks (if the play arrives in safety) ; for I have a good opinion of the piece, as poetry : it is in my gay metaphysical style, and in the *Manfred* line.

You must at least commend my facility and variety, when you consider what I have done within the last fifteen months, with my head, too, full of other and of mundane matters. But no doubt you will avoid saying any good of it, for fear I should raise the price upon you : that's right—stick to business ! Let me know what your other ragamuffins are writing, for I suppose you don't like starting too many of your Vagabonds at once. You may give them the start, for any thing I care.

If this arrives in time to be added to the other two dramas, publish them *together* : if not, publish it separately, in the *same* form, to tally for the purchasers. Let me have a proof of the whole speedily. It is longer than *Manfred*.

Why don't you publish my *Pulci*? [1] the best thing I ever wrote, with the Italian to it. I wish I was alongside of you : nothing is ever done in a man's absence ; every body runs counter, because they *can*. If ever I *do* return to England,

---

[1] Byron's translation of the first Canto of Luigi Pulci's *Morgante Maggiore*, with the Italian, was published in the *Liberal*.

(which I shan't though,) I will write a poem to which *English Bards*, etc., shall be New Milk, in comparison. Your present literary world of mountebanks stands in need of such an Avatar ; but I am not yet quite bilious enough : a season or two more, and a provocation or two, will wind me up to the point, and then, have at the whole set !

I have no patience with the sort of trash you send me out by way of books ; except Scott's novels, and three or four other things, I never saw such work or works. Campbell is lecturing, Moore idling, Southey twaddling, Wordsworth driveling, Coleridge muddling, Joanna Baillie piddling, Bowles quibbling, squabbling, and sniveling. Milman will *do*, if he don't cant too much, nor imitate Southey : the fellow has poesy in him ; but he is envious, and unhappy, as all the envious are. Still he is among the best of the day. Barry Cornwall will do better by and bye, I dare say, if he don't get spoilt by green tea, and the praises of Pentonville and Paradise Row. The pity of these men is, that they never lived either in *high life*, nor in *solitude* : there is no medium for the knowledge of the *busy* or the *still* world. If admitted into high life for a season, it is merely as *spectators*—they form no part of the Mechanism thereof. Now Moore and I, the one by circumstances, and the other by birth, happened to be free of the corporation, and to have entered into its pulses and passions, *quarum partes fuimus*. Both of us have learnt by this much which nothing else could have taught us.

Yours, B.

P.S.—I saw one of your brethren, another of the Allied Sovereigns of Grub-Street, the other day, viz. : Mawman the Great, by whom I sent due homage to your imperial self. To-morrow's post may perhaps bring a letter from you ; but you are the most ungrateful and ungracious of correspondents. But there is some excuse for you, with your perpetual levee of politicians, parson-scribblers, and loungers : some day I will give you a *poetical* Catalogue of them.

The post is come : no letter, but never mind.

How is Mrs. Murray, and Gifford ? Better ? Say *well*.

My Compliments to Mr. Heber [1] upon his Election.

---

[1] Richard Heber (1773–1833) was elected M.P. for the University of Oxford, August 24th, 1821.

TO THOMAS MOORE   *Ravenna, September 19, 1821*

I am in all the sweat, dust, and blasphemy of an universal packing of all my things, furniture, etc., for Pisa, whither I go for the winter.   The cause has been the exile of all my fellow Carbonics, and, amongst them, of the whole family of Madame G. ; who, you know, was divorced from her husband last week, " on account of P.P. clerk of this parish ",[1] and who is obliged to join her father and relatives, now in exile there, to avoid being shut up in a monastery, because the Pope's decree of separation required her to reside in *casa paterna*, or else, for decorum's sake, in a convent.   As I could not say with Hamlet, " Get thee to a nunnery ", I am preparing to follow them.

It is awful work, this love, and prevents all a man's projects of good or glory.   I wanted to go to Greece lately (as every thing seems up here) with her brother, who is a very fine, brave fellow (I have seen him put to the proof), and wild about liberty.   But the tears of a woman who has left her husband for a man, and the weakness of one's own heart, are paramount to these projects, and I can hardly indulge them.

We were divided in choice between Switzerland and Tuscany, and I gave my vote for Pisa, as nearer the Mediterranean, which I love for the sake of the shores which it washes, and for my young recollections of 1809.   Switzerland is a curst selfish, swinish country of brutes, placed in the most romantic region of the world.   I never could bear the inhabitants, and still less their English visitors ; for which reason, after writing for some information about houses, upon hearing that there was a colony of English all over the cantons of Geneva, etc., I immediately gave up the thought, and persuaded the Gambas to do the same.

By the last post I sent you " The Irish Avatar ",[2]—what think you?   The last line—" a name never spoke but with curses or jeers "—must run either " a name only uttered with curses or jeers ", or, " a wretch never named but with curses or jeers ".   Be*case* as *how*, " spoke " is not grammar, except in

---

[1] Alluding to Pope's *Memoirs of P. P. Clerk of this Parish.*
[2] " Lord B.'s tremendous verses against the King and the Irish " (as Moore called them) were inspired by George IV's triumphal expedition to Dublin, soon after the Queen's death.

the House of Commons ; and I doubt whether we can say " a name *spoken* ", for *mentioned*. I have some doubts, too, about " repay ",—" and for murder repay with a shout and a smile ". Should it not be, " and for murder repay him with shouts and a smile ", or " *reward* him with shouts and a smile "?

So, pray put your poetical pen through the MS. and take the least bad of the emendations. Also, if there be any further breaking of Priscian's head, will you apply a plaster? I wrote in the greatest hurry and fury, and sent it to you the day after ; so, doubtless, there will be some awful constructions, and a rather lawless conscription of rhythmus.

With respect to what Anna Seward calls " the liberty of transcript ",—when complaining of Miss Matilda Muggleton, the accomplished daughter of a choral vicar of Worcester Cathedral, who had abused the said " liberty of transcript ", by inserting in the *Malvern Mercury* Miss Seward's " Elegy on the South Pole ", as her *own* production, with her *own* signature, two years after having taken a copy, by permission of the authoress—with regard, I say, to the " liberty of transcript ", I by no means oppose an occasional copy to the benevolent few, provided it does not degenerate into such licentiousness of Verb and Noun as may tend to " disparage my parts of speech " by the carelessness of the transcribblers.

I do not think that there is much danger of the " King's Press being abused " upon the occasion, if the publishers of journals have any regard for their remaining liberty of person. It is as pretty a piece of invective as ever put publisher in the way to " Botany ". Therefore, if *they* meddle with it, it is at *their* peril. As for myself, I will answer any jontleman—though I by no means recognise a " right of search " into an unpublished production and unavowed poem. The same applies to things published *sans* consent. I hope you like, at least the concluding lines of the *Pome*?

What are you doing, and where are you? in England? Nail Murray—nail him to his own counter, till he shells out the thirteens. Since I wrote to you, I have sent him another tragedy—*Cain* by name—making three in MS. now in his hands, or in the printer's. It is in the *Manfred* metaphysical style, and full of some Titanic declamation ;—Lucifer being one of the *dram. pers.*, who takes Cain a voyage among the stars,

670

and afterwards to " Hades ", where he shows him the phantoms of a former world, and its inhabitants.   I have gone upon the notion of Cuvier, that the world has been destroyed three or four times, and was inhabited by mammoths, behemoths, and what not ; but *not* by man till the Mosaic period, as, indeed, is proved by the strata of bones found ;—those of all unknown animals, and known, being dug out, but none of mankind.   I have, therefore, supposed Cain to be shown, in the *rational* Preadamites, beings endowed with a higher intelligence than man, but totally unlike him in form, and with much greater strength of mind and person.   You may suppose the small talk which takes place between him and Lucifer upon these matters is not quite canonical.

The consequence is, that Cain comes back and kills Abel in a fit of dissatisfaction, partly with the politics of Paradise, which had driven them all out of it, and partly because (as it is written in Genesis) Abel's sacrifice was the more acceptable to the Deity.   I trust that the Rhapsody has arrived—it is in three acts, and entitled " *A Mystery* ", according to the former Christian custom, and in honour of what it probably will remain to the reader.

Yours, etc.

TO JOHN MURRAY   *R^a Septr 20th 1821*

DEAR MURRAY,—You need not send " *The Blues* ", which is a mere buffoonery, never meant for publication.

The papers to which I allude, in case of Survivorship, are collections of letters, etc., since I was sixteen years old, contained in the trunks in the care of Mr. Hobhouse.   This collection is at least doubled by those I have now here ; all received since my last Ostracism.   To these I should wish the Editor to have access, *not* for the purpose of *abusing confidences*, nor of *hurting* the feelings of correspondents living, or the memories of the dead ; but there are things which would do neither, that I have left unnoticed or unexplained, and which (like all such things) Time only can permit to be noticed or explained, though some are to my credit.   The task will, of course, require delicacy ; but that will not be wanting, if

Moore and Hobhouse survive me, and, I may add, yourself; and that you may all three do so, is, I assure you, my very sincere wish. I am not sure that long life is desirable for one of my temper and constitutional depression of Spirits, which of course I suppress in society; but which breaks out when alone, and in my writings, in spite of myself. It has been deepened, perhaps, by some long past events (I do not allude to my marriage, etc.—on the contrary, *that* raised them by the persecution giving a fillip to my Spirits); but I call it constitutional, as I have reason to think it. You know, or you do *not* know, that my maternal Grandfather (a very clever man, and amiable, I am told) was strongly suspected of Suicide (he was found drowned in the Avon at Bath), and that another very near relative of the same branch took poison, and was merely saved by antidotes. For the first of these events there was no apparent cause, as he was rich, respected, and of considerable intellectual resources, hardly forty years of age, and not at all addicted to any unhinging vice. It was, however, but a strong suspicion, owing to the manner of his death and to his melancholy temper. The *second had* a cause, but it does not become me to touch upon it; it happened when I was far too young to be aware of it, and I never heard of it till after the death of that relative, many years afterwards. I think, then, that I may call this dejection *constitutional*. I had always been told that in *temper* I more resembled my maternal Grandfather than any of my *father's* family—that is, in the gloomier part of his temper, for he was what you call a good natured man, and I am not.

The Journal here I sent by Mawman to Moore the other day; but as it is a mere diary, only *parts* of it would ever do for publication. The other Journal, of the tour in 1816, I should think Augusta might let you have a copy of; but her nerves have been in such a state since 1815, that there is no knowing. Lady Byron's people, and L^y Caroline Lamb's people, and a parcel of that set, got about her and frightened her with all sorts of hints and menaces, so that she has never since been able to write to *me* a *clear common letter*, and is so full of mysteries and miseries, that I can only sympathize, without always understanding her. All my loves, too, make a point of calling upon her, which puts her into a flutter (no difficult matter);

and, the year before last I think, Lady F. W. W. marched in upon her, and Lady Oxford, a few years ago, spoke to her at a party; and these and such like calamities have made her afraid of her shadow. It is a very odd fancy that they all take to her: it was only six months ago, that I had some difficulty in preventing the Countess G. from invading her with an Italian letter. I should like to have seen Augusta's face, with an Etruscan Epistle, and all its Meridional style of *issimas*, and other superlatives, before her.

I am much mortified that Gifford don't take to my new dramas: to be sure, they are as opposite to the English drama as one thing can be to another; but I have a notion that, if understood, they will in time find favour (though *not* on the stage) with the reader. The Simplicity of plot is intentional, and the avoidance of *rant* also, as also the compression of the Speeches in the more severe situations. What I seek to show in *The Foscaris* is the *suppressed* passion, rather than the rant of the present day. For that matter—

> " Nay, if thou'lt mouth,
> I'll rant as well as thou "—

would not be difficult, as I think I have shown in my younger productions—*not dramatic* ones, to be sure. But, as I said before, I am mortified that Gifford don't like them; but I see no remedy, our notions on the subject being so different. How is he? well, I hope: let me know. I regret his demur the more that he has been always my grand patron, and I know no praise which would compensate me in my own mind for his censure. I do not mind *reviews*, as I can work them at their own weapons.

Yours ever and truly, B.

P.S.—By the way, on our next settlement (which will take place with Mr. Kinnaird), you will please to deduct the various sums for *books*, packages *received* and *sent*, the *bust*, tooth-powder, etc., etc., expended by you on my account.

Hobhouse, in his preface to " *Rimini* ", will probably be better able to explain my dramatic system, than I could do, as he is well acquainted with the whole thing. It is more upon the Alfieri School than the English.

I hope that we shall not have Mr. Rogers here : there is a mean minuteness in his mind and tittle-tattle that I dislike, ever since I *found him out* (which was but slowly) ; besides he is not a good man : why don't he go to bed? What does he do travelling?

The Journal of 1814 I dare say Moore will give, or a copy. Has *Cain* (the dramatic third attempt), arrived yet? Let me know.

Address to me at *Pisa*, whither I am going. The reason is, that all my Italian friends here have been exiled, and are met there for the present ; and I go to join them, as agreed upon, for the Winter.

TO JOHN MURRAY   *Ravenna, September 24ᵗʰ 1821*

DEAR MURRAY,—I have been thinking over our late correspondence, and wish to propose to you the following articles for our future :—

1ˢᵗˡʸ That you shall write to me of yourself, of the health, wealth, and welfare of all friends ; but of *me* (*quoad me*) little or nothing.

2ᵈˡʸ That you shall send me Soda powders, tooth-powder, tooth-brushes, or any such anti-odontalgic or chemical articles, as heretofore, *ad libitum*, upon being re-imbursed for the same.

3ᵈˡʸ That you shall *not* send me any modern, or (as they are called) *new*, publications in *English whatsoever*, save and except-ing any writing, prose or verse, of (or reasonably presumed to be of) Walter Scott, Crabbe, Moore, Campbell, Rogers, Gifford, Joanna Baillie, *Irving* (the American), Hogg, Wilson (*Isle of Palms* Man), or *any* especial *single* work of fancy which is thought to be of considerable merit ; *Voyages* and *travels*, pro-vided that they are *neither in Greece, Spain, Asia Minor, Albania, nor Italy*, will be welcome : having travelled the countries mentioned, I know that what is said of them can convey nothing further which I desire to know about them. No other English works whatsoever.

4ᵗʰˡʸ That you send me *no periodical works* whatsoever— *no Edinburgh, Quarterly, Monthly*, nor any Review, Magazine, Newspaper, English or foreign, of any description.

5^{thly} That you send me *no* opinions whatsoever, either *good*, *bad*, or *indifferent*, of yourself, or your friends, or others, concerning any work, or works, of mine, past, present, or to come.

6^{thly} That all negotiations in matters of business between you and me pass through the medium of the Honble Douglas Kinnaird, my friend and trustee, or Mr. Hobhouse, as *Alter Ego*, and tantamount to myself during my absence, or presence.

Some of these propositions may at first seem strange, but they are founded. The quantity of trash I have received as books is incalculable, and neither amused nor instructed. Reviews and Magazines are at the best but ephemeral and superficial reading : *who thinks* of the *grand article* of *last year* in any *given review*? in the next place, if they regard *myself*, they tend to increase *Egotism* ; if favourable, I do not deny that the praise *elates*, and if unfavourable, that the abuse *irritates*— the latter may conduct me to inflict a species of Satire, which would neither do good to you nor to your friends : *they* may smile *now*, and so may *you* ; but if I took you all in hand, it would not be difficult to cut you up like gourds. I did as much by as powerful people at nineteen years old, and I know little as yet, in three and thirty, which should prevent me from making all your ribs Gridirons for your hearts, if such were my propensity. But it is *not*. Therefore let me hear none of your provocations. If any thing occurs so very *gross* as to require my notice, I shall hear of it from my personal friends. For the rest, I merely request to be left in ignorance.

The same applies to opinions, *good*, *bad*, or *indifferent*, of persons in conversation or correspondence : these do not *interrupt*, but they *soil* the *current* of my *Mind*. I am sensitive enough, but *not* till I am *touched*; and *here* I am beyond the touch of the short arms of literary England, except the few feelers of the Polypus that crawl over the Channel in the way of Extract.

All these precautions *in* England would be useless : the libeller or the flatterer would there reach me in spite of all ; but in Italy we know little of literary England, and think less, except what reaches us through some garbled and brief extract in some miserable Gazette. For *two years* (excepting two or three articles cut out and sent to *you*, by the post) I never read a newspaper which was not forced upon me by some accident, and know, upon the whole, as little of England as you all do of Italy, and God knows *that* is little enough, with all your travels, etc., etc., etc.   The English travellers *know Italy* as *you* know Guernsey : how much is *that*?

If any thing occurs so violently gross or personal as to require notice, Mr. Dˢ Kinnaird will let me *know* ; but of *praise* I desire to hear *nothing*.

You will say, " to what tends all this? "   I will answer THAT ;—to keep my mind *free and unbiassed* by all paltry and personal irritabilities of praise or censure ;—to let my Genius take its natural direction, while my feelings are like the dead, who know nothing and feel nothing of all or aught that is said or done in their regard.

If you can observe these conditions, you will spare yourself and others some pain : let me not be worked upon to rise up ; for if I do, it will not be for a little : if you can *not* observe these conditions, we shall cease to be correspondents, but *not friends* ; for I shall always be

Yours ever and truly, BYRON

P.S.—I have taken these resolutions not from any irritation against *you* or *yours*, but simply upon reflection that all reading, either praise or censure, of myself has done me harm.   When I was in Switzerland and Greece, I was out of the way of hearing either, and *how I wrote there !*   In Italy I am out of the way of it too ; but latterly, partly through my fault, and partly through your kindness in wishing to send me the *newest* and most periodical publications, I have had a crowd of reviews, etc., thrust upon me, which have bored me with their jargon, of one kind or another, and taken off my attention from greater objects.   You have also sent me a parcel of trash of poetry, for no reason that I can conceive, unless to provoke me to write a new *English Bards*.   Now *this* I wish to avoid ; for if ever I *do*, it will be a strong production ; and I desire peace, as long as the fools will keep their nonsense out of my way.

TO JOHN MURRAY   *Septʳ 28ᵗʰ 1821*

DEAR MORAY,—I add another cover to request you to ask Moore to obtain (if possible) my letters to the late Lady

Melbourne from Lady Cowper. They are very numerous, and ought to have been restored long ago, as I was ready to give back Lady M.'s in exchange: these latter are in Mr. Hobhouse's custody with my other papers, and shall be punctually restored if required. I did not choose before to apply to Lady Cowper, as her mother's death naturally kept me from intruding upon her feelings at the time of its occurrence. Some years have now elapsed, and it is essential that I should have my own epistles. They are essential as confirming that part of the " Memoranda " which refer to the two periods (1812 and 1814) when my marriage with her niece was in contemplation, and will tend to show what my real views and feelings were upon that subject, which have been so variously represented. You need not let *this motive* be stated to L^y C^r, as it in no degree concerns *her* particularly ; but *if* they refuse to give them up (or keep back *any*—recollect that they are in *great quantity*), it would become the duty of the Editor and my Executors to refer to parts of Lady Melbourne's letters—so that the thing is as broad as it is long. They involve also many other topics, which may or may not be referred to, according to the discretion of Moore, etc., when the time comes.

You need not be alarmed : the "*fourteen years*" will hardly elapse without some mortality amongst us ; it is a long lease of life to speculate upon. So your Cent per Cent Shylock Calculation will not be in so much peril, as the " Argosie " will sink before that time, and " the pound of flesh " be withered previously to your being so long out of a return.

I also wish to give you a hint or two (as you have really behaved very handsomely to M. in the business, and are a fine fellow in your line) for your advantage. *If* by your own management you can extract any of my epistles from L^y Caroline Lamb (mind she don't give you *forgeries* in my *hand*: she has done as much you *know* before now) they might be of use in your collection (sinking of course the *names* and *all such circumstances* as might hurt *living* feelings, or *those* of *survivors*) ; they treat of more topics than love occasionally.

As to those to other correspondents (female, etc.), there are plenty scattered about in the world ; but how to direct you to recover them, I know not : most of them have kept them—I hear at least that L^y O[xford] and F. W[ebster] have kept theirs; but these letters are of course inaccessible (and perhaps not desirable), as well as those of some others.

I will tell you who may *happen* to have some letters of mine in their possession: Lord Powerscourt, some to his late brother; Mr. Long of—(I forget his place)—but the father of Edward Long of the Guards, who was drowned in going to Lisbon early in 1809; Miss Elizabeth Pigot, of Southwell, Notts (she *may* be *Mistress* by this time, for she had more years than I): *they* were *not* love-letters, so that you might have them without scruple. There are, or might be, some to the late Revd J. C. Tattersall, in the hands of his brother (half-brother) Mr. Wheatley, who resides near Canterbury, I think. There are some to Charles Gordon, now of Dulwich; and some few to Mrs. Chaworth; but these latter are probably destroyed or inaccessible.

All my letters to Lady B., before and since her marriage, are in her possession, as well as her own which I sent to her: she had not the courtesy to restore me *mine*; but never mind; though they were too much to my credit for her to give them back, we can do without them.

I mention these people and particulars merely as *chances*: most of them have probably destroyed the letters, which in fact were of little import, most of them written when very young, and several at School and College.

Peel (the *second* brother of the Secretary) was a correspondent of mine, and also Porter, the son of the Bishop of Clogher; Lord Clare a very voluminous one; William Harness (a friend of Jew Milman's) another; Charles Drummond (son of the Banker); William Bankes (the Voyager); your friend R. C. Dallas, Esqre. Hodgson, Henry Drury, Hobhouse, you were already aware of.

I have gone through this long list of

" The cold, the faithless, and the dead ",

because I know that, like " the curious in fish sauce ", you are a researcher of such things.

Besides these, there are other occasional ones to literary men and so forth, complimentary, etc., etc., etc., not worth much more than the rest. There are some hundreds, too, of Italian notes of mine, scribbled with a noble contempt of the grammar and dictionary, and in very English Etruscan; for I *speak* Italian very fluently but write it carelessly and incorrectly to a degree.

TO THE HON. AUGUSTA LEIGH   *Octr 5th, 1821*

My dearest Augusta,—Has there been nothing to make it grey? to be sure the *years* have not. Your *parcel* will not find me here—I am going to *Pisa*, for the winter. The late political troubles here have occasioned the exile of all my friends and connections, and I am going there to join them. You know or you do not know that Madame La Comtesse G. was separated from her husband last year (on account of P.P. Clerk of this parish), that the Pope decided in her favor and gave her a separate maintenance and that we lived very quietly and decently—she at her father's (as the Pope decided) and I at home—till this Summer. When her father was exiled, she was obliged either to accompany him or retire into a Convent—such being the terms of His Holiness's deed of divorcement. They went to Pisa by my recommendation and there I go to join them.

So there's a *romance* for you. I assure you it was not my wish nor fault altogether. Her husband was old—rich—and must have left her a large jointure in a few years; but he was jealous, and insisted etc, and *she* like all the rest *would* have her own way. You know that all my loves go crazy, and make scenes—and so—" She is the sixteenth Mrs. Shuffleton ". Being very young—very romantic—and odd—and being contradicted by her husband besides, and being of a country where morals are no better than in England, (though elopements and divorces are rare—and *this* made an uncommon noise—the first that had occurred at Ravenna for two hundred years—that is in a *public* way with appeals to the Pope etc) you are not to wonder much at it; she being too a beauty and the great Belle of the four Legations, and married not quite a year (at our first acquaintance) to a man *forty* years older than herself who had had two wives already and a little suspected of having poisoned his first.

We have been living hitherto decently and quietly. These

679

things here do not exclude a woman from all society as in y^r hypocritical country. It is very odd that all my *fairs* are such romantic people; and always daggering or divorcing—or making scenes.

But this is " positively the last time of performance " (as the playbills say), or of my getting into such scrapes for the future. Indeed—I have had my share. But this is a finisher; for you know when a woman is separated from her husband for her *Amant,* he is bound both by honour (and inclination at least I am), to live with her all his days; as long as there is no misconduct.

So you see that I have closed as papa *begun,* and *you* will probably never see me again as long as you live. Indeed you don't deserve it—for having behaved so *coldly—when I was ready to have sacrificed every thing for you—and after [you had] taken the farther* [indecipherable] *always* [indecipherable] [1]

It is nearly three years that this "liaison" has lasted. I was dreadfully in love—and she blindly so—for she has sacrificed every thing to this headlong passion. That comes of being romantic. I can say that, without being so *furiously* in love as at first, I am more attached to her than I thought it possible to be to any woman after three years—*(except one and who was she can* YOU *guess)* [1] and have not the least wish nor prospect of separation from her.

She herself, (and it is now a year since her separation, a year too of all kinds of vicissitudes et^c) is still more decided. Of course the *step* was a decisive one. If Lady B. would but please to die, and the Countess G.'s husband (for Catholics can't marry though divorced), we should probably have to marry—though I would rather *not*—thinking it the way to hate each other—for all people whatsoever.

However you need not calculate upon seeing me again in a hurry, if ever. How have you sent the *parcel,* and how am I to receive it at Pisa? I am anxious about the Seal—not about Hodgson's nonsense. What is the fool afraid of the *post* for? it is the *safest*—the only *safe* conveyance. They never meddle but with political packets.

Yours.

---

[1] The words in italics have been erased—apparently not by Byron.

P.S.—*You* ought to be a great admirer of the *future* Lady B. for *three* reasons, 1^{stly} She is a grand patroness of the present Lady B. and always says " that she has no doubt that " she was exceedingly ill-used by me—2dly She is an admirer of yours ; and I have had great difficulty in keeping her from writing to you eleven pages, (for she is a grand Scribe), and 3dly she having read " Don Juan " in a *French* translation—made me promise to write *no more* of it, declaring that it was abominable etc etc that *Donna Inez* WAS meant for Lady B. and in short made me vow *not* to continue it—(this occurred lately) and since the last cantos were sent to England last year). Is this not altogether odd enough? She has a good deal of *us* too. I mean that turn for ridicule like Aunt Sophy and you and I and all the B's. Desire Georgiana to write me a letter. I suppose she can by this time.

Opened by me—and the Seal taken off—so—don't accuse the post-office without cause.

B—that's a sign—a written one where the
wax was.

TO LADY BYRON[1]   *Pisa, November 17, 1821*
(To the care of the Hon. Mrs. Leigh, London.)

I have to acknowledge the receipt of " Ada's hair ", which is very soft and pretty, and nearly as dark already as mine was at twelve years old, if I may judge from what I recollect of some in Augusta's possession, taken at that age. But it don't curl,—perhaps from its being let grow.

I also thank you for the inscription of the date and name, and I will tell you why ;—I believe that they are the only two or three words of your hand-writing in my possession. For your letters I returned ; and except the two words, or rather the one word, " Household ", written twice in an old account book, I have no other. I burnt your last note, for two reasons :— firstly, it was written in a style not very agreeable ; and, secondly, I wished to take your word without documents,

---

[1] This letter, never sent to Lady Byron, was enclosed by Byron in a letter to Lady Blessington (May 6th, 1823).

which are the worldly resources of suspicious people.

I suppose that this note will reach you somewhere about Ada's birthday—the 10th of December, I believe. She will then be six, so that in about twelve more I shall have some chance of meeting her ;—perhaps sooner, if I am obliged to go to England by business or otherwise. Recollect, however, one thing, either in distance or nearness ;—every day which keeps us asunder should, after so long a period, rather soften our mutual feelings, which must always have one rallying-point as long as our child exists, which I presume we both hope will be long after either of her parents.

The time which has elapsed since the separation has been considerably more than the whole brief period of our union, and the not much longer one of our prior acquaintance. We both made a bitter mistake ; but now it is over, and irrevocably so. For, at thirty-three on my part, and a few years less on yours, though it is no very extended period of life, still it is one when the habits and thought are generally so formed as to admit of no modification ; and as we could not agree when younger, we should with difficulty do so now.

I say all this, because I own to you, that, notwithstanding every thing, I considered our re-union as not impossible for more than a year after the separation ;—but then I gave up the hope entirely and for ever. But this very impossibility of re-union seems to me at least a reason why, on all the few points of discussion which can arise between us, we should preserve the courtesies of life, and as much of its kindness as people who are never to meet may preserve perhaps more easily than nearer connections. For my own part, I am violent, but not malignant ; for only fresh provocations can awaken my resentments. To you, who are colder and more concentrated, I would just hint, that you may sometimes mistake the depth of a cold anger for dignity, and a worse feeling for duty. I assure you that I bear you *now* (whatever I may have done) no resentment whatever. Remember, that *if you have injured me* in aught, this forgiveness is something ; and that, if I have *injured you*, it is something more still, if it be true, as the moralists say, that the most offending are the least forgiving.

Whether the offence has been solely on my side, or reciprocal, or on yours chiefly, I have ceased to reflect upon any but two things,—viz. that you are the mother of my child, and that we shall never meet again. I think if you also consider the two corresponding points with reference to myself, it will be better for all three.

Yours ever,
NOEL BYRON [1]

TO JOHN MURRAY   *Pisa, December 4, 1821*

DEAR SIR,—By extracts in the English papers,—in your holy Ally, Galignani's *Messenger*,—I perceive that " the two greatest examples of human vanity in the present age " are, firstly, " the ex-Emperor Napoleon ", and secondly, " his Lordship, etc., the noble poet ", meaning your humble servant, " poor guiltless I ".

Poor Napoleon ! he little dreamed to what " vile comparisons " the turn of the Wheel would reduce him ! I cannot help thinking, however, that had our learned brother of the newspaper office seen my very moderate answer to the very scurrile epistle of my radical patron, John Hobhouse, M.P., he would have thought the thermometer of my " Vanity " reduced to a very decent temperature. By the way you do not happen to know whether Mrs. Fry had commenced her reform of the prisoners at the time when Mr. Hobhouse was in Newgate? there are some of his phrases, and much of his style (in that same letter), which led me to suspect that either she had not, or that he had profited less than the others by her instructions. Last week I sent back the deed of Mr. Moore signed and witnessed. It was inclosed to Mr. Kinnaird with a request to forward it to you. I have also transmitted to him my opinions upon your proposition, etc., etc., but addressed them to himself.

I have got here into a famous old feudal palazzo, on the Arno, large enough for a garrison, with dungeons below and cells in the walls, and so full of *Ghosts*, that the learned Fletcher (my valet) has begged leave to change his room, and then refused to occupy his *new* room, because there were more ghosts

---

[1] When, on the death of her mother, Lady Byron succeeded to the Wentworth estate, Byron adopted the additional name of Noel.

there than in the other. It is quite true that there are most extraordinary noises (as in all old buildings), which have terrified the servants so as to incommode me extremely. There is one place where people were evidently *walled up* ; for there is but one possible passage, *broken* through the wall, and then meant to be closed again upon the inmate. The house belonged to the Lanfranchi family, (the same mentioned by Ugolino in his dream, as his persecutor with Sismondi,) and has had a fierce owner or two in its time. The staircase, etc., is said to have been built by Michel Agnolo [*sic*]. It is not yet cold enough for a fire. What a climate !

I am, however, bothered about these spectres, (as they say the last occupants were, too,) of whom I have as yet seen nothing, nor, indeed, heard (*myself*) ; but all the other ears have been regaled by all kinds of supernatural sounds. The first night I thought I heard an odd noise, but it has not been repeated. I have now been here more than a month.

Yours, BYRON

P.S.—Pray send me two or three dozen of " *Acton's corn-rubbers* " in a parcel by the post—*packed dry* and well—if you can.

I have received safely the parcel containing the Seal—the *E. Review*—and some pamphlets, etc. The others are I presume upon their way.

Are there not designs from *Faust*? Send me some, and a translation of it,—if such there is. Also of Goethe's life if such there be ; if not—the original German.

TO SIR WALTER SCOTT   *Pisa, January 12, 1822*

My dear Sir Walter,—I need not say how grateful I am for your letter, but I must own my ingratitude in not having written to you again long ago.   Since I left England (and it is not for all the usual term of transportation) I have scribbled to five hundred blockheads on business, etc., without difficulty, though with no great pleasure; and yet, with the notion of addressing you a hundred times in my head, and always in my heart, I have not done what I ought to have done.   I can only account for it on the same principle of tremulous anxiety with which one sometimes makes love to a beautiful woman of our own degree, with whom one is enamoured in good earnest; whereas, we attack a fresh-coloured housemaid without (I speak, of course, of earlier times) any sentimental remorse or mitigation of our virtuous purpose.

I owe to you far more than the usual obligation for the courtesies of literature and common friendship; for you went out of your way in 1817 to do me a service, when it required not merely kindness, but courage to do so: to have been recorded by you in such a manner, would have been a proud memorial at any time, but at such a time, when " all the world and his wife ", as the proverb goes, were trying to trample upon me, was something still higher to my self-esteem,—I allude to the *Quarterly Review* of the Third Canto of *Childe Harold*, which Murray told me was written by you,—and, indeed, I should have known it without his information, as there could not be *two* who *could* and *would* have done this at the time.   Had it been a common criticism, however eloquent or panegyrical, I should have felt pleased, undoubtedly, and grateful, but not to the extent which the extraordinary good-heartedness of the whole proceeding must induce in any mind capable of such sensations.   The very *tardiness* of this acknow-ledgment will, at least, show that I have not forgotten the obligation; and I can assure you that my sense of it has been out at compound interest during the delay.   I shall only add one word upon the subject, which is, that I think that you, and Jeffrey, and Leigh Hunt, were the only literary men, of numbers whom I know (and some of whom I had served), who dared venture even an anonymous word in my favour just then : and that, of those three, I had never seen *one* at all —of the second much less than I desired—and that the third was under no kind of obligation to me, whatever; while the other *two* had been actually attacked by me on a former occasion; *one*, indeed, with some provocation, but the other wantonly enough. So you see you have been heaping " coals of fire ", etc., in the true gospel manner, and I can assure you that they have burnt down to my very heart.

I am glad that you accepted the Inscription. I meant to have inscribed *The Foscarini* to you instead; but, first, I heard that *Cain* was thought the least bad of the two as a composition; and, 2dly, I have abused Southey like a pickpocket, in a note to *The Foscarini*, and I recollected that he is a friend of yours (though not of mine), and that it would not be the handsome thing to dedicate to one friend any thing containing such matters about another. However, I'll work the Laureate before I have done with him, as soon as I can muster Billingsgate therefor. I like a row, and always did from a boy, in the course of which propensity, I must needs say, that I have found it the most easy of all to be gratified, personally and poetically. You disclaim " jealousies "; but I would ask, as Boswell did of Johnson, " of *whom could* you be *jealous?* "—of none of the living certainly, and (taking all and all into consideration) of which of the dead? I don't like to bore you about the Scotch novels, (as they call them, though two of them are wholly English, and the rest half so), but nothing can or could ever persuade me, since I was the first ten minutes in your company, that you are *not* the man. To me those novels have so much of " Auld lang syne " (I was bred a canny Scot till ten years old), that I never move without them; and when I removed from Ravenna to Pisa the other day, and sent on my library before, they were the only books that I kept by me, although I already have them by heart.

January 27, 1822

I delayed till now concluding, in the hope that I should have got *The Pirate*, who is under way for me, but has not yet hove in sight. I hear that your daughter is married, and I suppose by this time you are half a grandfather—a young one, by the way. I have heard great things of Mrs. Lockhart's

personal and mental charms, and much good of her lord :
that you may live to see as many novel Scotts as there are
Scott's novels, is the very bad pun, but sincere wish of
Yours ever most affectionately, etc.

P.S.—Why don't you take a turn in Italy? You would
find yourself as well known and as welcome as in the Highlands among the natives. As for the English, you would be with
them as in London ; and I need not add, that I should be
delighted to see you again, which is far more than I shall ever
feel or say for England, or (with a few exceptions " of kith,
kin, and allies ") any thing that it contains. But my " heart
warms to the tartan ", or to anything of Scotland, which reminds me of Aberdeen and other parts, not so far from the
Highlands as that town, about Invercauld and Braemar,
where I was sent to drink goat's *whey* in 1795-6, in consequence
of a threatened decline after the scarlet fever. But I am
gossiping, so, good night—and the gods be with your dreams !

Pray, present my respects to Lady Scott, who may, perhaps,
recollect having seen me in town in 1815.

I see that one of your supporters (for, like Sir Hildebrand,
I am fond of Guillim,) is a *mermaid*; it is my *crest* too, and with
precisely the same curl of tail. There's concatenation for you :
—I am building a little cutter at Genoa, to go a cruising in the
summer. I know *you* like the sea too.

TO ROBERT SOUTHEY*   *Pisa, Fy 7th, 1822*

SIR,[1]—My friend, the Honourable Douglas Kinnaird, will
deliver to you a message from me, to which an answer is
requested.
I have the honour to be
Your very obedt. humble Servnt. BYRON

TO THE HON. DOUGLAS KINNAIRD *   [*Feb. 7th 1822*]

P.S.—I give you a " Carte blanche " in Southey's business.
If you agree with me that he ought to be called to account, I

[1] As a result of calumnious statements he was alleged to have made, Byron
proposed to call out Southey.

beg you to convey my invitation to meet when and where he may appoint, to settle this with him and his friend, and to let me know in as few posts as possible, that I may join you. This will (or ought) to prevent unnecessary delay. I wish you to observe that if I come to England with this object, *before* my message is delivered and the preliminaries fixed, my arrival would transpire in the interim of the arrangement; whereas, if all is settled before hand, we may bring the affair to a decision on the day of my landing.

Better on the coast of France, as less liable to interruption or publicity, but I presume Mr. S. is too great a patriot to come off the soil for such a purpose. The grounds are, that after the language he has both used and preached, this is the only honourable way of deciding the business.

I enclose your credentials in a note to Mr. Southey. I require satisfaction for the expression in his letter in the Newspapers; that will be the tenor of the Message, as you are well aware. Of course you will suspend the publication of " the Vision " [of Judgement] till we know whether the business can be settled in a more proper manner.

TO THOMAS MOORE · *Pisa, March 4, 1822*

Since I wrote the enclosed, I have waited another post, and now have your answer acknowledging the arrival of the packet—a troublesome one, I fear, to you in more ways than one, both from weight external and internal.

The unpublished things in your hands, in Douglas K.'s, and Mr. John Murray's, are, *Heaven and Earth*, a lyrical kind of Drama upon the Deluge, etc.;—*Werner, now with you*;—a translation of the First Canto of the *Morgante Maggiore*;—*ditto* of an Episode in Dante;—some stanzas to the Po, June 1st, 1819;—*Hints from Horace*, written in 1811, but a good deal, *since*, to be omitted; several prose things, which may, perhaps, as well remain unpublished;—*The Vision*, etc., of Quevedo Redivivus, in verse.

Here you see is " more matter for a May morning "; but how much of this can be published is for consideration. The

Quevedo (one of my best in that line) has appalled the Row already, and must take its chance at Paris, if at all. The new Mystery is less speculative than *Cain*, and very pious; besides, it is chiefly lyrical. The *Morgante* is the *best* translation that ever was or will be made; and the rest are—whatever you please to think them.

I am sorry you think *Werner* even *approaching* to any fitness for the stage, which, with my notions upon it, is very far from my present object. With regard to the publication, I have already explained that I have no exorbitant expectations of either fame or profit in the present instances; but wish them published because they are written, which is the common feeling of all scribblers.

With respect to " Religion ", can I never convince you that *I* have no such opinions as the characters in that drama, which seems to have frightened every body? Yet *they* are nothing to the expressions in Goethe's *Faust* (which are ten times hardier), and not a whit more bold than those of Milton's Satan. My ideas of a character may run away with me: like all imaginative men, I, of course, embody myself with the character while I *draw* it, but not a moment after the pen is from off the paper.

I am no enemy to religion, but the contrary. As a proof, I am educating my natural daughter a strict Catholic in a convent of Romagna; for I think people can never have *enough* of religion, if they are to have any. I incline, myself, very much to the Catholic doctrines; but if I am to write a drama, I must make my characters speak as I conceive them likely to argue.

As to poor Shelley, who is another bugbear to you and the world, he is, to my knowledge, the *least* selfish and the mildest of men—a man who has made more sacrifices of his fortune and feelings for others than any I ever heard of. With his speculative opinions I have nothing in common, nor desire to have.

The truth is, my dear Moore, you live near the *stove* of society, where you are unavoidably influenced by its heat and its vapours. I did so once—and too much—and enough to give a colour to my whole future existence. As my success in society was *not* inconsiderable, I am surely not a prejudiced judge upon the subject, unless in its favour; but I think it, as now constituted, *fatal* to all great original undertakings of every kind. I never courted it *then*, when I was young and high in blood, and one of its " curled darlings " ; and do you think I would do so *now*, when I am living in a clearer atmosphere? One thing *only* might lead me back to it, and that is, to try once more if I could do any good in *politics* ; but *not* in the petty politics I see now preying upon our miserable country.

Do not let me be misunderstood, however. If you speak your *own* opinions, they ever had, and will have, the greatest weight with *me*. But if you merely *echo* the *monde*, (and it is difficult not to do so, being in its favour and its ferment,) I can only regret that you should ever repeat any thing to which I cannot pay attention.

But I am prosing. The gods go with you, and as much immortality of all kinds as may suit your present and all other existence.

Yours, etc.

TO SIR GODFREY WEBSTER [1]*   *Pisa, April 12th 1822*

DEAR W.—Why don't you take a tour in Italy? I should be delighted to see you again which is far more than I shall ever say or feel for your island, or anything therein. They complain of my abusing England—my mother-country—a step-dame, I take it. I made out a list the other day of all the things and persons I have been compared to. It begins well with Alcibiades, but it ends with the Swiss giantess or the Polish dwarf—I forget which. I have now to add another description sermonised, lately by Parson Styles, depicting me as " a denaturalized being, who, having drained the cup of sin to its bitterest dregs, is resolved to show that he is no longer human, even in his frailties, but a cool, unconcerned fiend ". That's damnably cool—that's flat—Parson ! Well, I hope that neighbour-loving divine's holy rage will not put you in bodily fear of being cannibalized by such an *ogre* as the author of sundry blasphemous works, should you cross the Alps. A fig for all their clamours—" Come one—come all " we will fight it out. When I once take pen in hand, it will be difficult for me not " to

---

[1] The son of Lady Holland by her first marriage.

make sport for the Philistines ". Now we look upon ourselves as something, oh!—fellow with some pith—how we could lay it on. I think I see them wincing under the thong the pompous poltroons—Sunburn me if I don't tan their asses' skins for them. As to what I have said about you—never mind—it was only behind your back, and under those legitimate circumstances— why even our best friends cannot expect us to spare them— Pray—reply. Views are worth money. Believe me always yours very affectionately

BYRON

TO JOHN MURRAY   *Pisa, April 22ᵈ 1822*

DEAR SIR, You will regret to hear that I have received intelligence of the death of my daughter Allegra of a fever in the Convent of Bagna Cavallo, where she was placed for the last year, to commence her education. It is a heavy blow for many reasons, but must be borne,—with time.

It is my present intention to send her remains to England for sepulture in Harrow Church (where I once hoped to have laid my own), and this is my reason for troubling you with this notice. I wish the funeral to be very private. The body is embalmed, and in lead. It will be embarked from Leghorn. Would you have any objection to give the proper directions on its arrival?

I am yours, etc., N. B.

P.S.—You are aware that protestants are not allowed holy ground in Catholic countries.

TO PERCY BYSSHE SHELLEY   *April 23, 1822*

The blow was stunning and unexpected; for I thought the danger over, by the long interval between her stated amelioration and the arrival of the express. But I have borne up against it as I best can, and so far successfully, that I can go about the usual business of life with the same appearance of composure, and even greater. There is nothing to prevent your coming to-morrow; but, perhaps, to-day, and yester-evening, it was better not to have met. I do not know that I have any thing to reproach in my conduct, and certainly nothing in my feelings and intentions towards the dead. But it is a moment when we are apt to think that, if this or that had been done, such event might have been prevented,—though every day and hour shows us that they are the most natural and inevitable. I suppose that Time will do his usual work—Death has done his.

Yours ever, N. B.

TO SIR WALTER SCOTT   *Pisa, May 4, 1822*

My dear Sir Walter,—Your account of your family is very pleasing : would that I " could answer this comfort with the like " ! but I have just lost my natural daughter, Allegra, by a fever. The only consolation, save time, is the reflection that she is either at rest or happy ; for her few years (only five) prevented her from having incurred any sin, except what we inherit from Adam.

" Whom the gods love die young."

I need not say that your letters are particularly welcome, when they do not tax your time and patience ; and now that our correspondence is resumed, I trust it will continue.

I have lately had some anxiety, rather than trouble, about an awkward affair here, which you may perhaps have heard of ; but our minister has behaved very handsomely, and the Tuscan Government as well as it is possible for such a government to behave, which is not saying much for the latter. Some other English and Scots, and myself, had a brawl with a dragoon, who insulted one of the party, and whom we mistook for an officer, as he was medalled and well mounted, etc. ; but he turned out to be a serjeant-major. He called out the guard at the gates to arrest us (we being unarmed) ; upon which I and another (an Italian) rode through the said guard ; but they succeeded in detaining others of the party. I rode to my house, and sent my secretary to give an account of the attempted and illegal arrest to the authorities, and then, without dismounting, rode back towards the gates, which are near my present mansion. Half-way I met my man vapouring away and threatening to draw upon me (who had a cane in my hand, and no other arms). I, still believing him an officer, demanded his name and address, and gave him my hand and glove thereupon. A servant of mine thrust in between us (totally without orders), but let him go on my command. He then rode off at full speed; but about forty paces further was stabbed, and very dangerously (so as to be in peril), by some *Callum Beg* or other of my people (for I have some rough-handed folks about me), I need hardly say without my direction or approval. The said dragoon had been sabring our unarmed countrymen, however, at the *gate, after they were in arrest*, and held by the guards, and wounded one, Captain Hay, very severely. However, he got his paiks—having acted like an assassin, and being treated like one. *Who* wounded him, though it was done before thousands of people, they have never been able to ascertain, or prove, nor even the *weapon*; some said a *pistol*, an *air-gun*, a stiletto, a sword, a lance, a pitchfork, and what not. They have arrested and examined servants and people of all descriptions, but can make out nothing. Mr. Dawkins, our minister, assures me that no suspicion is entertained of the man who wounded him having been instigated by me, or any of the party. I enclose you copies of the depositions of those with us, and Dr. Crauford, a canny Scot (*not* an acquaintance), who saw the latter part of the affair. They are in Italian.

These are the only literary matters in which I have been engaged since the publication and row about *Cain*;—but Mr. Murray has several things of mine in his obstetrical hands. Another *Mystery*—a *Vision*—a Drama—and the like. But *you won't* tell me what *you* are doing—however, I shall find you out, write what you will. You say that I should like your son-in-law—it would be very difficult for me to dislike any one connected with you; but I have no doubt that his own qualities are all that you describe.

I am sorry you don't like Lord Orford's new work. My aristocracy, which is very fierce, makes him a favourite of mine. Recollect that those " little factions " comprised Lord

Chatham and Fox, the father ; and that *we* live in gigantic and exaggerated times, which make all under Gog and Magog appear pigmean. After having seen Napoleon begin like Tamerlane and end like Bajazet in our own time, we have not the same interest in what would otherwise have appeared important history. But I must conclude.

Believe me ever and most truly yours, NOEL BYRON

TO LORD HOLLAND*   *Pisa, May 11th, 1822*

MY DEAR LORD HOLLAND,—Let me thank you for your kind letter. What you say respecting poor Allegra is but too true. Her death, I confess, chilled my blood with horror. It was perhaps the most lively sorrow I have ever felt. With respect to the calumnies heaped upon me, I confess, though I am accustomed to all sorts of accusations, there are calumnies against which innocence itself loses courage. What of the— but the subject is too painful to me to touch upon. Great as my affliction may be, I beg to assure you, that I neither seek for, nor require the pity of any man ; and, although I by no means reject the sympathy of my friends, yet I feel that, if it were not expressed with greater delicacy of sentiment than *the party* appears to possess, it would be more chilling to my heart than the blasts of a Siberian winter.

The war of " *Church and State* " has astonished me more than it disturbs ; for I really thought " *Cain* " a speculative and hardy—but still a harmless—production. That crazy forgotten book, the " Pursuits of Literature ", contains one observation insisting notice. " Literature ", says the writer, " well or ill conducted, is the great engine by which all civilized states must ultimately be supported or overthrown." It were a difficult point to decide whether religion, education or litera- ture, in the hands of power, would tend most to its stability. It is certain, however, if by any means it could obtain all three, its influence would be unbounded, and a nation so enslaved would enjoy only an automaton existence, following every impulse of its rulers.

Let me hear from you when convenient, and believe me
Yours ever most affectionately, N. BYRON

TO JOHN MURRAY *Montenero, May 26ᵗʰ 1822, near Leghorn*

DEAR SIR,—The body is embarked, in what ship I know not, neither could I enter into the details; but the Countess G. G. has had the goodness to give the necessary orders to Mr. Dunn, who superintends the embarkation, and will write to you. I wish it to be buried in Harrow Church: there is a spot in the Church*yard*, near the footpath, on the brow of the hill looking towards Windsor, and a tomb under a large tree (bearing the name of Peachie, or Peachey), where I used to sit for hours and hours when a boy: this was my favourite spot; but, as I wish to erect a tablet to her memory, the body had better be deposited in the Church. Near the door, on the left hand as you enter, there is a monument with a tablet containing these words:—

" When Sorrow weeps o'er Virtue's sacred dust,
    Our tears become us, and our Grief is just:
    Such were the tears she shed, who grateful pays
    This last sad tribute of her love and praise ".

I recollect them (after seventeen years), not from any thing remarkable in them, but because from my seat in the Gallery I had generally my eyes turned towards that monument: as near it as convenient I could wish Allegra to be buried, and on the wall a marble tablet placed, with these words:—[1]

In memory of
Allegra,
daughter of G. G. Lord Byron,
who died at Bagnacavallo,
in Italy, April 20th, 1822,
aged five years and three months.

" I shall go to her, but she shall not return to me."
2d Samuel, xii. 23

The funeral I wish to be as private as is consistent with decency; and I could hope that Henry Drury will, perhaps, read the service over her. If he should decline it, it can be done by the usual Minister for the time being. I do not know that I need add more just now.

[1] Byron's wishes were not carried out.

I will now turn to other subjects. Since I came here, I have been invited by the Americans on board of their Squadron, where I was received with all the kindness which I could wish, and with *more ceremony* than I am fond of. I found them finer ships than your own of the same class, well manned and officered. A number of American gentlemen also were on board at the time, and some ladies. As I was taking leave, an American lady asked me for a *rose* which I wore, for the purpose, she said, of sending to America something which I had about me, as a memorial. I need not add, that I felt the compliment properly. Captain Chauncey showed me an American and very pretty edition of my poems, and offered me a passage to the United States, if I would go there. Commodore Jones was also not less kind and attentive. I have since received the enclosed letter, desiring me to sit for my picture for some Americans. It is singular that, in the same year that Lady Noel leaves by will an interdiction for my daughter to see her father's portrait for many years, the individuals of a nation, not remarkable for their liking to the English in particular, nor for flattering men in general, request me to sit for my " pourtraicture ", as Baron Bradwardine calls it. I am also told of considerable literary honours in Germany. Goethe, I am told, is my professed patron and protector. At Leipsic, this year, the highest prize was proposed for a translation of two Cantos of *Childe Harold*. I am not sure that this was at *Leipsic*, but Mr. Bancroft was my authority—a good German Scholar (a young American), and an acquaintance of Goethe's.

Goethe and the Germans are particularly fond of *Don Juan*, which they judge of as a work of Art. I had heard something like this before through Baron Lutzerode. The translations have been very frequent of several of the works, and Goethe made a comparison between *Faust* and *Manfred*.

All this is some compensation for your English native brutality, so fully displayed this year (I mean *not your* individually) to its brightest extent.

I forgot to mention a little anecdote of a different kind. I went over the Constitution (the Commodore's flag ship), and saw, among other things worthy of remark, a little boy *born* on board of her by a sailor's wife. They had christened him " Constitution Jones ". I, of course, approved the name;

and the woman added, " Ah, Sir, if he turns out but half as good as his name ! "

Yours ever and truly, N. B.

TO THE HON. DOUGLAS KINNAIRD *   *Montenero, Leghorn,*
May 27th, 1822

MY DEAR DOUGLAS,—My above address, as at Pisa, may probably be the same in Sept., and I need not add that you will be welcome there, as any where else that may happen to [be] my residence.

I have received the enclosed letter from Mr. Hanson Jr. When I constituted you my *Power of* Attorney, I meant it to be also *Power over* my Attorney. And so deal with the Attornd according to your despotism. Does he mean that the *whole* balance, or *his separate* balance, is £600 ? For if I recollect rightly, they set up a sort of *separate* claim, and a double claim besides. I see no use in their appealing to me, because if I empowered you to act during my absence, it was with the wish that you should do so. Else *why* make you my Potestas at all ?

You see they are getting on but slowly with that eternal mortgage. If the funds fall, (and war seems imminent) I shall lose all owing to the cursed dilatoriness of trustees and Solicitors, and yet he seems eager enough for his bill. Hanson is always too sanguine about Rochdale matters. However, the sum obtained for the tolls is better than nothing. I wonder when that blessed Appeal on the minerals will be heard and decided. I suppose my politics will prevent its success. " Well, Heaven's above all ! " As to the temporary and precarious tenure of the Noel affairs, manage it as you please. With those two fellows for trustees, I expect little profit, and less comfort.

Hobhouse proposed to ensure *her* life for *twenty* instead of *ten* thousand pounds. What think you ? *When* and *how* and *where* are the *rents* paid, or to be paid when they are due, or are they overdue ? What sum do you think I should set aside for liquidations etc. ? On all these points I desiderate illumination.

What *is* Lady N. B.'s *complaint* ? For of this even I know nothing.   There is another thing I wish to say.   As Mr. Murray should not run risks unnecessarily while I am going down hill in the world of scribbling, I will be at the *whole* expense of the publications of the things in hand, and any little profit which may accrue, I can take, or at any rate undergo the probable loss.   I care nothing about the Edinburgh Review (which I have not seen), though it will do much harm.   I have no hesitation in saying that the late volume contains by far the best of my writings, and the time will come when it will be thought so.

You must also advance for me to Murray the expense of poor little Allegra's funeral.   I have directed that she may be buried at Harrow on the Hill, and committed the care of the funeral (which I wish to be as private as is consistent with decency) to Mr. M. not wishing to trouble *you*.

Yours ever,   N. B.

TO THOMAS MOORE   *Montenero, Villa Dupuy, near Leghorn,*
June 8, 1822

I have written to you twice through the medium of Murray, and on one subject, *trite* enough,—the loss of poor little Allegra by a fever : on which topic I shall say no more—there is nothing but time.

A few days ago, my earliest and dearest friend, Lord Clare, came over from Geneva on purpose to see me before he returned to England.   As I have always loved him (since I was thirteen, at Harrow) better than any (*male*) thing in the world, I need hardly say what a melancholy pleasure it was to see him for a *day* only ;   for he was obliged to resume his journey immediately.   * * * I have heard, also, many other things of our acquaintances which I did not know ;   amongst others, that * * *   Do you recollect, in the year of revelry 1814, the pleasantest parties and balls all over London? and not the least so at * *'s.   Do you recollect your singing duets with Lady * *, and my flirtation with Lady * *, and all the other fooleries of the time? while * * was sighing, and Lady * * ogling him with her clear hazel eyes. *But* eight years have passed, and, since that time, * * has * * * * * * ;—— has run away with * * * * * ; and *mysen* (as my Nottinghamshire friends call themselves) might as well have thrown myself out of the window while you were singing, as intermarried where I did. You and * * * * have come off the best of us. I speak merely of my marriage, and its consequences, distresses, and calumnies ; for I have been much more happy, on the whole, *since*, than I ever could have been with * * * * * *.

I have read the recent article of Jeffrey in a faithful transcription of the impartial Galignani. I suppose the long and short of it is, that he wishes to provoke me to reply. But I won't, for I owe him a good turn still for his kindness by-gone. Indeed, I presume that the present opportunity of attacking me again was irresistible ; and I can't blame him, knowing what human nature is. I shall make but one remark :—what does he mean by elaborate? The whole volume was written with the greatest rapidity, in the midst of evolutions, and revolutions, and persecutions, and proscriptions of all who interested me in Italy. They said the same of *Lara*, which, *you* know, was written amidst balls and fooleries, and after coming home from masquerades and routs, in the summer of the sovereigns. Of all I have ever written, they are perhaps the most carelessly composed ; and their faults, whatever they may be, are those of negligence, and not of labour. I do not think this a merit, but it is a fact.

Yours ever and truly, N. B.

P.S.—You see the great advantage of my new signature ;— it may either stand for " Nota Bene " or " Noel Byron ", and, as such, will save much repetition, in writing either books or letters. Since I came here, I have been invited on board of the American squadron, and treated with all possible honour and ceremony. They have asked me to sit for my picture ; and, as I was going away, an American lady took a rose from me (which had been given to me by a very pretty Italian lady that very morning), because, she said, " She was determined to send or take something which I had about me to America ". *There* is a kind of Lalla Rookh incident for you ! However, all these American honours arise, perhaps, not so much from their

enthusiasm for my " Poeshie ", as their belief in my dislike to
the English,—in which I have the satisfaction to coincide with
them. I would rather, however, have a nod from an American,
than a snuff-box from an emperor.

TO ISAAC D'ISRAELI [1]   *Montenero, Villa Dupuy, nr Leghorn,*
(to ye care of John Murray, Esqre)   *June 10th 1822*

DEAR SIR,—If you will permit me to call you so. I had
some time ago taken up my pen at Pisa to thank you for the
present of your new Edition of the *Literary Character*, which has
often been to me a consolation, and always a pleasure. I was
interrupted, however, partly by business, and partly by vexations of different kinds, for I have not very long ago lost a
child by a fever, and I have had a good deal of petty trouble
with the laws of this lawless country, on account of the prosecution of a servant for an attack upon a cowardly Scoundrel of a
dragoon, who drew his Sword upon some unarmed Englishmen ; and whom I had done the honour to mistake for an
officer, and to treat like a Gentleman. He turned out to be
neither—like many others with medals and in uniform ; but
he paid for his brutality with a severe and dangerous wound
inflicted by nobody knows whom : for of three suspected and
two arrested they have been able to identify neither, which is
strange, since he was wounded in the presence of thousands in
a public Street during a feast day and full promenade.

But to return to things more analogous to the *Literary
Character*. I wish to say that had I known that the book was
to fall into your hands, or that the MSS. notes you have
thought worthy of publication would have attracted your
attention, I would have made them more copious and perhaps
not so careless.

I really cannot know whether I am or am not the Genius
you are pleased to call me, but I am very willing to put up with
the mistake, if it be one. It is a title dearly enough bought by
most men, to render it endurable, even when not quite clearly

[1] Author of *Curiosities of Literature, Calamities of Authors*, etc., etc., father of the
statesman.

made out, which it never *can* be till the Posterity, whose decisions are merely dreams to ourselves, has sanctioned or denied it, while it can touch us no further.

Mr. Murray is in possession of an MSS. Memoir of mine (not to be published till I am in my grave) which, strange as it may seem, I never read over since it was written and have no desire to read over again. In it I have told what, as far as I know, is the *truth—not* the *whole* truth—for if I had done so I must have involved much private and some dissipated history; but, nevertheless, nothing but the truth, as far as regard for others permitted it to appear.

I do not know whether you have seen those MSS.; but as you are curious in such things as relate to the human mind, I should feel gratified if you had.

I also sent him (Murray) a few days since, a commonplace book, by my friend Lord Clare, containing a few things which may perhaps aid his publication in case of his surviving me.

If there are any questions which you would like to ask me as connected with your Philosophy of the literary Mind (*if* mine be a literary mind), I will answer them fairly or give a reason for *not*—good, bad, or indifferent. At present I am paying the penalty of having helped to spoil the public taste, for, as long as I wrote in the false exaggerated style of youth and the times in which we live, they applauded me to the very echo; and within these few years, when I have endeavoured at better things and written what I suspect to have the principle of duration in it, the Church, the Chancellor, and all men— even to my grand patron Francis Jeffrey Esqre of the *E.R.*— have risen up against me and my later publications. Such is Truth! Men dare not look her in the face, except by degrees : they mistake her for a Gorgon, instead of knowing her to be a Minerva.

I do not mean to apply this mythological simile to my own endeavours. I have only to turn over a few pages of your volumes to find innumerable and far more illustrious instances.

It is lucky that I am of a temper not to be easily turned aside though by no means difficult to irritate. But I am making a dissertation instead of writing a letter. I write to you from the Villa Dupuy, near Leghorn, with the islands of Elba and Corsica visible from my balcony, and my old friend the Mediterranean rolling blue at my feet. As long as I retain my feeling and my passion for Nature, I can partly soften or subdue my other passions and resist or endure those of others.

I have the honour to be, truly, your obliged
and faithful Ser^{t}, NOEL BYRON

TO E. J. DAWKINS *   *Pisa, July 4th 1822*
[British Minister at Florence]

DEAR SIR,—I regret to say that my anticipations were well founded. The Gamba family received on Tuesday an order to quit the Tuscan States in four days.[1] Of course this is virtually my own exile, for where they go I am no less bound by honour than by feeling to follow. I believe we shall try to obtain leave to remain at Lucca—if that fails, Genoa—and, failing that, possibly America; for both Captain Chauncey of the American Squadron (which returns in September) and Mr. Bruen an American Merchant man at Leghorn offered me a passage in the handsomest manner—the latter sent to me to say that he would even send his vessel round to Genoa for us, if we chose to accept his offer. With regard to the interpretation which will be put upon my departure at this time, I hope that you will do me the favour of letting the truth be known, as my own absence will deprive me of the power of doing so for myself, and I have little doubt that advantage will be taken of that circumstance.

This letter will be presented to you by Mr. Taaffe, who is in considerable confusion at a measure to which his own heedlessness has a good deal contributed. But—poor fellow—I suppose that he meant no harm. He wanted the Countess Guiccioli to go to Florence and fling herself at the feet of the Grand Duchess—

a supplicant to wait
While Ladies interpose, and Slaves debate

I can only say, that if she did anything of the kind, I would never fling myself at *her* feet again.

Collini's office has now become a Sinecure, and I wish him

[1] For an account of the affray which led to the Gambas being exiled from the Tuscan States, see Byron's letter to Sir Walter Scott, May 4th, 1822.

joy of it.   The inconvenience and expense to me will be very
considerable, as I have two houses, furniture, Wines, Dinner
Services—linen,—books, my Schooner—and in short—a whole
establishment for a family—to leave at a moment's warning—
and this without knowing where the Gambas will be permitted
to rest, and of course where I can rest also.

The whole thing—the manner in which it was announced,
by the Commissary etc. was done in the most insulting manner.
The Courier treated as if he were a delinquent, and sent away
with Soldiers to take charge of him and lodged in the prison of
Pisa, by way of Hostel.

I trust that this just Government is now content, my
countrymen have been insulted and wounded by a rascal,
and my Servants treated like Criminals though guiltless, while
a noble and respectable family including a sick lady are
ordered away like so many felons, without a shadow of justice,
or even a *pretence* of *proof*.

With regard to yourself, I can only add that my obligations
and feelings towards you are the same as if your exertions had
been attended with Success.   I certainly did at one time think,
that whether they considered the person who applied in our
behalf, or the persons in whose behalf the application was
made, we should at least have had a *fair* trial, as I afforded
every facility for the investigation.   As it is, I will *not* express
my sentiments—at least for the present I cannot—as no words
could be at all adequate to describe my Sense of the manner
in which the whole has been conducted by these people who
call themselves a Government.

TO E. J. DAWKINS *   *Pisa, July 6th 1822*
[British Minister at Florence]

DEAR SIR,—Certainly, if anything will be of use at Lucca,
it is probable that a letter from you may have that effect.   I
should be sorry to give you the personal trouble of a journey,
on any account.   With regard to the Gambas I beg leave to
observe that the Countess Guiccioli is *not* an exile, and her
passport is or *was* given in the usual manner.   When she was
separated from her husband in 1820, by the Pope's decree,

it was enjoined by His Holiness that she was to reside with her father—or otherwise to forfeit the alimony or *any* money (or whatever the word may be in the Roman or Romagnole Doctors' Commons) allotted to her from her husband's estates by the Papal order. When her father and brother were exiled for political reasons, Count Guiccioli as was natural and conjugal applied to have her shut up in a Convent, on the plea that she was no longer residing with her family. A Minister of the Legation gave me notice of this application and its probable result in time for her to rejoin her relations in Tuscany. I could not then accompany her in person, as it would have [been] construed into an Elopement; but I joined her afterwards at Pisa. If you can obtain permission for *them* or for *her* at least to reside within the Lucchese territory, it would be a great service, till I can make arrangements for the removal of my establishment. I shall go with them, but could then return here to settle my business.—I do not even know upon what pretext She was ordered to quit Tuscany, or even if she really was so, since her name is not in the letter, nor is she an exile, and is besides in very delicate health as Sr Vacca testified and can testify.

Believe me yrs very truly
and obliged
NOEL BYRON

P.S.—Would you like to take a cruise in my little Schooner? it would console me for not being allowed to use it myself, if it could be of any pleasure to you while at Leghorn.

TO THOMAS MOORE *Pisa, August 8, 1822*

You will have heard by this time that Shelley and another gentleman (Captain Williams) were drowned about a month ago (a *month* yesterday), in a squall off the Gulf of Spezia. There is thus another man gone, about whom the world was ill-naturedly, and ignorantly, and brutally mistaken. It will, perhaps, do him justice *now*, when he can be no better for it.

I have not seen the thing you mention, and only heard of it casually, nor have I any desire. The price is, as I saw in some advertisements, fourteen shillings, which is too much to pay for a libel on oneself. Some one said in a letter, that it was a Dr. Watkins, who deals in the life and libel line. It must have diminished your natural pleasure, as a friend (*vide* Rochefoucault), to see yourself in it.

With regard to the Blackwood fellows, I never published any thing against them ; nor, indeed, have seen their magazine (except in Galignani's extracts) for these three years past. I once wrote, a good while ago, some remarks on their review of *Don Juan*, but saying very little about themselves, and these were *not* published. If you think that I ought to follow your example (and I like to be in your company when I can) in contradicting their impudence, you may shape this declaration of mine into a similar paragraph for me. It is possible that you may have seen the little I *did* write (and never published) at Murray's :—it contained much more about Southey than about the Blacks.

If you think that I ought to do any thing about Watkins's book, I should not care much about publishing *my Memoir now*, should it be necessary to counteract the fellow. But, in *that* case, I should like to look over the *press* myself. Let me know what you think, or whether I had better *not* :—at least, not the second part, which touches on the actual confines of still existing matters.

I have written three more cantos of *Don Juan*, and am hovering on the brink of another (the ninth). The reason I want the stanzas again which I sent you is, that as these cantos contain a full detail (like the storm in Canto Second) of the siege and assault of Ismael, with much of sarcasm on those butchers in large business, your mercenary soldiery, it is a good opportunity of gracing the poem with * * *. With these things and these fellows, it is necessary, in the present clash of philosophy and tyranny, to throw away the scabbard. I know it is against fearful odds ; but the battle must be fought ; and it will be eventually for the good of mankind, whatever it may be for the individual who risks himself.

What do you think of your Irish bishop? Do you remember Swift's line, " Let me have a *barrack*—a fig for the *clergy* "? This seems to have been his reverence's motto.
* * * * *

Yours, etc.

It is boring to trouble you with " such small gear " ; but it must be owned that I should be glad if you would enquire whether my Irish subscription ever reached the committee in Paris from Leghorn. My reasons, like Vellum's, " are three-fold " :—First, I doubt the accuracy of all almoners, or re-mitters of benevolent cash ; second, I do suspect that the said Committee, having in part served its time to time-serving, may have kept back the acknowledgment of an obnoxious politician's name in their lists ; and third, I feel pretty sure that I shall one day be twitted by the government scribes for having been a professor of love for Ireland, and not coming forward with the others in her distresses.

It is not, as you may opine, that I am ambitious of having my name in the papers, as I can have that any day in the week gratis. All I want is to know if the Reverend Thomas Hall did or did not remit my subscription (200 scudi of Tuscany, or about a thousand francs, more or less,) to the Committee at Paris.

The other day at Viareggio, I thought proper to swim off to my schooner (the Bolivar) in the offing, and thence to shore again—about three miles, or better, in all. As it was at mid-day, under a broiling sun, the consequence has been a feverish attack, and my whole skin's coming off, after going through the process of one large continuous blister, raised by the sun and sea together. I have suffered much pain ; not being able to lie on my back, or even side ; for my shoulders and arms were equally St. Bartholomewed. But it is over,—and I have got a new skin, and am as glossy as a snake in its new suit.

We have been burning the bodies of Shelley and Williams on the sea-shore, to render them fit for removal and regular interment. You can have no idea what an extraordinary effect such a funeral pile has, on a desolate shore, with moun-tains in the back-ground and the sea before, and the singular appearance the salt and frankincense gave to the flame. All of Shelley was consumed, except his *heart*, which would not take the flame, and is now preserved in spirits of wine.

Your old acquaintance Londonderry has quietly died at North Cray ! and the virtuous De Witt was torn in pieces by the populace! What a lucky * * the Irishman has been in his life and end. In him your Irish Franklin *est mort*!

Leigh Hunt is sweating articles for his new Journal; and both he and I think it somewhat shabby in *you* not to contribute. Will you become one of the *properrioters*? " Do, and we go snacks." I recommend you to think twice before you respond in the negative.

I have nearly (*quite three*) four new cantos of *Don Juan* ready. I obtained permission from the female Censor Morum of *my* morals to continue it, provided it were immaculate; so I have been as decent as need be. There is a deal of war—a siege, and all that, in the style, graphical and technical, of the shipwreck in Canto Second, which " took ", as they say in the Row.

Yours, etc.

P.S.—That * * * Galignani has about ten lies in one paragraph. It was not a Bible that was found in Shelley's pocket, but John Keats's poems. However, it would not have been strange, for he was a great admirer of Scripture as a composition. *I* did not send my bust to the academy of New York; but I sat for my picture to young West, an American artist, at the request of some members of that Academy to *him* that he would take my portrait,—for the Academy, I believe.

I had, and still have, thoughts of South America, but am fluctuating between it and Greece. I should have gone, long ago, to one of them, but for my liaison with the Countess G[uiccioli]; for love, in these days, is little compatible with glory. *She* would be delighted to go too; but I do not choose to expose her to a long voyage, and a residence in an unsettled country, where I shall probably take a part of some sort.

TO MRS. SHELLEY   *6ᵗʰ October, 1822*

The sofa—which I regret is *not* of your furniture—it was purchased by me at Pisa since you left it.

It is convenient for my room, though of little value (about 12 pauls), and I offered to send another (now sent) in its stead. I preferred retaining the purchased furniture, but always intended that you should have as good or better in its place. I have a particular dislike to anything of Shelley's being within the same walls with Mrs. Hunt's children. They are dirtier and more mischievous than Yahoos. What they can't destroy with their filth they will with their fingers. I presume you received ninety and odd crowns from the wreck of the *Don Juan*, and also the price of the boat purchased by Captain R., if not, you will have *both*. Hunt has these in hand.

With regard to any difficulties about money, I can only repeat that I will be your banker till this state of things is cleared up, and you can see what is to be done; so there is little to hinder you on that score. I was confined for four days to my bed at Lerici. Poor Hunt, with his six little blackguards, are coming slowly up; as usual he turned back once—was there ever such a *kraal* out of the Hottentot country.

N. B.

TO THE HON. AUGUSTA LEIGH   *Albaro, Genoa, Nov. 7ᵗʰ 1822*

My Dearest A.,—I have yours of the 25ᵗʰ. My illness is quite gone, it was only at Lerici. On the fourth night I had got a little sleep, and was so wearied, that, though there were three slight shocks of an Earthquake that frightened the whole town into the streets, neither they nor the tumult awakened me.

We have had a deluge here, which has carried away half the country between this and Genoa (about two miles or less distant) but being on a hill we were only nearly knocked down by the lightning and battered by columns of rain, and our lower floor afloat, with the comfortable view of the whole landscape under water, and people screaming out of their garret windows; *two bridges* swept down, and our next door neighbours, a Cobbler, a Wigmaker, and a Ginger-bread baker, delivering up their whole stock to the elements, which marched away with a quantity of shoes, several Perukes, and Gingerbread in all its branches. The whole came on so suddenly that there was no time to prepare. Think only, at the *top* of a hill of the road being an impassable cascade, and a child being drowned a few yards from its own door (as we heard say) in a place where Water is in general a rare commodity.

Well, after all this comes a preaching Friar and says that the day of Judgement will take place positively on the *4ᵗʰ* with all kinds of tempest and what not, in consequence of which the whole City (except some impious Scoffers) sent him presents to avert the wrath of Heaven by his prayers, and even the *public authorities* had warned the Captains of Ships, who, to mend the matter, almost all bought *new Cables* and anchors by way of weathering the Gale.

But the fourth turned out a very fine day. All those who had paid their money are excessively angry, and insist either upon having the day of judgement or their cash again. But the Friar's device seems to be " no money to be returned ", and he says that he merely made a mistake in the time, for the day of Judgement will certainly come for all that, either here or in some other part of Italy.

This has a little pacified the expectants. You will think this a fiction. Enquire further then. The populace actually used to kiss the fellow's feet in the streets. His Sermon, how-ever, had small effect upon some, for they gave a ball on the 3ᵈ, and a tradesman brought me an *over*charge on the same day, upon which I threatened him with the friar ; but he said that was a reason for being paid on the 3ᵈ as he had a sum to make up for his last account.

There seem [1] * * *

TO LADY [HARDY]   *Albaro, November 10, 1822*

*   *   *   *   *   *   *

The Chevalier [2] persisted in declaring himself an ill-used gentleman, and describing you as a kind of cold Calypso, who lead astray people of an amatory disposition without giving them any sort of compensation, contenting yourself, it seems, with only making *one* fool instead of two, which is the more approved method of proceeding on such occasions. For my part, I think you are quite right ; and be assured from me that

---

[1] The conclusion of this letter is missing.
[2] James Wedderburn Webster, who was now separated from his wife, Lady Frances. Byron's correspondent was the widow of the naval officer who attended Nelson's death-bed.

a woman (as society is constituted in England) who gives any advantage to a man may expect a lover, but will sooner or later find a tyrant; and this is not the man's fault either, perhaps, but is the necessary and natural result of the circumstances of society, which, in fact, tyrannise over the man equally with the woman; that is to say, if either of them have any feeling or honour.

You can write to me at your leisure and inclination. I have always laid it down as a maxim, and found it justified by experience, that a man and a woman make far better friendships than can exist between two of the same sex; but *these* with this condition, that they never have made, or are to make, love with each other. Lovers may, and, indeed, generally *are* enemies, but they never can be friends; because there must always be a spice of jealousy and a something of self in all their speculations.

Indeed, I rather look upon love altogether as a sort of hostile transaction, very necessary to make or to break matches, and keep the world going, but by no means a sinecure to the parties concerned.

Now, as my love perils are, I believe, pretty well over, and yours, by all accounts, are never to begin, we shall be the best friends imaginable, as far as both are concerned; and with this advantage, that we may both fall to loving right and left through all our acquaintance, without either sullenness or sorrow from that amiable passion, which are its inseparable attendants.

Believe me, etc., N. B.

TO THE HON. DOUGLAS KINNAIRD [?]   *Genoa,*
                                                   November, 1822

My dear [Douglas],—I have finished the twelfth canto of *Don Juan*, which I will forward when copied. With the sixth, seventh, and eighth in one volume, and the ninth, tenth, eleventh, and twelfth in another, the whole may form two volumes, of about the same size as the two former. There are some good things in them, as perhaps may be allowed. Perhaps one volume had better be published with one publisher, and the other with another; it would be a new experiment: or one in one month, and another in the next; or both at once. What thinkest thou?

Murray, long after the " piracies ", offered me a thousand pounds (guineas) a canto for as many as I might choose to write. He has since departed from this proposal, for it was too much, and I would not take advantage of it.

You must, however, use your own judgement with regard to the MSS. and let me know what you propose; presuming always (what may at last be but a presumption) that the seven new cantos are, on the whole, equal to the five former.

Suppose Hunt, or somebody else, were to publish one canto a week, upon the same size and paper, to correspond with the various former editions?—but this is merely as a vision, and may be very foolish, for aught I know.

I have read the defence of *Cain*, which is very good; who can be the author? As to myself I shall not be deterred by any outcry; your present public hate me, but they shall not interrupt the march of my mind, nor prevent me from telling those who are attempting to trample on all thought, that their thrones shall yet be rocked to their foundations. It is Madame de Stael who says, that " all talent has a propensity to attack the strong ". *I* have never flattered—whether it be or be not a proof of talent.

I have just seen the illustrious * * * [Wedderburn Webster] who came to visit me here. I had not seen him these ten years. He had a black wig, and has been made a knight for writing against the queen. He wants a diplomatic situation, and seems likely to want it.

He found me thinner even than in 1813; for since my late illness at Lerici, in my way here, I have subsided into my more meagre outline, and am obliged to be very abstinent by medical advice, on account of liver and what not.

But to the point—or at least my point in mentioning this new chevalier. Ten years ago I lent him a thousand pounds on condition that he would not go to the Jews; he took the moneys, and went to the Jews. Now, as Mr. —— [Hanson] is a purchaser of bonds, will he purchase this of me? or will any body else, at a discount?

I have been invited by the Americans on board of their squadron here, and received with the greatest kindness, and rather *too much* ceremony. They have asked me to sit for my picture to an American artist now in Florence. As I was preparing to depart, an American lady took a rose which I wore, from me, and said that she wished to send something which I had about me to America. They showed me, too, American editions of my poems, and all kinds of attention and good-will.

I also hear that, as an author, I am in high request in Germany. All this is some compensation for the desertion of the English.

Would you write a German line to Goethe for me, explaining the omission of the dedication to *Sardanapalus*, by the fault of the publisher, and asking his permission to prefix it to the forthcoming volume of *Werner* and the *Mystery*.

Are you quite well yet? I hope so. I am selling two more horses, and dismissing two superfluous servants. My horses now amount to *four*, instead of *nine* : and I have arranged my establishment on the same footing. So you perceive that I am in earnest in my frugalities.

Yours ever affectionately, N. B.

TO JOHN MURRAY [FRAGMENT]   [*Genoa, 10ᵇʳᵉ 9, 1822*]

Very willing to lighten any losses (" go to " ; thou art " a fellow that hath had losses ", like Dogberry, is it not so?) which you may experience from my becoming obnoxious to the Blue people.

I hope that you have a milder winter than we have here. We have had inundations worthy of the Trent or Po, and the Conductor (Franklin's) of my house was struck (or supposed to be stricken) by a thunderbolt. I was so near the window that I was dazzled and my eyes hurt for several minutes, and every body in the house felt an electric shock at the moment. Madame Guiccioli was frightened, as you may suppose.

I have thought since, that your bigots would have " saddled me with a judgement " (as Thwackum did Square when he bit his tongue in talking Metaphysics), if any thing had happened of consequence. These fellows always forget Christ in their Christianity, and what he said when " the tower of Siloam fell ".

To-day is the 9th, and the 10th is my surviving daughter's birthday. I have ordered, as a regale, a mutton chop and a bottle of ale. She is seven years old, I believe. Did I ever tell you that the day I came of age I dined on eggs and bacon and a bottle of ale for once in a way? They are my favourite dish and drinkable; but as neither of them agree with me, I never use them but on great jubilees—once in four or five years or so.

I see some booby represents the Hunts and Mrs. Shelley as living in my house : it is a falsehood. They reside at some distance, and I do not see them twice in a month. I have not met Mr. H[unt] a dozen times since I came to Genoa, or near it.

Yours ever, N. B.

TO JOHN CAM HOBHOUSE *Genoa, 10bre 14th, 1822*

MY DEAR H.,—Y[ou]rs of Turin arrived yesterday. If Lady M[organ] arrives safely, she will be received ; but I suspect the Dogana will detain her. We are all in great surprise and displeasure at the Marchesa's mancanza, which is the more extraordinary as she is a particular friend of the Count G[amba] (the father who gave the letter), who, it is supposed, went still further than Pius 6th with her in their Gioventù, and at this very time, as all along, she has been a staunch supporter of Me. Guiccioli's suit against her sposo, still pending in appeal before his Papal Majesty. Be this as it may, Count G[amba] writes to enquire and remonstrate. She must have known you, as being herself a friend, and what's more, a witness of the late Queen's ; and must have heard your name, in the course of that conflict of testimonies. But we have had a complaint from Florence from Madame Regnier, that you either did not or would not avail yourself of your letter to Madame Regnier, who says she would have been glad to see you. By my own experience, and that of all I ever heard of, I know what Italian introductions [are] ; the stranger pays the visit, and invites to dinner; and perhaps the *visit* is repaid. This is generally the case, unless you settle in a place, and then you may have enough of mummery and maccaroni, opera boxes, and conversazioni (criminal ditto included); but a flying stranger must take " Folly as it flies ".

You ask after my health; it has been worse since I saw you, is better now, and may be better still, without being what Scrope used to call " rude health ". I never quite recovered that stupid long swim in the broiling sun and saline sea of August. At Lerici I was in my bed for four days; and it is not the best place for beds, and physicians. The doctor made his debut by talking of *Hippocratè*; in consequence of which, I sent him away; but the women being clamorous as usual, and myself, as Fribble says, in " exquisite torter ", he was recalled; and after several formidable administrations of medicines which would not remain in the stomach; and of glysters which could not be persuaded to quit it again, Nature, I presume, did the business, and saved me from a threatened inflammation of the bowels; during which (by way of rocking my cradle) we had a slight shock of an earthquake, such as we felt at Athens, probably an echo of that of Aleppo. Well, I scuttled out of bed the moment I was convalescent, got to Sestri by dint of rowing, in twelve hours; and came on per terra, to Genoa the same night; verily believing that the journey did me more good than the physic, or the physicianer. All went on very well till about a month ago, when I had, and have a *cutaneous* and very uncomfortable eruption, for which, by the advice of an English physician, I am taking what he calls a " *decoction of Woods* " (and of *Forests* too, I should think by its variety of tastes), and I am so pleased with the name that I swallow a pint daily with more faith than effect hitherto.

Since I have been here I have seen Dick Fitzgibbon (Lord Clare's brother, and your brother M.P.), Lady Hardy, and various of your country-people, and lastly, that little and insane James Wedderburn Webster, now converted into a Knight (but of no order—a regular Address and City Knight), yclept Sir James Wedderburn. I saw little change in him, except that his countenance rather more resembled his *backside* (do you remember Mr. Frank, of the coffee house's, accentuation of that injured word?) than heretofore; and that he had gotten a new wig, and says he means to marry, having a wife living, from whom he cannot get divorced.

You will have heard before this reaches you that our friend D[ouglas] K[innaird] has had *another* fall, from *another* horse, and thereby brake his collar-bone, besides being grievously contused; but he is getting well, and I wish that he would choose his stud better. I should look in vain for such another Potestas of Attorneo, and still more vainly for a similar friend; that is to say, who could unite the power and the will to under-go the drudgery he has done for " P.P., Clerk of this Parish ".

I trust that this will find you flourishing, in speech as in health. I doubt if the Congressors will be so pacific as you anticipate.

Henry Hunt is out of prison, and John Hunt is in a fair way of going into it, by what I hear; all you predicted has come to pass. I have gotten myself into a scrape with the very best intentions (i.e., to do good to these Sunday paper patriots). Doug. will narrate as much as you care to listen to. Leigh Hunt is discomposed because said Murray showed (and be d—d to him) a letter in which I qualified that illustrious editor as " a bore ", and I have offended everybody, like the old man and his ass. What is to be done with mine?

Pray excuse this long epistle. All here salute you with meridian cordiality; remember me to Burdett, and the Dougal, and etc., etc., believing me

Ever yours and faithfully, N. B.

TO JOHN MURRAY   *Genoa, 10bre 25º, 1822*

I had sent you back the *Quarterly*, without perusal, having resolved to read no more reviews, good, bad, or indifferent; but " who can control his fate? " Galignani, to whom my English studies are confined, has forwarded a copy of at least one half of it, in his indefatigable Catch-penny weekly compila-tion; and as, " like Honour, it came unlooked for ", I have looked through it. I must say that, upon the *whole*, that is, the whole of the *half* which I have read (for the other half is to be the Segment of Gal.'s next week's Circular), it is extremely handsome, and any thing but unkind or unfair. As I take the good in good part, I must not, nor will not, quarrel with the bad: what the Writer says of *Don Juan* is harsh, but it is inevitable. He must follow, or at least not directly oppose, the opinion of a prevailing, and yet not very firmly seated, party: a review may and will direct or " turn awry " the Currents of opinion, but it must not directly oppose them. *Don Juan* will be known by and bye, for what it is intended,—a *Satire* on *abuses* of the present states of Society, and not an eulogy of vice: it may be now and then voluptuous: I can't help that. Ariosto is worse; Smollett (see Lord Strutwell in vol. 2ᵈ of *R[oderick] R[andom]*) ten times worse; and Fielding no better. No Girl will ever be seduced by reading *D.J.*:—no, no; she will go to Little's poems and Rousseau's romans for that, or even to the immaculate De Stael: they will encourage her, and not the Don, who laughs at that, and—and—most other things. But never mind—Ça ira!

And now to a less agreeable topic, of which *pars magna es*—you Murray of Albemarle Sᵗ and the other Murray of Bridge Street—" Arcades Ambo " (" *Murrays both* ") " et *cant*-are pares ": ye, I say, between you, are the Causes of the prosecution of John Hunt, Esqʳᵉ on account of the *Vision*.[1] You, by sending him an incorrect copy, and the other, by his function. Egad, but H.'s Counsel will lay it on you with a trowel for your tergiversifying as to the MSS., etc., whereby poor H. (and, for anything I know, myself—I am willing enough) is likely to be impounded.

Now, do you see what you and your friends do by your injudicious rudeness?—actually cement a sort of connection which you strove to prevent, and which, had the H.'s *prospered*, would not in all probability have continued. As it is, I will not quit them in their adversity, though it should cost me character, fame, money, and the usual et cetera.

My original motives I already explained (in the letter which you thought proper to show): they are the *true* ones, and I abide by them, as I tell you, and I told Lʰ Hᵗ when he

---

[1] *The Vision of Judgement*, which Byron had presented to Leigh Hunt and his brother. When John was prosecuted for publishing it—at the instance of a society called the Constitutional Association, to which Charles Murray of Bridge Street acted as legal adviser—Byron provided funds for his defence. Hunt was convicted and fined.

questioned me on the subject of that letter. He was violently hurt, and never will forgive me at bottom ; but I can't help that. I never meant to make a parade of it ; but if he chose to question me, I could only answer the plain truth : and I confess I did not see anything in the letter to hurt him, unless I said he was " a *bore* ", which I don't remember. Had their Journal gone on well, and I could have aided to make it better for them, I should then have left them, after my safe pilotage off a lee shore, to make a prosperous voyage by themselves. As it is, I can't, and would not, if I could, leave them amidst the breakers.

As to any community of feeling, thought, or opinion, between L. H. and me, there is little or none : we meet rarely, hardly ever ; but I think him a good principled and able man, and must do as I would be done by. I do not know what world he has lived in, but I have lived in three or four ; and none of them like his Keats and Kangaroo *terra incognita*. Alas ! poor Shelley ! how he would have laughed had he lived, and how we used to laugh now and then, at various things, which are grave in the Suburbs !

You are all mistaken about Shelley. You do not know how mild, how tolerant, how good he was in Society ; and as perfect a Gentleman as ever crossed a drawing-room, when he liked, and where he liked.

I have some thoughts of taking a run down to Naples (*solus*, or, at most, *cum solâ*) this Spring, and writing, when I have studied the Country, a fifth and sixth Canto of *Ch^e Harolde* : but this is merely an idea for the present, and I have other excursions and voyages in my mind. The busts are finished : are you worthy of them?

Yours, etc., N. B.

P.S.—Mrs. Shelley is residing with the Hunts at some distance from me : I see them very seldom, and generally on account of their business. Mrs. S., I believe, will go to England in the Spring.

Count Gamba's family, the father and Son and daughter, are residing with me by Mr. Hill's (the minister's) recommendation, as a safer asylum from the political persecutions than they could have in another residence ; but they occupy one part of a

large house, and I the other, and our establishments are quite
separate.

Since I have read the *Q*[*uarterly*], I shall erase two or three
passages in the latter 6 or 7 Cantos, in which I had lightly
stroked over two or three of your authors; but I will not
return evil for good.   I liked what I read of the article much.

Mr. J. Hunt is most likely the publisher of the new Cantos;
with what prospects of success I know not, nor does it very
much matter, as far as I am concerned; but I hope that it
may be of use to him, for he is a stiff, sturdy, conscientious man,
and I like him : he is such a one as Prynne or Pym might be.   I
bear you no ill will for declining the *D. Js.*, but I cannot commend your conduct to the H.'s.

Have you aided Madame de Yossy, as I requested?   I sent
her 300 francs.   Recommend her, will you, to the Literary
F[und], or to some benevolence within your Circles.

TO THE HON. AUGUSTA LEIGH   *Genoa. J^u 27th 1823*

My dearest Augusta,—Your informant was as usual in error. Do not believe all the lies you may hear. Hobhouse can tell you that I have *not* lost *any* of my *teeth hitherto*, since I was 12 years old, and had a back one taken out by Dumergue to make room for others growing, and so far from being fatter —at *present* I am much thinner than when I left England, when I was not very stout—the *latter* you will regret, the *former* you will be glad to hear. Hobhouse can tell you all particulars, though I am much reduced since he saw me, and more than *you* would like. I write to you these few lines in haste, perhaps we may meet in Spring, either *here*, or in England. Hobhouse says your coming out would be the best thing which you could do, for yourself and me too—ever yrs most affectly

N. B.

TO THOMAS MOORE   *Genoa, April 2, 1823*

I have just seen some friends of yours, who paid me a visit yesterday, which, in honour of them and of you, I returned to-day ;—as I reserve my bear-skin and teeth, and paws and claws, for our enemies.

I have also seen Henry Fox, Lord Holland's son, whom I had not looked upon since I left him a pretty, mild boy, without a neck-cloth, in a jacket, and in delicate health, seven long years agone, at the period of mine eclipse—the third, I believe, as I have generally one every two or three years. I think that he has the softest and most amiable expression of countenance I ever saw, and manners correspondent. If to those he can add hereditary talents, he will keep the name of Fox in all its freshness for half a century more, I hope. I speak from a transient glimpse—but I love still to yield to such impressions ; for I have ever found that those I liked longest and best, I took to at first sight ; and I always liked that boy—perhaps, in part, from some resemblance in the less fortunate part of our destinies—I mean, to avoid mistakes, his lameness. But there is this difference, that *he* appears a halting angel, who has tripped against a star ; whilst I am *Le Diable Boiteux*,—a soubriquet, which I marvel that, amongst their various *nominis umbræ*, the Orthodox have not hit upon.

Your other allies, whom I have found very agreeable personages, are Milor Blessington and *épouse*, travelling with a very handsome companion, in the shape of a " French Count " [1] (to use Farquhar's phrase in the *Beaux Stratagem*), who has all the air of a *Cupidon déchaîné*, and is one of the few specimens I have seen of our ideal of a Frenchman *before* the Revolution—an old friend with a new face, upon whose like I never thought that we should look again. Miladi seems highly literary, to which, and your honour's acquaintance with the family, I attribute the pleasure of having seen them. She is also very pretty even in a morning,—a species of beauty on which the sun of Italy does not shine so frequently as the chandelier. Certainly, English women wear better than their continental neighbours of the same sex. Mountjoy seems very good-natured, but is much tamed, since I recollect him in all the glory of gems and snuff-boxes, and uniforms, and theatricals, and speeches in our house—" I mean, of peers ",—(I must refer you to Pope—whom you don't read and won't appreciate —for that quotation, which you must allow to be poetical,) and sitting to Stroelling, the painter, (so you remember our visit, with Leckie, to the German?) to be depicted as one of the heroes of Agincourt, " with his long sword, saddle, bridle, Whack fal de ", etc., etc.

I have been unwell—caught a cold and inflammation, which menaced a conflagration, after dining with our ambassador, Monsieur Hill,—not owing to the dinner, but my carriage broke down in the way home, and I had to walk some miles, up hill partly, after hot rooms, in a very bleak, windy evening, and over-hotted, or over-colded myself. I have not been so robustious as formerly, ever since the last summer, when I fell ill after a long swim in the Mediterranean, and have never been quite right up to this present writing. I am thin,—perhaps thinner than you saw me, when I was nearly transparent, in 1812,—and am obliged to be moderate of my mouth; which, nevertheless, won't prevent me (the gods willing) from dining with your friends the day after to-morrow.

[1] Count Alfred d'Orsay.

They give me a very good account of you, and of your nearly Emprisoned *Angels*. But why did you change your title?—you will regret this some day. The bigots are not to be conciliated; and, if they were—are they worth it? I suspect that I am a more orthodox Christian than you are; and, whenever I see a real Christian, either in practice or in theory, (for I never yet found the man who could produce either, when put to the proof,) I am his disciple. But, till then, I cannot truckle to tithe-mongers,—nor can I imagine what has made *you* circumcise your Seraphs.

I have been far more persecuted than you, as you may judge by my present decadence,—for I take it that I am as low in popularity and bookselling as any writer can be. At least, so my friends assure me—blessings on their benevolence! This they attribute to Hunt; but they are wrong—it must be, partly at least, owing to myself; be it so. As to Hunt, I prefer *not* having turned him to starve in the streets to any personal honour which might have accrued from some genuine phil-anthropy. I really act upon principle in this matter, for we have nothing much in common; and I cannot describe to you the despairing sensation of trying to do something for a man who seems incapable or unwilling to do any thing further for himself,—at least, to the purpose. It is like pulling a man out of a river who directly throws himself in again. For the last three or four years Shelley assisted, and had once actually extricated him. I have since his demise,—and even before,—done what I could: but it is not in my power to make this permanent. I want Hunt to return to England, for which I would furnish him with the means in comfort; and his situation *there*, on the whole, is bettered, by the payment of a portion of his debts, etc.; and he would be on the spot to continue his Journal, or Journals, with his brother, who seems a sensible, plain, sturdy, and enduring person. * *

TO THE EARL OF BLESSINGTON   *April 5, 1823*

MY DEAR LORD,—How is your gout? or rather, how are you? I return the Count D'Orsay's Journal, which is a very extraordinary production, and of a most melancholy truth in all that regards high life in England. I know, or knew personally, most of the personages and societies which he describes; and after reading his remarks, have the sensation fresh upon me as if I had seen them yesterday. I would however plead in behalf of some few exceptions, which I will mention by and by. The most singular thing is, *how* he should have penetrated *not* the *fact*, but the *mystery* of the English *ennui* at two-and-twenty. I was about the same age when I made the same discovery, in almost precisely the same circles,—(for there is scarcely a person mentioned whom I did not see nightly or daily, and was acquainted more or less intimately with most of them,)—but I never could have described it so well. *Il faut être Français*, to effect this.

But he ought also to have been in the country during the hunting season, with " a select party of distinguished guests ", as the papers term it. He ought to have seen the gentlemen after dinner (on the hunting days), and the soirée ensuing thereupon,—and the women looking as if they had hunted, or rather been hunted; and I could have wished that he had been at a dinner in town, which I recollect at Lord Cowper's— small, but select, and composed of the most amusing people. The dessert was hardly on the table, when, out of twelve, I counted *five asleep*; of that five, there were *Tierney*, Lord Lansdowne, and Lord Darnley—I forget the other two, but they were either wits or orators—perhaps poets.

My residence in the East and in Italy has made me somewhat indulgent of the siesta;—but then they set regularly about it in warm countries, and perform it in solitude (or at most in a tête-à-tête with a proper companion), and retire quietly to their rooms to get out of the sun's way for an hour or two.

Altogether, your friend's Journal is a very formidable production. Alas! our dearly beloved countrymen have only discovered that they are tired, and not that they are tiresome; and I suspect that the communication of the latter unpleasant verity will not be better received than truths usually are. I have read the whole with great attention and instruction. I am too good a patriot to say *pleasure*—at least I won't say so, whatever I may think. I showed it (I hope no breach of confidence) to a young Italian lady of rank, *très instruite* also;

and who passes, or passed, for being one of the three most celebrated belles in the district of Italy, where her family and connections resided in less troublesome times as to politics, (which is not Genoa, by the way,) and she was delighted with it, and says that she has derived a better notion of English society from it than from all Madame de Stael's metaphysical disputations on the same subject, in her work on the Revolution. I beg that you will thank the young philosopher, and make my compliments to Lady B. and her sister.

Believe me your very obliged and faithful   N.B.

P.S.—There is a rumour in letters of some disturbance or complot in the French Pyrenean army—generals suspected or dismissed, and ministers of war travelling to see what's the matter. " Marry (as David says), this hath an angry favour."

Tell Count D'Orsay that some of the names are not quite intelligible, especially of the clubs; he speaks of *Watts*—perhaps he is right, but in my time *Watier's* was the Dandy Club, of which (though no dandy) I was a member, at the time too of its greatest glory, when Brummel and Mildmay, Alvanley and Pierrepoint, gave the Dandy Balls; and we (the club, that is,) got up the famous masquerade at Burlington House and Garden, for Wellington. He does not speak of the *Alfred*, which was the most *recherché* and most tiresome of any, as I know, by being a member of that too.

TO THE EARL OF BLESSINGTON   *April 14, 1823*

I am truly sorry that I cannot accompany you in your ride this morning, owing to a violent pain in my face, arising from a wart to which I by medical advice applied a caustic. Whether I put too much, I do not know; but the consequence is, that not only I have been put to some pain, but the peccant part and its immediate environ are as black as if the printer's devil had marked me for an author. As I do not wish to frighten your horses, or their riders, I shall postpone waiting upon you until six o'clock, when I hope to have subsided into a more christian-like resemblance to my fellow-creatures. My infliction has partially extended even to my fingers; for on trying to get the black from off my upper lip at least, I have only transferred a portion thereof to my right hand, and neither lemon-juice nor eau de Cologne, nor any other eau, have been able as yet to redeem it also from a more inky appearance than is either proper or pleasant. But " out, damn'd spot "— you may have perceived something of the kind yesterday; for on my return, I saw that during my visit it had increased, was increasing, and ought to be diminished; and I could not help laughing at the figure I must have cut before you. At any rate, I shall be with you at six, with the advantage of twilight.

Ever most truly, etc.

Eleven o'clock

P.S.—I wrote the above at three this morning. I regret to say that the whole of the skin of about an *inch* square above my upper lip has come off, so that I cannot even shave or masticate, and I am equally unfit to appear at your table, and to partake of its hospitality. Will you therefore pardon me, and not mistake this rueful excuse for a " *make-believe* ", as you will soon recognise whenever I have the pleasure of meeting you again, and I will call the moment I am, in the nursery phrase, " fit to be seen ". Tell Lady B., with my compliments, that I am rummaging my papers for a MS. worthy of her acceptation. I have just seen the younger Count Gamba; and as I cannot prevail on his infinite modesty to take the field without me, I must take this piece of diffidence on myself also, and beg your indulgence for both.

TO THE COUNT D'ORSAY   *April 22, 1823*

My dear Count D'Orsay (if you will permit me to address you so familiarly),—You should be content with writing in your own language, like Grammont, and succeeding in London as nobody has succeeded since the days of Charles the Second and the records of Antonio Hamilton, without deviating into our barbarous language,—which you understand and write, however, much better than it deserves.

My " approbation ", as you are pleased to term it, was very sincere, but perhaps not very impartial ; for, though I love my country, I do not love my countrymen—at least, such as they now are. And, besides the seduction of talent and wit in your work, I fear that to me there was the attraction of vengeance. I have *seen* and *felt* much of what you have described so well. I have known the persons, and the re-unions so described,— (many of them, that is to say,) and the portraits are so like that I cannot but admire the painter no less than his performance.

But I am sorry for you ; for if you are so well acquainted with life at your age, what will become of you when the illusion is still more dissipated ? But never mind—*en avant !*—live while you can ; and that you may have the full enjoyment of the many advantages of youth, talent, and figure, which you possess, is the wish of an—Englishman,—I suppose, but it is no treason ; for my mother was Scotch, and my name and my family are both Norman ; and as for myself, I am of no country. As for my " Works ", which you are pleased to mention, let them go to the Devil, from whence (if you believe many persons) they came.

I have the honour to be your obliged, etc., etc.

TO THE EARL OF BLESSINGTON .   *April 22nd, 1823*

Milor,—I received your billet at dinner, which was a good one—with a sprinkling of female foreigners, who, I dare say, were very agreeable. As I have formed a sullen resolution about presentations, which I never break (above once a month), I begged —— to dispense me from being introduced, and intrigued for myself a place as far remote as possible from his fair guests, and very near a bottle of the best wine to confirm my misogyny. After coffee, I had accomplished my retreat as far as the hall, on full tilt towards your *thé*, which I was very eager to partake of, when I was arrested by —— requesting that I would make my bow to the French Ambassadress, who it seems is a Dillon, Irish, but born or bred in America ; has been pretty, and is a *blue*, and of course entitled to the homage of all persons who have been printed. I returned, and it was then too late to detain Miss P——[1] over the tea-urn. I beg you to accept my regrets, and present my regards to Milady, and Miss P——, and Comte Alfred, and believe me

Ever yours, NOEL BYRON

TO THE COUNTESS OF BLESSINGTON   *May 3, 1823*

DEAR LADY BLESSINGTON,—My request would be for a copy of the miniature of Lady B. which I have seen in possession of the late Lady Noel, as I have no picture, or indeed memorial of any kind of Lady B., as all her letters were in her own possession before I left England, and we have had no correspondence since—at least on her part.

My message, with regard to the infant, is simply to this effect—that in the event of any accident occurring to the mother, and my remaining the survivor, it would be my wish to have her plans carried into effect, both with regard to the education of the child, and the person or persons under whose care Lady B. might be desirous that she should be placed. It is not my intention to interfere with her in any way on the subject during her life; and I presume that it would be some consolation to her to know, (if she is in ill health, as I am given to understand,) that in *no* case would any thing be done, as far as I am concerned, but in strict conformity with Lady B.'s own wishes and intentions—left in what manner she thought proper.

Believe me, dear Lady B., your obliged, etc.

TO THE COUNTESS OF BLESSINGTON   *Albaro, May 6, 1823*

MY DEAR LADY ——,—I send you the letter which I had forgotten, and the book, which I ought to have remembered. It contains (the book, I mean,) some melancholy truths; though I believe that it is too triste a work ever to have been popular. The first time I ever read it (not the edition I send

[1] Miss Power, Lady Blessington's sister.

you,—for I got it since,) was at the desire of Madame de Stael, who was supposed by the good-natured world to be the heroine ; —which she was not, however, and was furious at the supposition. This occurred in Switzerland, in the summer of 1816, and the last season in which I ever saw that celebrated person.

I have a request to make to my friend Alfred (since he has not disdained the title), viz. that he would condescend to add a *cap* to the gentleman in the jacket,—it would complete his costume,—and smooth his brow, which is somewhat too inveterate a likeness of the original, God help me !

I did well to avoid the water-party,—*why*, is a mystery, which is not less to be wondered at than all my other mysteries. Tell Milor that I am deep in his MS., and will do him justice by a diligent perusal.

The letter which I enclose I was prevented from sending by my despair of its doing any good. I was perfectly sincere when I wrote it, and am so still. But it is difficult for me to withstand the thousand provocations on that subject, which both friends and foes have for seven years been throwing in the way of a man whose feelings were once quick, and whose temper was never patient. But " returning were as tedious as go o'er ". I feel this as much as ever Macbeth did ; and it is a dreary sensation, which at least avenges the real or imaginary wrongs of one of the two unfortunate persons whom it concerns.

But I am going to be gloomy ;—so " to bed, to bed ". Good night,—or rather morning. One of the reasons why I wish to avoid society is, that I can never sleep after it, and the pleasanter it has been the less I rest.

Ever most truly, etc., etc.

TO JOHN BOWRING[1]   *Genoa, May 12, 1823*

SIR,—I have great pleasure in acknowledging your letter, and the honour which the Committee have done me :—I shall endeavour to deserve their confidence by every means in my power. My first wish is to go up into the Levant in person, where I might be enabled to advance, if not the cause, at least

[1] Sir John Bowring, secretary of the Greek Committee founded to assist the cause of Greek freedom.

the means of obtaining information which the Committee might be desirous of acting upon ; and my former residence in the country, my familiarity with the Italian language, (which is there universally spoken, or at least to the same extent as French in the more polished parts of the Continent,) and my *not* total ignorance of the Romaic, would afford me some advantages of experience. To this project the only objection is of a domestic nature, and I shall try to get over it ;—if I fail in this, I must do what I can where I am ; but it will be always a source of regret to me, to think that I might perhaps have done more for the cause on the spot.

Our last information of Captain Blaquiere is from Ancona, where he embarked with a fair wind for Corfu, on the 15th ult. ; he is now probably at his destination. My last letter *from* him personally was dated Rome ; he had been refused a passport through the Neapolitan territory, and returned to strike up through Romagna for Ancona :—little time, however, appears to have been lost by the delay.

The principal material wanted by the Greeks appears to be, first, a park of field artillery—light, and fit for mountain-service ; secondly, gunpowder ; thirdly, hospital or medical stores. The readiest mode of transmission is, I hear, by Idra, addressed to Mr. Negri, the minister. I meant to send up a certain quantity of the two latter—no great deal—but enough for an individual to show his good wishes for the Greek success, —but am pausing, because, in case I should go myself, I can take them with me. I do not want to limit my own contribution to this merely, but more especially, if I can get to Greece my-self, I should devote whatever resources I can muster of my own, to advancing the great object. I am in correspondence with Signor Nicolas Karrellas (well known to Mr. Hobhouse), who is now at Pisa ; but his latest advice merely stated, that the Greeks are at present employed in organising their *internal* government, and the details of its administration : this would seem to indicate *security*, but the war is however far from being terminated.

The Turks are an obstinate race, as all former wars have proved them, and will return to the charge for years to come, even if beaten, as it is to be hoped they will be. But in no case can the labours of the Committee be said to be in vain ; for in the event even of the Greeks being subdued, and dispersed, the funds which could be employed in succouring and gathering together the remnant, so as to alleviate in part their distresses, and enable them to find or make a country (as so many emigrants of other nations have been compelled to do), would "bless both those who gave and those who took", as the bounty both of justice and of mercy.

With regard to the formation of a brigade, (which Mr. Hobhouse hints at in his short letter of this day's receipt, enclosing the one to which I have the honour to reply,) I would presume to suggest—but merely as an opinion, resulting rather from the melancholy experience of the brigades embarked in the Columbian service than from any experiment yet fairly tried in GREECE,—that the attention of the Committee had better perhaps be directed to the employment of *officers* of experience than the enrolment of *raw British* soldiers, which latter are apt to be unruly, and not very serviceable, in irregular warfare, by the side of foreigners. A small body of good officers, expecially artillery ; an engineer, with quantity (such as the Committee might deem requisite) of stores of the nature which Captain Blaquiere indicated as most wanted, would, I should conceive, be a highly useful accession. Officers, also, who had previously served in the Mediterranean would be preferable, as some knowledge of Italian is nearly indispensable.

It would also be as well that they should be aware, that they are not going "to rough it on a beef-steak and bottle of port ",—but that Greece—never, of late years, very plentifully stocked for a *mess*—is at present the country of all kinds of *privations*. This remark may seem superfluous ; but I have been led to it, by observing that many *foreign* officers, Italian, French, and even Germans (but *fewer* of the *latter*), have returned in disgust, imagining either that they were going up to make a party of pleasure, or to enjoy full pay, speedy promotion, and a very moderate degree of duty. They complain, too, of having been ill received by the Government or inhabitants ; but numbers of these complainants were mere adventurers, attracted by a hope of command and plunder, and disappointed of both. Those Greeks I have seen strenuously deny the charge of inhospitality, and declare that they shared their pittance to the last crum[b] with their foreign volunteers.

I need not suggest to the Committee the very great advantage which must accrue to Great Britain from the success of the Greeks, and their probable commercial relations with England in consequence; because I feel persuaded that the first object of the Committee is their EMANCIPATION, without any interested views. But the consideration might weigh with the English people in general, in their present passion for every kind of speculation,—they need not cross the American seas for one much better worth their while, and nearer home. The resources even for an emigrant population, in the Greek islands alone, are rarely to be paralleled; and the cheapness of every kind of, not *only necessary*, but *luxury*, (that is to say, *luxury* of *nature*,) fruits, wine, oil, etc., in a state of peace, are far beyond those of the Cape, and Van Diemen's Land, and the other places of refuge, which the English people are searching for over the waters.

I beg that the Committee will command me in any and every way. If I am favoured with any instructions, I shall endeavour to obey them to the letter, whether conformable to my own private opinion or not. I beg leave to add, personally, my respect for the gentleman whom I have the honour of addressing,

And am, Sir, your obliged, etc.

.P.S.—The best refutation of Gell [1] will be the active exertions of the Committee;—I am too warm a controversialist; and I suspect that if Mr. Hobhouse have taken him in hand, there will be little occasion for me to " encumber him with help ". If I go up into the country, I will endeavour to transmit as accurate and impartial an account as circumstances will permit.

I shall write to Mr. Karrellas. I expect intelligence from Captain Blaquiere, [2] who has promised me some early intimation from the seat of the Provisional Government. I gave him a letter of introduction to Lord Sydney Osborne, at Corfu; but as Lord S. is in the government service, of course his reception could only be a *cautious* one.

[1] Sir William Gell, in his *Narrative of a Journey in the Morea*, had suggested that the substitution of Russian for Turkish rule might, from the Greek point of view, be not without its advantages.

[2] At the first meeting of the Greek Committee, Edward Blaquiere, author and translator, had volunteered to visit Green and collect information.

TO THE HON. DOUGLAS KINNAIRD †   *Genoa, May 21st, 1823*

MY DEAR DOUGLAS,—I enclose you another corrected proof of D. J., and also a note of Mr. Barry, the acting partner of Messrs. Webbs, on the proposed credit in case I go up to the Levant. I do not quite know what to name as the amount —undoubtedly about 5000, in addition to what I already have in your circular notes, and in Webb's bank, would be more than sufficient for my own personal wants for *good four years*, for my habits are simple, and you are aware that I have lately reduced my other expences of every kind. But, if I do go up among the Greeks, I may have occasion to be of service to them. • There may be prisoners to ransom, some cash to advance, arms to purchase, or if I was to take an angry turn some sulky morning, and raise a troop of my own (though this is unlikely), any or all of these would require a command of credit and require my resources. You will let me have what you think proper *not under* the sum above stated ; but there is no *immediate* hurry, as I shall not sail till about July, if at all. It is to be understood that the *letter of credit for two thousand pounds* which I have *now untouched* is to be *returned* or left to be returned *untouched* in the hands of Messrs. Webb for your house the moment I receive the more extended credit. It is also [to] be understood that, if I receive this extended credit, and from any circumstances do not go up into the Levant, then that credit is to be null and void as it would then become quite superfluous to my present occasion. I am doing all I can to get away, but I have all kinds of obstacles thrown in my way by the " absurd womankind ", who seems determined on sacrificing herself in every way, and preventing me from doing any good, and all without reason ; for her relations, and her husband (who is moving the Pope and the Government here to get her to live with him again) and everybody, are earnest with her to return to Ravenna. She wants to go up to Greece too ! forsooth, a precious place to go to at present ! Of course the idea is ridiculous, as everything must there be sacrificed to seeing her out of harm's way. It is a case too, in which interest does not enter, and therefore hard to deal with ; for I have no kind of control in that way, and if she makes a scene (and she has a turn that way) we shall have another romance, and tale of

731

ill-usage, and abandonment, and Lady Carolining, and Lady Byroning, and Glenarvoning, all cut and dry.   There never was a man who gave up so much to women, and all I have gained by it has been the character of treating them harshly. However I shall do what I can, and have hopes; for her father has been recalled from his political exile; but with this proviso, that he do not return without his daughter.   If I left a woman for another woman, she might have cause to complain, but really when a man merely wishes to go on a great duty, for a good cause, this selfishness on the part of the " feminie " is rather too much.

Ever yrs., N. B.

I add the enclosed letter from Mr. J. M. which does him credit : also another M.S.S. for a proof from the same.

TO HENRI BEYLE[1]   *Genoa, May 29, 1823*

SIR,—At present, that I know to whom I am indebted for a very flattering mention in the *Rome, Naples, and Florence*, in 1817, by Mons. Stendhal, it is fit that I should return my thanks (however undesired or undesirable) to Mons. Beyle, with whom I had the honour of being acquainted at Milan, in 1816.   You only did me too much honour in what you were pleased to say in that work; but it has hardly given me less pleasure than the praise itself, to become at length aware (which I have done by mere accident) that I am indebted for it to one of whose good opinion I was really ambitious.   So many changes have taken place since that period in the Milan circle, that I hardly dare recur to it;—some dead, some banished, and some in the Austrian dungeons.—Poor Pellico! I trust that, in his iron solitude, his Muse is consoling him in part—one day to delight us again, when both she and her Poet are restored to freedom.

Of your works I have only seen *Rome*, etc., the Lives of Haydn and Mozart, and the *brochure* on Racine and Shakespeare.   The *Histoire de la Peinture* I have not yet the good fortune to possess.

---

[1] The novelist had originally encountered Byron at Milan in 1816.

There is one part of your observations in the pamphlet which I shall venture to remark upon;—it regards Walter Scott. You say that " his character is little worthy of enthusiasm ", at the same time that you mention his productions in the manner they deserve. I have known Walter Scott long and well, and in occasional stiuations which call forth the *real* character—and I can assure you that his character *is* worthy of admiration—that of all men he is the most *open*, the most *honourable*, the most *amiable*. With his politics I have nothing to do : they differ from mine, which renders it difficult for me to speak of them. But he is *perfectly sincere* in them : and Sincerity may be humble, but she cannot be servile. I pray you, therefore, to correct or soften that passage. You may, perhaps, attribute this officiousness of mine to a false affectation of *candour*, as I happen to be a writer also. Attribute it to what motive you please, but *believe* the *truth*. I say that Walter Scott is as nearly a thorough good man as man can be, because I *know* it by experience to be the case.

If you do me the honour of an answer, may I request a speedy one?—because it is possible (though not yet decided) that circumstances may conduct me once more to Greece. My present address is Genoa, where an answer will reach me in a short time, or be forwarded to me wherever I may be.

I beg you to believe me, with a lively recollection of our brief acquaintance, and the hope of one day renewing it,

Your ever obliged
And obedient humble servant, NOEL BYRON

TO THE COUNTESS OF BLESSINGTON   *Albaro, June 2, 1823*

MY DEAR LADY BLESSINGTON,—I am *superstitious*, and have recollected that memorials with a *point* are of less fortunate augury ; I will, therefore, request you to accept, instead of the *pin*, the enclosed chain, which is of so slight a value that you need not hesitate. As you wished for something *worn*, I can only say, that it has been worn oftener and longer than the other. It is of Venetian manufacture ; and the only peculiarity about it is, that it could only be obtained at or from Venice. At Genoa they have none of the same kind. I also enclose a ring, which I would wish *Alfred* to keep ; it is too large to *wear* ; but is formed of *lava*, and so far adapted to the fire of his years and character. You will perhaps have the goodness to acknowledge the receipt of this note, and send back the pin (for good luck's sake), which I shall value much more for having been a night in your custody.

Ever and faithfully your obliged, etc.

P.S.—I hope your *nerves* are well to-day, and will continue to flourish.

TO J. J. COULMANN *Genoa, July 12* [?], *1823*

MY DEAR SIR,—Your letter, and what accompanied it, have given me the greatest pleasure. The glory and the works of the writers who have deigned to give me these volumes, bearing their names, were not unknown to me, but still it is more flattering to receive them from the authors themselves. I beg you to present my thanks to each of them in particular ; and to add, how proud I am of their good opinion, and how charmed I shall be to cultivate their acquaintance, if ever the occasion should occur. The productions of M. Jouy have long been familiar to me. Who has not read and applauded *The Hermit* and *Scylla*? But I cannot accept what it has pleased your friends to call their *homage*, because there is no sovereign in the republic of letters ; and even if there were, I have never had the pretension or the power to become a usurper.

I have also to return you thanks for having honoured me with your own compositions ; I thought you too young, and probably too amiable, to be an author. As to the Essay, etc., I am obliged to you for the present, although I had already seen it joined to the last edition of the translation. I have nothing to object to it, with regard to what concerns myself personally, though naturally there are some of the facts in it discoloured, and several errors into which the author has been led by the accounts of others. I allude to facts, and not criticisms. But the same author has cruelly calumniated my father and my grand-uncle, but more especially the former. So far from being " brutal ", he was, according to the testimony of all those who knew him, of an extremely amiable and (*enjoué*) joyous character, but careless (*insouciant*) and dissipated. He had, consequently, the reputation of a good officer, and showed himself such in the Guards, in America. The facts themselves refute the assertion. It is not by " brutality " that a young Officer in the Guards seduces and carries off a Marchioness, and marries two heiresses. It is true that he was a very handsome man, which goes a great way. His first wife (Lady Conyers and Marchioness of Carmarthen) did not die of grief, but of a malady which she caught by having imprudently insisted upon accompanying my father to a hunt, before she was completely recovered from the accouchement which gave birth to my sister Augusta.

His second wife, my respected mother, had, I assure you, too proud a spirit to bear the ill-usage of any man, no matter who he might be ; and this she would have soon proved. I should add, that he lived a long time in Paris, and was in habits of intimacy with the old Marshal Biron, Commandant of the French Guards ; who, from the similitude of names, and Norman origin of our family, supposed that there was some distant relationship between us. He died some years before the age of forty, and whatever may have been his faults, they were certainly not those of harshness and grossness (*dureté et grossièreté*). If the notice should reach England, I am certain that the passage relative to my father will give much more pain to my sister (the wife of Colonel Leigh, attached to the Court of the late Queen, *not* Caroline, but Charlotte, wife of George III.), even than to me ; and this she does not deserve, for there is not a more angelic being upon earth. Augusta and I have always loved the memory of our father as much as we loved each other, and this at least forms a presumption that the stain of harshness was not applicable to it. If he dissipated his fortune, that concerns us alone, for we are his heirs ; and till we reproach him with it, I know no one else who has a right to do so. As to Lord Byron, who killed Mr. Chaworth in a duel, so far from retiring from the world, he made the tour of Europe, and was appointed Master of the Staghounds after that event, and did not give up society until his son had offended him by marrying in a manner contrary to his duty. So far from feeling any remorse for having killed Mr. Chaworth, who was a fire-eater (*spadassin*), and celebrated for his quarrelsome disposition, he always kept the sword which he used upon that occasion in his bed-chamber, where it still was *when he died*. It is singular enough, that when very young, I formed a strong attachment for the grand-niece and heiress of Mr. Chaworth, who stood in the same degree of relationship [to him] as myself to Lord Byron; and at one time it was thought that the two families would have been united in us. She was two years older than me, and we were very much together in our youth. She married a man of an ancient and respectable family; but her marriage was not a happier one than my own. Her conduct, however, was irreproachable, but there was no sympathy between their characters, and a separation took place. I had not seen her for many years. When an occasion offered, I was upon the point, with her consent, of paying her a visit, when my sister, who has always had more influence over me than anyone else, persuaded me not to do it. " For," said she, " if you go, you will fall in love again, and then there will be a scene; one step will lead to another, *et cela fera un éclat* ", etc. I was guided by these reasons, and shortly after I married; with what success it is useless to say. Mrs. C. some time after, being separated from her husband, became insane; but she has since recovered her reason, and is, I believe, reconciled to her husband. This is a long letter, and principally about my family, but it is the fault of M. Pichot, my benevolent biographer. He may say of me whatever of good or evil pleases him, but I desire that he should speak of my relations only as they deserve. If you could find an occasion of making him, as well as M. Nodier, rectify the facts relative to my father, and publish them, you would do me a great service, for I cannot bear to have him unjustly spoken of. I must conclude abruptly, for I have occupied you too long. Believe me to be very much honoured by your esteem, and always your obliged and obedient servant,

NOEL BYRON

P.S.—The tenth or twelfth of this month I shall embark for Greece. Should I return, I shall pass through Paris, and shall be much flattered in meeting you and your friends. Should I not return, give me as affectionate a place in your memory as possible.

6

Greece

September 1823 to April 1824

Byron did not expect that he would return from Greece—so he declared to his last confidante, the garrulous Lady Blessington; nor did he suppose that, while he still existed to further the cause of Hellenic freedom, his service would be easy. But he had accepted the Committee's invitation to represent them, and was resolved to do his utmost. Unfortunately neither was he a diplomatist, nor had he the training of a straightforward man of action. From the outset he encountered reverses. The Greeks were divided among themselves; each party was eager to lay hold of Byron's war-chest; and, having reached Cephalonia at the beginning of August 1823, he remained there till the end of the year, endeavouring to assess the claims and compose the differences of various rival parties. On January 5th, 1824, he at length gained Missolonghi, a squalid and inhospitable town among unhealthy marshlands. The story of Byron's life at Missolonghi is one of unending exasperation and ceaseless disappointment. He died of fever, after a brief but painful illness, on April 19th. His body was shipped to England and buried near Nottingham, in the village church of Hucknall Torkard.

JOURNAL IN CEPHALONIA

June 19ᵗʰ 1823

The dead have been awakened—shall I sleep?
The World's at war with tyrants—shall I crouch?
The harvest's ripe—and shall I pause to reap?
    I slumber not ; the thorn is in my Couch ;
Each day a trumpet soundeth in mine ear,
    Its echo in my heart—

1823

Mataxata, Cephalonia, Sepᵗ 28

On the sixteenth (I think) of July, I sailed from Genoa in
the English brig *Hercules* : Jⁿᵒ Scott, Master. On the 17ᵗʰ, a
Gale of wind occasioning confusion and threatening damage
to the horses in the hold, we bore up again for the same port,
where we remained four and twenty hours longer, and then
put to sea, touched at Leghorn, and pursued our voyage by the
straits of Messina for Greece. Passing within sight of Elba,
Corsica, the Lipari islands including Stromboli, Sicily, Italy,
etc., about the 4ᵗʰ of August we anchored off Argostoli, in the
chief harbour of the Island of Cephalonia.

Here I had some expectation of hearing from Capt.
B[laquiere], who was on a mission from the Gᵏ Committee in
London to the Provisional Govᵗ of the Morea, but, rather to my
surprise, learned that he was on his way home, though his
latest letters to me from the peninsula, after expressing an
anxious wish that I should come up without delay, stated
further that he intended to remain in the country for the
present. I have since received various letters from him addrest
to Genoa, and forwarded to the Islands, partly explaining the
cause of his unexpected return, and also (contrary to his former
opinion) requesting me not to proceed to Greece *yet*, for sundry
reasons, some of importance. I sent a boat to Corfu in the hopes
of finding him still there, but he had already sailed for Ancona.

In the island of Cephalonia, Colonel Napier commanded
in chief as Resident, and Col. Duffie the 8ᵗʰ, a King's Regiment
then forming the Garrison. We were received by both those
Gentlemen, and indeed by all the officers, as well as the

Civilians, with the greatest kindness and hospitality, which, if we did not deserve, I still hope that we have done nothing to forfeit, and it has continued unabated, even since the Gloss of new Acquaintance has been worn away by frequent intercourse.

We here learned, what has since been fully confirmed, that the Greeks were in a state of political dissention amongst themselves; that Mavrocordato was dismissed, or had resigned (*L'un vaut bien l'autre*); and that Colocotroni, with I know not what or whose party, was paramount in the Morea. The Turks were in force in Acarnania, etc., and the Turkish fleet blockaded the coast from Messolonghi to Chiarenza, and subsequently to Navarino. The Greek fleet, from the want of means or other causes, remained in port in Hydra, Ipsara, and Spetzas, and, for aught that is yet certainly known, may be there still. As, rather contrary to my expectations, I had no advices from Peloponnesus, and had also letters to receive from England from the Committee, I determined to remain for the interim in the Ionian Islands, especially as it was difficult to land on the opposite coast without risking the confiscation of the vessel and her contents, which Captn Scott, naturally enough, declined to do, unless I would ensure to him the full amount of his possible damage.

To pass the time we made a little excursion over the mountain to Saint Euphemia, by worse roads than I ever met in the course of some years of travel in rough places of many countries. At Santa Euphemia we embarked for Ithaca, and made the tour of that beautiful Island, which I had visited several years before. The hospitality of Capt. Knox (the Resident) and his lady was in no respect inferior to that of our military friends of Cephalonia. That gentleman, with Mrs. K., and some of their friends, conducted us to the fountain of Arethusa, which alone would be worth the voyage; but the rest of the Island is not inferior in attractions to the admirers of Nature. The arts and traditions I leave to the Antiquaries, and so well have those Gentlemen contrived to settle such questions, that, as the existence of Troy is disputed, so that of Ithaca (as Homer's Ithaca, *i.e.*) is not yet admitted.

Though the month was August, and we had been cautioned against travelling in the sun, yet, as I had during my former experience never suffered from the heat as long as I continued in *motion*, I was unwilling to lose so many hours of the day on account of a sunbeam more or less, and, though our party was rather numerous, no one suffered either illness or inconvenience, as far as could be observed, though one of the servants (a Negro) declared that it was as hot as in the West Indies. I had left our thermometer on board, so could not ascertain the precise degree. We returned to Saint Euphemia, and passed over to the monastery of Samos on the opposite part of the bay, and proceeded next day to Argostoli by a better road than the path to Saint Euphemia. The land journey was made on mules.

Some day after our return, I heard that there were letters for me at Zante ; but a considerable delay took place before the Greek, to whom they were consigned, had them properly forwarded, and I was at length indebted to Col. Napier for obtaining them for me ; *what* occasioned the demur or delay was never explained.

I learned, by my advices from England, the request of the Committee that I would act as their representative near the Greek Gov^t, and take charge of the proper disposition and delivery of certain stores, etc., etc., expected by a vessel which has not yet arrived up to the present date (Septr 28).

Soon after my arrival, I took into my own pay a body of forty Suliotes under their chiefs Photomara, Giavella, and Drako, and would probably have increased the number, but I found them not quite united among themselves in any thing except raising their demands on me, although I had given a dollar per man more each month than they could receive from the G^k Gov^t, and they were destitute, at the time I took them, of everything. I had acceded to their own demand, and paid them a month in advance. But, set on probably by some of the trafficking shopkeepers with whom they were in the habit of dealing on credit, they made various attempts at what I thought extortion, so that I called them together, stating my view of the case, and declining to take them on with me. But I offered them another month's pay, and the price of their passage to Acarnania, where they could now easily go, as the Turkish fleet was gone, and the blockade removed.

This part of them accepted, and they went accordingly. Some difficulty arose about restoring their arms by the Septinsular Gov^t, but these were at length obtained, and they are now with their compatriots in Etolia or Acarnania.

I also transferred to the resident in Ithaca the sum of two hundred and fifty dollars for the refugees there, and I had conveyed to Cephalonia a Moreote family who were in the greatest helplessness, and provided them with a house and decent maintenance under the protection of Messrs. Corgialegno, wealthy merchants of Argostoli, to whom I had been recommended by my correspondents.

I had caused a letter to be written to Marco Bozzaris, the acting commander of a body of troops in Acarnania, for whom I had letters of recommendation. His answer was probably the last he ever signed, or dictated, for he was killed in action the very day after its date, with the character of a good soldier, and an honourable man, which are not always found together nor indeed separately. I was also invited by Count Metaxa, the Governor of Messolonghi, to go over there ; but it was necessary, in the present state of parties, that I should have some communication with the existing Gov^t on the subject of their opinion *where* I might be, if not *most* useful, at any rate *least* obnoxious.

As I did not come here to join a faction but a nation, and to deal with honest men and not with speculators or peculators, (charges bandied about daily by the Greeks of each other) it will require much circumspection to avoid the character of a partizan, and I perceive it to be the more difficult as I have already received invitations from more than one of the contending parties, always under the pretext that *they* are the " real Simon Pure ". After all, one should not despair, though all the foreigners that I have hitherto met with from amongst the Greeks are going or gone back disgusted.

Whoever goes into Greece at present should do it as Mrs. Fry went into Newgate—not in the expectation of meeting with any especial indication of existing probity, but in the hope that time and better treatment will reclaim the present burglarious and larcenous tendencies which have followed this General Gaol delivery.

When the limbs of the Greeks are a little less stiff from the shackles of four centuries, they will not march so much " as if they had gyves on their legs ". At present the Chains are broken indeed; but the links are still clanking, and the Saturnalia is still too recent to have converted the Slave into a sober Citizen. The worst of them is that (to use a coarse but the only expression that will not fall short of the truth) they are such damned liars; there never was such an incapacity for veracity shown since Eve lived in Paradise. One of them found fault the other day with the English language, because it had so few shades of a Negative, whereas a Greek can so modify a " No " to a " Yes ", and *vice versa*, by the slippery qualities of his language, that prevarication may be carried to any extent and still leave a loop-hole through which perjury may slip without being perceived. This was the Gentleman's own talk, and is only to be doubted because in the words of the Syllogism " Now Epimenides was a Cretan ". But they may be mended by and bye.

Sept. 30th.

After remaining here some time in expectation of hearing from the G^k G^t I availed myself of the opportunity of Messrs. B[rowne] and T[relawny] proceeding to Tripolitza, subsequently to the departure of the Turkish fleet, to write to the acting part of the Legislature. My object was not only to obtain some accurate information so as to enable me to proceed to the Spot where I might be, if not most safe, at least more serviceable, but to have an opportunity of forming a judgement on the real state of their affairs. In the meantime I hear from Mavrocordato and the Primate of Hydra, the latter inviting me to that island, the former hinting that he should like to meet me there or elsewhere.

1823.

10bre 17th

My Journal was discontinued abruptly and has not been resumed sooner, because on the day of its former date I received a letter from my sister Augusta, that intimated the illness of my daughter, and I had not then the heart to continue it. Subsequently I had heard through the same channel that she was better, and since that she is well; if so, for me all is well.

But although I learned this early in 9th 9bre, I know not why I have not continued my journal, though many things which would have formed a curious record have since occurred.

I know not why I resume it even now, except that, standing at the window of my apartment in this beautiful village, the calm though cool serenity of a beautiful and transparent Moonlight, showing the Islands, the Mountains, the Sea, with a distant outline of the Morea traced between the double Azure of the waves and skies, has quieted me enough to be able to write, from which (however difficult it may seem for one who has written so much publicly to refrain) is, and always has been, to me a task and a painful one. I could summon testimonies, were it necessary; but my hand-writing is sufficient. It is that of one who thinks much, rapidly, perhaps deeply, but rarely with pleasure.

But—*En avant.* The Greeks are advancing in their public progress, but quarrelling amongst themselves. I shall probably, *bon grè mal grè*, be obliged to join one of the factions, which I have hitherto strenuously avoided in the hope to unite them in one common interest.

Mavrocordato has appeared at length with the Hydriote Squadron in these seas, which apparition would hardly have taken place had I not engaged to pay two hundred thousand piastres (10 piastres per dollar being the present value on the Greek continent) in aid of Messolonghi, and has commenced operations somewhat successfully but not very prudently.

Fourteen (some say seventeen) Greek ships attacked a Turkish vessel of 12 Guns, and took her. This is not quite an Ocean Thermopylæ, but *n'importe*; they (*on dit*) have found on board 50,000 dollars, a sum of great service in their present exigencies, if properly applied. This prize, however, has been made within the bounds of Neutrality on the coast of Ithaca, and the Turks were (it is said) pursued on shore, and some slain. All this may involve a question of right and wrong with the not very tolerant Thomas Maitland, who is not very capable of distinguishing either. I have advanced the sum above noted to pay the said Squadron; it is not very large but is double that which Napoleon, the Emperor of Emperors, began his campaign in Italy withal—*vide Las Cases, passim,* vol. i. (*tome premier*).

The Turks have retired from before Messolonghi—nobody knows why—since they left provisions and ammunition behind them in quantities, and the Garrison made no sallies, or none to any purpose. They never invested Messolonghi this year, but bombarded Anatoliko (a sort of village which I recollect well, having passed through the whole of that country with fifty Albanians in 1809, Messolonghi included) near the Achelous. Some say Vrioni Pacha heard of an insurrection near Scutari, some one thing, some another. For my part, I have been in correspondence with the Chiefs, and their accounts are not unanimous.

The Suliotes, both there, here, and elsewhere, having taken a kind of liking *to*, or at least formed or renewed a sort of acquaintance *with*, me—(as I have aided them and their families in all that I could, according to circumstances) are apparently anxious that I should put myself forward as their Chief (if I may so say). I would rather not for the present, because there are too many divisions and Chiefs already. But if it should appear necessary, why—as they are admitted to be the best and bravest of the present combatants—it might, or may, so happen that I could, would, should, or shall take to me the support of such a body of men, with whose aid I think something might be done both *in* Greece and *out* of it (for there is a good deal to put to rights in both). I could maintain them out of my own present means (always supposing my present income and means to be permanent). They are not above a thousand, and of these not six hundred *real* Suliotes ; but then they are allowed to be equal (that seems a bravado though, but it is in print recently) *one* to 5 European Moslems, and ten Asiatics ! Be it as it may, they are in high esteem, and my very good friends.

A soldier may be maintained on the Mainland for 25 piastres (rather *better than two* dollars a month) monthly, and find his rations out of the country, or for *five dollars*, including his paying for his rations. Therefore for between two and three thousand dollars a month (and the dollar here is to be had for 4 and 2 pence instead of 4 and 6 pence, the price in England), I could maintain between five hundred and a thousand of these warriors for as long as necessary, and I have more means than are (supposing them to last) [sufficient] to do so. For my own personal wants are very simple (except in horses as I am no great pedestrian), and my income considerable for any country but England (being equal to the President's of the United

States! the English Secretaries of States or the French Ambassador's at Vienna and the greater Courts—150,000 Francs, I believe), and I have hope to have sold a Manor besides for nearly 3,000,000 francs more. Thus I could (with what we should extract according to the usages of war also), keep on foot a respectable clan, or Sept, or tribe, or horde, for some time, and, as I have not any motive for so doing but the well-wishing to Greece, I should hope with advantage.

TO THE COUNTESS GUICCIOLI [1] *October 7*

Pietro has told you all the gossip of the island,—our earthquakes, our politics, and present abode in a pretty village. As his opinions and mine on the Greeks are nearly similar, I need say little on that subject. I was a fool to come here; but, being here, I must see what is to be done.

October ——

We are still in Cephalonia, waiting for news of a more accurate description; for all is contradiction and division in the reports of the state of the Greeks. I shall fulfil the object of my mission from the Committee, and then return into Italy; for it does not seem likely that, as an individual, I can be of use to them;—at least no other foreigner has yet appeared to be so, nor does it seem likely that any will be at present.

Pray be as cheerful and tranquil as you can; and be assured that there is nothing here that can excite any thing but a wish to be with you again,—though we are very kindly treated by the English here of all descriptions. Of the Greeks, I can't say much good hitherto, and I do not like to speak ill of them, though they do of one another.

October 29

You may be sure that the moment I can join you again, will be as welcome to me as at any period of our recollection. There is nothing very attractive here to divide my attention; but I must attend to the Greek cause, both from honour and inclination. Messrs. B[rowne] and T[relawny] are both in the Morea, where they have been very well received, and both of

[1] Extracts from letters to the Countess Guiccioli, printed in Moore's *Life*.

them write in good spirits and hopes. I am anxious to hear how the Spanish cause will be arranged, as I think it may have an influence on the Greek contest. I wish that both were fairly and favourably settled, that I might return to Italy, and talk over with you *our*, or rather Pietro's adventures, some of which are rather amusing, as also some of the incidents of our voyages and travels. But I reserve them, in the hope that we may laugh over them together at no very distant period.

TO THE HON. AUGUSTA LEIGH †   *Cephalonia, 8ᵇʳᵉ 12ᵗʰ 1823*

MY DEAREST AUGUSTA,—Your three letters on the subject of Ada's indisposition have made me very anxious to hear further of her amelioration. I have been subject to the same complaint, but not at so early an age, nor in so great a degree. Besides, it never affected my eyes but rather my hearing, and that only partially and slightly and for a short time. I had dreadful and almost periodical headaches till I was fourteen, and sometimes since ; but abstinence and a habit of bathing my head in cold water every morning cured me, I think, at least I have been less molested since that period. Perhaps she will get quite well when she arrives at womanhood. But that is some time to look forward to, though if she is of so sanguine a habit it is probable that she may attain to that period earlier than is usual in our colder climate ; * * * * * * You will excuse me touching on this topic *medically* and " en passant " because I cannot help thinking that the determination of blood to the head so early unassisted may have some connection with a similar tendency to earlier maturity. Perhaps it is a phantasy. At any rate let me know how she is. I need not say how *very* anxious I am (at this distance particularly) to hear of her welfare.

You ask why I came up amongst the Greeks? It was stated to me that my so doing might tend to their advantage in some measure in their present struggle for independence, both as an individual and as a member for the Committee now in England. How far this may be realized I cannot pretend to anticipate, but I am willing to do what I can. They have at length found leisure to quarrel among themselves, after repelling their other enemies, and it is no very easy part that I may have to play to avoid appearing partial to one or other of their factions. They have turned out Mavrocordato, who was the only *Washington* or *Kosciusko* kind of man amongst them, and they have not yet sent their deputies to London to treat for a loan, nor in short done themselves so much good as they might have done. I have written to Mr. Hobhouse three several times with a budget of documents on the subject, from which he can extract all the present information for the Committee. I have written to their Gov^t at Tripolizza and Salamis, and am waiting for instructions *where* to proceed, for things are in such a state amongst them, that it is difficult to conjecture where one could be useful to them, if at all. However, I have some hopes that they will see their own interest sufficiently not to quarrel till they have received their national independence, and then they can fight it out among them in a domestic manner—and welcome. You may suppose that I have something to *think* of at least, for you can have no idea what an intriguing cunning unquiet generation they are, and as emissaries of all parties come to me at present, and I must act impartially, it makes me exclaim, as Julian did at his military exercises, " Oh ! Plato, what a task for a Philosopher ! "

However, *you* won't think much of *my philosophy*; nor do I, *entre nous*———

If you think this epistle or any part of it worth transmitting to L^y B. you can send her a copy, as I suppose—unless she is become I know not what—she cannot be altogether indifferent as to my " whereabouts " and *what*abouts.

I am at present in a very pretty village (Metaxata in Cephalonia) between the mountains and the sea, with a view of Zante and the Morea, waiting for some more decisive intelligence from the provisional Gov^t in Salamis.—— But here come some visitors.

I was interrupted yesterday by Col. Napier and the Captain of a King's ship now in the harbour. Col. N. is Resident or Governor here and has been extremely kind and hospitable, as indeed have been all the English here. When their visit was over a Greek arrived on business about this eternal siege of Mesalonghi (on the Coast of Acarnania or Etolia) and some convoys of provisions which we want to throw in; and after this was discussed, I got on horseback (I brought up my horses with me on board and troublesome neighbours they were in blowing weather) and rode to Argostoli and back; and then I had one of my *thunder* headaches (*you* know how my head acts like a barometer when there is electricity in the air) and I could not resume till this morning. Since my arrival in August I made a tour to Ithaca (which you will take to be Ireland, but if you look into Pope's *Odyssey*, you will discover to be the antient name of the Isle of Wight) and also over some parts of Cephalonia.

We are pretty well in health, the Gods be thanked! By the way, who is this Dr. Tipperary or Mayo or whatever his name is? I never heard of anything of the name except an Irish County. Laurence the Surgeon, if he be the man who has been persecuted for his metaphysics, is, I have heard, an excellent professional man. But I wonder Ldy. B. should employ (so tell her) a Papist or a Sceptic. I thought that like " douce David Deans " she would not have allowed " a Goutte of physic to go through any of the family " unless she was sure that the prescriber was a Cameronian.

There is a clever but eccentric man here, a Dr. Kennedy, who is very pious and tries in good earnest to make converts; but his Christianity is a queer one, for he says that the priesthood of the Church of England are no more Christians than " Mahound or Termagant " are. He has made some converts, I suspect rather to the beauty of his wife (who is pretty as well as pious) than of his theology. I like what I have seen of him, of *her* I know nothing, nor desire to know, having other things to think about. *He* says that the dozen shocks of an Earthquake we had the other day are a sign of his doctrine, or a judgement on his audience, but this opinion has not acquired proselytes. One of the shocks was so prolonged that, though not very heavy, we thought the house would come down, and as we have a staircase to dismount *out* of the house (the buildings here are different from ours), it was judged expedient by the inmates (all *men* please to recollect, as if there had been females we must have helped them out or broken our heads for company) to make an expeditious retreat into the court-yard. *Who* was *first* out of the door I know not, but when I got to the bottom of the stairs I found several arrived before me, which could only have happened by their jumping out of the windows or down *over* or from the stairs (which had no balustrade or bannisters) rather than in the regular way of descent. The scene was ludicrous enough, but we had several more slight shocks in the night but stuck quietly to our beds, for it would have been of no use moving, as the house would have been down first, had it been to come down at all.

There was no great damage done in the Island (except an old house or two cracking in the middle), but the soldiers on parade were lifted up as a boat is by the tide, and you could have seen the whole line waving (though no one was in motion) by the heaving of the ground on which they were drawn up. You can't complain of this being a brief letter.

I wish you would obtain from Lady B. some account of Ada's disposition, habits, studies, moral tendencies, and temper, as well as of her personal appearance, for except from the miniature drawn five years ago (and she is now double that age nearly) I have no idea of even her aspect. When I am advised on these points, I can form some notion of her character and what way her dispositions or indispositions ought to be treated. At *her* present age I have an idea that I had many feelings and notions which people would not believe if I stated them *now*, and therefore I may as well keep them to myself. Is she social or solitary, taciturn or talkative, fond of reading or otherwise? And what is her *tic?*—I mean her foible. Is she passionate? I hope that the Gods have made her anything save *poetical*—it is enough to have one such fool in a family. You can answer all this at your leisure : address to *Genoa* as usual, the letters will be forwarded better by my Correspondents there.

Yours ever, N. B.

P.S.—Tell Douglas K^d I have only just got his letter of August 19th, and not only approve of his accepting a sum not under ten or twelve thousand pounds for the property in question, but also of his getting as much as can be gotten *above* that price.

TO DAVID GRANT*   *Cephalonia, 9ᵇʳᵉ 13th, 1823*

SIR,—I answered your obliging letter of the 12th of August by Capt. Symonds, and have now to avail myself of the advantage of your correspondence.

I yesterday drew bills for four thousand pounds sterling on my bankers in London, Messrs. Ransom and Co., Pall Mall East, in favour of the Greek Provisional Government to enable part of their fleet to succour Missolonghi now in a state of blockade. My letter of credit on Messrs. Ransom and the bills will be presented to your house by Mr Hamilton Browne, who is authorized to receive the amount in dollars and to convey these to this Island, the Greek Deputies paying the insurance and other expences incidental to business. I have to request that you will have the goodness to remit the sum as soon as possible. The bills are thirty days after sight, and I believe that Messrs. Webb can and have assured you of the goodness of the house on which they are drawn. I do not know what the present exchange is at Malta; but I should prefer infinitely negotiating with your house to transacting any business with the merchants of the Ionian Islands.

I have the honour to be your obliged and
very obedt. humble Sevt., NOEL BYRON

TO THE HON. DOUGLAS KINNAIRD*   *10ᵇʳᵉ 10th, 1823*

DEAR DOUGLAS,—This will be delivered by Col. Napier, whom I request you to present to the Committee. He is too well known to require me to say more than I have already said in my letter to Mr. Bowring—which see.

I have had only *two* letters from you, both (I think) of August: one, however, is without date. I have often written to acknowledge both, and to sanction or approve your acceptance of the Rochdale proposition.

I have been expending monies on the Greek cause. I shall probably have to expend *more*, and therefore require *more* to *expend*. As I hope that you have gotten together the Kirkby Mallory dues—also arrears—also mine own especial fees and funds, the Rochdale produce and my income for the ensuing year (and I have still of the present year something in hand, including my Genoese credit) ought to make a pretty sufficient sort of sum to take the field withal ; and I like to do so with all I can muster, in case of anything requiring the same. I shall be as saving of my purse and person as you recommend ; but you know that [it] is as well to be in readiness with one or both in the event of either being required.

Yrs, ever and faithfully, N. B.

P.S.—Col. Napier will tell you the recent events.

TO THE HON. DOUGLAS KINNAIRD [?] * 10bre 11th, 1823
[P.S. to a letter not preserved]

P.S.—I presume that you have also come to some agreement with Mr. M. about " Werner ". The year is more than out since he published it. Although the copyright should only be worth two or three hundred pounds, I will tell you what can be done with them. For three hundred pounds I can maintain in Greece at more than *fullest pay* of the Provisional Govt., *rations* included, one hundred armed men *for three months* ! It is not that I am in any pressing need of monies, especially of this kind, but it is better to have all financial matters arranged of whatever description—rents, funds, purchase-monies or printer's products. I presume that there is or will be something from " the Island " also, and from the sale of the other writings ; but I do not reckon much on anything of that kind. H. ought to have collected the works by this time, as before directed, and published the whole eleven new D.J.s.

I am particular on this point only because a sum of trifling account even for a Gentleman's *personal* expences in *London* or *Paris* in Greece can arm and maintain hundreds of men. You may judge of this when I tell you that the four thousand pounds advanced by me is likely to set a fleet and an army in motion for some months.

I request you to avoid all unnecessary disbursements (excepting for the Insurances) in England. Whatever remains to be paid to lawyers and creditors (and you yourself say that it is but a sum not exceeding much my *whole*, Kirkby Mallory included, *half* year's income) can be settled after the Greek war, or the Greek Kalends; for the dogs, especially the lawyers, have already had more than ever was justly owing to them. But they shall have fair play—and I too, I hope and trust; but prithee look to these recommended affairs.

TO THE HON. DOUGLAS KINNAIRD † *10bre 23rd, 1823*

DEAR DOUGLAS,—A quarter of a year has elapsed since I have heard from you, but I have written through various channels to approve of your *Rochdale proposition* which I hope has gone on *well*.

A Greek vessel has arrived from the squadron to convey me to Missolonghi, where Mavrocordato now is, and has assumed the command, so that I expect to embark immediately. Address, however, to Cephalonia, (through Messrs. Webb and Barry of Genoa, as usual); and get together all the means and credit of mine you can, to face the war establishment, for it is " in for a penny, in for a pound ", and I must do all that I can for the Ancients. I have advanced them four thousand pounds, which got the squadron to sea, and I made them forward the Deputies for the Loan, who ought to be soon in England, having sailed some weeks ago. I have already transmitted to you a copy of their agreement etc.—and to Hobhouse and Bowring various dispatches with copies or originals of correspondence more or less important. I am labouring to reconcile their parties, and there is some hope *now* of succeeding. Their *public* affairs go on well. The Turks have retreated from Acarnania without a battle, after a few fruitless attempts on Anatoliko and Corinth is taken, and the Greeks have gained a battle in the Archipelago and the squadron here, too, has taken a Turkish corvette with some money and a cargo. In short, if they can obtain a Loan, I am of opinion that matters will assume and preserve a steady and favourable aspect for their independence.

In the mean time I stand paymaster, and what not; and lucky it is that, from the nature of the warfare and of the country, the resources even of an individual can be of partial and temporary service.

Colonel Stanhope is at Messolonghi. Probably we shall attempt Patras next. The Suliotes, who are friends of mine, seem anxious to have me with them, and so is Mavrocordato. If I can but succeed in reconciling the two parties (and I have left no stone unturned therefor), it will be something; and if not, why we must go over to the Morea with the Western Greeks—who are the bravest, and at present the strongest, now that they have beaten back the Turks—and try the effect of a little *physical* advice, should they persist in rejecting *moral* persuasion. I suppose you know the state and names of the parties from my letters to Hobhouse and Bowring. Once more (as usual) recommending to you the reinforcement of my strong box and credit from all lawful sources and *re*sources of mine to their practicable extent (and after all, it is better playing at nations than gaming at Almack's or Newmarket or piecing or dinnering) and also requesting Your Honour to write now and then one of those pithy epistles " touching the needful " so agreeable to the distant traveller,

I remain ever yours, N. B.

P.S.—Please to transmit any further credits through Messrs. Webb and Barry who have been very civil and useful, all throughout.

My dear Muir,[1]—I wish you many returns of the season, and happiness therewithal. Gamba and the Bombard (there is a strong reason to believe) are carried into Patras by a Turkish frigate, which we saw chase them at dawn on the 31st: we had been close under the stern in the night, believing her a Greek till within pistol shot, and only escaped by a miracle of all the Saints (our captain says), and truly I am of his opinion, for we should never have got away of ourselves. They were signalising their consort with lights, and had illuminated the ship between decks, and were shouting like a mob;—but then why did they not fire? Perhaps they took us for a Greek brûlot, and were afraid of kindling us—they had no colours flying even at dawn nor after.

At daybreak my boat was on the coast, but the wind unfavourable for *the port*;—a large vessel with the wind in her favour standing between us and the Gulf, and another in chase of the Bombard about twelve miles off, or so. Soon after they stood (*i.e.* the Bombard and frigate) apparently towards Patras, and, a Zantiote boat making signals to us from the shore to get away, away we went before the wind, and ran into a creek called Scrofes, I believe, where I landed Luke and another (as Luke's life was in most danger), with some money for themselves, and a letter for Stanhope, and sent them up the country to Messolonghi, where they would be in safety, as the place where we were could be assailed by armed boats in a moment, and Gamba had all our arms except two carbines, a fowling-piece, and some pistols.

In less than an hour the vessel in chase neared us, and we dashed out again, and showing our stern (our boat sails very well), got in before night to Dragomestri, where we now are. But where is the Greek fleet? I don't know—do you? I told our master of the boat that I was inclined to think the two large vessels (there were none else in sight) Greeks. But he answered, "They are too large—why don't they show their colours?" and his account was confirmed, be it true or false, by several boats which we met or passed, as we could not at any rate have got in with that wind without beating about for

[1] Dr. Henry Muir was health officer of Argostoli.

a long time; and as there was much property, and some lives to risk (the boy's especially) without any means of defence, it was necessary to let our boatmen have their own way.

I despatched yesterday another messenger to Messolonghi for an escort, but we have yet no answer. We are here (those of my boat) for the fifth day without taking our clothes off, and sleeping on deck in all weathers, but are all very well, and in good spirits. It is to be supposed that the Government will send, for their own sakes, an escort, as I have 16,000 dollars on board, the greater part for their service. I had (besides personal property to the amount of about 5000 more) 8000 dollars in specie of my own, without reckoning the Committee's stores: so that the Turks will have a good thing of it, if the prize be good.

I regret the detention of Gamba, etc., but the rest we can make up again; so tell Hancock[1] to set my bills into cash as soon as possible, and Corgialegno to prepare the remainder of my credit with Messrs. Webb to be turned into monies. I shall remain here, unless something extraordinary occurs, till Mavrocordato sends, and then go on, and act according to circumstances. My respects to the two colonels, and remembrances to all friends. Tell " *Ultima Analise* " that his friend [P]raidi did not make his appearance with the brig, though I think that he might as well have spoken with us *in* or *off* Zante, to give us a gentle hint of what we had to expect.

Yours ever affectionately, N. B.

P.S.—Excuse my scrawl on account of the pen and the frosty morning at daybreak. I write in haste, a boat starting for Kalamo. I do not know whether the detention of the Bombard (if she be detained, for I cannot swear to it, and I can only judge from appearances, and what all these fellows say), be an affair of the Government, and neutrality, and, etc.—but *she was stopped at least* twelve miles distant from any port, and had all her papers regular from *Zante* for *Kalamo* and *we also*. I did not land at Zante, being anxious to lose as little time as possible; but Sir F. S. came off to invite me, etc., and every body was as kind as could be, even in Cephalonia.

[1] Messrs. Samuel Barff and Charles Hancock were bankers of Zante and Argostoli.

TO CHARLES HANCOCK　　　　*Missolonghi, February 5, 1824*

DEAR SIR,—Dr. Muir's letter and yours of the 23d reached me some days ago. Tell Muir that I am glad of his promotion for his sake, and of his remaining near us for our sakes ; though I cannot but regret Dr. Kennedy's departure, which accounts for the previous earthquakes and the present English weather in this climate. With all respect to my medical pastor, I have to announce to him, that amongst other fire-brands, our fire-master Parry (just landed) has disembarked an elect black-smith, entrusted with three hundred and twenty-two Greek Testaments. I have given him all facilities in my power for his works spiritual and temporal ; and if he can settle matters as easily with the Greek Archbishop and hierarchy, I trust that neither the heretic nor the supposed sceptic will be accused of intolerance.

By the way, I met with the said Archbishop at Anatolico (where I went by invitation of the Primates a few days ago, and was received with a heavier cannonade than the Turks, probably), for the second time (I had known him here before) ; and he and P. Mavrocordato, and the Chiefs and Primates and I, all dined together, and I thought the metropolitan the merriest of the party, and a very good Christian for all that. But Gamba (we got wet through on our way back) has been ill with a fever and colic ; and Luke (not the Evangelist, but a disciple of mine) has been out of sorts too, and so have others of the people, and I have been very well,—except that I caught cold yesterday, with swearing too much in the rain at the Greeks, who would not bear a hand in landing the Committee stores, and nearly spoiled our combustibles ; but I turned out in person, and made such a row as set them in motion, blas-pheming at them all from the Government downwards, till they actually did *some* part of what they ought to have done several days before, and this is esteemed, as it deserves to be, a wonder.

Tell Muir that, notwithstanding his remonstrances, which I receive thankfully, it is perhaps best that I should advance with the troops ; for if we do not do something soon, we shall only have a third year of defensive operation and another siege, and all that. We hear that the Turks are coming down in force, and sooner than usual: and as these fellows do mind me a little, it is the opinion that I should go,—firstly, because they will sooner listen to a foreigner than one of their own people, out of native jealousies: secondly, because the Turks will sooner treat or capitulate (if such occasion should happen) with a Frank than a Greek; and, thirdly, because nobody else seems disposed to take the responsibility—Mavrocordato being very busy here, the foreign military men too young or not of authority enough to be obeyed by the natives, and the Chiefs (as aforesaid) inclined to obey any one except, or rather than, one of their own body. As for me, I am willing to do what I am bidden, and to follow my instructions. I neither seek nor shun that nor any thing else that they may wish me to attempt: as for personal safety, besides that it ought not to be a consideration, I take it that a man is on the whole as safe in one place as another; and, after all, he had better end with a bullet than bark in his body. If we are not taken off with the sword, we are like to march off with an ague in this mud basket; and to conclude with a very bad pun, to the ear rather than to the eye, better *martially* than *marsh-ally*;—the situation of Messolonghi is not unknown to you. The dykes of Holland when broken down are the Deserts of Arabia for dryness, in comparison.

And now for the sinews of war. I thank you and Mr. Barff for your ready answer, which, next to ready money, is a pleasant thing. Besides the assets and balance, and the relics of the Corgialegno correspondence with Leghorn and Genoa, (I sold the dog's flour, tell him, but not at *his* price,) I shall request and require, from the beginning of March ensuing, about five thousand dollars every two months, *i.e.* about twenty-five thousand within the current year, at regular intervals, independent of the sums now negotiating. I can show you documents to prove that these are considerably *within* my supplies for the year in more ways than one; but I do not like to tell the Greeks *exactly what* I *could* or would advance on an emergency, because, otherwise, they will double and triple their demands (a disposition that they have already sufficiently shown): and though I am willing to do all I can *when* necessary, yet I do not see *why* they should not help a little; for they are not quite so bare as they pretend to be by some accounts.

February 7, 1824

I have been interrupted by the arrival of Parry,[1] and afterwards by the return of Hesketh, who has not brought an answer to my epistles, which rather surprises me. You will write soon, I suppose. Parry seems a fine rough subject, but will hardly be ready for the field these three weeks : he and I will (I think) be able to draw together,—at least, *I* will not interfere with or contradict him in his own department. He complains grievously of the mercantile and *enthusymusy*, as Braham pronounces enthusiasm, part of the Committee, but greatly praises Gordon and Hume. Gordon *would* have given three or four thousand pounds and come out *himself*, but Kennedy or somebody else disgusted him, and thus they have spoiled part of their subscription and cramped their operations. Parry says Blaquiere is a humbug, to which I say nothing. He sorely laments the printing and civilising expenses, and wishes that there was not a Sunday-school in the world, or *any* school *here* at present, save and except always an academy for artilleryship.

He complained also of the cold, a little to my surprise; firstly, because, there being no chimneys, I have used myself to do without other warmth than the animal heat and one's cloak, in these parts ; and, secondly, because I should as soon have expected to hear a volcano sneeze, as a firemaster (who is to burn a whole fleet) exclaim against the atmosphere. I fully expected that his very approach would have scorched up the town like the burning-glasses of Archimedes.

Well, it seems that I am to be Commander-in-Chief, and the post is by no means a sinecure, for we are not what Major Sturgeon calls " a set of the most amicable officers ". Whether we shall have " a boxing bout between Captain Sheers and the Colonel ", I cannot tell ; but, between Suliote chiefs, German barons, English volunteers, and adventurers of all nations, we are likely to form as goodly an allied army as ever quarrelled beneath the same banner.

February 8, 1824

Interrupted again by business yesterday, and it is time to conclude my letter. I drew some time since on Mr. Barff for

---

[1] William Parry, firemaster R.N., had been sent out to Greece by the Committee, with eight English workmen, to help prepare the insurgents' artillery.

a thousand dollars, to complete some money wanted by the Government. The said Government got cash on that bill *here*, and at a profit; but the very same fellow who gave it to them, after proposing to give me money for other bills on Barff to the amount of thirteen hundred dollars, either could not, or thought better of it. I had written to Barff advising him, but had afterwards to write to tell him of the fellow's having not come up to time. You must really send me the balance soon. I have the artillerists and my Suliotes to pay, and Heaven knows what besides; and as every thing depends upon punctuality, all our operations will be at a stand-still unless you use despatch. I shall send to Mr. Barff or to you further bills on England for three thousand pounds, to be negotiated as speedily as you can. I have already stated here and formerly the sums I can command at home within the year,—without including my credits, or the bills already negotiated or negotiating, or Corgialegno's balance of Messrs. Webb's letter,—and my letters from my friends (received by Mr. Parry's vessel) confirm what I already stated. How much I may require in the course of the year I can't tell, but I will take care that it shall not exceed the means to supply it.

Yours ever, N. B.

P.S.—I have had, by desire of a Mr. *Gerosstati*, to draw on Demetrius Delladecima (is it our friend *in ultima analise?*) to pay the Committee expenses. I really do not understand what the Committee mean by some of their proceedings. Parry and I get on well *hitherto*: how long this may last, Heaven knows, but I hope it will, for a good deal for the Greek service depends upon it; but he has already had some *miffs* with Col. S[tan-hope], and I do all I can to keep the peace amongst them. However, Parry is a fine fellow, extremely active, and of strong, sound, practical talent, by all accounts. Enclosed are bills for three thousand pounds, drawn in the mode directed (*i.e.* parcelled out in smaller bills). A good opportunity occurring for Cephalonia to send letters on, I avail myself of it. Remembrances to Stevens and all friends. Also my compliments and every thing kind to the colonels and officers.

February 9, 1824

P.S.—2d or 3d. I have reason to expect a person from

England directed with papers (on business) for me to sign, somewhere in the Islands, by and by : if such should arrive, would you forward him to me by a safe conveyance, as the papers regard a transaction with regard to the adjustment of a lawsuit, and a sum of several thousand pounds, which I, or my bankers and trustees for me, may have to receive (in England) in consequence. The time of the probable arrival I cannot state, but the date of my letters is the 2d. Nov., and I suppose that he ought to arrive soon.

FROM THE MANUSCRIPT BOOK CONTAIN-
ING THE JOURNAL IN CEPHALONIA   *Febry. 15th, 1824*

Upon February 15th—(I write on the 17th of the same month) I had a strong shock of a convulsive description, but whether Epileptic, Paralytic, or Apoplectic, is not yet decided by the two medical men, who attend me ; or whether it be of some other nature (if such there be). It was very painful, and, had it lasted a minute longer, must have extinguished my mortality—if I can judge by sensations. I was speechless with the features much distorted, but *not* foaming at the mouth, they say, and my struggles so violent that several persons— two of whom, Mr. Parry the engineer, and my Servant Tita the Chasseur, are very strong men—could not hold me. It lasted about ten minutes, and came on immediately after drinking a tumbler of Cider mixed with cold water in Col. Stanhope's apartments. This is the first attack that I have had of the kind to the best of my belief. I never heard that any of my family were liable to the same, though my mother was subject to *hysterical affections.*

Yesterday (the 16th) leeches were applied to my temples. I had previously recovered a good deal, but with some feverish and variable symptoms. I bled profusely, and, as they went too near the temporal artery, there was some difficulty in stopping the blood even with the Lunar Caustic. This, how- ever, after some hours was accomplished about eleven o'clock at night, and this day (the 17th), though weakly, I feel tolerably convalescent.

With regard to the presumed causes of this attack, as far as I know, there might be several. The state of the place and the weather permit little exercise at present. I have been violently agitated with more than one passion recently, and a good deal occupied, politically as well as privately, and amidst conflicting parties, politics, and (as far as regards public matters) circumstances. I have also been in an anxious state with regard to things which may be only interesting to my own private feelings, and, perhaps, not uniformly so temperate as I may generally affirm that I was wont to be. How far any or all of these may have acted on the mind or body of one who had already undergone many previous changes of place and passion during a life of thirty-six years, I cannot tell, nor—— But I am interrupted by the arrival of a report from a party returned from reconnoitring a Turkish Brig of War, just stranded on the Coast, and which is to be attacked the moment we can get some guns to bear upon her. I shall hear what Parry says about it. Here he comes——

TO THE HON. AUGUSTA LEIGH   *Missolonghi,*
                                [*Monday*] *Feby 23^d 1824*

MY DEAREST AUGUSTA,[1]—I received a few days ago yours and Lady B's report of Ada's health, with other letters from England for which I ought to be and am (I hope) sufficiently thankful, as they were of great comfort and I wanted some, having been recently unwell, but am now much better. So that you need not be alarmed.

You will have heard of our journeys and escapes, and so forth, perhaps with some exaggeration; but it is all very well now, and I have been for some time in Greece, which is in as good a state as could be expected considering circumstances. But I will not plague you with politics, wars, or *earthquakes*, though we had another very smart one three nights ago, which produced a scene ridiculous enough, as no damage was done except to those who stuck fast in the scuffle to get first out of the doors or windows, amongst whom some recent importations,

---

[1] This letter was found unfinished on Byron's writing-table after his death.

fresh from England, who had been used to quieter elements, were rather squeezed in the press for precedence.

I have been obtaining the release of about nine and twenty Turkish prisoners—men, women, and children—and have sent them at my own expense home to their friends, but one, a pretty little girl of nine years of age named Hato or Hatagée, has expressed a strong wish to remain with me, or under my care, and I have nearly determined to adopt her. If I thought that Lady B. would let her come to England as a Companion to Ada—(they are about the same age), and we could easily provide for her; if not, I can send her to Italy for education. She is very lively and quick, and with great black oriental eyes, and Asiatic features. All her brothers were killed in the Revolution; her mother wishes to return to her husband who is at Prevesa, but says that she would rather entrust the child to me in the present state of the Country. Her extreme youth and sex have hitherto saved her life, but there is no saying what might occur in the course of the *war* (and of *such* a war), and I shall probably commit her to the charge of some English lady in the islands for the present. The Child herself has the same wish, and seems to have a decided character for her age. You can mention this matter if you think it worth while. I merely wish her to be respectably educated and treated, and, if my years and all things be considered, I presume it would be difficult to conceive me to have any other views.

With regard to Ada's health, I am glad to hear that it is so much better. But I think it right that Lady B. should be informed, and guard against it accordingly, that her description of much of her indisposition and tendencies very nearly resemble my *own* at a similar age, except that I was much more impetuous. Her preference of *prose* (strange as it may seem) *was* and indeed *is* mine (for I hate *reading* verse, and always did), and I never invented anything but " *boats—ships* " and generally relating to the Ocean. I shewed the report to Col. Stanhope, who was struck with the resemblance of *parts* of it to the *paternal* line even *now*. But it is also fit, though unpleasant, that I should mention that my recent attack, and a very severe one, had a strong appearance of *epilepsy*. *Why*— I know not, for it is late in life—its first appearance at thirty-six—and, as far as I *know*, it is not *hereditary*, and it is that it may not *become* so, that you should tell Lady B. to take some precautions in the case of Ada. My attack has not yet returned, and I am fighting it off with abstinence and exercise, and thus far with success; if merely casual, it is all very well.

TO JOHN MURRAY *Missolonghi, February 25, 1824*

I have heard from Mr. Douglas Kinnaird that you state " a report of a satire on Mr. Gifford having arrived from Italy, *said* to be written by *me*! but that *you* do not believe it ". I dare say you do not, nor any body else, I should think. Whoever asserts that I am the author or abetter of anything of the kind on Gifford lies in his throat. I always regarded him as my literary father, and myself as his prodigal son; if any such composition exists, it is none of mine. *You* know as well as any body upon *whom* I have or have not written; and *you* also know whether they do or did not deserve that same. And so much for such matters.

You will perhaps be anxious to hear some news from this part of Greece (which is the most liable to invasion); but you will hear enough through public and private channels. I will, however, give you the events of a week, mingling my own private peculiar with the public; for we are here jumbled a little together at present.

On Sunday (the 15th, I believe), I had a strong and sudden convulsive attack, which left me speechless, though not motionless—for some strong men could not hold me; but whether it was epilepsy, catalepsy, cachexy, or apoplexy, or what other *exy* or *epsy*, the doctors have not decided; or whether it was spasmodic or nervous, etc.; but it was very unpleasant, and nearly carried me off, and all that. On Monday, they put leeches to my temples, no difficult matter, but the blood could not be stopped till eleven at night (they had gone too near the temporal artery for my temporal safety), and neither styptic nor caustic would cauterise the orifice till after a hundred attempts.

On Tuesday, a Turkish brig of war ran on shore. On Wednesday, great preparations being made to attack her, though protected by her consorts, the Turks burned her and retired to Patras. On Thursday, a quarrel ensued between the Suliotes and the Frank guard at the arsenal : a Swedish officer was killed, and a Suliote severely wounded, and a general fight expected, and with some difficulty prevented. On Friday, the officer was buried ; and Captain Parry's English artificers mutinied, under pretence that their lives were in danger, and are for quitting the country :—they may.

On Saturday we had the smartest shock of an earthquake which I remember, (and I have felt thirty, slight or smart, at different periods ; they are common in the Mediterranean,) and the whole army discharged their arms, upon the same principle that savages beat drums, or howl, during an eclipse of the moon :—it was a rare scene altogether—if you had but seen the English Johnnies, who had never been out of a cockney workshop before !—or will again, if they can help it—and on Sunday we heard that the Vizier is come down to Larissa, with one hundred and odd thousand men.

In coming here, I had two escapes ; one from the Turks, (*one* of my vessels was taken, but afterwards released,) and the other from shipwreck. We drove twice on the rocks near the Scrofes (Islands near the coast).

I have obtained from the Greeks the release of eight-and-twenty Turkish prisoners, men, women, and children, and sent them to Patras and Prevesa at my own charges. One little girl of nine years old, who prefers remaining with me, I shall (if I live) send, with her mother, probably, to Italy, or to England, and adopt her. Her name is Hato, or Hatagée. She is a very pretty lively child. All her brothers were killed by the Greeks, and she herself and her mother merely spared by special favour and owing to her extreme youth, she being then but five or six years old.

My health is now better, and I ride about again. My office here is no sinecure, so many parties and difficulties of every kind ; but I will do what I can. Prince Mavrocordato is an excellent person, and does all in his power ; but his situation is perplexing in the extreme. Still we have great hopes of the success of the contest. You will hear, however, more of public news from plenty of quarters : for I have little time to write.

Believe me, yours, etc., etc., N. Bn.

TO THE EARL OF CLARE *Missolonghi, March 31, 1824*

MY DEAREST CLARE,—This will be presented to you by a live Greek deputy, for whom I desiderate and solicit your countenance and goodwill. I hope that you do not forget that I always regard you as my dearest friend and love you as when we were Harrow boys together; and if I do not repeat this as often as I ought, it is that I may not tire you with what you so well know.

I refer you to Signor Zaimie, the Greek deputy, for all news, public and private. He will do better than an epistle in this respect.

I was sorry to hear that Dick had exported a married woman from Ireland, not only on account of morals but monies. I trust that the jury will be considerate. I *thought* that Richard looked sentimental when I saw him at Genoa, but little expected what he was to land in. Pray who *is* the lady? The papers merely inform us by dint of asterisks that she is somebody's wife and has children, and that Dick (as usual) was the intimate friend of the confiding husband. It is to be hoped that the jury will be bachelors.

Pray take care of *yourself* Clare, my dear, for in some of your letters I had a glimpse of a similar intrigue of yours. Have a care of an *éclat*. Your Irish juries lay it on heavy; and then besides you would be fixed for life with a *second-hand épouse*, whereas I wish to see you lead a virgin heiress from Saville Row to Mount Shannon.

Let me hear from you at your best leisure, and believe me ever and most truly, my dearest Clare,

Yours, NOEL BYRON

P.S.—The Turkish fleet are just bearing down to blockade this port; so how our deputy is to get by is a doubt, but the island boats frequently evade them.

The sight is pretty, but much finer for a limner than a lodger. It is the Squadron from the Gulf of Corinth (Hooke-Gulf of Lepanto); they (the Greeks, I mean) are all busy enough, as you may suppose, as the campaign is expected to commence next month. But as aforesaid I refer you for news to the bearer.

TO CHARLES F. BARRY   *April 9th 1824*

DEAR BARRY,[1]—The Account up to 11th July was 40,541, etc., Genoese livres in my favour : since then I have had a letter of Credit of Messrs. Webb for 60,000 Genoese livres, for which I have drawn ; but how the account stands *exactly*, you do not state. The balance will of course be replaced by my London Correspondent, referring more particularly to the Honble Douglas Kinnaird, who is also my Agent and trustee, as well as banker, and a friend besides since we were at College together—which is favourable to business, as it gives confidence, or ought to do so.

I had hoped that you had obtained the price of the Schooner from Ld Blessington : you must really tell him that I must make the affair public, and take other steps which will be agreeable to neither, unless he speedily pays the money, so long due, and contracted by his own headstrong wish to purchase. You *know* how fairly I treated him in the whole affair.

Every thing except the best (*i.e.* the Green travelling Chariot) may be disposed of, and that speedily, as it will assist to balance our accompt. As the Greeks have gotten their loan, they may as well repay mine, which they no longer require : and I request you to forward a copy of the agreement to Mr. Kinnaird, and direct him from me to claim the money from the Deputies. They were welcome to it in their difficulties, and also for good and all, supposing that they had not got out of them ; but, as it is, they can afford repayment, and I assure you that, besides *this*, they have had many " a strong and long pull " at my purse, which has been (and still is) disbursing pretty freely in their cause : besides, I shall have to *re-expend* the same monies, having some hundred men under orders, at my own expense, for the Gk. Government and National service.

Of all their proceedings here, health, politics, plans, acts, and deeds, etc.—good ,or otherwise, Gamba or others will tell you—truly or not truly, according to their habits.

Yours ever, N. B^N.

---

[1] On the evening of the day on which this letter was written, Byron came home wet after a ride, and complained of feeling feverish. He died on April 19th, 1824.

APPENDIX

LETTERS HITHERTO UNPUBLISHED
Marked in the text with *

TO MRS. BYRON	[?] 1804	*Sir John Murray*
,, LORD CLARE	AUG. 20, 1807	*Yale University Library*
,, JOHN CAM HOBHOUSE	MAR. 26, 1808	*Sir John Murray*
,, JOHN CAM HOBHOUSE	APR. 15, 1808	*Sir John Murray*
,, FRANCIS HODGSON	NOV. 18, 1808	*Sir John Murray*
,, EDWARD ELLICE	JUNE 25, 1809	*Russell Ellice, Esq.*
,, EDWARD ELLICE	JULY 4, 1810	*Russell Ellice, Esq.*
,, JOHN CAM HOBHOUSE	MAR. 5, 1811	*Sir John Murray*
,, JOHN CAM HOBHOUSE	FEB. 10, 1812	*Sir John Murray*
,, MISS MERCER ELPHINSTONE	JULY 29, 1812	*The Marquess of Lansdowne*
,, LADY MELBOURNE	[AUG. 12. 1812]	*Sir John Murray*
,, LADY CAROLINE LAMB	JAN. 1813	*Sir John Murray*
,, JOHN CAM HOBHOUSE	JAN. 17, 1813	*Sir John Murray*
,, E. D. CLARKE	DEC. 15, 1813	*British Museum*
,, MISS MERCER ELPHINSTONE	MAY 3, 1814	*The Marquess of Lansdowne*
,, HENRIETTA D'USSIÈRES	JUNE 8, 1814	*Sir John Murray*
,, S. T. COLERIDGE	OCT. 18, 1815	*Yale University Library*
,, MISS MERCER ELPHINSTONE	APR. 11, 1816	*The Marquess of Lansdowne*
,, THE HON. DOUGLAS KINNAIRD	JULY 20, 1816	*Lord Kinnaird*
,, THE HON. AUGUSTA LEIGH	OCT. 13, 1816	*Sir John Murray*
,, THE HON. AUGUSTA LEIGH	NOV. 2, 1816	*Sir John Murray*
,, THE HON. DOUGLAS KINNAIRD	JAN. 12, 1817	*Lord Kinnaird*
,, THE HON. DOUGLAS KINNAIRD	JULY 15, 1818	*Lord Kinnaird*
,, THE COUNTESS GUICCIOLI	APR. 25, 1819	*Count Carlo Gamba* (translated by the Marchesa Origo)
,, THE LORD KINNAIRD	MAY 15, 1819	*Lord Kinnaird*
,, THE LORD KINNAIRD	MAY 26, 1819	*Lord Kinnaird*
,, THE LORD KINNAIRD	JULY 5, 1819	*Lord Kinnaird*
,, THE HON. AUGUSTA LEIGH	JULY 26, 1819	*The Pierpont Morgan Library, New York*
,, ALEXANDER SCOTT	JULY 31, 1819	*The Pierpont Morgan Library, New York*
,, CAPTAIN HAY	SEPT. 1819	*From a copy, made in Nantes in 1925, in Sir John Murray's Collection*

TO	THE HON. DOUGLAS KINNAIRD	JAN. 2, 1820	*Sir John Murray*
,,	RICHARD BELGRAVE HOPPNER	MAR. 31, 1820	*Henry E. Huntingdon Library*
,,	THE HON. DOUGLAS KINNAIRD	MAY 3, 1820	*Lord Kinnaird*
,,	JOHN CAM HOBHOUSE	JUNE 8, 1820	*Sir John Murray*
,,	THE HON. DOUGLAS KINNAIRD	JULY 20, 1820	*Lord Kinnaird*
,,	THE COUNTESS GUICCIOLI	AUG. 7, 1820	*Count Carlo Gamba (translated by the Marchesa Origo)*
,,	THE HON. DOUGLAS KINNAIRD	SEPT. 17, 1820	*Yale University Library*
,,	THE HON. AUGUSTA LEIGH	OCT. 1820	*Sir John Murray (from a copy)*
,,	THE HON. DOUGLAS KINNAIRD	FEB. 1, 1821	*Sir John Murray*
,,	JOHN CAM HOBHOUSE	FEB. 22, 1821	*Sir John Murray*
,,	THE HON. DOUGLAS KINNAIRD	FEB. 26, 1821	*Sir John Murray*
,,	THE HON. DOUGLAS KINNAIRD	MAR. 23, 1821	*Sir John Murray*
,,	THE HON. DOUGLAS KINNAIRD	APR. 26, 1821	*Sir John Murray*
,,	THE HON. DOUGLAS KINNAIRD	JULY 24 [? 14] 1821	*Sir John Murray*
,,	THE HON. DOUGLAS KINNAIRD	AUG. 23, 1821	*Sir John Murray*
,,	OCTAVIUS GILCHRIST	SEPT. 5, 1821	*Henry E. Huntingdon Library*
,,	ROBERT SOUTHEY	FEB. 7, 1822	*Lord Kinnaird*
,,	THE HON. DOUGLAS KINNAIRD	[FEB. 7, 1822]	*Lord Kinnaird*
,,	SIR GODFREY WEBSTER	APR. 12, 1822	*Dr. Eric Millar*
,,	LORD HOLLAND	MAY 11, 1822	*Historical Society of Pennsylvania*
,,	THE HON. DOUGLAS KINNAIRD	MAY 27, 1822	*Lord Kinnaird*
,,	E. J. DAWKINS	JULY 4, 1822	*University of Texas*
,,	E. J. DAWKINS	JULY 6, 1822	*University of Texas*
,,	DAVID GRANT	NOV. 13, 1823	*Sir John Murray*
,,	THE HON. DOUGLAS KINNAIRD	DEC. 10, 1823	*Sir John Murray*
,,	THE HON. DOUGLAS KINNAIRD [?]	DEC. 11, 1823	*Sir John Murray*

LETTERS INCLUDING HITHERTO UNPUBLISHED PASSAGES

Marked in the text with †

,,	JOHN CAM HOBHOUSE	FEB. 27, 1808	*Sir John Murray*
,,	MRS. BYRON	JUNE 28, 1810	*Correspondence of Lord Byron, edited by R. C. Dallas (suppressed)*
,,	JOHN CAM HOBHOUSE	JULY 29 AND 30, 1810	*Sir John Murray*
,,	JOHN CAM HOBHOUSE	AUG. 16, 1810	*Sir John Murray*

TO	JOHN CAM HOBHOUSE	AUG. 23, 1810	*Sir John Murray*
,,	JOHN CAM HOBHOUSE	SEPT. 25, 1810	*Sir John Murray*
,,	JOHN CAM HOBHOUSE	OCT. 2, 1810	*Sir John Murray*
,,	JOHN CAM HOBHOUSE	OCT. 4, 1810	*Sir John Murray*
,,	JOHN CAM HOBHOUSE	JUNE 19, 1811	*Sir John Murray*
,,	JOHN CAM HOBHOUSE	OCT. 22, 1811	*Sir John Murray*
,,	LADY CAROLINE LAMB	MARCH OR APRIL 1812	*Sir John Murray*
,,	LADY MELBOURNE	SEPT. 21, 1813	*Sir John Murray*
,,	JOHN CAM HOBHOUSE	MAY 1, 1816	*Sir John Murray*
,,	THE HON. AUGUSTA LEIGH	NOV. 6, 1816	*Sir John Murray*
,,	THE HON. AUGUSTA LEIGH	DEC. 19, 1816	*Sir John Murray*
,,	JOHN MURRAY	JAN. 2, 1817	*Sir John Murray*
,,	JOHN CAM HOBHOUSE	MAR. 31, 1817	*British Museum*
,,	JOHN MURRAY	APR. 2, 1817	*Sir John Murray*
,,	JOHN MURRAY	AUG. 21, 1817	*Sir John Murray*
,,	JOHN MURRAY	JAN. 27, 1818	*Sir John Murray*
,,	JOHN CAM HOBHOUSE AND THE HON. DOUGLAS KINNAIRD	JAN. 19, 1819	*Sir John Murray*
,,	JOHN CAM HOBHOUSE	APR. 6, 1819	*Sir John Murray*
,,	JOHN CAM HOBHOUSE	[APR. 20 1819]	*Sir John Murray*
,,	THE HON. DOUGLAS KINNAIRD	APR. 24, 1819	*Sir John Murray*
,,	RICHARD BELGRAVE HOPPNER	JUNE 20, 1819	*Sir John Murray*
,,	JOHN CAM HOBHOUSE	JULY 30, 1819	*Sir John Murray*
,,	JOHN MURRAY	AUG. 1, 1819	*Sir John Murray*
,,	THE HON. DOUGLAS KINNAIRD	OCT. 26, 1819	*British Museum*
,,	RICHARD BELGRAVE HOPPNER	OCT. 29, 1819	*Sir John Murray*
,,	JOHN CAM HOBHOUSE	MAR. 3, 1820	*British Museum*
,,	JOHN CAM HOBHOUSE	MAR. 29, 1820	*Sir John Murray*
,,	THE HON. DOUGLAS KINNAIRD	NOV. 22, 1820	*Sir John Murray*
,,	THE HON. DOUGLAS KINNAIRD	MAY 21, 1823	*Sir John Murray*
,,	THE HON. AUGUSTA LEIGH	OCT. 12, 1823	*Sir John Murray*
,,	THE HON. DOUGLAS KINNAIRD	DEC. 23, 1823	*Sir John Murray*

INDEX

665, 681, 696, 705, 707, 710-11,
716, 718, 731, 752 ; Byron defends
its indelicacy, 435, 439, 441, 449,
479-80, 491, 716 ; his answer to
Blackwood's Observations on,
515 ; popularity in Germany,
696 ; "female Censor Morum",
707
Donna Josepha, 54
Dorant's, 95, 100 ; Byron's letters
from, 39-42
D'Orsay, Count Alfred, 720 n.,
721-3, 726-7, 734 ; Byron's letter
to, 724
Dorset, George John Frederick, 4th
Duke of, 2
Dorville, Vice-Consul at Venice,
493, 512
Downing Fellowship, 535, 538
Dragomestri, Byron's letter from,
755
Drake, George (Draco), Suliot
chief, 741
Drummond, Charles, 678
Drummond, Sir William, 421, 448,
678
Drunken Barnaby's Journal, 170
Drury, Rev. Henry Joseph, 10, 43-4,
46, 52, 67, 69, 122, 161, 678, 695 ;
Byron's quarrel with, 4, 5 and
n. ; his letters to, 63, 100
Drury, Dr. Joseph, Headmaster of
Harrow, 5 and n., 9-10, 13, 612,
642
Drury, Martin, 9-10
Drury Lane Theatre, 166, 216, 402,
426, 664 n. ; Committee and
plays sent to, 310, 315-17, 320
and n., 384, 390 and n., 633-5 ;
Byron's *Monody on Death of Sheridan*
delivered at, 340-41
Dryden, John, 208, 463, 561, 601 ;
Huntsman's Ghost, 587
Dudley, 4th Earl of. *See* Ward,
Hon. J. W.
Duff, Helen, 223
Duff, Mary (Mrs. Robert Cock-
burn), 211 and n., 222 and n.,
223-4
Duffie, Colonel John, 739
Dumergue, dentist, 719
Duncan, Byron's writing-master at
Aberdeen, 606
Dundas, Henry. *See* Melville,
Viscount
Dunn, Henry (Leghorn), 695

D'Ussières, Henrietta, Byron's
letter to, 286 and n.
Dutens, 421
Dwyer, 52, 66
Dyer, *Grongar Hill,* 595

Eardley, Lord, 289
Earthquake in Cephalonia, Byron's
description of, 749-50, 762-3,
765
Eccelino, 254
Edgecombe, Richard, 459, 471,
492-3
Edgeworth, Maria, 533, 568 and n.,
569, 631 ; *Patronage,* 248, 253
Edgeworth, R. L., 533, 569, 581,
631-2 ; *Memoirs,* 568, 581
Edgeworth, Mrs. R. L. (Beaufort),
533, 569, 631
Edinburgh Annual Register, 122
Edinburgh Magazine, Blackwood's.
See *Blackwood's Edinburgh Magazine*
Edinburgh Review, 40-41, 66, 95 n.,
117, 119, 169, 171, 214, 225, 237,
253, 274-5, 329, 384, 386, 396-7,
402, 405, 434, 526, 533, 601, 607,
674, 684, 698, 701
Edleston, John, Byron's "Cor-
nelian", 3, 28 and n., 29-30,
119-20, 124 n., 133
Eigher, Grosser and Kleiner, 353
Ekenhead, 592
Elba, 257
Eldon, Lord, 135, 625
Elegy on the South Pole. See Seward,
Anna
Elgin, Lord, 119
Elis, marshes of, 401
Elizabeth, Queen, 527
Ellice, Edward ("Bear Ellice"),
488, 490 ; Byron's letters to,
50 and n., 73
Elliot, Sir Gilbert, 612
Ellis, George, 210
Ellis, Mr. Russell, xv
Elliston, Robert William, 653 n.,
655
Elphinstone, Margaret Mercer,
Baroness Keith (Madame de
Flahault), 549 and n. ; Byron's
letters to, 139, 282, 332
Endymion. See Keats, John
England and the English, Byron's
opinion of, 133, 341, 434, 465,
485-6, 525, 640, 650, 653, 675-6,
687

Norfolk, Duke of, 624
North, Frederick. *See* Guilford, 5th Earl of
North, Mr., at Athens, 74, 78
Northampton, Byron's letter from, 195
Nourjahad (attributed to Byron), 225, 227
Nourse, 77
Novelle. See Bandello, M.

Oakes, General, 96
Oberhasli, valley of, 354
Octavius, 605
Ode on Venice, 450, 467, 502
Ode to King William, 541
Odes on Razors, 239
Odyssey, trans. *See* Pope, Alexander
O'Higgins, Mr., 634
Ohio, 230
Okeden, Mr., 347
Olympia, 84, 531
Olympus, 322
O'Neil, Miss, 417
On the Causes and Consequences of the War with France. See Erskine, Lord
Opie, 421
Orange, William, Prince of, 199 and n., 212, 219
" Orange Boven ", 213, 219
Orestes. See Sotheby, W.
Orford, Lord. *See* Walpole, Horace
Origo, Marchesa Iris, *The Last Attachment*, xv, 445 n.
Osborne, Dorothy, x
Osborne, Lord Sidney Godolphin, 6, 8, 573, 730
Ossian, 41, 109, 568
Ossulston, Lady, 164, 198, 200, 212, 237
Ossulston, Lord, 198-9, 212, 237
Ostend, 334-5
Otello. See Rossini
Othello. See Shakespeare
Otway, 174, 371, 404
Ouchy, Byron at, 347 ; letters from, 339, 345
Ovioli *or* Oviuoli, Domenico, 651
Owls Club (" Fly by Night "), 619
Oxford, 389, 538, 636
Oxford, Countess of (Jane Elizabeth Scott), 105, 154, 157, 159-61, 162 and n., 166, 177, 188-90, 211, 523, 673, 677

Oxford, Edward Harley, 5th Earl of, 153, 159-60 n., 162 and n., 166, 177, 194

Packwood, Mrs. George, 239
Padua, 459
Paer, General, 483
Paine, Tom, 504
Pallet, artist, 337
Pamela. See Richardson, S.
Paolo, 452
Papadopoli, Signor, 401
Paris, 50, 583 ; in 1814, 256, 274, 276, 315
Parisina, 463
Parker, Augusta, 639
Parker, Margaret, 3 n., 638-9
Parker, Mr., 46
Parker, Mrs. (Charlotte Augusta Byron), Byron's letters to, viii, 3 and n.
Parkyns, Mrs., 3
Parliamentary Register, 135
Parnassus, 64, 101, 254, 601, 640
Parr, Dr. Samuel, 111, 435 and n., 533, 569, 632
Parry, Captain, 491
Parry, William (firemaster, R.N.), 757, 759 and n., 760-62, 765
Partridge, John, 181, 395, 401
Pasquale, Father, 386, 389, 420, 629
Paston and Quennell, *To Lord Byron*, 130 n., 139 n., 286 n., 664 n.
Paterson, Byron's tutor at Aberdeen, 606
Patras, 57, 61-2, 75, 78, 401, 531, 754-5 ; Byron's letters from, 74, 82-7
Patronage. See Edgeworth, Maria
Paul, Mr., 77
Pausanias. See Taylor
Pauw, Cornelius de, 119
Pavia, battle of, 654
Payne, Mr., 122 and n.
Peachey, John, 695
Pearce, Henry, 39
Peel, Sir Robert, 480, 531, 610, 619, 642, 678
Peel, Sir Robert's 2nd brother, 642, 678
Pellico, Silvio, 732
Peloponnesus, 740
Penn, William, 218
Perceval, Spencer, 138 n.
Peregrine Pickle. See Smollett, Dr. T.